The Continental Actress

The Continental Actress

European Film Stars of the Postwar Era

Biographies, Criticism, Filmographies, Bibliographies

Kerry Segrave
and
Linda Martin

McFarland & Company, Inc., Publishers
Jefferson, North Carolina and London

British Library Cataloguing-in-Publication data are available

Library of Congress Cataloguing-in-Publication Data

Segrave, Kerry, 1944–
    The continental actress : European film stars of the postwar era —
biographies, criticism, filmographies, bibliographies / by Kerry
Segrave and Linda Martin.
        p.   cm.
    [Includes index.]
    ISBN 0-89950-510-4 (lib. bdg. : 50# alk. paper) ∞
    1. Motion picture actors and actresses — Europe — Biography.
2. Motion pictures — Europe — Bio-bibliography.   I. Martin, Linda,
1950–   . II. Title.
PN2570.S4   1990
791.43′028′09224 — dc20   89-13878
                                                                        CIP

Manufactured in the United States of America

McFarland & Company, Inc., Publishers
  Box 611, Jefferson, North Carolina 28640

Table of Contents

Introduction

Sweden's Bibi Andersson once said that American audiences wanted American actors, and they did not want to read subtitles. This may partially explain the difficulty that foreign actresses have had in cracking the United States market. American producers often make it even harder for foreign actresses by miscasting them. Hanna Schygulla was miscast opposite Chuck Norris in *The Delta Force,* a violent macho movie. That Schygulla accepted such a role attests to Hollywood's allure for an actress, especially in economic terms.

The era of the silent film was an easier time to become an international star in the cinema world. With no dialogue, a film from one country could be shown in any other, with no loss in audience enjoyment or comprehension. The few intertitle cards could be easily done in another language or even omitted. The major beneficiaries were the Americans since they had a well-developed film industry and plenty of money. American films went overseas but the reverse seldom occurred. The European industry was less advanced, the area financially less prosperous and the continent damaged by the First World War.

It was the 1930s before Europe began to recover and the talkies had arrived. Dialogue was then pivotal and motion pictures could not move easily from one country to another. From 1930 until the end of World War II, few foreign films were shown in the United States. France was the continental country with the most vigorous film industry but it did not compare to Hollywood. In 1938 France produced 120 motion pictures while Hollywood produced 550. The real difference, however, lay in cost—$75,000 on average per French film and $1,500,000 per film in the United States.

The arts of subtitling and dubbing were then only fledgling and inadequate, even if the public had been willing to accept them. Foreign actresses, such as Greta Garbo, Ingrid Bergman and Marlene Dietrich, did succeed in America, but often they did so by becoming Americans. They went to America and built their reputation there, often giving up their European identities.

1

The European film industry attracted wide attention in America after the Second World War due to the quality of the product. With realistic plots and characters and exotic locales, it was a powerful antidote to the generally uplifting, silly and contrived material churned out by Hollywood. The American audiences usually resisted films with subtitles, or dubbed into English, but despite these handicaps European films drew an enthusiastic audience in some markets and among some groups. It was 1951, however, before a major film company, Columbia, distributed a foreign film in the United States.

For the first time, it became possible to become a film superstar without making a Hollywood film. European audiences, more accustomed to a diversity of languages, were much less loathe to view a film not in their native language. The vigorous growth of the continental film industry made it possible for actresses to work as often as they wished in several different countries and build a strong international following—not necessarily English-speaking. As European economies prospered, the North American audience was less vital to the success of a film.

Hollywood's response was as it had been before the war; to import foreign actresses and turn them into "American" stars. It did not work as well this time. Many of the women tried it, then returned to their homeland. The money was good, usually much better than at home, and the lure and mystique of the film capital remained strong, even though the reality rarely measured up. The studio system was gone, however, and there was no way to hold these women for the long term. In a sense the Europeans were lucky because they could return to their native country and continue their careers in another language when the glitter of Hollywood paled—something that native American actresses could not do.

A few of the actresses in this book have never been to Hollywood, never made a film in English, yet have still become superstars. Most, though, have been to Hollywood and seemed to welcome the opportunity. Some worked in America for several years, but the stay was short for most. One or two films was often enough to disillusion even the most determined actress. Virtually all were used badly in Hollywood, appearing in stereotypical roles, in appallingly poor vehicles. Their best work has been done in Europe.

Despite the mainly negative experiences of Europeans in Hollywood, each new generation of actresses is still eager to try for American stardom, convinced perhaps that with them it will be different. Most are disappointed. The quality of Hollywood films has continued to decline and challenging roles are limited for actresses of any nationality. European films are not always better. Europe produces its share of B movies but a much higher proportion are quality films, with a larger range and wider variety of roles for women. The gap between the European and American films has widened—in favor of the Europeans.

In one respect the two areas are equal. Both treat aging actresses poorly.

Once a woman passes 40 or 45, roles of any kind diminish drastically, while males continue on in films as lovers, fighters etc., into their 50s and 60s.

Subtitled films have a limited market in America relying almost exclusively on large city audiences to survive. This is unfortunate because the best actresses in the business are no longer exclusively American. Over the years the 41 actresses who are profiled in this book have appeared in 1,799 motion pictures— almost 44 each—an incredible total. In each actress profile, a complete theatrical filmography is given. These filmographies do not include made-for-television movies.

With regard to our selection of actresses for this book we have included only actresses who have become prominent since the end of World War II, who were born or did much of their work in continental Europe, and who achieved recognition as international stars in the press in North America.

We found that these women operated from Italy, France and Germany, with a secondary group from Scandinavia and Greece. Clearly the European film industry is dominated by these countries, at least in terms of producing actresses of international repute.

Initially we have envisioned more countries being represented but our research uncovered less than anticipated. We placed each woman in the country in which she was born or where she did the greatest number of her films. Countries such as Spain, Portugal, Belgium, the Netherlands, etc., are not represented because they produced no actresses which met our critieria in terms of international repute.

Seven of the actresses profiled in this book were born in a country other than the one in which we placed them. Most did the bulk of their European work in their country of birth. Two of those seven changed countries when they were very young. Simone Signoret was born in Germany and moved to France when she was two years old. Hanna Schygulla moved from Poland to Germany as a young child. Ursula Andress was born in Switzerland but made no films there. Laura Antonelli was born in Yugoslavia but made no films there. Of the six actresses in the German section only two were born in that country. In addition to Schygulla, the others are Senta Berger, Romy Schneider and Maria Schell, all of whom were born in Austria. Romy went to Germany as a teen while Schell went to Switzerland for her first two films. Berger made her first two films in Austria before she too went to Germany. Schell is an example of the mobility many of these actresses have, and of the difficulties involved in placing them in one country. She made films in six or more languages, in as many countries in her early career, but Germany became her base fairly early. These mobile actresses were categorized in the country where they made the greatest number of films.

The talent of these 41 women is recognized in many parts of the world.

Chapter 1

Italian Actresses

Among the continental countries of Europe it was Italy that first rose to prominence in film after World War II. Led by filmmakers like Vittorio de Sica and Roberto Rossellini and featuring the gritty realism of *Bicycle Thief* and *Rome, Open City,* Italian films achieved worldwide recognition and praise—and so did some of the country's actresses. By the end of the 1940s, Italy had three actresses of international stardom, more than the rest of continental Europe combined.

That first group of three was somewhat incongruous with the ones that would follow since they were not obviously sex objects. The Italian neorealist style dealt with ordinary impoverished people living in mean dwellings, dressed in threadbare clothes and trying to survive in a war-ravaged country. There was no place for heavy makeup, scanty clothing and numerous costume changes. The films were about survival.

Anna Magnani was the most incongruous of the three. She was over 35 years old before she became a film star. Somewhat overweight, Magnani used virtually no makeup and always did her own hair. With a reputation for being fiery and emotional, Anna often essayed the earth mother role, the easy to rile and hot-blooded Italian. Nevertheless, she was Italy's most popular star at the end of the 1940s and one of the highest paid actresses in the world. She made a few Hollywood films and, after a number of personality clashes in Italy, claimed everything was better in America. The films she made in the United States were the worst of her career.

Silvana Mangano approached the traditional sex object role, particularly in the film that brought her international fame, *Bitter Rice.* Considered by many to be more talented than her contemporaries, Mangano was an erratic individual who could not resolve the conflicts of being a wife and mother with the demands of a career as an actress. She was also an intensely private person who disliked giving media interviews in a business where they were expected. Ultimately her personality held her back from the kind of stardom her acting talents entitled her to.

Giulietta Masina, wife of director Federico Fellini, specialized in a cross between comedy and tragedy. She did so well in her work in *La Strada,* and as a wistful waif in *The Nights of the Cabiria.* Being married to Fellini, Giulietta did not have trouble getting parts, but often other directors feeling she was Fellini's property, were reluctant to use her. Fellini tended to make the decisions for his wife and she regularly deferred to him.

Pier Angeli was only 16 when she made her first film, in which she played a vulnerable teenager. The film brought her instant fame. Rushed to Hollywood, she displayed a pure innocence and specialized in "vulnerable" parts. Pier enjoyed financial success here, if not artistic satisfaction, but by 1960 work was gone. Angeli went back to Europe but her roles were generally poor. Her personal life was troubled and she died at age 39.

The middle '50s brought four more Italian actresses to prominence. These women were openly viewed as sex objects and lusted after for their full figures. An actress' physical measurements became all important. Acting ability was secondary and these women had to work harder to establish themselves as something other than a body.

Gina Lollobrigida spent most of her time on screen either undressed or in skimpy costumes. Hollywood made extensive use of her in much the same way as in Europe. Gina's image had never made her happy and she eventually tried to change it, but with little success. Once she passed 40, demand for her waned, as it did for many sex objects past that age.

One of the most popular actresses to emerge from Italy is Sophia Loren. Prodded into the entertainment business by an ambitious mother, Sophia became a protégée of producer Carlo Ponti and soon married him. Her figure got her parts in over two dozen films while her acting impact was minimal. After Sophia became popular in Italy, Ponti arranged lucrative deals in Hollywood for his wife. They were dismal films and Loren retreated back to Italy where she established a fine reputation as a dramatic actress in such vehicles as *Two Women.* She also showed a flair for comedy in a number of screen unions with Marcello Mastroianni.

Modeling gave Elsa Martinelli her start and she was unusual in that she made her film debut in the United States after being discovered by Kirk Douglas. Speaking almost no English and with her thick Italian accent, she played a native Indian—an example of the miscasting which often plagued most of the women in this book. Elsa has made films all over the world although her best work has been in Italian films. Almost totally absent from the screen for the last decade and a half, Martinelli has kept busy with a second career as a clothes designer.

Virna Lisi also began as a sex object used mostly in decorative roles. When Hollywood "discovered" her they increased the sex object image by dyeing her hair blond and giving her roles which required nudity. The experience was an unhappy one for Lisi who returned to Europe where she gave a number of fine performances in a variety of roles. Equally adept at drama and comedy, her career had more staying power than many of her peers.

The 1960s saw a new threesome of sex goddesses come to the fore in Italy. A vacuum of sorts had been created by a defection of some of the earlier women such as Lollobrigida and Loren to Hollywood, although their stays would not be permanent.

Claudia Cardinale was groomed as the Italian Brigitte Bardot and while she never equalled the French star in media attention or box office clout, she had a greater variety of roles and has given some excellent dramatic performances. Ironically Claudia, who was born in Tunisia, spoke no Italian at all until she started making films in Italy. Claudia's husband, producer Franco Cristaldi, ran her career for almost two decades.

Monica Vitti escaped much of the sex object stereotyping when she made several films with director Michelangelo Antonioni and starred as his brooding and anguished leading lady in the early part of her career. These roles brought her international fame. When she and Antonioni separated, Vitti made her mark as Italy's foremost comic actress, often being paired on the screen with Mastroianni and Alberto Sordi. Monica was unusual in that she never went to Hollywood and rarely worked in the English language.

Swiss born Ursula Andress was one of the more notable sex bombs of the 1960s. She started her career with a handful of Italian films before being lured to Hollywood. Not particularly ambitious, Ursula did not learn English and thus was not used. She met and married John Derek and, after a seven-year absence, returned to the screen under Derek's direction, and achieved an international reputation as a sexpot. Whether she worked in the United States or in Europe, she was cast in particularly poor roles and rarely got the chance to display the acting ability she may have had.

The most recent Italian actress to achieve fame has been Laura Antonelli who dazzled the screen in the 1970s. Removing her clothes was all that was expected of her in the first few years. Later, good notices for her acting began to appear and some better parts came her way. Antonelli hoped for a Hollywood career but the call never came. She has never worked in the English language.

The least active of these women (Masina and Antonelli) have appeared in 29 films each while the most prolific have been featured in 78 and 76 films (Loren and Lisi respectively). Together these 12 actresses have made 595 films.

Anna Magnani

Anna Magnani was an unlikely candidate to be the first foreign actress to achieve international stardom after the Second World War. She was past 35, somewhat plump, used almost no makeup except lipstick and always did her own hair which perpetually framed her face in a disheveled manner. Despite these uncommon characteristics she was Italy's most popular star and one of the highest paid actresses in the world for over a decade.

She epitomized what the rest of the world considered to be the stereotypical Italian — flamboyant and emotional. With her luminous dark eyes and earthy sensuality, she brought a fiery and hot tempered presence to both the screen and her private life which helped her to gain popularity and to usher in the Italian neorealist style of filmmaking during the late 1940s.

Magnani was born out of wedlock on March 7, 1908, in a poor section of Rome, the daughter of seamstress Marina Casadei and Francesco Magnani. Her father left within a month of her birth and when she was about two her mother went to Egypt and would not see her child again for 12 years. In later years Anna would rarely speak of her mother and when she did it was with an undertone of resentment although she once remarked, "I am really grateful to Marina. Had she been the usual sort of mother, I would probably never have become an actress. But she was violent, willful and romantic — I take after her. Egypt was her escape. Acting is mine."

After her mother departed, Anna was left with her grandparents to be raised by the large Casadei family who lived a financially precarious existence. Due to pampering by her grandparents and money sent by Marina, Anna fared better than most children in the neighborhood and other kids often tore her dresses in envy and taunted her with epithets like "Dung Princess." She grew up somewhat frail and forlorn, yet having the language and manners of a tough street kid. She later proclaimed, "I am antibourgeois. I hate respectability. Give me the life of the streets, of common people."

At seven she was placed in a French convent school in Rome where she studied the piano, learned French and had her first acting experience in a Christmas play staged at the convent. A decade later she finished her schooling at the convent and enrolled at Rome's Academy of Dramatic Art using money from her mother for the tuition. Of her decision to study acting, Magnani recalled, "I couldn't stand my life any more. I wanted to break out. I was stifling."

After a year there and midway through her course, Magnani was interviewed by the manager of a touring repertory company who needed extras. Anna jumped at the chance and joined the troupe. Although she was paid little more than one dollar a day, she never again needed financial help from her mother.

For the next six years Anna toured Italy with one impoverished troupe after another, never making more than a subsistence wage but slowly getting better stage parts. Her meager salary had to cover her expenses as well as buy dresses for contemporary plays although period costumes were supplied.

To supplement her income during this period, Anna, who had a good

Anna Magnani with Sidney Lumet in *The Fugitive Kind*.

singing voice, moonlighted in Roman variety halls where she specialized in singing rowdy Italian songs. She watched a leading Italian variety comic of the time and soon began to emulate his style of making the audience part of the show through wisecracks and bawdy ad-libbing. It was a completely different stage approach from the one Anna had learned at the Academy and one which stood her in greater stead as she wisecracked her way into the main spot on the bill.

In 1933 Magnani was doing stage work in Rome when she drew the attention of film director Goffredo Alessandrini who was attracted to her fieriness.

The couple married in 1935 and separated about seven years later although they would never get a divorce. Anna gave birth to her only child, a son named Luca, in 1942.

Through Goffredo, Anna made contact with film people and made her motion picture debut in the unsuccessful 1934 release *La cieca di Sorrento* in which she had a starring role as the villain's mistress. The actress retired to devote herself to her husband, however, and later said, "I suffered horribly away from the theater but I could bear to be away from Goffredo even less." Alessandrini began womanizing and passion soon cooled between the pair. Anna abandoned her short retirement to return to the stage. She was then leaning toward what would become neorealism, saying, "The classic poses, the cultured accents—tripe! For me, acting should be as natural as life."

Before Anna and her husband split up, the actress had asked Goffredo to let her star in one of his films. The director did not really have any faith in her and instead tried to get her to go to the United States as a nightclub singer — something that did not interest Anna. "I want to act in movies. I know I'm ugly, but must movies show only beautiful, well-dressed women?" said Magnani to Goffredo, "Why not ordinary, down-to-earth women for a change, women of the people—like me?" To which the director replied, "Dismiss it from your mind, my dear. The cinema can never be for you."

Despite his reservations, Magnani's husband gave her a supporting role in his 1936 release *Cavalleria* as a café singer. Over the next eight years Anna appeared in about 14 films mostly in supporting roles but sometimes as the star. Director Vittorio de Sica cast her in *Theresa Venerdi* and Anna starred in a thriller *L'ultima carrozzella* and in the comedy *Campo dei fiori* where she was a vegetable-selling street vendor temporarily deserted by her man for a silly blonde.

The actress returned to the stage to play a variety of what she termed "delinquent heroines." War came to Italy and with it a banning of most foreign plays which dried up most of her stage work. Personal tragedy struck in 1944 when her son was stricken with polio and lost the use of his legs. He would spend the next couple of decades at a clinic in Switzerland. It was the split with her husband which was said to have given the public the Magnani they would come to know and love. Taking the separation very emotionally, Anna began wearing odd clothes, mostly black, without regard to fashion and let her hair grow in an unkempt manner.

Up to that point in her career, the actress had enjoyed some success but was not a superstar in her native Italy. Outside of Italy she was unknown. Her biggest success to that point came with the American occupation of Rome when she scored a big hit dancing, singing and telling racy stories in scenery-less reviews put on for servicemen, the vast majority of which could not understand a word she said.

The film that made her an international superstar was Roberto Rossellini's *Roma città aperta (Rome, Open City)*, a gritty and realistic tale of the last days of the German occupation of the city. Roberto began shooting clandestinely even as the Germans were leaving the city. Filming was done on a shoestring budget and often delayed when money was short. Most of the cast were residents of the areas in which filming was done and turned into actors overnight. Since studios were few and expensive, most shooting was done outdoors. Workers lent their shanties for interiors and helped man the lights. The first money raised for the film came from a black-market butcher.

Originally Rossellini was unimpressed by Magnani and began shooting with another actress but she quit after a few days, having neither faith nor foresight in the financial stability of the now famous production. Anna came in as a replacement and delivered a powerful performance as a fierce and pregnant widow shot down by the Nazis.

The Italian press disliked the film and it flopped at Cannes but was a big hit with the public in Italy and France and went on to even greater international success. When the film reached the United States in 1946 it had long runs in many cities and played New York for over a year. That year Anna won the United States National Board of Review award as best foreign actress for *Rome, Open City* and in 1947 the Venice Film Festival named her best international actress for her work in that film and in *Angelina*.

The actress was an overnight sensation and also embarked on a brief and stormy affair with Rossellini. The public began to call her "Nannarella" (little Anna) and she quickly demanded and got the largest sums of money ever paid to a European actress for her film work. Her salary was sometimes more than one third of a film's total production costs. So popular was she that she received the supreme accolade of imitation. Hopeful starlets began going to work with their hair unwashed, uncombed, parted in the middle and hanging into their eyes. They lowered their voices to a rasp and talked out of the corners of their mouths, hoping they would follow Anna down the road to fame. Known as "Magnanini" (little Magnanis) they usually got no farther than a director who told them to "go home and clean up."

Several more films followed over the next couple of years but none were widely seen outside of Italy until the 1947 release *L'onorevole Angelina (Angelina)* in which Magnani had another earthy role as the leader of some Rome tenement dwellers protesting their conditions. Of her performance in that film, a British critic remarked she was "probably as fine an all-round actress as the current cinema has to offer." Another reviewer noted she was "unencumbered by glamour as we know it," but still called her "the most potent female on the contemporary screen."

Magnani teamed up with Rossellini again for *Amore (The Miracle)* which earned the actress the Italian equivalent of an Oscar but which ran afoul of American censors. The film consisted of two unrelated parts. The first part was "The Human Voice," a one-character twenty-minute monolgoue in which a woman pled on the telephone with the lover who had just jilted her. The piece was usually performed in low key but "Magnani shed a Niagara of tears, howled like Medea and rolled on the floor in her anguish."

The other part of the film drew the wrath of the American censors. In "The Miracle" Anna played a demented peasant, seduced and impregnated by a stranger, who then fancied she was carrying the Christ Child. The New York Commissioner of Licenses found the picture "blasphemous" and banned it. The ban was later revoked but then finally upheld by the courts.

Toward the end of the 1940s, Anna was the highest paid and most successful international film star and offers poured in. She rejected them all, however, waiting for Roberto to provide a promised part for her. She was idle for over a year. Trouble came when the director became attracted to actress Ingrid Bergman. Anna and Roberto had always fought loudly and publicly but more so after the actress learned of the director's new affair. Once while physically fighting about Ingrid in a taxi, the driver tried to intervene and was beaten up by Magnani. When the pair finally split up, Anna threatened to "break every plate of spaghetti in Rome over his head."

Her fiery temper was part of the Magnani mystique. At the 1948 Venice Film Festival, the actress did not get an award she felt she deserved and stormed out of the hotel screaming, "Goddam them, they didn't give me the prize!" Years later she chased a lover of the time up and down the Via Veneto in Rome until she was able to force his car to the curb with her own, whereupon she let loose with a patented stream of Magnani profanity. After Rossellini took up with Bergman, friends feared for the physical safety of Ingrid if Magnani and Bergman ever met; fortunately they did not.

The film Rossellini had picked for Anna was *Stromboli* but he gave the part to Bergman and the couple quickly disappeared to the tiny volcanic island of that name near Sicily for location shooting. Not to be outdone, the enraged Magnani orchestrated a similar film of her own, *Vulcano,* shot on the tiny volcanic island of Vulcano only twelve miles from Stromboli. Neither island had running water, electricity or much food and shelter.

American director William Dieterle and starlet Geraldine Brooks were imported from Hollywood for *Vulcano* while English was dubbed for Magnani. It was the first Italian film made primarily for the American market. Bemused Romans watched "the battle of the islands" wondering who would finish their picture first. Both films were bad and did not further anyone's career. Anna's trademark of frantic fury and seething emotionalism was lost in the dubbing.

After that debacle Magnani gave several outstanding performances in the early 1950s, one of which was in Visconti's *Bellissima* in which she played a mother determined to make her child a movie star. The film prompted the *New York Times* to call her "a searing symbol of gutter femininity." Other excellent performances were in *Camicie rosse* and in Renoir's *Le carrozza d'oro*

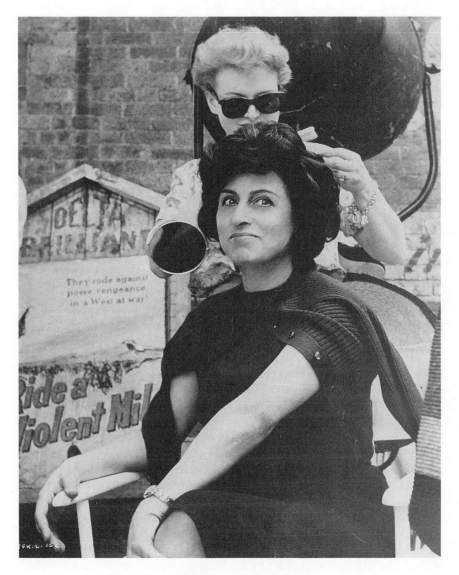

Anna Magnani in a publicity photo.

(The Golden Coach) which gave her an extravagant comedy role. Said critic Pauline Kael, "At her greatest, she, too, expresses the beauty in our common humanity . . . the most sensual of great actresses . . . the actress who has come to be the embodiment of human experience, the most 'real' of actresses."

Magnani was at her peak then and director Jean Renoir said she was "probably the greatest actress I have ever worked with. She is the complete animal—

an animal created for the stage and screen." Director Dieterle added with affection, "Magnani is the last of the great shameless emotionalists. You have to go back to the silent movies for that kind of acting. Most of the modern stars try to cultivate understatement and subtlety, but Magnani pulls out all the stops. The style is so old it looks new." Explained Anna, "I have so much boiling inside; if I hadn't chosen acting, I think I would have been a great criminal."

Film offers decreased and had dried up for the actress by 1954 and she briefly returned to vaudeville. Part of the reason lay in her supposed "difficult" nature as an actress. She was said to relentlessly try and control everything once a film was underway, to want to see the rushes and to stop work if she was not satisfied. Anna herself was tired of the films she found herself doing and said, "The things they always want me to do, the horrible ideas they get ... the characters they want me to act ... the dead chiché." A second reason for her career decline was the emergence of the buxom young sex goddess role of the 1950s which had seen the 46-year-old Magnani supplanted by the likes of Sophia Loren and Gina Lollobrigida.

American playwright Tennessee Williams had written *The Rose Tattoo* specifically with Magnani in mind but the actress declined to appear in the Broadway stage production feeling her English was not good enough. In 1954 Williams persuaded her to study the script and this time she agreed to do the film version — her first Hollywood film. She gave a dazzling performance as the mourning widow who succumbed to a lusty Burt Lancaster. The performance earned her an Oscar as best actress of 1955 as well as being named best actress by the New York Film Critics. The part was a natural for Anna as she essayed an earthy, lusty and loud-mouthed woman.

Curiously the film did poorly in Italy as the Romans were not pleased with the stereotype. It did revive a waning Magnani career, however. This film's reception was responsible for the praise she gave Hollywood. She claimed to love working in the United States where she said movies were a serious business, people were competent, producers were gentlemanly and directors kindly stopped shooting to let her rework her lines. In reality, her Hollywood vehicles were generally weaker than her Italian ones.

Her next Hollywood film was *Wild in the Wind,* an awkward and poorly crafted film about a mail order bride. Magnani's performance was the film's only virtue. Said George Cukor, the film's director, "I was happy to work with Magnani and I think she gave a very unusual performance, not her normal fiery thing, but more subtle, toned down." The picture was not a success nor was *The Fugitive Kind* in which Magnani played a love-starved storekeeper who picked up Marlon Brando. This part also was written specially for her by Tennessee Williams.

Between her American features, the actress made Italian films but most were unsuccessful and many did not get distribution in the Anglo-American markets. Anna had continued to give good performances in films such as *Mamma Roma,* created specifically for her by director Pier Paolo Pasolini but her career was in a steady decline.

By the end of the 1960s Magnani had not made a film for several years although she had done some stage work. Hollywood tapped her one last time for *The Secret of Santa Vittoria,* an unexceptional film in which the actress had a supporting role. Still bitter about the state of the Italian cinema, she said, "In Italy, all Westerns. You see me in a Western? Ha! They are terrible pictures made for the money. There is no part there for me." After that she had small roles in a few more Italian films, her last being *Fellini's Roma* before her death in Rome on September 26, 1973, from cancer of the pancreas at the age of 65.

Critics may have been divided on her abilities but the actress had always considered herself to be the best in the business. Once, when she was staying at the posh Beverly Hills Hotel, she was disturbed by noisy plumbing in the next suite and had a maid slip a note under the door which read, "Please don't use your bathroom in the mornings. You are disturbing the world's greatest actress." While fans had not flocked to her films in the last years the occasion of her burial was similar to a state funeral with thousands turning out for national mourning to pay tribute to the actress. On the tenth anniversary of her death, the International Anna Magnani Association held a week long program of ceremonies and restrospectives in Rome.

Her beginning in poverty had left its mark and early in her career she demanded the day's pay in cash at the end of each shooting day. It took quite awhile before she was trustful enough to wait till the end of the week and take a check. She often took indifferent films during the early years of her career with the idea of making enough money to take care of a son who would never be able to support himself. Her prime motivation, however, was her love of acting. Magnani once remarked, "The only thing that means anything for me is art in any form, any kind. For me it is acting. I live for this. I don't think a person can be a great actor if he is incomplete individual. He must be strong, powerful person."

Anna Magnani Filmography

La cieca di Sorrento [The Blind Woman of Sorrento] (1934)
Tempo massimo (1936)
Cavalliera (1936)
Trenta secondi d'amore (1936)
La principessa Tarakanova (1937)
Una lampada alla finestra (1939)
Finalmente soli (1940)

La fuggitiva (1941)
Teresa Venerdi (1941)
La fortuna viene dal cielo (1942)
L'ultima carrozzella (1943)
Campo dei fiori (1943)
T'amoro sempre (1943)
La vita è bella (1943)
Abbasso la miseria (1943)

L'avventura di Annabella (1943)
Il fiore sotto gli occhi (1943)
Roma città aperta [Rome, Open City]
  (1944)
Un uomo ritorna (1945)
Abbasso la ricchezza! (1945)
Il bandito (1946)
Davanti a lui tremava tutta Roma
  [Before Him All Rome Trembled;
  Tosca] (1946)
Lo sconosciuto di San Marino (1947)
Quartetto pazzo (1947)
L'onorevole Angelina [Angelina] (1947)
Assunta Spina (1948)
Molti sogni per le strade (1948)
Amore [The Miracle; Ways of Love;
  Woman] (1948)
Vulcano (1949)
Bellissima (1951)
Camicie rosse (1952)

La carrozza d'oro [The Golden Coach]
  (1952)
Siamo donne [We the Women] (1953)
The Rose Tattoo (1955)
Suor Letizia (1956)
Wild Is the Wind (1957)
Nella città l'inferno [Caged] (1958)
The Fugitive Kind (1960)
Risate di gioia [The Passionate Thief]
  (1960)
Mamma Roma (1962)
Le magot de Josefa (1963)
Volles Herz und leere taschen (1964)
Made in Italy (1965)
The Secret of Santa Vittoria (1969)
Nell' anno del signore (1969)
1870 [Correva l'anno di grazia 187]
  (1971)
Fellini's Roma (1972)

Sources

"Anna Magnani Lifted Int'l Stature of Italo Films, Dies in Rome at 65." *Variety*, 272:4, October 3, 1973.

"Anna Magnani, the Actress, Dies at 65." *New York Times*, September 27, 1973, p. 42.

Barzini, Luigi, Jr. "Italy's Greatest Actress." *Harper's Magazine*, 215:52–7, September 1957.

Cianfarra, Jane. "Tigress of Italy's Screen." *New York Times Magazine*, October 16, 1949, p. 28+.

Current Biography 1956. New York: H.W. Wilson, 1957, p. 400–402.

The International Dictionary of Films and Filmmakers: Volume III: Actors and Actresses. Chicago: St. James Press, 1986, p. 400–401.

Kobler, John. "Tempest on the Tiber." *Life*, 28:115–118+, February 13, 1950.

Lloyd, Ann, ed. *The Illustrated Who's Who of the Cinema*. London: Orbis, 1983, p. 284.

"Magnificent Magnani." *Newsweek*, 46:65–66, December 26, 1955.

Quinlan, David. *The Illustrated Directory of Film Stars*. London: B.T. Batsford, 1981, p. 303–304.

"Rome Re-remembers Magnani." *Variety*, 312:2, October 12, 1983.

Ross, Nancy L. "Anna Magnani, Fiery Italian Actress, Dies." *Washington Post*, September 27, 1973, p.C16.

Shipman, David. *The Great Movie Stars: The International Years*. London: Angus & Robertson, 1972, p. 307–311.

Shivas, Mark. "In the Beginning There Was Magnani. Then Came Loren." *New York Times*, September 29, 1968, sec. 2, p. 17.

Thompson, Howard. "Anna Magnani: Testament of a Tamed Tempest," *New York Times*, April 19, 1953, sec. 2, p. 5.

Thomson, David. *A Biographical Dictionary of Film*. New York: William Morrow, 1975, p. 349.

Wlaschin, Ken. *The Illustrated Encyclopedia of the World's Great Movie Stars and Their Films*. London: Salamander, 1979, p. 119.

Silvana Mangano

Of all the actresses who attained international fame from the Italian cinema after the end of the Second World War, none was more enigmatic than Silvana Mangano. She had more potential and perhaps more ability than others such as Gina Lollobrigida or Sophia Loren but her personality was not suited to the demands of stardom. While Loren had married her producer early on and had a good working relationship with him, Mangano had a less satisfactory one with the producer she had married at the start of her career. These factors, combined with Silvana's own disinterest in acting, meant she never reached her full potential.

Silvana was born in Rome, Italy, on April 21, 1930. She was one of four children born to an English mother, Ivy, and a Sicilian railway worker, Amedeo Mangano. Amedeo had met and married Ivy in London and then took her back to Italy. Mrs. Mangano had her daughter study ballet at the academy of Zhia Ruskaya in Rome from the time Silvana was seven until she was about fourteen years old. At one point during World War II the family moved from Rome to the city of Frascati to avoid the Allied bombings. When the German High Command later made the same move, the Manganos quickly returned to Rome. Silvana gave up ballet on the advice of doctors after her body started to swell in a nervous reaction to the bombings.

When the war was over the young girl sent her picture to a Roman beauty contest and suddenly found herself "Miss Rome" of 1946. This led to a career as a model which included a stint as a hat model in a Roman store. The contest win also led to bit parts in a few films with her debut in the 1947 release *Elixir of Love.* She was unsuccessful in her attempts to gain a major role until she was cast as the lead in *Bitter Rice,* the film that established the actress as a major star. It was the story of female rice pickers in the Po Valley and blended social significance with sex. Giuseppe de Santis directed the film and Dino De Laurentiis was the producer. Dressed in a black sweater, shorts and black stockings with her main interests being boogie-woogie, men and money, Silvana was described as "pneumatic and primitive" by critics. She gained a reputation as an earthy, neorealistic sex goddess, devoid of the usual makeup and high fashion associated with Hollywood goddesses.

Bitter Rice did well all over the globe and it enjoyed a long run in the United States. The *New York Times* enthused, "Anna Magnani minus 15 years, Ingrid Bergman with a Latin disposition and Rita Hayworth plus 15 pounds ... nothing short of a sensation ... full-bodied and gracefully muscular with a rich voice and a handsome pliant face." She had a chance to use her dancing skills with the dance sequences in the film but was not happy doing them since she felt they were too vulgar.

When de Santis was casting for the film he had been struck by the girl's freshness and beauty. She was one of many hopefuls and the director gave her a screen test and chose her. De Santis recalled, however, that Dino De Laurentiis did not feel the same way. "Dino refused to accept her. He said it was insane to build a film on someone so unknown. When I told him I was going to use her anyway, he became angry and quit ... though eventually he did return."

The actress had received only $800 for her work in *Bitter Rice* but that film shot her salary up to $100,000 per film. She was besieged by offers from Hollywood including one from Alexander Korda who wanted to put her under contract. Silvana turned down all Hollywood offers, saying, "I like to be able to walk about in public without incidents. I am not a protest meeting." Dino then offered her a long-term contract which Silvana refused, to his surprise. Mr. Mangano convinced his daughter to sign but as De Laurentiis remembered "she didn't like it. I should have known then that this was going to be the greatest anti-diva of all time."

A more personal offer came from the producer and the couple married in 1949. By 1950 Mangano had completed a few more films but appeared in only a couple more over the next five years. During this period she had three children, two boys and a girl. A third daughter followed in the early 1960s. Silvana's weight soared from 128 pounds to almost 200 pounds.

The actress was content to retire from acting and when asked if she was ready to sacrifice everything for her career, replied, "Definitely not!" Nor was she interested in becoming rich, saying, "I consider the desire to be rich for the sake of being rich some form of lunacy." Reluctantly and at the insistence of Dino, who would produce most of her films in the future, Mangano trimmed down and appeared in *Mambo* (1954). She found her part drastically altered from the original script to the final cut and was not well received by the critics. The actress admitted that film "was a disaster."

Better work followed in films such as *The Gold of Naples* where her portrayal of a prostitute trapped in a marriage of honor was acclaimed by reviewers. She portrayed a sophisticate in *Crimen,* displayed fine comic skills as a prostitute in *The Great War* as well as giving a good performance in *This Angry Age.* Mangano was always ill at ease in the world of film, timid, with a strong sense of privacy and little desire to do media interviews. "But for my husband, I would not be an actress. He is kind and sympathetic about everything except my wish to help him in his work in every way except acting. I want to be a great actress or not act at all. People came to *Bitter Rice* to see my legs, not my acting."

After *This Angry Age* the actress came home with incense and books on Oriental philosophy. She gave up makeup entirely, refused to do interviews and went on a crash diet. When Dino protested, Silvana blew up and said, "Let me alone! I didn't want to do films to start with. Now I don't want my career and private life mixed up. No, I won't see journalists, ever. And I don't want to be with people I don't like. Take me as I am or leave me!"

Silvana Mangano practices a dance routine for *Bitter Rice* while United States dance stylist Katherine Dunham beats the drums.

De Santis thought her wide swings in weight came about because "she hated *Bitter Rice*. She did not want to be an object, a sex symbol. So she withdrew, destroying everything as she went. She was a girl who did not want a physique that turned her into an object for men and made it difficult, if not impossible, to be a dignified human being."

Mangano continued to work steadily in films taking some that Dino suggested and some on her own, although her husband was always consulted. Her role as a mother came first, however, and she would never do any film shooting during her children's vacations. Many of the films miscast the actress and director Vittorio De Sica remarked that "it's a great loss — not only for her, but for cinema everywhere." De Santis said her greatest defect was that she had "no ambition."

Italian actor Alberto Sordi who costarred with Mangano in numerous films thought Dino had ruined his wife's career. "Dino never realized he had a trump card on which to base his cinema activity. Instead of building colossal film studios, he could have put more into Mangano — and be much better off today. Silvana, overpowered by Dino, withdrew to be mainly wife and mother. It's too bad because only now has Dino discovered that he lost a unique opportunity."

By the end of the 1960s Mangano was more selective in her work and acted mainly for Italian directors Pier Pasolini and Luchino Visconti. In *The Witches* she was the lead in the four different stories each by a different director. She had a wide range of parts and emotion and got good notices. Mangano delivered another excellent performance in *Teorema* by Pasolini, a mixture of eroticism and religion in which a university student visited an upper bourgeois household and presided over the disintegration of the family. Mangano played the mother.

For Visconti, she played the mother in *Death in Venice,* reportedly for no salary because she admired the story and the director. Her performance relied entirely on mime for its powerful effect. She was cast as Richard Wagner's mistress and gave another strong performance in *Ludwig.* A third teaming with Visconti was *Conversation Piece* where Mangano portrayed a woman who pushed herself and her family into the life of a reclusive professor played by Burt Lancaster. *Variety* called her "striking as the decadent noblewoman." Since the release of that film in 1975 Silvana has been absent from the screen with the exception of two small roles, 10th-billed as the Rev. Mother Ramallo in the 1984 big budget sci-fi epic *Dune,* and with Marcello Mastroianni in *Dark Eyes.*

She had begun to assert a little autonomy late in her career with *Teorema.* It was the first film she had done without going through her husband. When the film was finished De Laurentiis phoned producer Franco Rossellini and asked to see the picture before it was released. Rossellini agreed but Mangano exploded when she heard of it. "Show that film to De Laurentiis? Why? I've trusted you and Pasolini to do it with a taste which would not embarrass my children. That's good enough for me — and the entire De Laurentiis family." For once she prevailed although it took her eight months to work up the nerve to see the film. "I had trusted them so much," she said, "I wanted to keep that faith — even if it meant never seeing the film."

Silvana Mangano in *Anna*.

Her talent as an actress was recognized by those in the industry even if it was not always evident on the screen. Director Joseph Losey called her "one of the world's great screen actresses" while Visconti said she was an "actress who's done fewer films than Loren or Lollobrigida yet is without doubt our greatest star."

When asked about her need to avoid people, she said, "I have nothing of myself to give to people. I cannot speak well of cultural things. I prefer to be silent because I fear the poverty of my own opinion. I bore myself in the company of others. So I withdrew. I have all the defects that a woman can have and some that aren't typically feminine. I honestly don't think I can be proud of any of my qualities."

Such attitudes exasperated Dino. She was a star who would not do interviews and did not lend herself to promotion. Dino wondered, "What can you do with a woman like that?" Silvana was not overly enthusiastic about her husband either and while acknowledging he was a wonderful father and dedicated provider, complained, "De Laurentiis is not my ideal man. He has many defects. I wouldn't know where to begin listing them."

Dino De Laurentiis felt his wife had two problems as an actress. First was too much desire to be a mother and wife. The second lay at the start of her career when Dino felt he had the choice of putting himself at the service of his actress wife or working for himself. He said candidly, "I'll admit that if she has lacked the development her talent deserved, the fault is mine. She had enormous possibilities. But I never occupied myself with her as an actress — though I did use her in certain films for my own reasons, commercial ventures mainly, and often in roles not adapted to her. But it was no mistake for me. Ponti is content to put himself at the service of his wife [Sophia Loren], but I could never do such work."

Silvana Mangano Filmography

L'elisir d'amore [Elixir of Love] (1947)
Il delitto de Giovanni Episcopo [Flesh Will Surrender] (1947)
Gli uomini sono nemici (1948)
Riso amaro [Bitter Rice] (1948)
Cagliostro [Black Magic] (1949)
Il lupo della Sila [The Lure of the Sila] (1950)
Il brigante Musolino [Fugitive in 6B] (1950)
Anna (1951)
Mambo (1954)
Ulisse [Ulysses] (1954)
L'oro di Napoli [The Gold of Naples; Every Day's a Holiday] (1955)
Uomini e lupi (1956)
La diga sul Pacifico [The Sea Wall; This Angry Age] (1958)
La tempesta [Tempest] (1959)
La grande guerra [The Great War] (1959)
Jovanka e le altre [Five Branded Women] (1960)
Crimen [. . . And Suddenly It's Murder!; Killing in Monte Carlo] (1960)
Il giudizio universale [The Last Judgment] (1961)
Barabba [Barabbas] (1961)
Una vita difficile (1961)

Il processo di Verona [The Verona Trial] (1963)
La mia signora (1964)
Il disco volante [The Flying Saucer] (1965)
Io, io, io . . . e gli altri [I, I, I . . . and the Others] (1966)
Scusi, lei è favorevole o contrario? [Excuse Me, Are You For or Against?] (1967)
Edipo Re [Oedipus Rex] (1967)
Le streghe [The Witches] (1967)
Capriccio all'italiana (1968)
Viaggio de lavoro (1968)
Teorema (1968)
Medea (1969)
Morte a Venezia [Death in Venice] (1971)
Scipione detto anche l'Africano (1971)
Il Decamerone [The Decameron] (1971)
Ludwig (1971)
Lo scopone scientifico (1972)
D'amore si muore (1972)
Gruppo di famiglia in un interno [Conversation Piece] (1975)
Dune (1984)
Oci ciornie [Dark Eyes; Black Eyes] (1987)

Sources

"Bolster the New Italian Movie Industry." Newsweek, 42:67, August 31, 1953.
Candide. "The Most Beautiful Woman in the World." United Nations World, 4:26–27, December 1950.
D'Allessandro, Alan. "Italian Movie Stars." Cosmopolitan, 136:45+ , February 1954.
The International Dictionary of Films and Filmmakers: Volume III: Actors and Actresses. Chicago: St. James Press, 1986, p. 404.

Lloyd, Ann. ed. *The Illustrated Who's Who of the Cinema.* London: Orbis, 1983, p. 287.
"McCall's Visits." *McCall's,* 85:14+ , February 1958.
Pepper, Curtis Bill. "Secret Star." *Vogue,* 160:156+ , November 1, 1972.
"Silvana Mangano," *Focus on Film,* n23:8, Winter 1976.
Thomson, David. *A Biographical Dictionary of Film.* New York: William Morrow, 1975, p. 353.
Two Ways To Be a Woman. *Collier's,* 132:52+ , October 30, 1953.

Giulietta Masina

Known more for her wistful face, saucer eyes, waif image and combination of pathos and humor than for physical beauty, Giulietta Masina became an international star in the late 1950s. This was a considerable achievement since that was precisely the time of the ascent of voluptuous female screen stars such as Sophia Loren in Italy and Brigitte Bardot in France.

Her way was eased considerably by her long association with Italian director Federico Fellini both professionally, as one of his principal players, and personally — as his wife. The actress's performances are rarely discussed separately from the directorial achievements of Fellini and in some ways she has had difficulty in moving out from under his shadow.

She was born Giulia Anna Masina in Bologna, Italy, on February 22, 1920, the daughter of Gaetano and Angelo and one of four siblings. Most of the family had been teachers but Mr. Masina was briefly an exception. A musician, he was once first violinist at La Scala but after marriage became a teacher. Giulietta started acting in school plays when she was a teenager and continued with student dramatic productions during her years at the University of Rome. At university she specialized in Christian archeology and briefly taught Italian and Latin at the Massimo Gymnasium of Rome.

Acting was her first love, however, and she joined a Rome theater group making her professional acting debut in 1939 in a Thornton Wilder play. Over the next few years she gained a growing reputation as an actress, principally in radio work. In 1943 a 23-year-old writer of radio scripts was looking for someone to play a character in a soap opera when he spotted a picture of Masina in an Italian entertainment magazine.

In that way Fellini met her, and after she accepted a part, a courtship began. Giulietta then lived in Rome with her aunt and, in keeping with the code of honor, the aunt forbade the actress to see Fellini alone. The couple did manage to sneak off alone a few times and later that year were married. Masina then retired for several years and Fellini turned his attention to film work.

Bored with being at home, Giulietta returned to acting after the Second World War ended and appeared in a number of stage productions. Since

Giulietta Masina in *The Madwoman of Chaillot*.

Federico then moved with the film crowd Masina got her first film role in the 1946 release *Paisà* in which Fellini was involved, but it was just a bit part.

Her first major film role came two years later in *Senza pietà (Without Pity)* which was cowritten by Fellini. Masina played a prostitute and confidante to the female lead who was in love with a black American G.I. The film was not very good but Giulietta was, giving a fresh and funny performance which won her a Silver Ribbon (Italy's equivalent to the Oscar) as best supporting actress. *Senza pietà* received United States distribution and her acting was equally praised in that country.

Several more years passed before her next role in *Luci del varietà (Variety Lights)* in 1951. Masina was featured as the mistress of the lead in this tale of a third-rate touring company. Fellini wrote the script and codirected with Alberto Lattuada — his first venture into directing — and both men cast their wives in the film. After that Giulietta was incredibly busy appearing in 15 films from 1951 to 1955. Mostly she played support roles as either friend, mistress or prostitute. She was found in a bordello in *Persiane chiuse* and *Donne proibite* and friend to the female in outings such as *Sette ore di guai*, *Wanda la peccatrice* and *Europa '51* where she was socialite Ingrid Bergman's buddy.

Occasionally she starred as in *Lo sceicco bianco (The White Shiek)*, the comic tale of a wife who left her husband on their honeymoon to chase after a magazine pin-up boy. A warped comedy, it was the first film Fellini directed alone and did not do well critically although Masina earned praise for her comic and pantomime skills.

Fellini went on to great international success with his next film *I Vitelloni* and then prepared a starring vehicle for his wife, *La Strada*. One of the main characters in the film was a half wit girl bought by a traveling strong man to be his "slavey" and a clown in his act. Federico, who cowrote and directed, said, "The actress who could put across the comic-tragic interpretation called for was pretty close to home. In fact, she was right in my own home: my wife Giulietta."

As the optimistic clown Gelsomina, Masina smiled and laughed through her tears no matter how badly she was mistreated by chance or by the strong man (Anthony Quinn). Both the film and the actress drew rave reviews and *La Strada* was named best picture at more than one festival. *Newsweek* magazine called it the most popular foreign picture ever to play in the United States and attributed most of its success to the actress whose appeal "in her person and in the role she plays, ... represents to most moviegoers, in a distraught time, what one critic has called 'the triumph of modesty, of goodness, and a desire to live decently.'"

Another critic stated that "with her mobile features and eloquent eyes, this girl has a wide range of expression, flicking instantly and forcefully from mood to mood—laughter, pathos, sorrow, love. She should join Fellini on his new pedestal as one of the foremost current Italian film figures."

Despite all this praise Fellini had great difficulty in getting the film financed. Nobody wanted Masina for the part. The first producer Federico approached agreed to do the film but only if his girlfriend got the lead. Fellini declined.

A second producer broke down and cried after reading the script. Federico was delighted thinking the man was crying with emotion but chagrined to find out it was rage. "You can't put your wife in that, you need a child to play the part," Fellini recalled the producer saying.

Others told the director they would back him but only without Giulietta. Then Carlo Ponti and Dino De Laurentiis, producing together, offered Fellini a contract calling for Burt Lancaster and Silvana Mangano in the parts. Federico again refused, saying he wrote it for Masina, and he tore up the contract. The two producers then relented and accepted both spouses.

When *La Strada* was first released it generated a poor critical response in Italy although later it would be overwhelmingly favorable both there and internationally. This poor initial reaction worried Masina who thought it might be because her physical type was then not in fashion, having been replaced by the ripe beauty and physical characteristics associated with Sophia Loren and Gina

Lollobrigida. "Can you imagine my crisis," said Giulietta, "Because I thought I had ruined Federico."

Certainly Masina was no conventional beauty and one reviewer described her as having "button-eyes in a chalk-white golliwog face." Giulietta herself once wryly noted, "I'm not one of those actresses who act with their chests." But her popularity soared and her comic and pantomime abilities were often compared to those of Charlie Chaplin who was reported to have said Giulietta was the actress who had moved him the most.

She became known in Italy simply as "La Masina" and received more fan mail than any other actress in Italy during the latter part of the 1950s. Much of it was the standard sort but some was not. The actress recalled that letters came from "doctors, businessmen, lawyers—they don't ask for photographs, they don't want anything but advice . . . maybe I should have been a psychiatrist."

Masina identified with her clown image and once remarked, "I would like to be a clown but maintain my sex with a skirt. I know there have been women clowns, but always with pants, not skirts. I must wear a skirt. I would like to have a circus act and play Gelsomina."

The actress went on to other magnificent performances notably in *il Bidone (The Swindle)* and then in Fellini's *Le notti de Cabiria (The Nights of Cabiria)* where she again essayed her favorite role as the wistful waif. Playing a whore, she smiled her way through misfortune on the Appian Way. Masina received the Best Actress Award at the Cannes Film Festival as well as being judged Best Actress of the Year in Italy, Germany and Japan. Said one reviewer, "She is one of those performers you can't tear your eyes from, lest you miss a moment of her tragi-comic timing."

Several more films followed but none did well critically or at the box office. Reviewers grew tired of what they felt were excessive facial gestures. In *Fortunella* Giulietta was again a maltreated heartbreaker and *Variety* commented that "all four expressions are outrageously overworked." Anna Magnani and Masina were cast as convicts in *Nella città l'inferno* where the charge of "outrageous facial distortions" was again raised.

A big international coproduction was mounted, *Le grand vie* with Giulietta again cast a waif going from man to man. *Variety* was unrelenting and noted, "Actually Miss Masina has a tendency to mug rather than act, and it is hard to believe that she is physically appealing to the myriads of men in her life." The failure of that film took the bloom off the actress's career and except for a small role in one film she was off the screen for five years.

Fellini's *Giulietta degli spiriti (Juliet of the Spirits)* brought the actress back to prominence in 1965. The film was autobiograhical, exploring the relationship between Giulietta and Federico during his midlife artistic crises, and earned the actress high praise for her acting although traces of Gelsomina the waif were detected by some of her critics.

Giuletta Masina and Marcello Mastroianni in *Ginger and Fred*.

Minor roles in a few more films followed in the 1960s ending with her first English language film *The Madwoman of Chaillot* where she was one of Katherine Hepburn's pals. After that she was inactive in films for a decade and a half.

Her best work had been done in Fellini's films and so firmly linked with him was she that other directors sometimes did not offer her the number and variety of roles her talent entitled her to. The actress also had a tendency to stay with a certain kind of role and not try new things. She felt since she was known mostly as a clown or a prostitute the public might not accept her in a realistic role as a wife with a husband and lover. As a result she turned down offers that did come her way and joked that it was not hard turning them down since "they don't pay me like Al Pacino or De Niro."

Success had made her overly cautious and she remarked, "Success also means being careful not to make mistakes because you develop a certain kind of fear. You are scared to accept roles which are different. You are scared that you will cancel the success you had. You are scared to disappoint the critics and the public."

Fellini and Giulietta worked well together and Fellini usually accepted her suggestions but also tended to be more demanding and exacting with his wife than with other actresses. In turn she was usually docile in his presence. Her clown character worked brilliantly under Fellini but too often became a cliché under other directors, and more and more she relied on her husband for guidance. Giulietta turned down offers from other directors claiming to not "feel" the part. A more plausible reason was that she suffered when away from Federico. "I'd rather cook for Federico for the rest of my life than get into a picture he felt I was not ready for," said Masina.

During her long hiatus from the screen in the 1970s and 1980s Masina filled her time with several Italian television appearances, volunteer work for UNICEF, a decade of writing an advice column and tending to Fellini. "First of all I run my house," she said, "Federico is not too demanding, but let's say I spoil him a bit like a good Italian woman."

In 1985 she had a part in *Frau Holle,* a Czech and West German production of a Brothers Grimm fairy tale with Giulietta as a white fairy. It received little distribution outside of eastern Europe. The next year, however, she received international attention again, and wide critical praise, with the release of Fellini's *Ginger and Fred.* Masina and Marcello Mastroianni portrayed ballroom dancers retired for decades who are brought back to try and strut their stuff once again on a zoo-like television variety show. The film was widely viewed as a satire on the quality of television. Although Masina and Mastroianni had both worked extensively for Fellini, it was their first time together, except for a stage appearance in a play almost four decades previous.

The idea for that film ironically came from a television project. Masina was thinking of a series of six short television films on different types of female characters to try and change the image of Italian women. One of the characters for this series was "Ginger" and when Masina discussed it with producer Alberto Grimaldi he insisted that Fellini make a separate big screen film about her. The result was *Ginger and Fred.*

Giulietta had always been modest about her own accomplishments and abilities as an actress and once asked, "Do you think I physically could hope to fill the stockings of an Anita Ekberg, or wear veils in the manner of Anouk Aimee? ... I didn't decide anything. It was destiny which decided for me."

Decades after it was made, people still asked her about *La Strada,* a film which was her favorite and provided enough satisfaction to last a lifetime. "If an actress has the luck to do an important film with an important director, and in an important role," said Masina, "it's natural that it remains."

Giulietta Masina Filmography

Paisà [Paisan] (1946)
Senza pietà [Without Pity] (1948)
Luci del varietà [Variety Lights] (1951)
Persiane chiuse [Behind the Closed Shutters] (1951)
Sette ore di guai (1951)
Cameriera bella presenza offresi (1951)
Europa '51 [The Greatest Love] (1952)

Lo sceicco bianco [The White Sheik] (1952)
Wanda la peccatrice (1952)
Romanze della mia vita (1952)
Al margini della metropoli (1953)
Donne proibite [Angel of Darkness] (1953)
Via Padova 46 (1953)

La Strada (1954)
Cento anni d'amore (1954)
Il bidone [The Swindle] (1955)
Buonanotte, avvocato! (1955)
Le notti di Cabiria [The Nights of Cabiria; Cabiria] (1956)
Fortunella (1958)
Nella città l'inferno [And the Wild, Wild Women] (1958)
La Donna dell' Altro (1959)
La grande vie [Le gran vita] (1960)

Landru (1963)
Giulietta degli spiriti [Juliet of the Spirits] (1965)
Scusi, lei è favorevolo o contrario? (1966)
Non stuzzicare la zanzara (1967)
The Madwoman of Chaillot (1969)
Frau Holle (1985)
Ginger et Fred [Ginger and Fred] (1986)

Sources

Current Biography 1958. New York: H.W. Wilson, 1959, p. 275–6.

Davis, Melton S. "First the Pasta, Then the Play." *New York Times Magazine,* January 2, 1966, p. 10–11+.

Dionne, E.J., Jr. "Giulietta Masina: Film's Eternal Waif." *New York Times,* March 23, 1986, sec. 2, p. 1, 21.

"Foreign Accents in Starlets." *Coronet,* 40:57, August 1956.

The International Dictionary of Films and Filmmakers: Volume III: Actors and Actresses. Chicago: St. James Press, 1986, p. 415.

"A Sad and Saucy Star." *Life,* 41:48, August 6, 1956.

Shipman, David. *The Great Movie Stars: The International Years.* London: Angus & Robertson, 1972, p. 321–23.

"That Round-Eyed Girl." *Newsweek,* 50:99–100, December 9, 1957.

Wlaschin, Ken. *The Illustrated Encyclopedia of the World's Great Movie Stars and Their Films.* London: Salamander, 1979, p. 122.

Pier Angeli

She had barely gotten started in Italian films before Hollywood discovered her and launched Pier Angeli in a career as a Hollywood leading lady. Mostly she was cast as a fragile and innocent heroine and, while she had a couple of good roles, her vehicles were generally undistinguished. Her American career faded away and Pier returned to Europe where she appeared in many more forgettable films. With a stormy private life that belied her sunny screen persona, and unable to adjust to stardom, Angeli died from an overdose of barbituates before she was 40.

The actress was born Anna Maria Pierangeli, June 19, 1932, in Cagliari, Sardinia, Italy, along with her twin sister Marisa. The girls were the daughters of construction engineer Luigi Pierangeli and his wife Enrica who was an enthusiastic amateur actress. When the twins were three the family moved to Rome where they grew up quietly in a expensive apartment and neighborhood.

The girls were brought up in a rigorous and secluded way and Pier had few friends. She turned to the company of animals, picking up stray dogs and hiding them in her room until they were discovered by her parents who sent them on their way. After losing 17 dogs she went on to cats and saw 25 come and go before Mrs. Pierangeli called a truce and promised to buy her daughter a dog if Pier did better at school.

She grew up closer to her father than to any other family member but he never got to see his daughter as a film star since he died of a stroke in 1950 at the age of 41. Relations with Marisa were less cordial and Pier recalled an intense rivalry and constant fights. "We quarreled often. If I say green, she say red. If I say big, she say little," she said.

The family's comfortable existence changed drastically in 1940 when Italy went to war. Over the next four years the young girl came to know what it meant to go without meals and to lie awake at night wondering if her mother would return from food hunting trips. She saw a young boy shot to death on the street by a Nazi, she once fled screaming from a German solider who tried to accost her and while visiting Milan the young girl saw people pumping bullets into Mussolini's dead body hanging from a beam. Throughout the war years Pier continued to attend school every day, hiding in doorways or bomb shelters when planes flew by. In the spring of 1944 Pier fell ill with a strange fever, partly from the shock of war and partly from malnutrition. She was bedridden for three months and by the time she was beginning to recover American troops had reached Italy and for Pier the war was over.

Growing up Pier enjoyed the theater and loved going to the opera with her parents. At ten she sang a popular Italian song of that year so well at a Rome radio audition that the director wanted to take her on as a student. Angeli quickly declined, however, not wishing to leave her relatively cloistered life. Other than this one audition, Pier had had no public performances, no acting lessons nor had she shown any indication that she wanted to be an actress. Her artistic outlet was painting and sketching which she was studying at art school in her mid teens. Her mother had a different future in mind for her daughter, however.

In 1948 Mrs. Pierangeli arranged a tea at the home of a retired actress where Pier was introduced to a French producer and director by the name of Leonide Moguy. For several years Moguy had put off making his film *Tomorrow Is Too Late* in the hope of finding the right actress for the lead role of Mirella — a combination of adolescense and maturity. Upon meeting Pier, Leonide immediately said, "This is my girl — this is Mirella." At first Pier resisted the idea of becoming an actress but after several visits to the director's home accompanied by her mother, and a reading of the script, she changed her mind and starred in that 1950 release.

The film was about sexual enlightenment and concerned one teenager (Angeli) who was destroyed after being wrongly suspected of having had carnal knowledge of a young man. The actress went on to win the Best Actress Award at the Venice Film Festival for her work in that film. Critics praised her for her ability to mix wisdom with naïveté and childishness with maturity. She went on to do a sequel with Moguy, *Tomorrow Is Another Day,* and then began the Hollywood phase of her career.

Stewart Stern, who coauthored the 1951 release *Teresa,* was in Rome for MGM studios. He was looking for a girl to play the title role and picked Pier over 300 other hopefuls on the strength of her first film and on the recommendation of the head of a Rome acting school. In that film Pier portrayed a cheerful adolescent coming to grips with a woman's problems. Teresa left her war-ravaged Italian family to marry an American soldier thinking he was a hero only to discover in America that he was a shiftless and poor, mother-dominated weakling.

Angeli was the best thing about the picture and earned excellent notices. The last few months of shooting were done in New York and Pier and her mother and sister were soon settled in Hollywood. For her Italian films the actress had used her given name but for her American features Hollywood gave her a new name by splitting up her surname.

The naïveté displayed on the screen by Angeli was real and before her arrival in Hollywood she had never drank, smoked or used makeup, even in films. During her first film the director told her the heroine thought she was going to have a baby because she had kissed a boy. Pier thought that was true and Moguy had to tactfully explain the facts of life to her.

Vittorio De Sica acted in that film and helped in the direction of the young actress. In vain, De Sica pleaded with Pier to kiss the leading man as the script called for, saying, "Please Pier, don't be silly. What is it—just one little kiss?" Angeli continued to refuse and did not relent until the entire production crew heckled her in unison.

That same problem cropped up during the filming of *Teresa,* with Pier making countless attempts, including faking ill health, to avoid embracing the actor who played her husband. Director Fred Zinnemann had desperate thoughts of abandoning the project before he got the actress to cooperate.

Despite these problems both men had nothing but praise for Angeli as an actress. "This is not an actress; this is a real human being with an animal quality," said Vittorio, "There is a purity of soul. And an intelligence. She absorbs and she executes. It is material with which you can do anything." Zinnemann commented, "She has a God-given ability to transmit emotion without seeming to do anything—and an unerring instinct for the truth."

Temperamental and childish behavior were also hallmarks of her personality on the sets of her early films. During the shooting of *Teresa* Stewart Stern was awakened in the middle of the night by a phone call from Mrs. Pierangeli frantically saying her daughter was ill and weeping.

Familiar with her behavior by then and thinking over the day's events,

Pier Angeli in *Sodom and Gomorrah*.

Stern remembered that no one had praised Pier's performance after the rushes and he hurried over to her apartment. Armed with a five-pound box of chocolates as a peace offering, the writer told the actress how wonderful she was while Pier lay in bed with her head under the pillow. After about two hours the actress came out and accepted the peace offering.

Angeli's bedroom was crowded with a collection of 27 toy animals and dolls and on the set it was not uncommon to see her reciting nursery rhymes to a doll or sucking on a lollipop. Mrs. Pierangeli did not allow her daughter to go out on her first unchaperoned date until early in 1952. The actress explained her behavior by saying, "I don't like to grow up. I saw many things before I was thirteen that nobody saw in their whole life — and I had to understand them all by myself. We grew up too fast during the war, in Italy. Now I just want to be young and have fun."

Pier was the most natural and unspoilt female to hit Hollywood in a long time and in her next American feature, *The Light Touch,* the cinematographer Robert Surtees said, "For the first time in my career I ordered a leading lady to wear no makeup." Praise flowed from all quarters and *New York Times'* film critic Bosley Crowther said, "Miss Angeli is a young lady with a spindly figure and a wistful face but a wealth of revealing expressions and a beautifully warming smile." Another critic said, "Pier Angeli, sloe-eyed, solemn and boyish, is the best discovery the screen has made since Garbo was a girl." While many hailed her as the next Greta Garbo she never matched those hopes.

None of her films over the next few years lived up to *Teresa.* In *The Light Touch* jewel thief and cad Stewart Granger reformed for the love of the young and innocent Angeli, while she played a German B-girl in *The Devil Makes Three.* Several clunkers followed including *Sombrero* and *The Flame and the Flesh* wherein she lost her man to Lana Turner. As a Spanish café singer she was miscast and ill-at-ease in the melodrama *Port Afrique.* She did not do well in another melodrama *The Vintage* and finished off her MGM contract, and Hollywood career, with her 12th American feature as Danny Kaye's leading lady in *Merry Andrew.*

Only in the 1956 release *Somebody Up There Likes Me* did she achieve the same kind of critical and box office success as she had for *Teresa.* She was cast as Mrs. Rocky Graziano (opposite Paul Newman) as the long-suffering wife of the slum hoodlum who fought his way up to the middleweight boxing championship of the world. "She is gentle and courageous, and proves herself a fine and lovely actress," wrote one critic.

Sister Marisa, overshadowed when she first arrived in Hollywood with her family, soon launched her own acting career as Marisa Pavan. Some thought she had more talent than Pier but her career was cut short when she retired after marrying Jean-Pierre Aumont.

Pier had had an affair with actor James Dean, ending with his death, and then married singer Vic Damone in 1954. The couple had one son named Perry after Damone's friend and idol, singer Perry Como. The marriage lasted until 1958. Bitter court fights over custody of the child, which were well headlined by the press, went on for years and it was 1965 before a settlement was reached. Angeli married Italian bandleader Armando Travajoli in 1962 but that union also ended in divorce, in 1966.

She was off the screen for a couple of years at the end of the 1950s and then started a second phase of her career in European films in 1960, appearing in productions in many different countries including France, Italy, Britain and Israel. Most of these films were minor and some simply sexploitation. She would never again reach the heights of stardom she had once enjoyed.

Angeli was cast as an air hostess in *SOS Pacific* and then as Richard Attenborough's Italian wife in *The Angry Silence,* a role she handled very well. Film roles then got worse as Pier appeared opposite Aldo Ray in *Musketeers of the Sea.* She was in a convict ship melodrama *L'Ammutinamento (White Slave*

Pier Angeli in a tense moment in *White Slave Ship*.

Ship), and in *Sodom and Gomorrah*, the actress was turned into a pillar of salt.

Angeli then reverted to her real name for film work. The parts got no better as she appeared in spy thrillers opposite American male stars who were no longer popular in the United States and seeking work in Europe. She appeared with Dana Andrews in *Spy in Your Eye* and with George Sanders in *One Step to Hell*, where she was cast as a saloon girl who was tortured to death.

Work was steady for the actress but most of her films were little seen in the United States. In the 1969 release *Addio, Alexandra (Love Me, Love My Wife)* Pier was reduced to sexploitation as she often appeared in the nude. A few more films followed and then Pier made her first Hollywood film in more than a decade with a role in the minor film *Octaman*.

The start of a possible comeback was cut short when the actress was found dead in her Beverly Hills apartment on September 10, 1971, at the age of 39. The cause of death was listed as a drug overdose and likely suicide for Pier had never adjusted to stardom or to the decline in her career. Leonide Moguy commented that he felt he was to blame for her death since he had discovered her.

Pier Angeli Filmography

Domani e troppo tardi [Tomorrow Is Too Late] (1950)
Domani e un altro giorno [Tomorrow Is Another Day] (1951)
Teresa (1951)
The Light Touch (1951)
The Devil Makes Three (1952)
Mam'zelle Nitouche [Oh No, Mam'- zelle] (1953)
The Story of Three Loves (1953)
Sombrero (1953)
The Flame and the Flesh (1954)
The Silver Chalice (1954)
Santarellina (1955)
Somebody Up There Likes Me (1956)
Port Afrique (1956)
The Vintage (1957)
Merry Andrew (1958)
The Angry Silence (1960)
SOS Pacific (1960)
I Moschettiere del mare [Musketeers of the Sea] (1960)

Sodoma e Gomorra [Sodom and Go- morrah] (1961)
L'Ammutinamento [White Slave Ship] (1962)
Banco a Bangkok pour OSS 117 [Shadow of Evil] (1964)
Battle of the Bulge (1965)
Berlin, appuntamento per le spie [Spy in Your Eye] (1965)
MMM 83 [Million Bloody Mary] (1965)
Per mille dollari al giorno (1966)
Rose rosse per il Fuhrer [Code Name Red Roses] (1967)
One Step to Hell [King of Africa] (1967)
Vive America (1969)
Addio, Alexandra [Love Me, Love My Wife] (1969)
Les enemoniades (1970)
Every Bastard a King (1970)
Nelle pieghe della carne (1971)
Octaman (1971)

Sources

"A Fine Part for Pier." *Life,* 41:41–2+, July 30, 1956.
Katz, Ephraim. *The Film Encyclopedia.* New York: Thomas Y. Crowell, 1979, p. 33.
Lloyd, Ann, ed. *The Illustrated Who's Who of the Cinema.* London: Orbis, 1983, p. 11.
"A New Star from Italy." *Life,* 30:77–8+, March 19, 1951.
"Pier Angeli, Actress, 39, Dies." *New York Times,* September 11, 1971, p. 14.
Quinlan, David. *Quinlan's Illustrated Directory of Film Stars.* London: B.T. Batsford, 1986, p. 10–11.
Shipman, David. *The Great Movie Stars: The International Years.* London: Angus & Robertson, 1972, p. 11–13.
Strauss, Theodore. "Hollywood Natural." *Colliers,* 129:52+, April 26, 1952.
"Transition." *Newsweek,* 78:71, September 20, 1971.
Watson, E.M.D. "Italy's Twin Sisters." *Cosmopolitan,* 137:28+, September 1954.

Gina Lollobrigida

Hot bombshell, volcanic seductress, smoldering siren—Gina Lollo- brigida's sex appeal conjures up these terms that are rarely used to label women in the late '80s. These terms were very much in vogue during the 1950s

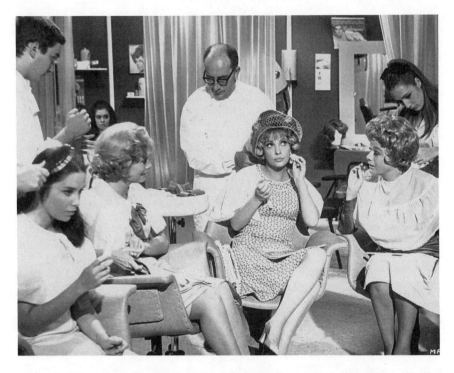

At the hairdresser, Carla (Gina Lollobrigida) listens to Shirley Newman (Shelley Winters) *right,* and Lauren Young (Marian Moses) talk about their Italian trip in *Buona Sera, Mrs. Campbell. At left* is Gia (Janet Margolin), Carla's daughter.

and 1960s, the peak years of Lollobrigida's fame. Her exquisite nubile beauty made up for any lack of acting skills, and Gina became one of the most popular stars of the Italian cinema.

Gina was born Luiga Lollobrigida on July 4, 1927 in Subiaco, Italy, a small town near Rome. The pet form of her name was Luigina, and from this she derived Gina. Her father was a furniture manufacturer and Gina was the second of four daughters. As a child, she received private lessons in singing, dancing, drawing and languages. During World War II Subiaco was bombed and the family home and factory were destroyed. The Lollobrigidas were eventually evacuated to Rome where they lived in a penniless state in a single room. Gina brought in some money by sketching portraits of American G.I.'s and posing for Italian comics that used actual people rather than drawings of cartoon characters. When Gina's father inherited money from a relative, she was able to resume singing lessons.

Lollobrigida won a scholarship to Rome's Academy of Fine Arts where she studied sculpture and painting for three years. In 1946 Italian director Mario Costa spotted Gina on the street. When he approached her and suggested she

Gina Lollobrigida with unidentified actor in *Where the Hot Wind Blows.*

perform in one of his films, Gina thought he was just giving her a line and told him to get lost. He had to show her his identity card before she was convinced that the offer was legitimate. Gina had a few bit parts, earning a little over $3 per day, before working with Costa himself, making her debut in *L'aquila nera.* Her Catholic parents were concerned about their daughter becoming an actress, but when they saw how determined she was, they relented. Gina also entered a couple of beauty contests and was "Miss Rome" in 1947.

In 1950 Gina had her first major role in a part she knew well. She played a beauty contestant in *Miss Italia.* Gina had posed for some pin-up posters and one of the photos showing her in a bikini came to the attention of Howard Hughes. In 1949 he invited Lollobrigida to Hollywood with the intention of using her in his movies. She signed a contract but no roles materialized. Gina claimed she was kept in a hotel room for six weeks, given some English lessons, and taken dining and dancing by Hughes. When she finally got frustrated by the lack of work, she returned to Europe. The contract she signed with Hughes gave him the exclusive right to cast Gina in American films, but he never exercised the option. In 1959 he finally sold his rights to MGM and Gina was free to work in the States.

In the meantime she kept busy in European films. Several of these were

released in the States including the popular *Fanfan the Tulip*. Critic Bosley
Crowther of the *New York Times* called Gina "most fetching ... with ample
charms," in the role of a sergeant's daughter.

She costarred with Vittorio de Sica in *Times Gone By* in which she played
a woman accused of murder. Several films followed including *La Provinciale*
directed by Mario Soldati. The plot was based on a Moravian short story about
a professor's wife who had two men on the side. Gina also starred with Errol
Flynn in *Crossed Swords*. Her acting was considered competent if not always
entirely convincing.

Lollobrigida costarred with other Americans in films that were shot outside the United States. In *Beat the Devil*, directed by John Huston, she played
Humphrey Bogart's wife, and in *Trapeze* she was part of a love triangle that
included Burt Lancaster and Tony Curtis.

The film that really established her reputation in North America was
Bread, Love and Dreams released there in 1954. Gina played a farm girl who
became a love interest for a policeman in her village. Gina entranced critics and
fans with her tight jeans and T-shirted décolletage. She won a Silver Ribbon
for her acting, the Italian equivalent of an Oscar. The movie was so successful
that a sequel called *Bread, Love and Jealousy* was quickly released.

Suddenly everyone was interested in Gina's measurements (36,22,35) and
personal life. It was discovered that she owned 250 outfits and 70 pairs of shoes.
Gina had made sketches of her entire wardrobe and numbered each item so
that her maid could retrieve them quickly. *Life* magazine published the drawings in a 1954 issue. The press also learned that Gina was a married woman.
In 1950 she wed Drago Milko (sometimes spelled Mirko) Skofic, a Yugoslavian-
born physician. She had met him at a New Year's Eve party. Her career then
became so successful that Skofic gave up medicine and became Gina's business
manager.

By 1954 Lollobrigida was one of the highest paid actresses in the world,
earning about $100,000 per picture. Bogart said Gina made "Marilyn Monroe
look like Shirley Temple." Columnist Walter Winchell coined the term
"Lollopalooza" and a Parisian brassiere was advertised as "les lollos."

At times Gina became defensive about her sexuality. Movies always emphasized her body. In *Night Beauties* she had to take a nude milk bath, and
in *Beware of the Bandits* her bosom was so ostentatious that an Italian movie
critic wrote a disparaging review about her "udder." Lollobrigida was highly
offended and sued for libel. The critic and his editor were fined $176 and costs.

Lollobrigida made an extra effort to be professional because she knew it
would earn her respect. She always memorized the script in advance and was
never late for the studio. She took pride in her stardom and had scrapbooks
full of clippings and the dozens of magazine covers that she had appeared on.

In 1955 Gina was cast as soprano Lina Cavalieri in *The World's Most
Beautiful Woman*. Lollobrigida did her own singing in the movie, much to the

dismay of the critics. But audiences loved the film and it was a huge box-office hit in Italy.

In 1957 Gina gave birth to a son, but this did not slow down her career. She stayed in the public eye and in 1959 she appeared in her most notorious film *Solomon and Sheba,* directed by King Vidor. Tyrone Power was originally cast as Solomon but he died during production. Yul Brynner was hired to replace him so much of the movie had to be reshot. Gina had a much heralded bathtub scene, but was not actually naked during the filming. She wore a flesh colored leotard. Still the movie was steamy enough. After one erotic segment, Gina commented in heavily accented English: "I think this is not good. Did you see the way Yul—the way he massage my stomach? Oho! Those censors in Boston will be very much unhappy—I think it is too much."

Gina also protested that one of her costumes was too skimpy. "It ashames me," she complained. "They make me a skirt. And what for above? Nothing. What do I put here? . . . a scarf? Like peasant? . . . I am suppose to be queen, I am supposed to be well dressed." Lolobrigida got her way and the veil-like top was replaced by a sturdier halter bra which was still plenty revealing. Gina also refused to dance in a vulgar manner. When the director, Ted Richmond, threatened to hire a belly-dancer as a stand-in, Gina became furious. When Richmond reminded her that it was a pagan dance, Gina retorted, "They are the pagans. I am the queen," and did the dance her way.

Lollobrigida owned a percentage of the film. During the shooting she decided it was going to be a flop due to the delays caused by Power's death and the circus-like atmosphere on the set. She sold her interest back to United Artists, a decision she later regretted. The movie was a box-office hit and grossed millions.

In Italy a Roman Catholic priest wrote an article on how scandalous the Sheba movie was. He castigated Lollobrigida for immorality and said she showed a censored version of the movie to her son, thus proving that she herself knew how corrupting certain scenes were. Gina sued the paper and pointed out the absurdity of the accusation since her son was only two years old and had never seen the film at all. Lollobrigida withdrew the suit after the paper printed a retraction.

Gina's husband was still in charge of the business side of her career and friends noted, "When he's on hand, she's the dutiful wife." But Gina realized, "My husband is in a psychologically difficult position, with a famous wife." She told a reporter that she was willing to give up acting if her husband wanted her to.

Lollobrigida continued to work steadily in the 1960s. In European pictures she had a saucy, mischievous attraction that was sometimes lost to American audiences. The problem was that her English was poor and she was not always certain what she was saying. This gave her performances a wooden quality. Her roles were also partly to blame. She was often mere decoration as in *Never So*

Few, a male-action movie starring Frank Sinatra, or a prostitute as in *Go Naked in the World.* At least the pay was good. Gina earned about $250,000 per film.

At first it had not been easy for Gina to work with Sinatra. He was used to filming a scene in one take and had no patience for reshooting. He was also casual about time. When he showed up late one morning, Lollobrigida complained that she could have had some extra sleep if she'd known. Sinatra was furious that she dared criticize him and walked off the set. Gina apologized and after that relations improved between them.

In 1960 Lollobrigida vacated her beautiful Roman villa and established residence in Toronto, Canada. Some observers felt she moved for tax reasons, but Gina claimed it was necessary for her son. Her husband had been a war refugee and had a stateless passport. Under Italian law if the father is stateless, so is the son. The family planned to apply for Canadian citizenship.

Acting was still very important to Gina and although she felt that being a celebrity was like being on display in a zoo, she wanted to be respected for her talent. She was no longer content with just posing through a picture, and took acting lessons. "Was much easier before," she said of her early films. "All I did was talk, and I didn't think."

Come September, a comedy costarring Rock Hudson, was a successful vehicle for Gina, but even though her acting was good, it was her body that received the kudos. Even the film crew related to her as a sex symbol. In one scene where she had to walk seductively up a staircase, the entire crew began whistling and hooting. "Please!" Gina insisted. "If you do not become quiet with the noise, I cannot work."

Even though she wore loose clothing and scarves off-screen, fans usually recognized her, and men leered. "Always there is the wolf call," Gina sighed. "I yell back at them! Dog! Pig! Nasty!" Even more hurtful were the obscene phone calls and letters she received and the vulgar graffiti painted on her house. "My whole life is big, long battle to tell men I don't wish to take off the clothes . . . I cannot help the way I look."

Gina was in several more European movies, none of which made a big impact. An American project *Strange Bedfellows,* another comedy with Rock Hudson, did get some attention. In 1966 Gina and her husband separated. Rumors abounded that she was having an affair with famous heart surgeon Dr. Christiaan Barnard. The marriage never recovered and the couple divorced. Lollobrigida was criticized by the Vatican but Pope Paul VI deigned to shake her hand when she and several other performers visited him in 1967. "We are aware of the wall that separates your field from ours, the profane from the sacred," said the Pope.

Once again Gina's home base was Rome. She made 16 more films between 1966 and 1977 but none gave her the kind of fame she had enjoyed earlier in her career. Most were made in Europe and many were light comedies or thrillers. Gina passed the age of 40 during these years and her roles became less glamorous. Gina's buxom beauty was also no longer in style. She regretted that "nobody has taken the trouble to find out if I have any talent or brains."

By the mid–1970s Lollobrigida had switched her focus from acting to photography. She had always been interested in cameras and parlayed this hobby into a new career. Several books of her photographs have been published and she has taken portraits of Henry Kissinger, Neil Armstrong, Salvador Dali, Yevgeny Yevtushenko and Aristotle Onassis. In 1974 she visited Cuba and snapped Fidel Castro in various poses as well as directing a television documentary about him. Gina described Castro as surprisingly "gentle, very soft . . . those eyes of his! He still is a mysterious man."

Lollobrigida married again in 1969 to George Kaufman. At the age of 50 she became the artistic director of an interior design firm and the president of a cosmetics company. She still enjoyed being in the limelight, however, and always dressed like a star in public, wearing furs, jewels, and flashy makeup. A source of pride was the fact that the term "Lollobrigidian" had been added to the French dictionary. "It's used to describe a landscape with a lot of hills," she said with a wide smile.

Gina Lollobrigida Filmography

L'aquila nera (1946)
Lucia de Lammermoor (1946)
Il segreto di don Giovanni (1947)
Il delitto di Giovanni Episcopo (1947)
Vendetta nel sole [A Man About the House] (1947)
L'elisir d'amore (1947)
Follie per l'opera (1948)
I pagliacci (1948)
Campane a martello (1949)
La sposa non puo attendere (1949)
Miss Italia (1950)
Cuori senza frontiere (1950)
Vita de cani (1950)
Alina (1950)
Passaporto per l'Oriente [A Tale of Five Cities] (1951)
La città si difende (1951)
Enrico Caruso, leggenda di una voce [The Young Caruso] (1951)
Achtung banditi! [Beware of the Bandits] (1951)
Fanfan la tulipe [Fanfan the Tulip] (1951)

Amor non ho, pero, pero . . . (1951)
Altri tempi [Times Gone By] (1952)
La belle della notte [Les Belles de nuit; Night Beauties] (1952)
Moglie per una notte (1952)
Le infideli [The Wayward Wife] (1953)
La provinciale (1953)
Il maestro di don Giovanni [Crossed Swords] (1953)
Pane, amore e fantasia [Bread, Love and Dreams] (1953)
Pane, amore e gelosia [Bread, Love and Jealousy] (1953)
Beat the Devil (1953)
Il grande giuoco [Le Grand Jeu; The Card of Fate] (1954)
La romana [Woman of Rome] (1954)
La donna più bella del mondo (1955)
Trapeze (1956)
Notre-Dame de Paris [The Hunchback of Notre Dame] (1956)
Anna di Brooklyn [Anna of Brooklyn] (1958)

La Loi [Where the Hot Wind Blows]
  (1958)
Never So Few (1959)
Solomon and Sheba (1959)
Go Naked in the World (1959)
Come September (1961)
Venere imperiale (1962)
Mare matto (1963)
Woman of Straw (1963)
Le bambole [Four Kinds of Love]
  (1964)
Strange Bedfellows (1964)
Io, io, io ... e gli altri (1966)
Les Sultans [L'amante italiana] (1966)
Hotel Paradiso (1966)
Cervantes (1966)
Le piacevoli notti (1966)

*La morte ha fatto l'uovo [Plucked; A
  Curious Way to Love]* (1968)
The Private Navy of Sgt. O'Farrell
  (1968)
Un bellissimo novembre (1968)
Buona sera, Mrs. Campbell (1969)
Stuntman (1969)
*...e continuavano a fregarsi il milione
  di dollari* (1970)
Le avventura di Pinocchio (1971)
Herzbube [King, Queen, Knave]
  (1972)
Peccato mortale (1972)
*Roses rouges et piments vert [The
  Lonely Woman]* (1975)
Nido de viudas [Widow's Nest]
  (1977)

Sources

Angell, Roger. "World of Women: Italy Gina," *Holiday,* 17:91, February 1955.
Chusmir, Janet. "Says Gina Lollobrigida," *Biography News,* 1:67, January 1974.
Current Biography, 1959. New York: H.W. Wilson, 1960, p. 235–237.
Fajardo, Rolan. "Gina Says," *Interview,* n. 33:17–18, June 1973.
"Film-Press Group Received by Pope," *New York Times,* May 7, 1976, p. 86.
Gehman, Richard. "Gina," *Good Housekeeping,* 152:77+, February 1961.
"Hollywood on the Tiber," *Time,* 64:54+, August 16, 1954.
International Dictionary of Films and Filmmakers: Volume III: Actors and Actresses.
　　Chicago: St. James Press, 1986, p. 385–386.
Johns, Robert. "Saga of a Siren," *Saturday Evening Post,* 233:18+, August 13, 1960.
Klemesrud, Judy. "Gina Offers a Few Tips to Women," *New York Times,* January 23, 1969,
　　p. 53.
"Lollobrigida: Pin-Up," *Collier's,* 135:29+, January 21, 1955.
Morton, Frederic. "The Antic Art," *Holiday,* 25:111+, June 1959.
"People," *Time,* 104:58, September 30, 1974.
"People," *Time,* 111:85, April 24, 1978.
Quinlan, David. *The Illustrated Directory of Film Stars.* London: B.T. Batsford, 1981, p.
　　289.
Shipman, David. *The Great Movie Stars: The International Years.* London: Angus &
　　Robertson, 1972, p. 291+.
"Speaking of Pictures," *Life,* 37:18+, November 15, 1954.
"That Certain Something," *Newsweek,* 44:85–86, October 4, 1954.
Whitcomb, Jon. "Gina As Sheba," *Cosmopolitan,* 147:13+, August 1959.

Sophia Loren

　　　Famed for her earthy and voluptuous sensuality, Sophia Loren took the
Italian cinema by storm around 1954 and soon conquered the rest of the

cinematic world. Unlike so many other sex goddesses, Sophia engaged in very little nudity in her films and instead conveyed sexuality with her full figure and lusty, fiery characterizations.

In the beginning her acting ability was poor but Loren worked at it and eventually gave many exceptional performances. Hollywood beckoned and she made several films there in the late 1950s. None were very good and most wasted her talent or miscast her. She joined a long list of other foreign actresses who never returned to Hollywood.

The actress was born Sofia Scicolone on September 20, 1934, in Rome, Italy. Her parents, Riccardo Scicolone and Romilda Villani, never married although her father signed an affidavit attesting to the fact that Sophia was his issue, allowing her to use his name.

Romilda came from Pozzuoli, an impoverished industrial suburb of Naples, and by the time she was 17 she was an accomplished piano player. She also felt she bore a striking resemblance to actress Greta Garbo and that year entered a contest held by MGM to find a Garbo look-alike. Romilda beat out over 350 other contestants and won a trip to Hollywood where she would get a screen test. Sophia's grandmother stepped in, however, and refused to let her daughter go. She believed that Rudoph Valentino had been murdered by the Mafia in the United States and that the same fate would befall Romilda since fans of Garbo would be jealous of her and employ the Mafia. MGM officials went to Pozzuoli and tried to convince the woman, but to no avail. The prize was awarded to the second place finisher.

A frustrated Romilda went to Rome, without her mother's permission, and hung around the film studios trying to get acting work. Nothing came her way but she did meet Riccardo who did not work but drifted around on the fringes of show business. Soon Romilda found herself pregnant and gave birth to Sophia.

With her hopes of being a film star or a concert pianist gone, Romilda returned to Pozzuoli where Sophia was raised. Riccardo visited once in a while and another daughter was born four years later. Sophia rarely saw her father although he once started an unsuccessful legal action to try and get some money after Loren had become famous. Sophia's feelings for her father varied from ambivalence to outright dislike.

The family had little money in Pozzuoli and that came from Romilda playing piano in small cafés. Sophia attended a Catholic parochial school until she was 12. So frail was she from not having enough to eat that other children called her "stecchetto" (the stick) and "stuzzicadenti" (toothpick). The two sisters found their own diversions and whenever they got a few lire they bought colored paper with which they made costumes and then put on little presentations for their mother and other relatives.

As a youngster Loren was not considered attractive and her wet nurse recalled "Sophia was the ugliest child I ever saw in my life." She was also quiet

Sophia Loren

and sometimes did not speak for several days. "I've always been a very closed character," she said. Naples was a prime bomb target for the Allies during the war, because of its industries and port, and time got even harder for the family. They had to queue for food and sleep in a railway tunnel on many nights, which provided a bomb shelter.

At 12 Loren enrolled at a teacher training institute where she stayed until she was 15. Her intention then was to become a teacher and she explained "to be ugly is the worst thing that can happen to a girl. In Italy it means you must have a career. Italian girls have careers only if they cannot get married." She disliked teacher training but then at 15 her life changed. "Then I became nice," she said. "I stopped growing taller and began to grow the other ways, and men began to look at me when I walked down the street."

Romilda noticed the change also and in 1949 urged her daughter to enter a Queen of the Sea beauty contest in Naples. The shy daughter protested that she did not want to enter but her mother insisted. Loren entered and while she did not win she was named one of the 12 princesses and won a train ticket to Rome, a tablecloth and napkins, $35 and several rolls of wallpaper.

Romilda next enrolled her daughter at a Naples dramatic school, paying the tuition out of money she made giving piano lessons. Loren came home from acting lessons one day and told her mother that the teacher had said an American film production, *Quo Vadis?* was shooting in Rome and looking for hundreds of extras. Romilda made a quick decision and the family moved to Rome. That was the end of teacher training. Mother and daughter both got work as extras in that film and earned a total of $76 between them.

Loren searched for film work but was only able to find bit parts. Her main income came from the "fumetti." These were Italian magazines with a soap opera plot and which had dialogue coming in puffs out of the characters' mouths. They are similar to comic books, only then using real photos instead of drawings. She became quite popular posing in this field and appeared in literally hundreds of magazines.

Initially she had worked under her real name, Sofia Scicolone, in both the "fumetti" and films until a "fumetti" director changed her last name to Laz-zaro, feeling it was less comic and less difficult. The actress appeared under that name in a couple of films as well. A film director later decided she needed a different name. Sofia became Sophia because it was more exotic and Loren was chosen because it was short, easy to remember and less Italian.

After about a year in Rome, Sophia visited a nightclub with some friends on an evening when a beauty contest was to be held. An official from the jury came over and told Loren that Carlo Ponti, a movie producer and judge that evening, requested that she enter. She did and came in second. Later Ponti introduced himself and set up a screen test for Sophia on the following day. That test was a disaster but Ponti persisted and gave her a number of screen tests over the course of a year, each with a different cameraman. Each one was a disaster.

When the fourth test proved to be bad Ponti suggested Loren might "consider a little bit of modification." He had in mind some weight loss from the hips and a nose job. Sophia adamantly refused. Ponti did not lose interest and kept in contact with the young girl. When they first met Sophia had just turned 16 while Carlo was 37, and separated with two children.

Recalling how small her parts were in her early films, Sophia joked, "In my first picture I said, 'Good morning.' Then I made rapid progress in my second movie. I said, 'Good morning, madame.' In my third movie, I had a really big part. I said, 'Good morning, madame, how are you?'"

Meeting Ponti was a turning point for Loren, who said, "I was very, very young. I was impressed with his self-assurance, culture and intelligence. And I felt immediately a strong impulse to impress him." Ponti remembered being struck more by her personality than by her looks, and admitted, "I was first interested in Sophia as a woman, and only afterward as an artist." Carlo took her on as a protégée, bought her clothes, had her hair cut more fashionably, and sent her off to learn to use makeup. He also bought acting and diction lessons. Her Neapolitan accent was so strong in the beginning that her voice had to be dubbed a few times. Soon she had a more standard Italian accent.

Loren worked steadily in films in small parts and did her best to promote her career. She posed for cheesecake photos, wrapped in a bath towel, or having her bra adjusted by a male coworker. One magazine cover featured the actress with her skirt pulled up so high that the Italian police confiscated the entire issue. One of those films, *It's Him, Yes! Yes!* featured Sophia topless but generally she was properly clothed. Her first major part came in *Africa under the Sea,* a dismal low budget semidocumentary. It was for this film that she had her name changed to the now world famous Sophia Loren.

Next came *Aida* wherein Loren mouthed the lyrics while diva Renata Tebaldi sang. It brought the actress her first major salary, notices and publicity. She got the part only after reigning Italian movie queen Gina Lollobrigida had turned it down at the last moment, feeling it was beneath her dignity to act as a singer's stand-in. *Aida* prompted Ponti to sign Loren to a personal contract with him, as opposed to a studio contract. Romilda was against the idea, saying, "You should not be tied down to a contract. You are just starting your career. You should be free to do what comes along." It was advice Sophia ignored.

The year 1954 was a big one for the actress. She had major roles in several films such as playing a volatile shopkeeper in *The Treasure of Naples,* and wearing wet and revealing clothing and engaged in a passionate triangle in *Woman of the River.* That film was especially created for the actress by Ponti. She also played in a comedy *Too Bad She's Bad* wherein she was paired with Marcello Mastroianni, the first of ten films in which they would costar.

By the end of 1954 Loren had appeared in 29 films, was a major box office draw in Italy, and was being noticed in other parts of the world. The following year was definitely Sophia's year as she got worldwide publicity and supplanted Lollobrigida as Italy's favorite actress. A phoney feud between them was developed by publicity people who had Gina say, "Sophia is a very pretty girl but she cannot threaten me because she is incapable of playing my roles." They had Sophia respond, "Her personality is limited. She is good as a peasant but incapable of playing a lady."

Sophia Loren *(right)* and Marcello Mastroianni with an unidentified actress in *The Priest's Wife.*

Americans were also impressed with her, and veteran actor George Raft said, "She's Mount Vesuvius, Etna and Krakatoa all thrown into one." Marlon Brando commented that "when you see it you don't believe it. Then you look again . . . and still you don't believe it." Her acting ability was not generally considered to be responsible for her success. One critic said she "has gotten where she is with a minimum of dramatic ability and a maximum of everything else." Another said she "registered all emotion with her bosom," while one of her directors, Vittorio de Sica, diplomatically said, "Her acting ability is not quite as fully developed as her physical presence."

In 1955 the actress was presented to Queen Elizabeth and appeared on the cover of *Life* magazine. Ponti was concentrating on her career and told her not to limit herself to Italian films but to learn English so she could eventually work in Hollywood. Complying with the request, Loren had gotten no further than simple phrases such as "Please, pass the butter" when Ponti informed her he had signed her to costar in Stanley Kramer's, *The Pride and the Passion,* opposite Cary Grant.

United Artists, the producing company, wanted a name star and so did Grant, who had cast approval. Attempts were made to get several other actresses, including Ava Gardner, but none were available. Kramer, who had seen *Woman of the River,* kept pushing and finally got approval to cast Loren.

"You can stick me with this prediction: this girl will explode within two or three years as the world's greatest actress," said Kramer. "I've worked with some great talents, but in this twenty-two year old youngster I see the greatest of them all."

Happy to be working in an American picture, Loren said, "My figure made me famous and I am grateful. But now I want to be known as an actress." The only worry for that film was whether Sophia's command of English would be good enough. Before shooting began, Loren told Kramer, "By the time you are ready to shoot, I will be ready to speak my lines." She was.

The actress appeared in two other American-made films, *Boy on a Dolphin* opposite Alan Ladd, and *Legend of the Lost* as an Arab slave girl loved by John Wayne. These two and *The Pride and the Passion* were all filmed in Europe and she was miscast in all of them. She liked none of them and was particularly displeased with *Boy on a Dolphin*. She would not explain the reason saying only, "Go see it, and you will know." Because she was several inches taller than Ladd she "had to stand in a hole for half the picture" to make Ladd appear taller. One of her scenes had her emerge from the ocean in a wet and clinging dress. Hollywood directors then tried to ingeniously devise ways for her to appear in a similar condition in other films. "It seems to me," said Sophia, "that I spent years in the movies having people throw pails of water on me."

Ponti and Loren had begun dating not long after they met and the relationship came to a head during the filming of *The Pride and the Passion* when Loren and Grant fell in love. Loren wanted to get married and Grant had no strings attached but Ponti did. Finally Carlo married Sophia in 1957 in a proxy ceremony conducted in Mexico. This was after Ponti obtained a divorce, also in a Mexican proxy ceremony, since Italy did not grant divorce.

Italy recognized none of these ceremonies and a religious zealot charged the couple as being bigamists. To avoid the furor, and a possible jail sentence, the couple moved to Switzerland. However, wanting to work back home Ponti had the marriage annulled in 1962 and the couple lived together, although no longer subject to bigamy charges. Commenting on the bigamy charge, Loren said, "I was sued by a woman whose husband had left her. This woman didn't know me, but she was miserable and bitter and she said, 'I want to make every woman suffer.' If it is any satisfaction to her, I have suffered."

Loren appeared in several more American films including *Desire Under the Elms,* her first film that was actually shot in Hollywood. As the film was about New Englanders, Sophia was woefully miscast. The actress played a kept woman wooed by Tab Hunter in *That Kind of Woman,* starred in a ludicrous western *Heller in Pink Tights,* and then did better in two comedies *Houseboat* with Cary Grant, and *It Started in Naples* with Clark Gable. One of her better outings was in *The Black Orchid* as a widow courted by Anthony Quinn for which she won the Best Actress honors at the Venice Film Festival.

About acting, Sophia said, "I am worried. I worry all the time about a picture, a role I play. I worry about everything . . . it's easy to become a star by exposing the body and looking sultry. But if that is all you have, you go down fast in competition with a better body, better sultry looks." She said, "I love my business. I want to go on acting until I'm ninety. Acting for me is getting rid of my inhibitions. I do things in front of the camera that I would never, ever do in real life. So acting becomes a kind of vacation for me."

In 1959 she left Hollywood and never made another film there. Usually she was diplomatic about her experiences there and said, "From a schooling point of view, Hollywood was very good to me. I was fortunate to work with top stars, and I learned very much from them." Sometimes she let her real feelings out as when she said, "In America, people think in stereotypes. They think all Italians are either gangsters or waiters. And I would play their daughters. So when my contracts ran out, I decided to leave because I'd be playing gangsters' daughters forever . . . Americans have never been able to accept a foreign actress for what she is. They feel they have to change her. That's what happened to me." Loren was also unhappy about the sexpot image and commented, "I get so upset sometimes when I see so many people who think beautiful women are stupid and ugly women are always the best actresses and most intelligent."

In Italy Loren got a role in *Two Women,* the story of a widow and her daughter in war-torn Italy. Originally Anna Magnani was set as the mother with Loren as the daughter. When Magnani could not do the film, the ages of the characters were changed and the 27-year-old Loren was given a 13-year-old daughter. Loren gave a stunning performance and won the Best Actress Award at the Cannes Film Festival and at the New York Film Festival. The British Academy voted her Best Foreign Actress while the American Academy awarded her an Oscar as Best Actress — the first time a top Oscar had gone to a person in a foreign-language film.

During the 1960s the actress gave many fine performances as in *Yesterday, Today and Tomorrow* and *Marriage, Italian Style* for which the American Academy nominated her for an Oscar as Best Actress. She also appeared in many dismal films such as *The Condemned of Altona, Operation Crossbow* and Charlie Chaplin's *A Countess from Hong Kong.* The latter film was totally panned by the critics but Loren got some decent notices.

The marriage situation was resolved in 1966 after the couple renounced their Italian citizenship and moved to Paris, became French citizens, and were joined in that country by Ponti's first wife and children who also became French citizens. A French divorce for Ponti was followed by a French wedding and Loren and Ponti were legally married. Sophia had often tried to have a child but had numerous miscarriages. The couple finally had a son in 1968 and another one four years later. During both pregnancies Sophia had to spend many months almost completely in bed. Motherhood was very important for the actress, who said, "Now I am a complete woman."

Sophia Loren appears to be refereeing a fight in *Lady Liberty*.

By the time Sophia turned 40 in 1974 the best of her work, and the bulk of it, was behind her. She said she gave no thought to being 40, noting, "For an actress there's no problem really. If the age shows for a certain moment, you have to change your role. But I already changed 15 years ago . . . as for me, if I ever get to the point where I feel I can't throw myself enthusiastically into a movie, where I don't feel anything inside, I would quit."

The pictures she made tended to do well in Europe but less so in the English language world. Pairings with Mastroianni were particularly well received by cinemagoers. Loren's own favorite films were *Two Women* and *A Countess from Hong Kong*. The latter more for the opportunity to work with Charlie Chaplin than for the film.

Ponti and Loren ran into trouble with Italy again in 1977 when the couple were charged with trying to smuggle $12 million out of Italy. Sophia was acquited but Ponti was convicted — in absentia. He faced arrest and prison if he entered Italy again. In the early 1980s the couple abruptly moved to Geneva, Switzerland. The reason was never divulged although some speculated it was because Ponti was having trouble with the French tax authorities.

Sophia's film appearances declined toward the end of the 1970s, with her best performance coming in *A Special Day*, a drama in which she played a frumpy housewife with six children who struck up a friendship with Mastroianni, who was cast as a homosexual. Loren also appeared in *The Cassandra Crossing*, *Brass Target* and Lina Wertmuller's *Blood Feud*. None of these did well at the box office.

In 1982 the actress returned to Italy to make a film for director Wertmuller. Before shooting began, Loren was jailed for 30 days as a result of a tax evasion charge that went back to 1964. Sophia claimed her accountant had told her she did not have to file a return that year since she was then living in Switzerland. After 19 days in jail the actress was released. Ironically Wertmuller and Sophia had a disagreement and the actress withdrew from that film.

During the 1980s Loren moved into commercial endorsements and promoted a line of eyeglasses, a perfume named after her and a southern Florida resort in which she had an interest. A beauty book under her name, *Women and Beauty*, was published the month Loren turned 50. "You shouldn't drag yourself down because you turn 50," said Sophia. "If you have achieved something in life, age doesn't scare you." Her absence from films did not disturb her. She said, "I worked so much when I was young, starting at 15. My first choice is to be with the children."

Her marriage to Ponti has often been reported as rocky. Ponti has been accused of numerous infidelities while Sophia had one reported affair with a French doctor in the early '80s. Yet it survived. "I know what makes my marriage work," she said. "I make it work. Men don't make any real effort, which is my main objection to them."

While she has not been in a theatrical film since 1980, Loren has appeared on television a couple of times. One of those in 1984 was because one of her sons was making his acting debut. Speaking about the problems of women in films, Sophia said, "I love my work. Being an actress is something I've always wanted. And now that I've succeeded, I feel much more conscious of the problems an actress has to face . . . I like to play submissive women, because I think I can help some women to wake up. But what I represent for the public, I don't know."

By the end of the 1970s there were only four films that the actress was proud of, *Two Women*, *A Special Day*, *Yesterday, Today and Tomorrow* and *Marriage, Italian Style*. Of the rest, she said, "I made a lot of other films but I wasn't enchanted with them. You know, I'll consider myself lucky if I make six or seven valid films in my career, artistically. Not many actresses will, you know."

Sophia Loren Filmography

Quo Vadis? (1949)
Curoi sul mare [Hearts Upon the Sea]

(1950)
Il voto [The Vote] (1950)

Le sei moglie di Barbarbù [Bluebeard's Six Wives] (1950)
Io sono il capataz (1950)
Erà Lui, ... si! si! [It's Him, Yes! Yes!] (1951)
Milana miliardaria [Milana the Millionairess] (1951)
Anna (1951)
Il mago per forza [The Magician in Spite of Himself] (1951)
Il sogno di Zorro [The Dream of Zorro] (1951)
È arrivato l'accordatore [The Piano Tuner Has Arrived] (1951)
Lebfra bianca (1951)
La favorita [The Favorite] (1952)
Africa sotto i mari [Africa Under the Seas; Woman of the Red Seas] (1952)
La tratta delle bianche [The White Slave Trade; Girls Marked Danger] (1952)
Aida (1953)
La domenica della buona genti [Good People's Sunday] (1953)
Il paese dei campanelli [The Country of Bells] (1953)
Un giorno in pretura [A Day in Court] (1953)
Pellegrini d'amore [Pilgrim of Love] (1953)
Carosello Napoletano [Neapolitan Carousel] (1953)
Ci troviamo in galleria [We'll Meet in the Gallery] (1953)
Tempi nostri [Anatomy of Love] (1953)
Due notti con Cleopatra [Two Nights with Cleopatra] (1953)
Attila [Attila the Hun] (1953)
L'oro di Napoli [The Treasure of Naples; The Gold of Naples] (1954)
La donna del fiume [Woman of the River] (1954)
Miseria e nobiltà [Poverty and Nobility] (1954)
Pecatto che sia una canaglia [Too Bad She's Bad] (1954)
Il segno di Venere [The Sign of Venus] (1955)
La bella mugnaia [The Miller's Wife] (1955)
Pane, amore e ... [Scandal in Sorrento] (1955)
La fortuna di essere donna [Lucky to be a Woman] (1955)
The Pride and the Passion (1957)
Boy on a Dolphin (1957)
Legend of the Lost (1957)
Desire Under the Elms (1958)
Houseboat (1958)
The Key (1958)
The Black Orchid (1959)
That Kind of Woman (1959)
Heller in Pink Tights (1960)
It Started in Naples (1960)
A Breath of Scandal (1960)
The Millionairess (1960)
Lo ciociara [Two Women] (1961)
El Cid (1961)
Boccaccio '70 (1961)
Madame Sans-Gene [Madame] (1961)
La Couteau dans la plaie [Five Miles to Midnight] (1962)
I sequestrati di Altona [The Condemned of Altona] (1962)
Ieri, oggi e domani [Yesterday, Today and Tomorrow] (1963)
The Fall of the Roman Empire (1964)
Matrimonio all'italiana [Marriage, Italian Style] (1964)
Judith (1965)
Operation Crossbow [The Great Spy Mission] (1965)
Lady L (1965)
Arabesque (1966)
A Countess from Hong Kong (1966)
C'erà una volta [More than a Miracle; Cinderella, Italian Style] (1967)
Questi fantasmi [Ghosts, Italian Style] 1967
I girasoli [Sunflowers] (1969)
La mogli del prete [The Priest's Wife] (1970)
La mortadella [Lady Liberty] (1971)
Bianco, rosso, e... [The White Sister] (1971)
Man of La Mancha (1971)
Il viaggio [The Voyage] (1973)
Le testament [Jury of One, The Verdict] (1974)
Poopsie [Gun Moll] (1974)
Una giornata speciale [A Special Day] (1975)

The Cassandra Crossing (1976)
Angela (1976)
Brass Target (1978)
Firepower (1979)
Revenge (1979)

Blood Feud (1979)
Shimmy Lugano e tarantelle e vino
(1979)
Oopsie Poopsie (1980)

Sources

Battelle, Phyllis. "Sophia Loren," *Ladies' Home Journal,* 101:32+, July 1984.
Bentley, Logan. "After a Proud Moment, Sophia Loren Flies Off to a Harsh Homecoming," *People,* 17:34–35, June 7, 1982.
Bester, Alfred. "The Dilemma of Sophia Loren," *Holiday,* 26:87–92, September 1959.
Burke, Tom. "Now I Am a Complete Woman," *New York Times,* October 4, 1970, sec. 2, p. 13, 32.
Current Biography 1959. New York: H.W. Wilson, 1960, p. 266–267.
Hall, Jane. "Sophia's Choice," *People,* 22:121+, October 22, 1984.
Hamblin, Dora Jane. "Che Gioia, La Vita," *Life,* 51:50–60+, August 11, 1961.
Hamill, Pete. "First, I Am a Woman," *Saturday Evening Post,* 237:60–63, February 15, 1964.
Hotchner, A.E. "Sophia Loren," *McCall's* 106:77+, January 1979.
_____. "A Test of Her Strength," *Ladies' Home Journal,* 99:16+, March 1982.
The International Dictionary of Films and Filmmakers: Volume III: Actors and Actresses. Chicago: St. James Press, 1986, p. 387–389.
"Italy's Sophia Loren," *Newsweek,* 46:53–56, August 15, 1955.
Klemesrud, Judy. "There's More to Sophia Loren than Being a Sex Symbol," *New York Times,* September 22, 1977, p. C16.
Krims, Milton. "Sophia, Etc.," *Holiday,* 54:28+, December 1, 1973.
Levy, Alan. "Sophia Loren: My 20 Years with Carlo," *McCall's,* 104:16+, August 1977.
"Much Woman," *Time,* 79:78–82, April 6, 1962.
Pryor, Thomas. "Hollywood Luminary," *New York Times,* February 9, 1958, sec. 2, p. 5.
Quinlan, David. *The Illustrated Directory of Film Stars.* London: B.T. Batsford, 1981, p. 291–292.
Reed, Rex. "Sophia Loren," *Ladies' Home Journal,* 93:90+, April 1976.
Reese, John. "From Starvation to Stardom," *Saturday Evening Post,* 229:24–5+, October 20, 1956.
"A Saga of Sophia," *Life,* 39:43–4+, August 22, 1955.
"Sent for One," *Time,* 79:79–80, April 20, 1962.
Shipman, David. *The Great Movie Stars: The International Years.* London: Angus & Robertson, 1972, p. 293–299.
"Sophia at Peak of Her Busy Career," *Life,* 42:137–144, May 6, 1957.
"Sophia Faces 50," *McCall's,* 110:99+, July 1983.
"Sophia Loren," *Film Comment,* 19:46–47, April 1983.
"Sophia Loren: Spaghetti-Inspired Sex Appeal," *Coronet,* 41:8, February 1957.
"Sophia Tells," *People,* 11:105+, March 12, 1979.
Von Faber, Karin. "Profile of a Positive Person," *Biography News,* 1:1417–18, December 1974.
Werba, Hank. "Loren Disputes Account of 'Tieta' Pullout," *Variety,* 307:33, July 21, 1982.
Whitcomb, Jon. "Sophia Loren in America," *Cosmopolitan,* 144:77–79, February 1958.

Elsa Martinelli

While most of her films have been made in Europe, Elsa Martinelli is unusual in that her debut film was a Hollywood effort after she was discovered by actor Kirk Douglas. Her American career never really got started but for a number of years she was a high demand leading lady in Europe. More recently her screen appearances have been rare as she has turned to a second career as a fashion designer.

Elsa was born in 1932 in Grosseto, Italy, the daughter of a lower echelon government official. With nine children in the family, finances were tight and Elsa had to go to work at the age of 12. A couturier was attracted to her tall, lithe figure and the teenager began a modeling career at the age of 16. It took years to get established and she sometimes took other jobs to make extra money. One was as a barmaid. By the early 1950s she was earning $1,000 a week and her pictures appeared in high fashion magazines around the world.

In New York an agent saw some of these pictures and invited the model to come and work in the United States. Martinelli needed no coaxing. She quickly accepted and after only six months in this country Kirk Douglas phoned her and asked her to test for his new film *The Indian Fighter*. Elsa did not believe it was really Douglas and asked him to sing the song from the film *20,000 Leagues Under the Sea*. Kirk passed his test and later so did Elsa.

That film was released in 1955 but was a less than outstanding debut for the actress. She had the customary Hollywood nude scenes and had little to do except look stunning and provide a love interest for Douglas. She did not have many lines in the film which was just as well since she had a heavy Italian accent but was cast as a native Indian.

The actress then returned to Italy and made her Italian film debut the next year in *La Risaia*, a melodrama set in the rice fields of the Po Valley. It was a copy of *Bitter Rice*, a successful Italian film of a few years previous. The copy was done on the wide screen and in color but in all other ways it was a poor vehicle for the actress's home country debut. She did better later that year with the lead role in *Donatella*. Martinelli played a poor girl who worked as a personal secretary in a rich household. A visiting lawyer fell in love with her believing her to be wealthy. Complications followed but a happy ending eventually ensued in this Cinderella remake and Elsa got excellent notices and was named Best Actress at the Berlin Film Festival.

That year, 1956, was busy for the actress in other ways. In July she tried to park her car in a no-parking zone which the police refused to allow. An argument followed and the actress was charged with insulting three policemen. In Italy sentences of 12 months or less can be suspended for first offenders and at the trial the next year the prosecution asked for a six-month suspended sentence. The judge agreed but decided three policemen meant three offenses and came up with a sentence of eighteen months imprisonment. On appeal in 1958 the sentence was reduced to twelve months and then suspended.

Martinelli became a countess in 1957 when she married Count Franco Mancinelli Scotti. She had first met the Count in 1954 and the marriage took place despite the protests of the Count's mother who did not believe in a "mixed marriage between a nobleman and an actress." The couple had a daughter in 1958 but soon separated. In the 1960s Elsa married photographer Willy Rizzo, a union which ended in the 1970s.

Between these marriages Elsa kept busy in films. *Manuela* was set aboard an ocean freighter, with Martinelli being smuggled aboard by an engineer with lecherous intent. The captain discovered her and became involved. It was a man's picture with Martinelli being the only female in the cast. Despite her use as a sex object, she gave a good account of herself and was pronounced "pert and provocative." A fisherman stranded by a storm in a seaside village became involved with local girl Martinelli in *La mina,* and again she earned excellent reviews.

She followed with a role as the wife of a fruit peddler in the comedy *Costa Azzura* and then in Roger Vadim's strange and arty vampire film *Et Mourir de plaisir.* In the latter, she was engaged to marry a man, arousing the jealousy of the man's female cousin who became a vampire and took revenge on Elsa. *The Pigeon That Took Rome* was a bright and fast-paced comedy set in World War II Italy. The plot involved mix-ups with homing pigeons used by both sides to deliver messages. Elsa did well as the lead female and love interest to star Charlton Heston.

A different type of film was *The Trial,* Orson Welles' adaptation of Kafka's nightmare novel. It was an engrossing work and the actress was well received in a support role. She acted with Welles in two later films, but was never again under his direction. Welles always remained Martinelli's favorite director, however. A couple of big budget English-language features did little to enhance her reputation. *Rampage!* was a dismal safari yarn filled with clichés. The actress played Jack Hawkins' mistress who followed her aging big game hunter mate as he teamed up with trapper Robert Mitchum. The inevitable conflict saw Hawkins lose his mistress to Mitchum.

The V.I.P.s was a drama about a group of people stranded overnight by fog at London's airport, each of whom was desperate to leave the country. Martinelli was cast as the dumb film star protégée of a film director (Welles). She had an unrewarding part in a film dominated by stars Richard Burton and Elizabeth Taylor who were then popular in the media.

Better roles came when the actress returned to non–English films. *De l'amour* was a glib look at love in the French manner and Elsa was praised as being "shrewd and engaging." *Marco the Magnificent* was a costume epic about the explorer Marco Polo. The explorer found many obstacles before he reached Kublai Khan, one of which was Martinelli in Samarkand, billed only

Top: Elsa Martinelli in *Hatari*. *Bottom:* Elsa Martinelli is admired by Robert Mitchum in *Rampage*.

as "Woman with a Whip." A fine film called *The Tenth Victim* was a satiric stab at what life might be like a century in the future when people are licensed to hunt and kill each other for money. Elsa played the girlfriend of Marcello Mastroianni who had been patiently waiting 12 years for the church to annul his marriage. Critics found her "particularly effective."

Un Milliard dans un billard was a pedestrian comedy about thieves, with the actress giving an adequate performance as one of the crooks. She was a thief again in *Maroc 7*, a drama about a fashion magazine editor who went abroad claiming to do photo layouts but actually executing jewel robberies with the aid of her models. Martinelli was the chief model but had a poorly written role.

Based on a popular sex spoof book of the same name, *Candy* was a satire on pornographic stories with cameos by many stars. As Aunt Livia, Elsa more than held her own and was described by reviewers as "excellent." The actress played a psychotic wife in *Maldonne* and the high class mother of a student revolutionary in *Les chemins de Katmandou*.

By the end of the 1960s Elsa was getting only small roles in films though she often had much higher billing than her part warranted. In *OSS, 117* Martinelli was the first-billed female although her role was minor in that low-budget French version of the James Bond film. The same was true with *La part des lions* wherein the actress only briefly appeared as a crook's ever-waiting girlfriend.

Since 1971 she has been seen in only two films. She had a support role as a prostitute in the 1976 release *Il garofano rosso* and ten years after that she appeared in *Barbascio*. As demand waned for her services as an actress, Elsa turned to designing clothes—dresses, blouses, suits, coats and hats—and began showing and selling her designs. She had always been interested in clothing but turned to serious designing in the early 1970s while she was bedridden recovering from a broken leg.

Martinelli explained, "It's something I always wanted to do. I got a little bit tired of the movie business. People are changing and are not as interesting as they used to be, and films are made for men, more and more. Unless I have a beautiful man's role—which I don't play very well—it's very difficult to find a beautiful female role. I'm always working, I'm not what you would call a housewife, or someone who can just sit and have friends at the house, so I really need to work. That's why I decided to do what I like."

Elsa Martinelli Filmography

The Indian Fighter (1955)
La risaia [Rice Girl] (1956)
Donatella (1956)

Four Girls in Town (1956)
Manuela [Stowaway Girl] (1957)
La mina (1957)

I battellieri del Volga [The Boatmen; Prisoners of the Volga] (1958)
Tunisi top secret (1958)
Costa azzura (1959)
La notte brava (1959)
Ciao, ciao, bambina (1959)
Et mourir de plaisir [Blood and Roses] (1960)
Le capitane (1960)
La menace (1960)
Un amore a Roma (1960)
I piaceri del sabato notte (1960)
Il carro armato dell'8 settembre [The Tank of 8 September] (1960)
The Pigeon That Took Rome (1962)
La pelle viva (1962)
Le proces [The Trial] (1962)
Hatari! (1962)
Rampage! (1962)
The V.I.P.s (1963)
De l'amour [All About Loving] (1964)
La Fabuleuse Aventure de Marco Polo [Marco the Magnificent] (1964)
La decima vittima [The Tenth Victim] (1965)
Je vous salue, mafia [Hail Mafia!] (1965)
L'Or du duc (1965)

Un Milliard dans un billard [Diamonds Are Brittle] (1965)
Maroc 7 (1966)
Un dollaro per setti vigliacchi [Madigan's Millions] (1966)
Come imparai ad amare le donne (1966)
The Oldest Profession (1967)
Woman Times Seven (1967)
Manon '70 (1967)
Qualcuno ha tradito [Requiem for a Rabble] (1967)
Belle Starr [The Belle Starr Story] (1968)
Candy (1968)
Maldonne (1968)
If It's Tuesday, This Must be Belgium (1969)
Una sull'altra [One On Top of the Other] (1969)
Les chemins de Katmandou (1969)
L'amica (1969)
OSS, 117, prend des vacances (1969)
L'araucana massacro degli dei (1970)
La part des lions (1971)
Il garofano rosso (1976)
Barbascio [Supernatural Man] (1986)

Sources

Burgos, Guy. "Elsa Martinelli," *Interview,* 7:18–19, May 1977.
"Foreign Accent in Starlets," *Coronet,* 40:54–55, August 1956.
Katz, Ephraim. *The Film Encyclopedia.* New York: Thomas Y. Crowell, 1979, p. 783.
"Newest Eyeful from Italy," *Life,* 43:115–6+, November 25, 1957.
"Prison Sentence on Italian Actress," *Times,* (London), April 10, 1957, p. 8.
Quinlan, David. *Quinlan's Illustrated Directory of Film Stars.* London: B.T. Batsford, 1986, p. 285.
Talese, Gay. "Accommodation—Italian style," *Esquire,* 59:89+, February 1963.

Virna Lisi

Her dazzling good looks and trim figure made it inevitable that Virna Lisi would often be cast in the sex object role. She has also made a name for herself in a number of comedy parts where she displayed her humorous skills. She has also given some fine dramatic performances. Europe provided her with a wider

Virna Lisi in a publicity pose.

range of roles in which she progressed from support player to leading lady. Hollywood imported her when she was a big name, groomed her into a sex object, and signed her to a long-term contract. As with so many other foreign imports, Lisi was unhappy with Hollywood and quickly departed.

The actress was born Virna Lisi Pieralisi on September 8, 1936, in Ancona, Italy, a city on the Adriatic Sea. She grew up in comfortable and prosperous circumstances and her father did well with his business of mining and exporting marble. After grade school, the youngster was sent to Rome where she was enrolled in a business and technical school. When she was 17 a film producer friend of the family "discovered" her and, after clearing the matter with her parents, offered her a part in a film starting the following week.

Virna accepted and made her film debut in 1953. She has been busy ever since and appeared in twelve films between 1954 and 1955. Most of her early parts were small and decorative as in *Lo Scapolo,* a comedy about a bachelor who exaggerated his conquests of the opposite sex for a more macho image.

Lisi was one of the conquests. She also had a small part in *Les Hussards,* a costume epic set during the Napoleonic invasion of Italy.

Even at that early stage of her career she was getting some star roles. Virna was the lead in the 1955 release *La donna del giorno,* a drama that dealt with the harsh world of show business success. Lisi played a girl who faked an attack to get publicity. With the situation out of hand she was forced to name her attackers before finally breaking down and telling the truth. The actress received excellent notices.

By 1960 she was a well established star in Europe and no longer did support roles, being first or second billed, although some of the parts were still purely decorative. *Duel of the Titans,* a musclebound epic which told the story of Romulus and Remus, had Lisi next billed but with nothing to do except look good.

She had more to do in *Eva* where she played the fiancée of a writer. The writer broke up with her and chose a prostitute. In *Les bonnes causes* she was one of the few decent people overcome by ruthless adversaries. *Black Tulip* was a swashbuckling epic set in the period of the French Revolution. Alain Delon played twin brothers, one of whom was a robber adopted as leader by the people. Virna scored well as his peasant girlfriend.

With some 30 films behind her, Hollywood "discovered" Lisi in 1963 and signed her to a seven-year contract. By then the actress was married to a Rome architect, Franco Pesci, and had a son born in 1962. Producer George Axelford found her in a Paris hotel, rushed her to Hollywood for a screen test and signed her up immediately even though Lisi spoke little English. The language barrier suited her first Hollywood film, *How to Murder Your Wife,* since Axelrod used her lack of English to symbolize a lack of communication between husband and wife. Lisi spoke Italian in the movie but when it was released in her native country her lines had to be dubbed in Greek since the couple were not supposed to be able to speak the same language.

In most of her European films Lisi appeared as she was—a brunette—a quietly dressed lady "who had barely bared a shoulder in earlier movies." Axelrod changed her into "a lacquered, convertible blonde sex goddess."

She costarred with Jack Lemon in *How to Murder Your Wife* and had to leap out of a cake in scanty attire and melt in Lemmon's arms during a stag party. Lemmon was impressed, and said, "She's a star. She has it, a real regality." Virna initially did not complain, at least in public, and said, "I don't mind being nude under a couple of sheets. For the moment, I'm only a body, and I don't want to be an actress with psychological problems."

Pesci, who had accompanied his wife to Hollywood, was not pleased. Pesci was particularly upset over the cake scene and executive producer Gordon Carrol recalled, "He had this peculiar bellowing noise. I spent the day playing matador to his bull . . . he is very much the Italian husband." During a publicity tour to promote that film, Pesci, then back in Rome, frequently called his

Producer-Director Stanley Kramer *(right)* tells Virna Lisi and Sergio Franchi how he sees their scene in *The Secret of Santa Vittoria.*

wife and told her to come home. "I think he prefer I stop working," said Lisi, "but it is not possible for me. Acting is so much important part of me, like it is essence . . . It's difficult to be very good wife, very good mother, very good actress at same time."

Axelrod spent a large amount of money promoting Virna around the country, and said, "I want to make her a household word like General Motors . . . You're not a star until you're a star in America. I found her, I invented her." Originally he had envisioned Marilyn Monroe for the part Lisi played in *How to Murder Your Wife* but that actress had died and Axelrod was determined to remake Virna as the new Marilyn.

Lisi soon tired of the stereotyping and roles she was expected to play in Hollywood. When she turned down the mindless *Barbarella,* the actress had to repay money on her contract. Her working relationship with Axelrod was over and the contract terminated. Virna returned to Europe where she enjoyed a greater variety of roles. She did make some American films in the future, however.

After her Hollywood experience she found she was in even greater demand with European directors and embarked on a decade of films in which she was usually top-billed or at least first-billed female. *Casanova 70* had Marcello Mastroianni as a contemporary Casanova aroused only when there was danger in the chase. Lisi played a virginal beauty who enchanted Marcello only until she decided to succumb. One critic said, "She is a pure delight, funny and affecting." In *Assault on a Queen* the actress was love interest and point of tension between Frank Sinatra and Tony Franciosa in an action film about robbing an ocean liner. Lisi had little to do except wear skimpy bathing suits.

Along the same lines was *Not with my Wife, You Don't,* a domestic comedy with Lisi giving an excellent performance as the woman being fought over by Tony Curtis and George C. Scott. A better part came her way in *The Girl and the General* in which she played a peasant helping an Italian soldier recapture an escaped Austrian general for part of the reward money, during World War I. One sequence where she met a group of Austrian soldiers and was forced to disrobe in exchange for food was out of place and an example of the gratuitous nudity so often required of actresses.

One of her best efforts came in the comedy *Arabella* which was a series of episodes focusing on Virna's larcenous activities as she tried to help her grandmother raise money to pay back taxes. It was a showcase for the actress and she excelled. One of the few times she was physically deglamorized was in *The 25th Hour* as the peasant wife of a Rumanian who was shunted around for years as a political pawn during the World War II. Back to comedy in *Tenderly,* she and George Segal, childhood friends, met again after fifteen years and started a romance despite differing backgrounds. As an unconventional member of society she gave a gripping performance and sustained the film.

Un beau monstre was about a psychotic ladies' man who drove his wives to suicide. Lisi starred as a wife and was rated "very effective." In the farcical comedy *The Statue,* Virna was the sculptress wife of a Nobel Prize winner commissioned to create a statue of him for a public square. Husband David Niven was incensed when he discovered the statue duplicated him except for the genitals. Convinced his wife was unfaithful, he set out to find the man who posed for that part of the statue. *Variety* called Lisi's performance "captivating as usual."

By the early 1970s Lisi worked steadily but was no longer top-billed. One such film was *Bluebeard,* a camp version with lots of nudity. Bluebeard (Richard Burton) guillotined his wife (Lisi) when he could not stand her constant singing. *Beyond Good and Evil* was an engrossing account of three people trying to live together in the late 19th century in a repressive Germany. The three were the philosopher Nietzsche, his friend and disciple and a liberated woman. Lisi was excellent as Nietzsche's hysterical sister.

Ernesto was the story of a young man's initiation into life, sex and class ways in pre–World War I Italy. Lisi did well cast as the mother of the boy. An Italian *American Graffiti* was *Sapore di mare,* a comic and nostalgic look at middle-class teens during the 1960s. One of the teens temporarily dropped his girlfriend for a frustrated but very sexy older woman, played by Virna Lisi. Her performance was termed outstanding and one critic wrote that she was "so vital and magnetic she injects believability into a clichéd role."

Lisi has taken a variety of roles and showed she has more staying power than the average sex symbol. She has appeared in 76 films.

Virna Lisi Filmography

. . .e Napoli canta (1953)
Lettera Napoletana (1954)
Il vetturale del Moncenisio (1954)
Cardinal Lambertini (1954)
La corda d'acciaio (1954)
Desiderio è sole (1954)
Violenza sul lago (1954)
Ripudiata Piccola santa (1954)
La donne del giorno [The Girl of the Day; The Doll That Took the Town] (1955)
Les Hussards (1955)
Luna nova (1955)
Lo scapolo (1955)
Vendicata (1955)
The Teenagers (1956)
La rossa (1956)
Le diciottenni (1957)
Il conte di Matera (1957)
Vita perduta (1958)
Caterina Sforza, leonessa di Romagna (1958)
Totò, Peppino e le fanatiche (1958)
Il padrone delle ferriere (1959)
Il mondo dei miracoli (1959)
Un militare e mezzo (1960)
Sua Eccellenza si fremo a mangiare (1961)
Cinque marine per cento ragazze (1961)
Romulus and Remus [Duel of the Titans] (1961)
Eva [Eve] (1962)
La Tulipe Noire [The Black Tulip] (1962)
Il giorno più corto [commedia umoristica] [The Shortest Day] (1963)
Les Bonnes Causes (1963)
Coplan prend des risques (1963)
Casanova 70 (1964)
I complessi (1964)

How to Murder Your Wife (1964)
Signore e signori [The Birds, the Bees and the Italians] (1965)
Oggi, domani e dopo domani (1965)
La donna del lago (1965)
Made in Italy (1965)
Una vergina per il principe [A Virgin for the Prince] (1965)
Possessed (1965)
Le bambole [Four Kinds of Love] (1965)
Paranoia [Kiss the Other Sheik] (1965)
La volta buona (1965)
Assault on a Queen (1966)
Not with my Wife, You Don't (1966)
La ragazza e il generale [The Girl and the General] (1966)
Arabella (1967)
Meglio vedova [Better a Widow] (1967)
Le dolci signore [Anyone Can Play] (1967)
La vingt-cinquieme heure [The 25th Hour] (1967)
Tenderly [The Girl Who Couldn't Say No] (1968)
The Christmas Tree (1969)
Les Temps des loups (1969)
The Secret of Santa Vittoria (1969)
If It's Tuesday, This Must be Belgium (1969)
Trigon (1969)
Giuochi particolari (1970)
Un Beau Monstre (1970)
Roma bene (1971)
The Statue (1971)
Barbe-Bleue [Bluebeard] (1972)
Les Galets d'entretat (1972)
Le serpent (1973)
White Fang (1974)
Love Me Strangely (1975)

Challenge to White Fang (1975)
Oltre il bene e il male [Beyond Good
and Evil] (1977)
Ernesto (1978)
Cocktails for Three (1978)
Footloose [Venetian Lies] (1979)

La cicala (1980)
Miss Right (1980)
Sapore di mare [A Taste of Sea] (1982)
Stelle emigrati (1983)
Amarsi un po' (1984)
I Love N.Y. (1986)

Sources

Furlong, William Barry. "How to Manufacture a Siren," New York Times, February 7, 1965, sec. 2, p. 1.
Hamilton, Jack. "Virna Lisi: Experiment in Star Making," Look, 29:61–2+, May 18, 1965.
Katz, Ephraim. The Film Encyclopedia. New York: Thomas Y. Crowell, 1979, p. 723.
"La Lisi," Time, 85:47, April 2, 1965.
Lloyd, Ann, ed. The Illustrated Who's Who of the Cinema. London: Orbia, 1983, p. 267.
Quinlan, David. Quinlan's Illustrated Directory of Film Stars. London: B.T. Batsford, 1986, p. 265.

Claudia Cardinale

Claudia Cardinale arrived on the Italian film scene at the time when reigning screen queens Sophia Loren and Gina Lollobrigida were both abandoning the country in favor of Hollywood. Claudia was able to step in and fill the void. She was groomed and marketed to be an Italian equivalent of Brigitte Bardot and an alphabet war ensued in which CC (Claudia Cardinale) was compared to BB (Brigitte Bardot). Cardinale never became quite as popular as Bardot but she lasted longer and appeared in better quality films as she worked with many top directors in Italy and other countries. She enjoyed a large international success, particularly during the 1960s. Ironically she was one of Italy's top actresses but did not speak Italian until she started making films.

Claudia was born on April 15, 1939, in Tunis, Tunisia, the daughter of an Italian railroad worker and a French mother who named her daughter Claude Josephine Rose. She was the oldest of four children. "I grew up mostly in Carthage," said the actress. "My parents and I spoke French. At that time, Tunisia belonged to France, although my parents, who were born in Tunis, are Italian. My great-grandfather came from Italy and his family kept their Italian citizenship."

Claudia also spoke some Arabic, attended a Catholic grammar school and then went on to a French lycée to continue her education. Just a few blocks from her home was a neighborhood cinema and the youngster attended faithfully every Sunday afternoon, fascinated by motion pictures, although she had no desire to become an actress.

Claudia Cardinale in publicity still.

As a child her social life was confined to the Italian colony, and she re-called, "My father was severe. I almost never went to a party. And though I went out with some boys, I never go steady, as you say in America . . . we had to be home at a certain time. If our grades were not what they should be, we could not go to the movies, and we were allowed to go only to movies my parents found acceptable."

While she had a bit part in a short film released in 1956, her ambition, in 1957, was to be a grade school teacher. She had started university but her education was permanently sidetracked that year. Mrs. Cardinale worked for a large charity, organized for the poor of Tunis. The group held a bazaar with Mrs. Cardinale as one of the members of the committee. One event was a beauty contest that Claudia was reluctant to enter. "They ask me to go on stage and I refuse," she said, "but when the contest is about to start, I am pushed on the stage. I am wearing a pony tail and a white dress, very tight, very low in the back, and I am very dark from the sun. Well, I win."

What she won was the title "Miss Italy of Tunis, 1957," and a trip to the Venice Film Festival with her mother. In Venice Claudia found herself besieged by producers offering her movie contracts. She, however, was unimpressed. "I couldn't understand why all those people were so excited," she said. "They talked so much, so loud. I didn't want to have anything to do with those crazy people."

At that time Cardinale regarded the whole excursion as just a tourist jaunt, saying, "I never had any thoughts of becoming an actress. I never admired actors and actresses as people; I wanted to be a schoolteacher in primary school." She did succumb to the temptation, however, and had a small role in one 1957 film *Goha*. Claudia next enrolled at Centro Sperimentale film school in Rome to study acting. She spent just one month there, and said, "I get homesick. I am thinking of Tunis and the whole city white and my family. I take the first plane home." Another reason for her quick departure was her dislike of the way acting was taught there. "I could not become a tree. At the school, I saw people acting like trees, and I thought they were all crazy. I think The Method — you call it that — is a very strange method."

Even though she was back in Africa she was not forgotten by the Italian cinema world. Magazines wrote stories of the girl who had given up a film career to be with her family and offers rolled in once again. Claudia refused them all for a few months but finally got such a good financial deal from Vides Films that by May, 1958, she was back in Rome, signed to a long-term contract. Vides's mastermind was a producer named Franco Cristaldi who took over Cardinale's life and career, making virtually all the decisions for her. The couple married and Franco ran her career for almost two decades. Around 1959 the actress had a son, Patrick. Not married at the time, it was a subject the actress did not discuss.

Cardinale took no more acting lessons. Her first few months in Italy were spent with language teachers who were teaching her Italian. She also posed for magazines in various cheesecake shots, such as emerging from the sea in a wet bikini or lying provocatively on a bed. Franco was busy grooming her as the Italian answer to France's Brigitte Bardot. "I didn't mind," she said. "As for the cheesecake, I never posed completely naked, and in Africa it was nothing to wear a bikini. My family understood that this is a business."

Cristaldi carefully selected roles for his protégée and her first appearance was as support in the well-received comedy *Big Deal on Madonna Street*. She went on to play Marcello Mastroianni's wife, making him anxious about his virility, in *Il bell'Antonio,* and then played the fiancée of the eldest brother in Visconti's *Rocco and His Brothers.* It was an excellent film about a southern Italian family's move north to a new life in Milan and the family's slow disintegration. *The Girl with the Suitcase* was a sensitive story about adolescent love with Claudia left with a child by a man who abandoned her. The actress earned rave reviews and was fast becoming an international film star.

From 1958 to 1964 the busy actress appeared in 25 films. The first twelve she did have her voice dubbed in, until she mastered the language. Later she learned English and thereafter she spoke Italian with a French accent and English with an Italian accent. While she had initially avoided becoming an actress, Claudia quickly got used to the idea, and said, "For sure I like the material things, and to be known to many strangers. It's nice to have a chauffeur always on hand, to stay in the best hotels, eat in the best restaurants and buy clothes from the best Paris designers. And I like diamonds, jewels and furs."

Though marketed as a sex symbol, her personal life was quiet. She did not drink or smoke nor did she have romances with her leading men. "In many ways, I suppose I am dull," Claudia offered. Of her first couple dozen films she felt *The Girl with the Suitcase* was her best role but was adamant that she was a dramatic actress and not a sexpot. "I never made sexy things in my films. It is so stupid all this sex talk. When I am in Paris making *Cartouche* with Jean-Paul Belmondo, everybody treated me like a boy."

Cardinale gave one excellent performance after another in the early 1960s as her international stature as a film star grew. *Senilità* was about a middle-aged man desperately grasping for the love of a young flirt, abandoning his work, friends and family to pursue her, not knowing he meant nothing to her and never would. Cardinale was outstanding as the flirt. A period drama set in 1885 Florence, *La viaccia* was about a man in love with a prostitute eventually disowned by his family. According to one reviewer Claudia excelled as the "voluptuous, hardened-by-life prostie."

Visconti cast her as the female lead, opposite Burt Lancaster, in *The Leopard* and drew gripping performances from both. Fellini's *8 1/2* was about a film director (Marcello Mastroianni) going through a series of personal crises. Cardinale appeared as Marcello's symbolic dream girl. *Variety* termed her to be "strikingly effective."

Her fame had reached such heights in the middle 1960s that the actress was summoned to meet Queen Elizabeth of England. Giovanni Gronchi, the President of Italy, designated her one of that country's finest artists. Writer Alberto Moravia was so struck by Cardinale that he wrote a book about her, asking her such strange questions as the size of her earlobes and the shape of her shoulders. Moravia declared her beauty came "from the very strong contrast between the small size of your head and the large size of your body."

Claudia Cardinale and George Chakiris in *Bebo's Girl*.

In 1963 Claudia appeared on the cover of over 250 European magazines. Fan letters came in at the rate of over one thousand a month of which seven hundred were, according to her agent, marriage proposals. A writer in Brazil was one of the many who proposed marriage by mail. He went a little farther by posting a marriage notice in his church and then changing his name to Mr. Cardinale.

Claudia regarded herself as an "instinctive actress—I prepare for a role by reading the script over and over again until I know the character completely." Despite her stardom she worried it might not last, saying, "There is no way to tell what will happen to you in films. Actors appear, disappear, often you never hear again of someone you have worked with. Who knows what happens to them?" Fame had never gone to her head. Visconti called her "a lovely, unsophisticated girl" and John Wayne said, "It's a pleasure to meet such an unspoiled young lady."

When asked what made her a star, she said, "Some actors are cinema-animals; they give off a certain excitement on the screen which the public wants. That is what makes a successful star. If an actor does not have it, he doesn't last. It is nothing one can acquire, either you have it or you do not." Modest about her own acting talents, she commented, "A director, if he's good enough, can take people off the street and make a great picture with them." Claudia enjoyed acting "because it is a way of keeping my private feelings to myself, to keep people from prying into who I am."

Cardinale was just as busy during the end of the '60s and early '70s as she appeared in 26 films from 1965 to 1974. *Circus World* was about an American circus in Europe circa 1910 with her cast as a foster daughter to John Wayne. She had some nude scenes and got generally good notices. Her American film debut came in *The Pink Panther* where she scored well in a support role and had a memorable scene with David Niven in which the pair were amorously drunk. *Blindfold* was a fluffy comedy starring Rock Hudson, with Claudia as a chorus girl who spent a lot of time naked. She had little to do in *The Professionals,* an action-adventure yarn set in 1917 wherein she was a kidnapped woman in need of rescue. What little she had to do though, she did well.

The Pink Panther was the first film she made in Hollywood although she had made a few English-language films previously. Cardinale was reluctant to work in Hollywood, fearing she might be overglamorized and exploited as she thought Sophia Loren had been. She was paid less in Europe, but said, "If I have to give up the money, I give it up. I do not want to become a cliché."

In Sergio Leone's Italian western *Once Upon a Time in the West,* Claudia and the three male leads, Henry Fonda, Jason Robards and Charles Bronson were each after the ownership of a crucial town which would lead to extreme wealth. The actress was second-billed and a critic described her as "extremely effective as a fancy lady from New Orleans."

Bardot and Cardinale finally met on the screen in a western *Les Petroleuses* in which they fought over an oil claim. Since French-speaking towns were few and far between in the American west the story got around this problem by explaining the town had been founded by French people who continued to speak that language. Of both actresses, *Variety* said, "They supply some pulpy and fading pulchritude, but the film remains quite chaste except for a long-shot nude scene." Reunited with Visconti and Burt Lancaster in *Conversation Piece,* the actress gave another excellent performance. By the middle 1980s the actress declared her favorite films to be *The Leopard, 8 1/2, Once Upon a Time in the West* and *The Professionals.*

Claudia made a drastic change in her life in 1975 when she and Cristaldi separated and the actress terminated her contract with Vides Films. The marriage had drifted to one of convenience and the couple had maintained separate households for years. "For more than 15 years, I was considered and treated like an object or a project to be manufactured and merchandised," said the actress. "For much of my adult life, I was someone else's creation — they decided what movies I should play in, what clothes to wear, how to have my hair done and even what friends to see. It was as if I were something operated by remote control."

The first step came when she began refusing roles "not because I was

Burt Lancaster carries Claudia Cardinale to train cab and hands her to Lee Marvin as they try to escape from Mexican revolutionaries in a scene from Columbia's *The Professionals*.

temperamental but because I wanted more intelligent parts. In Italy actresses are usually cast only as sex objects. It is really absurd to treat women this way — women, after all, are capable of more in life than making love — but it is very difficult to find intelligent parts for women in films."

She began living with director Pasquale Squitieri and had a child in June 1979, at the age of 40. Claudia became a grandmother that same month when her son's girlfriend also had a child. At home the actress cut back on her own staff in order to live a simpler life. She got rid of her cook, maid, agent, driver and personal secretary and took over most of their duties herself. While Cardinale did support some women's causes such as the movement for an abortion law she did not consider herself to be a militant feminist.

The 1980s have seen Claudia enter a still busy but more mature phase of her career. She teamed with Mastroianni in Liliana Cavani's *La pelle,* the grim memoirs of American liberation troops and the vanquished people of Naples. *Le cadeau* was a routine sex farce about a bank clerk who got an unusual retirement gift—a high class call girl. The difference was that Claudia played the wife and not the call girl. She gave a good performance as the girlfriend in *Fitzcarraldo* and was excellent in *Enrico IV,* teamed once more with Mastroianni.

One of her best roles came in *Claretta* in which she was lead billed in the story of Claretta Petacci, mistress for ten years of Italian dictator Mussolini. Philippe Noiret and Claudia played the parents of a large brood who were torn apart but finally reunited in *L'ete prochain.* The acting was good but the story was too syrupy and sentimental.

Questioned about the difficulties of being a woman and independent, Cardinale reflected, "I think women everywhere have the same problems in trying to assert their independence. That doesn't mean that I am against men—quite the contrary—but I am for great independence for women. But being independent can be difficult for an actress. It means that you do not take the first part that comes along. It means reading scripts and talking to writers about creating intelligent parts for women. It means not working regularly."

Claudia Cardinale Filmography

Anneaux d'or (1956)
Goha (1957)
I soliti ignoti [Big Deal on Madonna Street] (1958)
Tre straniere a Roma (1958)
La prima notte (1958)
Toto e Marcellino (1958)
Il magistrato (1959)
Un maledetto imbroglio [The Facts of Murder] (1959)
Audace colpo dei soliti ignoti (1959)
Vento del sud (1959)
Upstairs and Downstairs (1959)
Austerlitz [The Battle of Austerlitz] (1959)
La ragazza con la valigia [The Girl with the Suitcase] (1960)
Il bell'Antonio (1960)
I delfini (1960)
Rocco e i suoi fratelli [Rocco and His Brothers] (1960)
Les Lions sont lâches (1961)
Cartouche [Swords of Blood] (1961)
Senilità (1961)
La viaccia [The Love Makers] (1961)
Il gattopardo [The Leopard] (1962)
Otto e mezzo [8 1/2] (1963)
Gli indifferenti [A Time of Indifference] (1963)
La ragazza di Bube [Bebo's Girl] (1963)
Circus World [The Magnificent Showmen] (1963)

The Pink Panther (1964)
Il magnifico cornuto [The Magnificent
    Cuckold] (1964)
Blindfold (1965)
Vaghe stelle dell'Orsa [Sandra, of a
    Thousand Delights] (1965)
Una rosa per tutti [A Rose for Every-
    one] (1966)
Le fate [Sex Quartet; The Queens]
    (1966)
Lost Command (1966)
The Professionals (1966)
Don't Make Waves (1967)
Piero Gherardi (1967)
The Hell with Heroes (1968)
A Fine Pair (1968)
C'erà una volta il West [Once Upon a
    Time in the West] (1968)
Il giorno della civettà (1968)
Krasnaya palatka [The Red Tent]
    (1969)
Nell'anno del signore (1969)
The Adventures of Gerard (1970)
Certo, certissimo, anzi ... probabile
    (1970)
Popsy Pop [The Butterfly Affair; The
    21 Carat Snatch] (1971)
Les Petroleuses [The Legend of
    Frenchie King] (1971)
L'undienza (1971)
Bello, onesto, emigrato Australia
    sposerebbe compaesana illibata (1971)
La scoumoune (1972)
Libera, amore mio (1973)
Un uomo (1973)
I guappi (1973)
Il giorno del furore [Days of Fury;

One Russian Summer] (1973)
Gruppo di famiglia in un interno
    [Conversation Piece] (1974)
A mezzanotte va la ronda del piacere
    (1975)
Qui comincia l'avventure [Lucky Girls;
    Midnight Pleasures] (1975)
Beato lore (1975)
Il communo senso del pudore (1976)
Un jour peut-etre a San Pedro ou ail-
    leurs (1977)
Il prefetto di ferro (1977)
La part du feu (1977)
Goodbye and Amen (1977)
Cocktails for Three (1978)
L'arma (1978)
La petite fille en velours bleu [The Lit-
    tle Girl in Blue Velvet] (1978)
Corleone (1978)
L'ingorgo [Traffic Jam] (1979)
Escape to Athena (1979)
Si salvi chi vuole (1980)
I briganti (1980)
La pelle (1981)
The Salamander (1981)
Le cadeau [The Gift] (1982)
Fitzcarraldo (1982)
Burden of Dreams (1982)
The Ruffian (1983)
Stelle emigranti (1983)
Enrico IV (1983)
Claretta (1984)
L'ete porchain (1985)
La storia [History] (1985)
The Woman of Wonders (1985)
A Man in Love (1987)

Sources

"Acting Italian Style," Film Comment, 19:46, April 1983.
"Clamor over Claudia," Look, 26:109–10+, June 19, 1962.
Hamilton, Pete. "The Square World of Claudia Cardinale," Saturday Evening Post, 237:62,
    February 29, 1964.
The International Dictionary of Films and Filmmakers: Volume III: Actors and Actresses.
    Chicago: St. James Press, 1986, p. 121–122.
Katz, Ephraim. The Film Encyclopedia. New York: Thomas Y. Crowell, 1979, p. 205.
Miller, Edwin. "Something of a Nomad," Seventeen, 25:145+, April 1966.
Mitgang, Herbert. "On Screen: Claudia Cardinale," Horizon, 5:38, January 1963.
"People," Time, 107:47, June 21, 1976.
"People Are Talking About ...," Vogue, 139:88, March 15, 1962.

"People on the Way Up," *Saturday Evening Post,* 235:26, February 3, 1962.
Quinlan, David. *Quinlan's Illustrated Directory of Film Stars.* London: B.T. Batsford, 1986,
    p. 68.
"She'd Rather Lose Money than Be a Cliché," *Life,* 61:52–6, July 8, 1966.
"Talk of Rome," *Washington Post Parade Magazine,* March 4, 1979, p. 15.
Thomson, David. *A Biographical Dictionary of Film.* New York: William Morrow, 1975,
    p. 77.
Tuohy, William. "The Liberation of Cardinale," *Los Angeles Times,* November 29, 1975,
    sec. 2, p. 10.
Wlaschin, Ken. *The Illustrated Encyclopedia of the World's Great Movie Stars and Their
    Films.* London: Salamander, 1979, p. 178.

Monica Vitti

Monica Vitta has enjoyed two distinct phases in her acting career. The first
was in the early 1960s when she was the muse to director Michelangelo Antonioni and starred in four of his films as a neurotic and alienated woman. When
the director and actress went their separate ways Vitti turned to comedy and
became Italy's favorite comic actress through the 1970s and into the '80s. The
films made big money at home but received little distribution in America. The
actress has never been in Hollywood and has made only a couple of films in
the English language.

She was born Maria Luisa Ceciarelli in Rome, Italy, on November 3, 1931,
to a Roman merchant father and a mother originally from Bologna. The family
spent about ten years in Milan during Monica's youth before returning to
Rome. By the time she was a teenager Monica wanted to be an actress but her
family was not pleased. "I was too different from all the other members of my
family," recalled the actress. "They not only didn't understand my ambition
to become an actress, but they tried to put obstacles before me. They detested
the idea."

A girlfriend was scheduled to do a little act at a benefit and asked 14-year-
old Monica to join her but her parents refused saying it "would shame them.
Even reading a little poem would be a crime." Her family was very traditional
and acting was not a profession that "nice" girls took up. Monica might never
have been able to overcome the objections had not fate intervened and the
family, including her parents and two brothers, went to America when she was
18 years old. Monica refused to go. Her parents were sure she would change
her mind or at least have to turn to them for money. However, Monica "used
their absence to become an actress."

She took the stage name of Monica Vitti because of her family's objections
to her acting aspirations. When they returned, however, Vitti noted that her
parents had to call her Monica and to acknowledge her as an actress. The strife

at home left its mark though. "The family is an ill-conceived proposition. How can parents help their children? I find it hard to imagine," said Vitti. "If you don't share similar opinions about things, about life, how can you live together? . . . That's why I never wanted to have a family of my own, and that's why I never got married."

She enrolled at Rome's National Academy of Dramatic Arts, graduating in 1953 and beginning her professional stage career that same year. One of her first stage roles was playing a woman of forty-five. She worked with the Teatro Nuovo in Milan and made her mark touring Italy and other countries in plays by Brecht, Molière, Ionesco and John Osborne.

Vitti's film debut came in 1955 with bit parts in a few films. Most of her work was on the stage and later she said she did not want to be in films because she had "seen what had happened to some of the Italian girls who were." Later she contradicted herself by saying, "Directors at the time didn't want actors to act, especially actresses — they were expected to be pretty. So they told me I should stick to the theater."

Monica was working on an Antonioni film in 1957 *Il grido* but only dubbing in a voice because it was all the film work she could get at the time. Working in the dubbing studio, Monica was unaware the director had entered the room and was watching her from behind until he said, "You have a beautiful neck. You could be in the movies." She became Antonioni's main female player for his next four films. The couple also established a personal relationship that lasted close to ten years.

L'avventura (1960) was their first collaboration but it took two years for the film to be made because, said the actress, "Nobody wanted to take a chance on it and on me, an unknown." Initially Vitti had resisted establishing a personal relationship, fearing the label "director's girl," but the couple decided they needed each other. Her other films for Antonioni were *La notte, L'eclisse* and *The Red Desert*.

Vitti's screen persona was basically the same in all of these films, playing a neurotic, passive and alienated modern woman who was bored, rich and unable to love or find out what love was as she desperately searched for something to believe in. The films were slow to catch on but eventually became worldwide successes, particularly with intellectuals, who elevated the director and his works to cult status. Much of the general population in provincial Italy found these films boring or pretentious. In those films Vitti was forever forgiving and consoling the men and her character was very much under the domination of the male leads. As one critic noted, the director had made Vitti's character a "helpless and indecisive neurotic." Another reviewer described her as "the thinking man's set star in pessimistic alienation fantasies."

The actress's own opinion of those films was again contradictory. She once said those films "were a part of me, and the characters I played reflected my state of mind and feelings. I had a lot of anguish, as I still do, and he used

Monica Vitti in a publicity photo.

it. I love *L'avventura* and *The Red Desert* the most because they're based most closely on my real life." Yet to another interviewer, she said of those same films, "I shouldn't want the public to think that the role I play in them is drawn from my real character in private life." She did feel that Antonioni was the only Italian director who then told the woman's story, the only creative person who took their problems seriously. The director said of his star, "I like to watch and to direct her, but the parts I give her are a long way from her own character."

She bought her Rome apartment in 1961 with money from her first Antonioni film but commented, "I was so insecure that I kept all my clothes at my mother's and used to go home to sleep." That soon ended when Antonioni moved into the apartment directly above hers with an inside staircase connecting the two units. The director continued to occupy the one above long after the couple broke up, with the staircase being left unused. Vitta still lives in the same apartment.

Monica's fame as an actress had grown and offers came rolling in. She refused all the ones from Hollywood but she made a few other European films in 1963–64. It was the first work she had done without Antonioni since they met. The actress had a desire to do comedy but Antonioni saw her only as a dramatic actress so, after *The Red Desert,* Vitti struck out on her own. "I felt like the greenest of actresses. I was terrorized, afraid that I could not make my way by myself. I had refused everyone in order to work and live with Michelangelo. And because I was too identified with him, other directors, like Fellini, would not use me," said Monica. "As an actress I must accept what is offered to me, although I can select. Money is no problem. I do, however, want to act . . . Yet I did not want to work with imitators of the Antonioni style." It was a deliberate effort on her part to create a new style for herself. She found it difficult at first to get the audience to accept her since they had come to expect "this tortured, neurotic woman."

She made several Italian comedy films in 1965 including *Le bambole* and *Il disco volante* where she was one of the population concerned with flying saucers. Offers from abroad continued to tempt her and she finally made her first English-language film, Joseph Losey's *Modesty Blaise* (1966). As the title character, Vitti was a karate-conscious female spy in a spoof of the James Bond films.

The film was loaded with gimmicks and Vitti had a purse with a pistol in the handle, a flame-throwing cigarette lighter and lipsticks that were tiny hand grenades. At the time she said she loved the film, but later admitted, "I did not like it. The director wanted one thing and I another. Maybe neither of us was right for it." *Modesty Blaise* was not a success either with the critics or at the box office but it did gain a certain status on university campuses, particularly radical ones. Its lack of success had much to do with the image it gave of a competent woman, not readily accepted by the public at that time.

The following year (1967) she starred in the comedy *The Girl with the Pistol* as a Sicilian peasant who was raped and kidnapped by a man who wanted to marry her. After the wedding he left her and she pursued him in a wild fury. Her work in that film won her the Italian equivalent of the Oscar and by 1970 Monica was established as the top comic actress in Italy, the equal of male comics such as Alberto Sordi.

The actress turned out hit after hit, mostly Italian comedy films as *Amore mio, aiutami,* a marital comedy with Sordi; *vedo nudo,* a sex comedy with Nino Manfredi; *The Pizza Triangle,* a comic vehicle with Marcello Mastroianni; and *Le coppie,* another marital comedy with Sordi. Mastroianni and Sordi were her favorite actors; Sordi in particular because of the many films they had done together. She felt they were known as Italy's "Comic Couple." Most of these films received little or no distribution in the English-speaking world but all were box office winners at home.

Vitti never considered herself to be a sex symbol and felt women identified with her because she was not inaccessible or beautiful. "I'm blonde, with freckles, and I don't have a big chest," she said. "In the beginning, all this made it very difficult for me, but in retrospect, it allowed me to do my own thing. I became a female protagonist, which is quite unusual in Italian cinema. In Italy, they still don't like to make films about women, because they don't believe they can make a profit that way."

Life as a woman and actress was not easy for Monica, who said, "I have many handicaps in Italy. Being a woman, unmarried, without children, and an actress besides, all puts you very low on the social scale. Acting is not considered a nice profession." She once remarked, "How I wish I could be a man. Perhaps women are not as important as men, but they have infinitely deeper feelings."

During the 1970s the actress appeared in 26 films, most of which were Italian comedies although she took the odd serious role. *Tigers in Lipstick* was an episodic comedy with Vitti giving an excellent performance posing as a nun and then a doddering old woman as she tried to steal an expensive necklace from a woman at a casino. She even tried producing with *Mimi bluette,* a film she bought the rights to from MGM in 1974. MGM had first acquired the rights in 1926 but had abandoned the project.

Monica did not make her second English-language film until *An Almost Perfect Affair* (1979). She did not think her command of English was adequate and she loathed traveling. The few films she made in English were shot in Europe. She has never been in California and her sole trip to the United States was in 1960 for the premiere of *L'avventura,* when she went no further than New York City, saying, "I was terrified in America, I didn't like to watch the way the women get old. Anyway, I have Europe, it's so original, so full of faults."

After she and Antonioni broke up, Vitti began a relationship with director Carlo di Palma, who directed her in four films. The relationship lasted about eight years. In the mid-1970s she began dating Roberto Russo, a cinematographer turned director, and the pair remain close. "I realize that the men I loved were those I could work with. And talk to. But I never chose anybody; they chose me. They always had to force, almost. I'm not a predator. I don't have the courage to choose anybody."

Vitti felt that comedy was the natural forum for her acting and remarked, "I act in order to get out of my reality, and the minute I do that I can no longer share my anguish with other people. So I'm funny. It's not easy to be me and I'm not sure what I can do about it, except resort to laughter." The public agreed and her good-natured, goofy and unpretentious screen persona has won the hearts of millions and made her a major box office draw with many smash hits.

Vitti has been much less active on the screen in the 1980s appearing in only five pictures. In one, *The Mystery of Oberwald,* she was reunited with Antonioni who was paid big money by Italian television to make an experimental picture on the use of video in filmmaking. The story cast Monica as a bereaved and lovesick queen and neither the film nor her performance were well received. The rest of her recent outings have been her forte—comedies.

Flirt, a comedy about insanity, was cowritten by Vitti and Russo. The actress played a wife who, after 22 years of marriage, discovered her husband was insane and carrying on an "affair" with a phantom woman. She gave her usual excellent performance and presented a powerful presence, as she did in most of her films. Her latest outing, *Francesca e mia,* was also cowritten by the pair. Vitti had also begun to teach at the National Academy in 1984, the same institute she had attended years earlier as a student.

She lived, she said, "a very simple life. When I'm not working I go to the cinema every night. Sometimes it's very difficult. I am three dangerous things, a woman, an actress and not married, so I suppose I'll work until I'm ninety."

Monica Vitti Filmography

Ridere, ridere, ridere (1955)
Adriana Lecouvreur (1955)
Una pelliccia di visone (1956)
Il guido [The Cry] (1957)
Le dritte [Smart Girls] (1958)
L'avventura (1960)
La notte (1961)
L'eclisse [The Eclipse] (1962)
Les Quatres Vérités [Three Fables of Love] (1962)
Château en Suède [Nutty, Naughty Chateau] (1963)
Dragées au poivre [Sweet and Sour] (1963)
Alta infedeltà [High Infidelity] (1964)
Il deserto rosso [The Red Desert] (1964)
Le bambole [Four Kinds of Love; The Dolls] (1965)
Il disco volante [The Flying Saucer] (1965)
Fai in fretta ad uccidermi . . . ho Freddo! (1965)
Modesty Blaise (1966)
Le fate [Sex Quartet; The Queens] (1966)
Le piacevoli notti (1966)
La ragazza con la pistola [The Girl with the Pistol] (1967)
Ti ho sposato per allegria [I Married You for Fun] (1967)
La Femme écarlate [The Scarlet Woman] (1968)
La cintura di castita [The Chastity Belt; On My Way to the Crusades . . .] (1969)
Vedo nudo (1969)
La moglie del Prete (1969)

Amore mio, aiutami [Help Me, Darling] (1969)
Nini Tirabuscio, la donna che invento la mossa (1970)
Dramma della gelosica — tutti i particolari in cronaca [The Pizza Triangle] (1970)
La pacifista [The Pacifist] (1971)
Le coppie [The Couples] (1971)
Lei (1971)
La supertestimone (1971)
Teresa la ladra [Teresa the Thief] (1972)
Gli ordini sono ordini (1972)
Noi donne siamo fatte così (1972)
Tosca (1973)
Polvere di stelle (1973)
La Fantôme de la liberté [The Phantom of Liberty] (1974)
Qui comincia l'avventura [Midnight Pleasures; Lucky Girls] (1975)
A mezzanotte va la ronda del piacere [The Immortal Bachelor] (1975)
Canard a l'orange [Duck in Orange Sauce] (1975)
L'anitra all'arancia (1975)
Mimi bluette (1976)
La Goduria (1976)
L'altra meta del cielo [The Other Half of Heaven] (1977)
Amore mei [My Loves] (1978)
La raison d'etat (1978)
Letti selvaggi [Tigers in Lipstick] (1979)
An Almost Perfect Affair (1979)
Take Two (1979)
Per vivere meglio [The Good Life] (1979)

The Mystery of Krantz (1979)
*Il mistero di Oberwald [The Mystery
  of Oberwald]* (1981)
Io so che tu sai che io so (1982)

Trenta minuti d'amore (1983)
Flirt (1983)
Francesca e mia (1986)

Sources

Buckley, Tom. "At the Movies," *New York Times,* May 11, 1979, p. C6.

Davis, Melton S. "Monica Laughs," *New York Times,* January 17, 1971, sec. 2, p. 17+.

The International Dictionary of Films and Filmmakers: Volume III: Actors and Actresses. Chicago: St. James Press, 1986, p. 633–634.

Katz, Ephraim. *The Film Encyclopedia.* New York: Thomas Y. Crowell, 1979, p. 1198.

"Monica Vitti," *Look,* 30:83+, June 14, 1966.

"Monica Vitti," *McCall's,* 96:99, March 1969.

"Moncia Vitti," *London Times Magazine,* January 2, 1977, p. 18.

Quinlan, David. *The Illustrated Directory of Film Stars.* London: B.T. Batsford, 1981, p. 470.

Shipman, David. *The Great Movie Stars: The International Years.* London: Angus & Robertson, 1972, p. 528.

Thomson, David. *A Biographical Dictionary of Film.* New York: William Morrow, 1975, p. 585.

Walter, Eugene. "Monica Vitti," *Vogue,* 147:123–5+, February 15, 1966.

Wlaschin, Ken. *The Illustrated Encyclopedia of the World's Great Movie Stars and Their Films.* London: Salamander, 1979, p. 225–6.

Yakir, Dan. "Monica Vitti," *Interview,* 16:87–8, July 1986.

Ursula Andress

When Ursula Andress strolled out of the sea dressed only in a bikini in the first James Bond film in the early 1960s, she made an immediate and international impact. From that moment on her future as a movie star was assured. With her luminous skin, voluptuous body and beautiful face she became one of the most popular sexpots of the middle '60s. Some gave her no credit for acting ability, and as one critic said, "She tends to be humorless, unanimated and preoccupied with the stiff-necked haughtiness of someone who has been taught to hold her breath so that her breasts stay high." She had talent but like many other sexpots she rarely got any decent roles.

Ursula was born March 19, 1936, in Berne, Switzerland, one of six children of German parents. She attended a private girls' school until she was in her teens and then spent a year in Paris studying art. She was on a holiday in Rome when she was 18 and was approached at a party by someone who wanted her to read for a film. "When you're a young girl, in Rome, they always want to put you in pictures," she said.

Andress got the part and appeared in four Italian films in 1954–55, pictures that did not achieve North American distribution and in which the actress had small roles. Ursula came to the attention of Marlon Brando who was impressed enough to introduce her to an agent for Paramount studios. Paramount flew her to London for a screen test and then shipped her to Hollywood where they hoped to groom her as another Marlene Dietrich. Ursula agreed to go because, she said, "I thought it might be fun to have a swimming pool and horses."

Once in the American film capital, Paramount never used her and after awhile she bought back her contract and ended the association. The problem was that Ursula never learned to speak English. She developed a friendship with James Dean.

The trip was not a total loss. The actress met actor producer John Derek in 1955 and the couple married in 1957. According to Ursula, "I married John because one day he said 'we're getting married in three days' time,' and I was still in a state of shock." John said she came to this country because "she's a Swiss mercenary at heart. Money is important to her, but she won't work for it. Why does she need a career for her vanity? She gets enough flattery from everybody she knows."

For the next four years the couple globetrotted and Andress made no more screen appearances until she landed a part in the 1962 release *Dr. No*, the first in the series of James Bond films. By then she was fluent in English, as well as German, Italian and Spanish. During those years away from film offers to do motion pictures had never stopped coming in. Andress chose not to accept any. In *Dr. No* the actress emerged from the sea, deeply tanned, beautiful, wearing a bikini with a knife at her waist — a dream-like sequence that is likely the most remembered scene from that film.

"*Dr. No* can't do her any good, or any harm either," said Derek, "she just plays a dame in an animated bikini." But it did her career a lot of good and her asking price moved from $10,000 to $50,000 per film. Derek was also a photographer and shot a nude layout of his wife which appeared in *Playboy* magazine in 1963, further increasing the demand for Ursula.

Derek believed his wife to have a lack of discipline, and remarked, "She wouldn't read a script beforehand, because she can't be bothered. Reading would mean she would have to be alone, and she's never been alone in her life. Scripts are sent to her, but she won't read them. They offer her parts anyhow. If she really wanted a career, she'd have had it years ago. She suddenly decided to go back to work again, and I don't know why . . . she has nothing to do all day long, but she keeps very busy doing it . . . Ursula never could be disciplined about anything."

Nevertheless Andress was able to get a job whenever she felt inclined. In 1963 she appeared in several films. In *Four for Texas* she was merely decoration in a farcical Western vehicle for Frank Sinatra and Dean Martin. *Nightmare in the Sun*, produced by and starring Derek, was an abysmal film about a man hunted for murder by people who knew he was innocent. Ursula played a bored

Ursula Andress demonstrates her bullet-shooting bra in *The 10th Victim*.

wife who slept around a lot and was murdered early in the picture. Critics felt the film was a nightmare on the screen with all the main actors branded as "terrible." Andress, however, was labeled as "passable," a compliment for that film.

The actress was again a decoration in *Fun in Acapulco* where she was an Elvis Presley love interest. "They wouldn't let me wear a real bikini and put a ruffled thing on me," said Andress, "they even stuck on a hair ribbon, stupidly thinking this would please the innocent little girls in Elvis's audiences." A bikini was the favored attire again in the farce *What's New, Pussycat?* with Ursula cast as a sex-mad parachutist. A much better role came her way in *The 10th Victim,* an Italian futuristic drama wherein people hunted and killed one another for big prize money in televised events. Ursula and Marcello Mastroianni were the main adversaries and the actress came equipped with a bullet-shooting brassiere. She got generally good notices.

About her own reluctance to work, the actress once said, "They all keep teasing me about such nice parts, and I get excited. Then one morning, I have to get up at 5:30 and things start to get complicated."

Her best known film is perhaps the 1965 release *She,* an adaptation of the H. Rider Haggard novel. Andress was top-billed as the cold-blooded Queen Ayesha of a lost kingdom. The queen pined for the return of a lover she had murdered ages in the past. Generally she earned praise for her acting and *Variety* said the film brought out "heretofore unknown depths in Miss Andress' acting. Role calls for sincere warmth as a woman in love, also brutal cruelty as queen, and she convinces." In *The Blue Max,* a World War I drama told from the German point of view, Andress was fought over by two German airmen. One reviewer pronounced her to be "an okay sexpot."

The marriage to Derek ended in divorce in 1966 and Ursula began an affair with French actor Jean-Paul Belmondo after the pair costarred in a French film. Belmondo left a wife and three children for Ursula and that affair lasted about six years. Over the years the actress claimed she remained devoted to Derek and once, in the 1980s, she and another ex-wife, Linda Evans, gathered with Derek and his current wife (Bo) to celebrate his birthday.

The Southern Star was an action film set in Africa in 1910 with the actress first-billed and giving a good performance as the girlfriend of an adventurer played by George Segal. As one of a trio of amoral thieves plotting a robbery in the crime comedy *Perfect Friday,* Andress spent much time undressed but, according to one critic, "demonstrated a flair for low-key comedy." In *Red Sun* the actress was merely decoration in this European-made Western.

Ursula did not want to get married again and, in the early 1970s, said, "I'd only marry if I had a child. Otherwise, only live together. Then you can leave without going to court. I don't want to be bothered with a $180,000 divorce. I've had one of those." Of her screen image, she said, "I think my image, especially to Americans, is that of a femme fatale, a man-eating woman. I'm not empty-headed or calculated and cool. But maybe my looks give that impression. I'm disciplined in my doings and undisciplined in my emotions. I can't control the things I feel or hide my feelings."

Ursula remained busy with film work through the 1970s, appearing in one to four films per year. The pictures were mostly low-budget European efforts, however, with titles such as *Stick 'Em Up Darlings!* and *Primitive Desires.* They received virtually no distribution in North America.

By the end of the 1970s she had become interested in photography and

Ursula Andress with unidentified actor in *Red Sun*.

had her pictures published in many magazines around the world. "I started when I got discouraged with films," she said. "It's such a rough, tough business, making movies. And I'm in it in only a limited way, after all, making action-adventure films. It's my fault, probably. I've always been scared of opening myself up, of trusting a director. But with a camera it's up to me. I don't have to rely on anyone else. And I like that."

Andress opposed women's liberation feeling women were lucky to be able to be somewhat independent as well as have the protection of men. She hoped the situation would not change. As for feminists the actress said, "I don't think I would like to live in a world of such women. The truth is I have more faith in men than in women. Really, you know, they are much nicer than we are."

The films Andress appeared in during the 1980s received a wider distribution and she has been more widely visible on American screens. The parts, however, often have tended to be dismal. Ursula had a support role in *Chanel solitaire* about the life of fashion designer Gabrielle Chanel. She played Aphrodite in *Clash of the Titans,* a film charitably described as an "unbearable bore."

Mexico in Flames was a picture about journalist John Reed during the years 1910–15 and his coverage of the Mexican Revolution. Andress played New York socialite Mabel Dodge with whom Reed had an affair in the film. Once again Andress was put in a no-win situation with a poor plot and vacuous dialog.

One of her best outings was in *Tigers in Lipstick,* filmed in 1979 but not released until 1985. It consisted of seven separate episodes emphasizing women as aggressors. Andress was top-billed over Laura Antonelli and Monica Vitti and was described as "the sexiest performer in the field." The actress played Marie Antoinette in *Liberty, Equality, Sauerkraut,* an historical spoof about the French Revolution. The Bastille was not a prison but a disco for aristocrats. The film was not well received.

After her breakup with Belmondo, Andress had affairs with several men including Ryan O'Neal, Marcello Mastroianni, Italian actor Fabio Testi and John DeLorean. During the filming of *Clash of the Titans,* she began an affair with costar Harry Hamlin. Ursula was then 43 while Hamlin was 28. The actress left her Rome apartment to live with the actor in Hollywood and in May 1980, gave birth to her first child, a boy. By 1983 the couple had split up.

In 1986 Ursula, then 50, started keeping company with a twenty-year-old Italian student named Fausto Fagone and took him to live with her in Beverly Hills. Fausto's father was upset and told a reporter, "She is nothing more than a cradle snatcher, and she will marry him over my dead body."

Speaking of her career, Andress said, "To me life is the most important thing. What is a career in life? What is success in life? Life is to love and share and create. How can you say you sacrificed for a career? I could never, ever do that."

Ursula Andress Filmography

Le avventure di Giacomo Casanova [Sins of Casanova; The Loves of Casanova] (1954)
Un Americano a Roma [An American in Rome] (1954)
La tempesta e parsata [The Tempest Has Gone] (1955)
La cantena dell'odio (1955)
Dr. No (1962)
Four for Texas (1963)
Nightmare in the Sun (1963)
Fun in Acapulco (1963)
Toys for Christmas (1964)
She (1965)
What's New, Pussycat? (1965)

La decima vittima [The 10th Victim] (1965)
Les Tribulations d'un Chicois en Chine [Chinese Adventures in China] (1965)
Once Before I Die (1966)
The Blue Max (1966)
Casino Royale (1967)
Le dolci signore [Anyone Can Play] (1967)
L'etoile du Sud [The Southern Star] (1968)
Perfect Friday (1970)
Soleil rouge [Red Sun] (1971)
Five Against Capricorn (1972)

L'ultima occasione [The Last Chance] (1973)
Colpo in canna [Stick 'Em up Darlings!] (1974)
Loaded Guns (1975)
L'infermiera [I Will If You Will] (1975)
40 grada sotto le lenzuola (1976)
Africa Express (1976)
Scaramouche [The Loves and Times of Scaramouche] (1976)
The Fifth Musketeer (1977)
Double Murders (1977)
Casanova and Co. [The Rise and Rise of Casanova] (1977)

Spoglilamoci cosi Senza Pudor [Love in Four Easy Lessons] (1977)
The Mountain in the Jungle [Primitive Desires; Prisoner of the Cannibal God] (1978)
Letti selvaggi [Tigers in Lipstick] (1979)
Una strana coppio di gangsters (1979)
Nobody's Perfect (1980)
Grip (1980)
Clash of the Titans (1981)
Chanel solitaire (1981)
Meksika v ogne [Mexico in Flames; Red Bells] (1982)
Liberte, egalite, choucroute (1985)

Sources

Allis, Tim. "Chatter," *People.* 28:150, September 14, 1987.
"A Fabulous Body at Any Age," *Harper's Bazaar,* 117:117+, May 1984.
Haber, Joyce. "Ursula Andress' Private Thoughts on Living, Loving," *Los Angeles Times,* July 30, 1972, Calendar sec., p. 15.
Hamilton, Jack. "Ursula Andress of *Dr. No,*" *Look,* 26:72+, December 31, 1962.
_____. "Ursula Andress: Success Story of a Lazy Beauty," *Look,* 27:54–7+, November 5, 1963.
Katz, Ephraim. *The Film Encyclopedia.* New York: Thomas Y. Crowell, 1979, p. 31.
Lloyd, Ann, ed. *The Illustrated Who's Who of the Cinema.* London: Orbis, 1983, p. 10.
Mann, Roderick. "Elusively Yours, Ursula Andress," *Los Angeles Times,* August 27, 1978, Calendar sec., p. 28.
Quinlan, David. *Quinlan's Illustrated Directory of Film Stars.* London: B.T. Batsford, 1986, p. 9.
Quinn, Joan. "Ursula Andress," *Interview,* 13:42+, August 1983.
Thomson, David. *A Biographical Dictionary of Film.* New York: William Morrow, 1975, p. 8.
Wallace, David. "I Want to Be with Him Says Ursula Andress," *People,* 20:34–5, July 4, 1983.
Wlaschin, Ken. *The Illustrated Encyclopedia of the World's Great Movie Stars and Their Films.* London: Salamander, 1979, p. 165.

Laura Antonelli

Laura Antonelli had a voluptuous body and was noted for a dual expression of sensuality and innocence. These factors combined to make Laura Antonelli one of the biggest film stars in Italy during the 1970s. With the release of several of her films in the United States within the space of a year, she enjoyed a short spate of international fame. Laura's hopes of a Hollywood career never materialized and she was largely forgotten in the United States.

Antonelli was born Laura Antonaz on November 28, 1941, in the small coastal town of Pola, Yugoslavia. When Marshal Tito assumed power in Yugoslavia in 1947 the Antonaz family fled to Italy where they spent several years living in refugee camps in Genoa and Venice. Mr. Antonaz finally got a job as a hospital administrator in Naples where Laura spent most of her youth, although the family felt uprooted and friendless.

Antonelli's early ambition was to become a math teacher but she changed her mind and obtained a degree as a gymnastics instructor instead — a qualification that could be obtained more swiftly. "My parents had made me take hours of gym classes during my teens," Laura said. "They felt I was ugly, clumsy, insignificant, and they hoped that I would at least develop some grace. I became very good, especially in rhythmical gym, which is a kind of dance."

Laura got a job as a high school gym teacher in Rome but found that she did not like it. Her circle of friends included a few minor artists, one of whom asked her to appear in television commercials for products such as bed sheets and beverages. This led to a job as an announcer on television but she was so wooden and awkward that she was fired within a month. She returned to commercials where one she made for a soft drink caught the interest of a film producer.

While she had never had any acting lessons nor expressed any early interest in acting as a career, she had already appeared in the 1966 release *Dr. Goldfoot and the Girl Bombs* in a bit part. The producer who saw her commercial offered her a part in his film *Sexual Revolution*. Laura took the two-month job which paid just $600 and changed her name to Antonelli.

That film was as bad as its title and Laura was notable only for the amount of nudity. Director Riccardo Ghione recalled, "Laura walked on the set, undressed in front of all of us without hesitation and with great ease." Antonelli remarked, however, "It wasn't easy. I knew I had to do it, that was what my role called for, so I acted as professionally as I could."

The actress's next ten films, made over three years, offered her little to do other than repeatedly remove her clothes. One of the exceptions was *Gradiva* where Laura was the lead female. It was the story of a young archaeologist who fell in love with an ancient bas-relief of a woman and then pursued a girl (Antonelli) whom he thought was a reincarnation of her. She turned out to be a wealthy playgirl. Laura got some good reviews for her acting as well as her body. *Sans mobile apparent* was a detective film modeled after the American ones of the '40s with Laura lending good support.

The actress enjoyed her work saying, "I have lots of fantasies and the possiblity to express them through acting gives me an incredible sense of satisfaction. It's like a constant game that I play with myself. The halo around the star-system doesn't interest me particularly. I'm an instinctive actress. I don't have any background, so I really live the lives of my characters." In 1970 Antonelli married publisher Enrico Piacentini. The couple divorced in 1973.

Laura Antonelli in a scene from *Till Marriage Do Us Part.*

More pictures requiring nudity followed. *Il merlo maschio* cast the actress as the wife of a musician who loved to impress his friends. Laura appeared nude in his violoncello case. Reviews were as bad as they had been for most of her films but this one got a few good reviews in other European countries as Antonelli enjoyed a growing reputation. *Il merlo* led her to work in France where she appeared in *Docteur Popoul*, an anarchic comedy about a woman-chasing doctor. Jean-Paul Belmondo played the doctor who thought ugly women were more exciting and was married to a homely woman. Antonelli did well as the woman's beautiful sister who gave Belmondo cause to question his philosophy. Off-screen she started a long-term affair with Belmondo which was the catalyst for her divorce.

That same year, 1972, she starred in the Italian film *Malizia,* an irreverent comedy about manners and morals. Laura was cast as a young country girl who took over as servant and surrogate mother in a Sicilian household where the mother had recently died. Soon the father and three adolescent sons were after her. She was outstanding and *Variety* called her, "An uncanny choice for the key role of the servant: almost angelic in beauty, but oozing pentup sensuality, the almost ideal-mistress dream fantasy, and she plays it extremely well." The actress picked up a Golden Globe award for that film and *Malizia* became a smash hit in Italy carrying Laura to superstardom.

Several more big hits followed in Italy. *Sex Crazy* was an episodic satire in nine parts with Antonelli in all but two and displaying plenty of nudity. In a sex comedy, *Venial Sin,* Laura played a bored wife at a seaside resort whose husband only showed up on the weekends. She alleviated her boredom by having an affair with an adolescent. *Till Marriage Do Us Part* was a satire on upperclass Sicilians with Antonelli playing a virgin bride doomed to unconsummated frustration after a last-minute exposure of the bride and groom as brother and sister. This film featured more nudity for Laura and even some gratuitous lesbian scenes.

All of the nudity required of her did not bother Antonelli, who said, "To be considered a sex symbol gratifies me. I'm not ashamed of any of the films in which I undressed, not even the cheaper ones. If I manage to communicate a kind of sensuality on the screen, it must mean that there is something in me that I can express. I am proud of it. The important thing is to never let it degrade into pornography. Naked beauty without intelligence fades quickly. I have a good sense of my limitations. I can see when something I play is ridiculous or tends to degenerate . . . I confess I never thought of myself as being particularly sexy. Others always see this quality in me, and this amuses me."

Perhaps her best film was Visconti's *The Innocent.* Set at the turn of the century the film looked at women trying to find freedom in a male-dominated world. Antonelli was lead-billed and earned excellent notices. When Visconti cast for that film he selected Laura because he had remembered, and been impressed by, her nude appearance in the musician's case from *Il merlo maschio.* Said the director, "That girl will go a long way, for she is malleable and has an urge to learn. She has that mysterious quality which I call charm, namely beauty plus intelligence."

Working for the famed Visconti was a great opportunity for the actress who found herself "paralyzed with fright" on the set and described him as "a perfectionist, imperious, arrogant." She also agreed that she learned a great deal from him. *Wifemistress* starred Antonelli as an apathetic housewife who liberated herself through sex and politics. Her husband, played by Marcello Mastroianni, fell victim to political intrigue and had to hide. This led Laura to think he was dead, take over his business, and find out what kind of a man he really was.

Several of her films received a wide distribution in the United States in 1978–79, on the heels of her success in *The Innocent.* The others were *Wifemistress, Till Marriage Do Us Part,* which was five years old, and *Malizia.* The latter was originally made in 1972, released in the United States with no success in 1974 and then rereleased in 1979 under the new title *Malicious* to try and take advantage of the actress's sudden fame.

The ads for those films concentrated mainly on sex appeal. The one for *The Innocent* showed Laura nude, from the back. *Till Marriage Do Us Part* used an ad featuring the actress lounging seductively in a haystack, while the one for *Malicious* had her attired in a flimsy nightie. "To Americans, I must look feminine, soft, elegant, and sexy," said Antonelli. "I am all that, of course, but I can also act. I love my calling. I worked hard to become an actress, and then a better actress—I'm not a dumb doll, I just play that role when I have to. . . . Because I am the absolute master of myself, nobody can really exploit me."

Her relationship with Belmondo was still active at the end of the 1970s. She lived quietly in Rome describing herself as an introvert who preferred to be alone or with a few friends from the days when she was an unknown. When she was free she would fly to Paris to join Belmondo or he would come to Rome. "Ours is a great passion," she said. "It has been going on now for eight years. He complains all the time that I act like a man, rather than a woman, just because I am independent. He says it's so un–Italian of me."

Laura openly hoped her spate of exposure in the United States would lead to a Hollywood career. In anticipation she worked on her English and said of Hollywood, "I'd be terrified, but very pleased if someone would call me. Many European actress have made big mistakes by moving to Hollywood, because they failed over there and they have lost their identity over here. I have to be careful. I have to think before I do anything." Laura has yet to make an American film, or even one in the English language.

More recently she has appeared in *Il malato immaginario,* a comedy burlesque of Molière, opposite Alberto Sordi. She also played a married woman having an affair in *Passione d'amore* and starred in *Tigers in Lipstick,* an episodic comedy made in 1979 but not released until 1985.

She accepts less film work now because she feels she has not been getting enough demanding roles. In her mind her greatest successes have been in films set in the past where she was cast as the classic beauty. What she looks for now is a contemporary character with contemporary clothes, or as she says, "an intelligent woman in a modern comedy with none of those stupid lines which cannot be read with conviction."

Dissatisfied on the whole with her work, she remarked, "First I had to build my own career all by myself. I never had a production company, or producer, or a husband behind me, and this is very rare in Italy. Second, I think I gave the best of myself in what I did, but of course the situation was limited."

Laura has also faced the stereotypical belief that beauty and brains are incompatible. "I have often heard from those who have directed me that they really took me for this or that role because of my looks. At the end of the film, they would always note with surprise that I could also act. The truth is that too many people think that beauty is synonymous with stupidity."

Laura Antonelli Filmography

Dr. Goldfoot and the Girl Bombs
  (1966)
L'arcangelo (1968)
La rivoluzione sessuale [Sexual Revolution] (1968)
Un detective (1969)
Venere Nuda (1969)
Sledge (1970)
Avventura a Bali (1970)
Stop Verushko (1970)
Gradiva (1970)
Les mariés de l'an deux (1971)
Sans mobile apparent (1971)
Il merlo maschio (1971)
All'onorevole piacciano le donne (1971)
Simona (1972)
Docteur Popoul (1972)

Malizia [Malicious] (1972)
Peccato veniale [Venial Sin] (1973)
Sesso matto [Sex Crazy] (1973)
Mio Dio, come sono caduta in basso!
  [Till Marriage Do Us Part] (1974)
Incontro d'amore (1974)
La divina creatura [The Divine Nymph]
  (1975)
La malizia di venere (1975)
L'Innocente [The Innocent] (1976)
Mogliamonte [Wifemistress] (1977)
Gran Bollito (1977)
Tre scimmie d'oro (1977)
Il malato immaginario (1979)
Passione d'amore (1982)
Letti Salvaggi [Tigers in Lipstick]
  (1985)

Sources

Anderson, Archie A. "The Voice Behind the Body," New York Magazine, 13:76, February 4, 1980.
Barzini, Ludina. "I Never Thought of Myself as Sexy," New York Times, July 15, 1979, sec. 2, p. 1, 13.
Haskell, Molly. "Laura Antonelli Acts Out Our Sexual Fantasies," Ms, 8:14, October 1979.
Morera, Daniela. "Sinsational Laura Antonelli," Interview, 9:68–69, Christmas 1979.
"La Vedette de la Semaine: Laura Antonelli," Ciné Revue, 50:61, October 18, 1979.

Chapter 2

Greek Actresses

Most of the actresses who have reached stardom have come from the Italian and French cinema, with lesser representation from Germany and Scandinavia. Usually the women became popular in the country of their birth but in a few cases their popularity was gained in another country such as the Swiss-born Ursula Andress became popular in Italy and the Austrian-born Maria Schell in Germany. Countries like Belgium, Switzerland, the Netherlands or Spain have yet to produce even one actress of international repute who has made her reputation in her home country's film industry.

Greece has managed to produce two. This is an anomaly given the country's experiences with right wing military regimes — a stifling influence on the development of a film industry — and its relatively low economic development compared with other European countries.

Irene Papas had a passion for acting that stretched back into her childhood and was later nurtured at Greece's National School of Dramatic Arts. Leaving Greece after her first film, because the Greeks branded her style as "noncommercial," Papas made a few movies in Italy before trying her luck in the United States. There was little demand for her services and a disheartened Papas returned to Greece. Over the years she has gradually built a fine reputation as the best interpreter of the Greek classics, both on the screen and on the stage. She made films in many other countries and underwent a period of exile from Greece when the military took over.

Melina Mercouri became interested in acting as a career early in her life. Her best and most well-known work, *Never on Sunday,* was with her husband, director Jules Dassin. Melina made a few pictures in the United States but never based herself there preferring to retain her national identity. After the Greek junta took over Mercouri was openly critical and for her pains was deprived of her citizenship and Greek property. When the junta collapsed in the mid–1970s the actress returned to Greece and divided her time between acting and politics, becoming a cabinet minister in Greece's socialist government.

Mercouri and Papas have appeared in 64 films.

91

Irene Papas

With fierce dark eyes flaming beneath bushy eyebrows, Irene Papas became one of Greece's best known actresses by the time she was in her early 20s. Papas quickly rose to the rank of international film star. She and Melina Mercouri were the only Greek actresses that attained worldwide recognition. Her strongest work has come in the ancient Greek tragedies brought to life on the screen and stage but it has tended to limit the roles she has been offered. Hollywood made a major effort to turn her into a starlet but often wasted her talents in dismal productions.

She was born Irene Lelekou on March 9, 1926, in Chiliomodian, Greece, a small village 60 miles from Athens. Papas was given the name Irene because it is the Greek word for peace. Mr. and Mrs. Lelekou were both teachers and her mother also wrote fairytales which helped to awaken the young child's imagination. Mr. Lelekou spent hours with his daughter teaching her classical drama. Irene studied and recited for him from the plays of the Greek tragedians.

Recalling her youth, the actress said, "As a child I was always acting. I made dolls out of sticks and rags. Once a tour came to the village and set up a tent and I saw women tearing their hair in the Greek tragedies and I liked that. After that, I would tie black kerchiefs around my head and charge the other children to watch me."

The family moved to Athens when Irene was seven years old. She attended the same school where her parents taught and performed and studied classical drama as part of the regular curriculum. Her dream was to be accepted by Greece's National School of Dramatic Arts. The youngster exercised vigorously hoping the activity would make her taller, stronger and older looking. Irene tried to enroll when she was 12 but the school was not fooled and politely told her to come back when she got older. She persisted in applying and was finally enrolled at 15, going to high school in the morning and drama school in the afternoon.

Under the tutelage of Greece's experts in acting technique, Papas flowered quickly playing a variety of parts from Greek classics to Shakespeare. At 18 she was awarded her license, something all actors had to have. "In Greece actors are respected because they have the most education. You can't be a dumb actor there," said Papas, "You must get a license or you can't work. It's like becoming a doctor in America. Without a license the police arrest you."

Her professional stage debut came in 1948 in a musical comedy. Over the next couple of years she became one of the most popular leading ladies in Greek theaters. Her approach, however, was controversial. The prevailing method of acting the classics was to use unnatural intonations and a lot of rhetorical flourish. Papas used her own style which was more contemporary and

Irene Papas in *A Dream of Kings.*

realistic. Older members of the Greek establishment were not pleased. Besides classical acting, she appeared in a number of variety shows as a singer and dancer.

In 1947 she married Alkis Papas but the union was dissolved in 1951. A 1957 marriage to José Kohn ended in annulment. Papas had made her film debut in the 1951 Greek release *Nekri Politeia* and worried when the Greek acting establishment branded her a "noncommercial actress." Signed up with the Italian film company Lux, Papas made six films in Italy from 1953 to 1954 but they were forgettable with titles such as *Theodora Slave Empress* and *Attila the Hun.*

Those films did bring her to the attention of Hollywood. Greek magnate Spyros Skouras brought Papas to the United States for the first time in 1954 where she did a screen test for director Elia Kazan. Though she got no work at first opportunity came the next year when she landed a seven-year contract with MGM. Her first film for them, *Tribute to a Bad Man,* had bad luck from the start. Originally it was to star Spencer Tracy and a young actor named Bob Francis. On location in Colorado Tracy fought with the director and walked out. Later Francis was killed in a plane crash.

Eventually the film was made with James Cagney as the male lead but Hollywood was not impressed with Papas. It was the only film she made under her contract which was soon terminated. Irene tried for other work but could not get hired. Of her Hollywood experience, the actress said simply, "I vanished."

After a winter spent attending the Actors' Studio, Papas returned to Greece in despair and went back to stage work. She toured for several years with the National Popular Theater appearing in Greek classics, Shakespeare, and more modern plays such as *Inherit the Wind.* Papas made no films for four years.

In 1960 she appeared in the screen version of *Antigone* and began to build a reputation as a fine interpreter of Greek classics on film. Two years later she scored a major international success starring in *Electra,* the first of several films she would make with director Michael Cacoyannis.

Electra went on to win many film awards with Papas drawing rave reviews. Two years later, in 1964, she teamed up again with Cacoyannis and played the widow in *Zorba the Greek,* winning more rave reviews and solidifying her growing reputation as an international film star. Yet Irene was not particularly happy and said, "After *Electra* won all the international film prizes, I didn't work for two years. After *Zorba* I didn't work for a year and a half. I'm loved and admired, then dismissed with laurels. It's never been an easy life, acting. Blood and sweat. I've never made much money. For *Zorba,* my most popular film, I made only $10,000. I am not a star people pay money to see. They take my blood instead and I'm always there to give it. Every time I begin a new project I nearly die."

She appeared in other films like *The Guns of Navarone* as well as in a number of other foreign films in the late 1960s. Most of these were in Italian — a language in which she was fluent. Her greatest success and impact, however, came in Greek films. Irene was back in the United States to make the 1968 release *The Brotherhood,* a dismal Mafia outing with Papas cast as Kirk Douglas's wife. "It's not such a great part, but I need the money," said the actress. "Like most Greeks, I am supporting several people back home."

Another notable film from that period was *Z* where she played the wife of an assassinated politician. She also gave an outstanding performance as Helen in the 1971 release *The Trojan Women,* directed by Cacoyannis.

Privately she lived simply — not drinking or smoking, dressing simply and using no makeup. Like Melina Mercouri Irene left Greece after the military took over the country in the mid–1960s, moved to the United States, and vigorously denounced the junta contemptuously calling it "the fourth Reich." When the government returned to civilian hands Papas returned home after an exile of eight years. "When we were liberated I didn't go immediately," said Papas, "I didn't feel I should share in the happiness since I didn't share in the suffering of those who stayed." During her exile the actress kept busy with films and made a number of stage appearances in the United States, one of which was a 1967 appearance opposite Jon Voight.

Her next major film role was in *Iphigenia* (1977), another Euripides classic directed by Cacoyannis. Papas played a mother caught up in the tragedy of war whose daughter was taken away as a sacrifice. Enthusiastic about the film, Papas said, "It is a shame to advertise *Iphigenia* as a classic Greek tragedy because it scares everyone away. . . . But I'm not modest about this film. I love it. . . . We are trying to bring the classics to the people. They belong on the stage or the screen and not back on the shelf." The script was approved and financed by the Greek Film Center but the stars and director got no money right away for the film since the Film Center had to be reimbursed before any money went to the cast.

In May 1976 Irene was cast in *The Greek Tycoon,* a film based loosely on the life of Aristotle Onassis, for a fee of $55,000. The preproduction period lasted a year and Papas' name was used extensively during that time as part of the effort to attract investors. Producer Nico Mastorakis kept telling her to remain free for the filming but when the shoot finally commenced another actress was used and there was no part for Papas. The actress sued for $55,000 in Athens, an action that was settled out of court.

Cacoyannis was the only director with whom Papas felt comfortable. About directors in general, she said, "My problem is I'm too obedient. I try to serve the director, make him the hero. That's why I may leave acting. I'm thinking about it. Because I can't stand this dictatorship over me. I think I am too intelligent to be an actress. It's very hard for an intelligent person to act because you have to be selfish to stand up for what you believe and I'm not selfish."

Her enormous reputation as a Greek tragedian of the first rank made it difficult for her to get different types of parts particularly in Hollywood where she was usually cast as the earth mother type who was required to do little more than suffer stoically or emote furiously. "To me, there's not enough variety in my career," said Papas, "I want to do a musical."

More recently Papas did well as a slightly comic maid in *Christ Stopped at Eboli,* followed by an able performance in a minor role as an earth

Irene Papas and Gian Maria Volonte in *We Still Kill the Old Way*.

mother in *Omar Mukhtar—Lion of the Desert*. In *Erendira*, an adaptation of
a Gabriel García Márquez novel, Irene portrayed a grandmother who sold her
granddaughter into prostitution.

Papas was back as a black clad earth mother in *Il disertore*, giving an excellent performance as a woman, having lost two sons to the war, trying to get
a war memorial erected in her small Sicilian village. *The Assisi Underground*
featured Irene with some good scenes as a mother superior trying to keep people seeking refuge from the war out of her convent which had not been entered
by men in 700 years. *Into the Night* was a comedy about jewel smuggling with
Papas having a small role as one of those in pursuit of the jewels but she had
little to do.

The 1987 release *Sweet Country* had Papas seventh-billed as the mother of a Chilean family drawn into political turmoil after the 1973 assassination of Marxist leader Salvador Allende. A year later she costarred with Jacqueline Bisset in *High Season,* a romantic comedy set in Rhodes. Irene was singled out for praise in an otherwise lackluster vehicle.

When asked if her best work was done in film or on the stage, the actress replied, "I haven't done my best work yet." Insecurity and a less than optimistic opinion of her profession also marked the actress's outlook. "Many things I do just for money because I don't know how to make a living any other way. I miss that, not having done something more important with my life. I'm very sad that I may have to spend the rest of my life as an actress . . . I feel I am not good enough. I'm always looking into people's eyes to see if they like me . . . I feel nervous, nauseated. I'm not a happy person. . . . I have no ego and no ambition. I'm like a cow you milk, milk and then it finally gives you a kick. I feel like kicking back, but I never do. . . . I live my whole life wondering — am I worth it?

Irene Papas Filmography

Nekri Politeia [Dead City] (1951)
Le infideli [The Unfaithfuls] (1953)
Dramma della Casbah [The Man from Cairo] (1953)
Vortice (1953)
Teodora, Imperatrice di Bisanzio [Theodora Slave Empress] (1954)
Attila, Flagello di Dio [Attila the Hun] (1954)
Tribute to a Bad Man (1955)
The Power and the Prize (1956)
Antigone (1960)
The Guns of Navarone (1961)
Electra (1962)
The Moon-Spinners (1964)
Zorba the Greek (1964)
Die Zeugin aus der Holle (1965)
Roger la Honte (1966)
Mas alla de las montanas [The Desperate Ones; Beyond the Mountains] (1967)
A ciascuno il sou [To Each His Own; We Still Kill the Old Way] (1967)
The Brotherhood (1968)
Ecce Homo (1968)
Z (1969)
A Dream of Kings (1969)

Anne of the Thousand Days (1969)
The Trojan Women (1971)
Roma Bene (1971)
N.P. il segreto (1971)
Un posto ideale per uccidere (1971)
Non si servizia un paperino (1972)
Piazza Pulita (1972)
Sutjeska (1972)
Le faro da padre [Bambina] (1974)
Moses (1975)
The Message [Mohammed, Messenger of God] (1976)
Bodas de sangre (1976)
L'uomo di Corleone (1977)
Un ombra nell' ombra (1977)
Iphigenia (1977)
Bloodline (1979)
Cristo si e fermato a Eboli [Christ Stopped at Eboli] (1980)
Omar Mukhtar — Lion of the Desert (1981)
Erendira (1982)
Il disertore [The Deserter] (1983)
The Assisi Underground (1984)
Into the Night (1985)
Sweet Country (1987)
High Season (1988)

Sources

The International Dictionary of Films and Filmmakers: Volume III: Actors and Actresses. Chicago: St. James Press, 1986, p. 494.

Katz, Ephraim. *The Film Encyclopedia.* New York: Thomas Y. Crowell, 1979, p. 893.

Lloyd, Ann, ed. *The Illustrated Who's Who of the Cinema.* London: Orbis, 1983, p. 338.

Maslin, Janet. "At the Movies," *New York Times,* April 27, 1984, p. C8.

"Papas Hits 'Tycoon' Prods. with $55,000 Pact Breach Charge," *Variety,* 288:53, September 7, 1977.

Reed, Rex. "Irene Doesn't Believe in Irene," *New York Times,* December 24, 1967, sec 2, p. 3, 9.

Root, Nanda. "Irene Papas," *Saturday Review of the Arts,* 1:64, April 1973.

Scott, Vernon. "Where Are Those Classic Greeks?" *Washington Post,* March 12, 1978, p. K10.

Thomas, Kevin. "Papas: Committed to Her Craft," *Los Angeles Times,* March 22, 1978, sec. 4, p. 13–14.

Melina Mercouri

Known as a fiery actress with a passion for politics, Melina Mercouri put Greece on the map both culturally and politically. Working mainly with her husband, director Jules Dassin, the couple have produced several interesting films and joined forces for many social causes.

Melina Mercouri was born in Athens on October 18, 1925. Her father, Stamatis Mercouris, was a member of the Greek Chamber of Deputies and had served several terms as the Minister of the Interior. Her mother Irene was the daughter of a man who was mayor of Athens for about 30 years. Stamatis was a womanizer and Irene later divorced him. Melina's name was derived from the Greek word for "honey," and she later dropped the "s" from her surname when she took up acting.

Mercouri traced her dramatic flare to early childhood. "I remember when I was three," she said, "my grandfather would drive me around Constitution Square — our principal public place — and he would say, 'Salute your subjects, my queen.' I would bow and wave, making an exhibition of myself, and I guess that it was my first step toward the theater." Once Melina ran off to a neighborhood café when she was five and was found singing and dancing on a table.

The Mercouri household was frequented by politicians, intellectuals, and artists and provided a stimulating environment for a young girl. Melina received a fine education and became fluent in French and German. She was quite a disobedient student, however, and attended several schools before graduating.

During her teens Mercouri decided she wanted to become an actress. Her

Melina Mercouri in *Topkapi.*

family disapproved of this ambition and so she married at 17 to free herself from family control. Her husband was an elderly, wealthy Greek who paid for Melina's training at the Academy of the National Theater in Athens. She attended for three years studying Greek tragedy.

Her stage debut in Athens came in 1946 in an avant-garde play by Alexis Solomis. Mercouri's stage roles continued to be in modern works and she never used her classical training in a direct way. She appeared in dramas by Eugene O'Neill and Tennessee Williams among others, and was invited to perform in several Paris productions as well. By 1965 she had performed in nearly 100 plays.

Mercouri received her first film offer in 1955 when she played the lead role in *Stella* by Greek director Michael Cacoyannis. The film was not a financial success, but did do well critically, and was popular in England. When it was released in the United States in 1957, one critic described Melina as "a mercurial wench who has magnificent vitality and range as an actress ... the broad-shouldered, sun-bleached good looks of Ingrid Bergman, the glamor of Lauren Bacall, the passion of Anna Magnani, and the absolute hedonistic flair for comedy of the late Carole Lombard."

Stella was entered in competition at the Cannes Film Festival in 1955. It lost to a crime thriller *Rififi* directed by Jules Dassin. Melina wept loudly when her film failed to win, and Dassin came over to her table to console her. Although he was already married to concert violinist Beatrice Launer, with whom he had three children, he became fascinated by Mercouri and followed her back to Greece.

Jules Dassin was born in Connecticut in 1911 to immigrant parents. He started his career in the Yiddish Theater and then wrote for radio and the Broadway stage. He moved to Hollywood at age 30 and became an assistant director working with Alfred Hitchcock. Promoted to full directorship, Dassin made several films in Hollywood in the 1940s, with *The Naked City* being his best known film from that period.

All this time came to an end when the McCarthy hearings of the House on un–American Activities Committee began their proceedings. Dassin's name was given by two fellow directors who testified that he was a communist. Dassin was never called to testify on his own behalf, but was simply blacklisted. He moved to Europe and continued to work as a director there. Looking back on this period Dassin could not speculate on what would have happened if he had not been forced to leave the United States. "But I would never, probably, have met Melina Mercouri," he said, "and that alone would have changed the direction of my life and career."

The first film that they made together was *He Who Must Die* (1957). Mercouri played Mary Magdalene in this Biblical parable. Profits from this project were meager but critics liked it. A *Washington Post* reviewer called it "a screen classic—beautiful in concept, exciting in execution, absorbing to think about." Melina was praised as "splendid" and able to give the role "conviction."

Dassin and Mercouri's relationship deepened and eventually both divorced their spouses. They married in 1966 after having lived together for over a decade, a situation that had generated much disapproving gossip. Mercouri never had children and did not regret it later in life saying, "I'm not bitter because I don't have a child. You don't make youself a martyr if you're not a mother."

Dassin directed Mercouri in several films during their careers but both worked independently as well. In 1958 Mercouri made a film with Joseph Losey called *The Gypsy and the Gentleman.* The movie was a disaster but Mercouri was considered a saving grace. A *Variety* critic wrote that Melina was "a flashing personality-plus actress" who brought "verve to a tired script."

Her next film *Where the Hot Wind Blows,* directed by Dassin, did not fare much better. The film costarred Gina Lollobrigida and Yves Montand. Melina played an older woman who had a tragic affair with a much younger man. Mercouri was unhappy during the shooting because of Lollobrigida and complained that Gina "was terrible for me to work with. I know that I am jealous, but I do not know how to be a star like *that*—to stop the picture and demand close-ups."

Many producers blamed Mercouri for the commercial failure of Dassin's films with her. He had had such a success with *Rififi* before meeting Melina, that some felt she was a bad influence on him, and he was "bending his talent to serve her." "Every producer in Europe hated me then," she recalled. Mercouri and Dassin often had difficulty in obtaining financial backing for the movies. Mercouri had few qualms about her association with Dassin. "He is a genius," she said, "and I use him." However, she later said she would have broken with him if she thought she was ruining his career.

Ironically, their next picture *Never on Sunday* would become a box-office smash. Dassin wrote and directed the movie. Melina played the starring role of Ilya, a warm-hearted Greek prostitute who shows a prudish American male tourist what the joys of life are all about. Dassin was able to get enough money from United Artists to hire a skeleton crew. They wanted Henry Fonda for the part of the naïve American but did not have enough cash to hire him, so Dassin took the role himself.

The film was entered in the Cannes Festival and was an immediate hit. Mercouri won the Cannes award for Best Actress and would later be nominated for an Academy Award. Some observers felt she failed to win the Oscar because she was "foreign." The movie ran in New York for a year and a half. Mercouri was modest about her acting ability and quipped, "They want me to laugh, I laugh. They want me to cry, I cry."

The *New York Times* said that Melina's depiction of Ilya was so full of "personal warmth, wit and vigor and she utterly transcends any stereotype implicit in the part." One critic called her "the greatest gift from Greece since Helen of Troy."

Because of the success of *Never on Sunday* Mercouri became an unofficial ambassadress for her country and tourism soared in Greece. Mercouri was very patriotic and pleased with the positive influence of her movie. "I am proud of my country," she said, "and glad to be a Greek."

Dassin and Mercouri had created their own company, Melina Films, to make *Never on Sunday,* and only spent $125,000 on production costs. Profits were so large that the movie was considered the most financially successful film ever made at that time.

Mercouri was only 35 when *Never on Sunday* was released, but she was already thinking of herself as an aging actress. "As a woman I don't fear age at all," she said. "But it's different for an actress . . . An actress must have heart as well as talent. Beauty fades." As sensitive as she was about her appearance, Melina refused to alter her looks in any way. "I am going to let time ruin me and I am going to enjoy every minute of it." When Dassin suggested she get her protuding teeth fixed, she resisted and after the success of *Never on Sunday* the subject was not mentioned again.

Dassin had no illusions about his own acting in *Never on Sunday*, but was enthusiastic about Mercouri's talent. "She seems to say, 'I love you all—love me too, and let's have fun together.' And audiences respond," said Dassin.

Fame and fortune brought Mercouri a great deal of international media attention. "I have been asked why I don't go to Hollywood," she noted, "but I am a European . . . I want to remain Greek. Bergman, Garbo, and Dietrich lost their national identity." Mercouri eventually did make a few films in the States but never based herself there.

Mercouri was interested in working with other directors and had many offers after *Never on Sunday*. Most were to play prostitutes and she usually turned those down. The only director she did not want to work with was Ingmar Bergman whom she felt was too preoccupied with death. Her next film *Vive Henri IV—Vive l'amour* was directd by Claude Autant-Lara, and the following one *The Last Judgment* was directed by Vittorio De Sica. Neither film gained Mercouri much attention in the United States.

In 1962 Melina appeared in another Dassin film *Phaedra*, a modern version of the Greek myth about the granddaughter of Zeus who fell in love with her stepson. Her costar was Tony Perkins. The film was well received in Europe but had a mixed reception in the States. Some critics felt she was an impressive tragedian while others found her talents "histrionic." Perkins was enthusiastic about working with Mercouri. "She has the most extraordinary vital energy I've ever beheld in an actress," he noted. "She transforms a group, electrifies it."

Mercouri was directed by Carl Foreman in her next film *The Victors*. The international cast included Jeanne Moreau, Romy Schneider, Eli Wallach, George Peppard, and Albert Finney. Melina played a prostitute again. The movie was controversial because it was antiwar and critical of American soldiers.

After observing Moreau's seductive behavior during filming, Mercouri said she would not allow Dassin to work with Moreau. "With a Jeanne Moreau, danger. I would walk out on him and kill," Melina warned.

Peppard found working with Mercouri in *The Victors* to be stimulating, and remarked, "She gives as an actress; she acts with you and for you, and she has a glorious sense of humor." Foreman recalled that Melina was accustomed to Dassin becoming emotional and shouting at her while directing, and she interpreted Foreman's cool behavior as a lack of concern. When he did lose his temper one day and yelled at her, Melina burst into tears.

Dassin and Mercouri teamed up again for the 1964 comedy *Topkapi* about jewel thieves in Istanbul. Melina was happy to be with Dassin and felt there was a sense of community during the shooting of his pictures. The fine cast included Maximilian Schell, Peter Ustinov and Robert Morley, but one reviewer said, "It's Miss Mercouri who holds the picture together. Her unique magnetism — long blonde hair, wide eyes, bold mouth, and fascinating Greek accent — acts as a focal point for all the shenanigans."

In 1965–66 Mercouri was in a few more films, two without Dassin and one directed by him. She claimed to be happy as a movie actress and said, "I am trapped by the camera, I adore it." Yet she never lost her love for the stage. "I can never give up the theater," she insisted. "The rehearsals are too beautiful. It is like making a child. Like a child it grows. In most cinema work you have not the time to make the character grow. And in the cinema you are a slave. It's terrible. If I have a blemish or a cold, I can't be filmed in close-up. What a fuss they make. In the theater . . . no one cares. In the theater you live with writers, designers . . . artists. In the films you live with the producers. Before I was an actress in the cinema, my interests were larger. Now my interests are more and more self-interests."

Mercouri had a chance to return to the stage in 1967 when she appeared on Broadway in *Ilya Darling*. The play was a theatrical version of *Never on Sunday* with Melina singing and dancing her way through the show. Most critics felt the stage version was a disappointment which did not match the quality of the movie. But fans lined up for tickets and packed every performance.

Mercouri was past 40 with wrinkles and dark circles under her eyes when she starred in *Ilya Darling*. She was surprised that reviewers were referring to her as a "splendid dish." "I am not Bardot," she insisted. "It takes great courage at my age to take my clothes off and show my body onstage. I am scared to death when they gasp." Mercouri was alluding to her scene in a brief bikini.

Mercouri received more bad news besides poor reviews during the run of *Ilya Darling*. First her father became ill and died, and then the democratic government in Greece was overthrown in a military coup by a right-wing junta. Melina was heard on American television and radio denouncing the coup and advising tourists to avoid Greece. She read a statement on *The Tonight Show* signed by Edward Albee, Leonard Bernstein, Irene Papas and Jules Dassin which said in part, "Greece, the birthplace of the democratic concept, is presently under the heel of a military dictatorship. Constitutional government and the rights of the people and the press thereunder have been repressed."

The Greek embassy in Washington warned her to be silent but Mercouri

Melina Mercouri in an argumentative mood in *The Gypsy and the Gentleman.*

refused to comply. She was then deprived of her Greek citizenship and her property in Greece was confiscated with the charge of "antinational activities."

Mercouri gave a statement to the New York press saying, "I was born a Greek and will die a Greek. Patakos (the military dictator) was born a fascist and will die a fascist." She also said she was willing to risk death rather than remain silent about the coup. FBI agents guarded her hotel suite, and Dassin hired 17 bodyguards to patrol her dressing room on Broadway.

Asked about the value of her lost property, Melina replied, "I don't know, I've never been interested in money." Another time she remarked, "It's much more fun doing things than having things.... You are less free if you have things." Mercouri knew that she might be accused of being a communist because of her stance, but claimed, "I hate extremism, all extremisms, including communism." In a more recent interview, however, when a journalist referred to her as a Marxist, she did not correct him.

Mercouri and Dassin changed their base of operations from Athens to Paris. In 1971 her autobiography *I Was Born Greek* was published by Doubleday. Melina continued to act on the stage and in films. In 1969 she played Queen Lil, a madam, in *Gaily, Gaily* directed by Norman Jewison, and in 1970 she appeared in *Promise at Dawn* based on the Romain Gary memoir and directed by Dassin. She worked in a few other films in the 1970s including Dassin's *A Dream of Passion* in 1978.

This latter film was a modern adaptation of the Greek tragedy, *Medea*. Medea killed her two children for revenge against her husband who betrayed her by falling in love with another woman. Mercouri had not been outspoken about feminism, and in 1971 she said, "I have never been discriminated against. I have made my life as a woman and that's not so bad."

By 1978 her perspective had changed. "Medea is the only Greek heroine to fight against the male establishment," she said. "It is comfortable for us to call her mad. It lets us off. We call her a monster, but that is not how the play was written. Euripides is for her. He's on her side."

Mercouri also admitted, "I am dependent on men. I felt it very much in exile. I relied on Jules for langauge, for a passport. Everything is men: newspaper publicity, politics, the seat of power. For thousands of years we were taught that the enemy was other women. Now I am learning about sister-hood," she added. "Actresses are especially dependent on men because men control the cinema."

In *A Dream of Passion* Dassin was trying to convey "the contradictions that a woman has to face in herself . . . and the terrible fear of solitude that sometimes goes with independence." The central question of the film was: "What desperation causes a woman to kill what she loves most in the world? What is it but the complete revolution when you sacrifice everything that is most dear to you to attain freedom?"

Since the mid–1970s Mercouri's career has focused as much on politics as on acting. When the military junta in Greece collapsed in 1974, Mercouri returned to her country and ran for parliament. She lost her first election but in 1977 was successfully voted in as a member of the Panhellenic Socialist Party (PASOK) representing the working class port city of Piraeus which had also been the setting for *Never on Sunday*. Mercouri saw no contradiction in the fact that she was living in a penthouse in a wealthy neighborhood. Her acting skills came in handy for her first speech in parliament which concerned sewage in Piraeus. "Never in my life," said one colleague, "have I heard anyone describe garbage with such deep passion."

When asked if her fame as a movie star had helped her get elected, she did not deny it and said, "What's wrong with using my popularity to get votes? . . . What's wrong with mixing art and politics?"

Mercouri was one of eleven women out of 300 members of the Greek parliament. She created a scandal by wearing pants to a parliamentary session. Asked if she preferred politics or acting, Mercouri replied, "An actress is a very lonely person; it's very egotistical to be an actress . . . Political work is to *forget* yourself." She intended to make her political work a priority and act only in the summers. The responsibility of her government activities and the attempt to juggle an acting career gave her an ulcer, however.

After the 1981 elections in Greece Mercouri was appointed Minister of Culture and Sciences in Greece's socialist government. Her mandate was to revitalize the independent film industry and encourage more creativity in Greek television. The latest film she has appeared in to date was the 1984 documentary *Not by Coincidence* which explored her relationship with Dassin.

Melina Mercouri could have capitalized on her beauty and charm for an easy life in Hollywood. She always downplayed these attributes, however. An American journalist once asked what her measurements were and Mercouri replied, "You measure actresses here the way we measure cattle. In Greece we measure an actress by the eyes, the soul and the acting ability."

Melina Mercouri Filmography

Stella (1955)
Celui qui droit mourir [He Who Must Die] (1957)
The Gypsy and the Gentleman (1958)
La Loi [Le Legge; Where the Hot Wind Blows] (1959)
Pote tin kyriaki [Never on Sunday] (1960)
Il giudizio universale [The Last Judgment] (1961)
Vive Henri IV — Vive l'amour (1961)
Canzoni nel mondo [38-24-36] (1962)
Phaedra (1962)
The Victors (1963)

Topkapi (1964)
Les Pianos mecaniques [The Uninhibited] (1965)
A Man Could Get Killed (1966)
10:30 PM Summer (1966)
Gaily, Gaily (1969)
La Promesse de l'aube [Promise at Dawn] (1970)
Once Is Not Enough (1975)
Nasty Habits (1976)
A Dream of Passion (1978)
Keine Zufallige Geschichte [Not by Coincidence] (1984)

Sources

Alleman, Richard. "Melina Mercouri: The Actress Finds a New Role — in Government," *Vogue*, 168:252+, November 1978.
Borsten, Joan. "One-Woman Greek Chorus," *Los Angeles Times*, Calendar section, August 20, 1978, p. 32.
Carter, Betsy. "Never Offstage," *Newsweek*, 87:8, February 23, 1976.
Cohen, Barry. "Cultural Passion," *New Statesman*, 105:16, June 3, 1983.
Crawley, Tony. "Greece Is the Word," *Films Illustrated*, 10:307–312, May 1981.
Current Biography 1964. New York: H.W. Wilson, 1965, p. 289–291.
Fallaci, Oriana. "Melina Mercouri," *Look*, 31:73–76, September 5, 1967.
Ginna, Robert Emmett. "Mercouri," *Saturday Evening Post*, 236:24–25, May 25, 1963.
Grenier, Cynthia. "The Mercouri Rises," *New York Times Magazine*, September 25, 1960, p. 90–92.
The International Dictionary of Films and Filmmakers: Volume III: Actors and Actresses. Chicago: St. James Press, 1986, p. 431–432.
Kernan, Michael. "Mercouri," *Washington Post*, August 22, 1978, p. E1+.
Kerr, Walter and Reed, Rex. "*Ilya* Isn't Darling . . . But Melina Is," *New York Times*, section 2, April 30, 1967, p. 1+.

Klemesrud, Judy. "She Can't Get Greece Out of Her Mind," *New York Times,* February 28, 1971, p. 62.
Knowles, John. "Melina the Greek," *Holiday,* 35:101+, January 1964.
Mansfield, Paul. "Greek Revival," *Sight & Sound,* 51:149–150, #3, 1982.
"Melina Mercouri Loses Citizenship," *New York Times,* July 13, 1967, p. 1+.
"Melina Mercouri Rehearses *Never on Sunday* for Broadway," *Look,* 31:66–71, January 24, 1967.
Nichols, Mark. "Melina Mercouri," *Coronet,* 49:10+, April 1961.
"On Location: Greek Goddess," *Newsweek,* 58:102, September 11, 1961.
Oringer, Judy. "Melina Mercouri....," *Ramparts,* 10:48–51, January 1972.
Quinlan, David. *The Illustrated Directory of Film Stars.* London: B.T. Batsford, 1981, p. 326.
Schoebrun, David. "Melina Mercouri on Love," *Esquire,* 57:62+, April 1962.
Shearer, Lloyd. "Woman at the Top," *Washington Post,* June 17, 1979, p. 6.
Shipman, David. *The Great Movie Stars: The International Years.* London: Angus & Robertson, 1972, p. 338–339.
Theodoridis, Michael. "Interview with Melina Mercouri," *Macleans,* 91:4+, February 20, 1978.
Wlaschin, Ken. *The Illustrated Encyclopedia of the World's Great Movie Stars and Their Films.* London: Salamander, 1979, p. 204.

Chapter 3
French Actresses

The French were a bit slower than the Italians in establishing actresses of international fame after the end of the Second World War. But since then they have rapidly produced popular actresses. In fact, over one-third of the women profiled in this book have come from the French cinema. France has also provided a wider diversity of quality roles for females and a smaller proportion of French actresses have been viewed primarily as sex objects.

Simone Signoret started her film career in the early 1940s and by the end of that decade was drawing considerable notice. Initially she was often cast as a femme fatale or a prostitute but then graduated to more mature parts after scoring heavily in *Room at the Top* as the older woman. She was married to Yves Montand and both were politically active. The couple was denied entry into the United States for many years. Simone avoided Hollywood although she received many offers. Her willingness to take less than glamorous parts helped keep her active in pictures right up to her death.

Another early arrival was Jeanne Moreau who had a strong theatrical background. She was very busy in B films during the 1950s but did not attract a great deal of notice at first. *The Lovers* brought her wide fame after a controversial scene in which she faked an orgasm on the screen. So realistic was it that her lover of the time, Louis Malle, left her shortly thereafter. Jeanne went on to work with a variety of directors and became perhaps France's most accomplished actress. An intellectual and outspoken woman, age has been no barrier to finding work. Moreau is the type of actress who could always rise above the material.

The career of Anouk Aimee has been more erratic than most. A 1948 French film brought her a chance in Britain where a couple of poor films stalled her career. Then it was back to the continent where she worked in some good, and some terrible, films before gaining wide attention again in Fellini's *La dolce vita*. A few years later she appeared in her most memorable film, *A Man and a Woman*. This film led her to Hollywood where she had several abysmal roles. Anouk then abruptly retired from 1969 to 1976 right at the peak of her stardom, after marrying Albert Finney. Divorce brought her back to filmmaking and since then she has been trying to rebuild her career.

American actor Gene Kelly happened to see a teenage ballet dancer in Paris one night and not too many years later Leslie Caron made her film debut in an American film. She became a big hit, mainly in musical extravaganzas, and spent more years in Hollywood, with greater success, than most other foreign actresses. As time went by she disliked her American films more and more and finally left for Europe with a reputation for being difficult. Back in Europe she had to struggle to revive her career and while she has appeared in many poor movies, the few decent parts she has gotten have been in European films.

France produced only one other star in the 1950s — Brigitte Bardot. Bardot was one of the few French actresses regarded solely as sexpots. With the exception of Marilyn Monroe no other actress has ever rivaled Bardot, before or after, in terms of sex appeal. Brigitte made a career out of running around in a towel, or nothing at all, while displaying little acting ability. Few cared about the acting ability. Bardot has not made a film for over 15 years, living in a semireclusive state and devoting herself to other causes, yet she still remains a big name.

One of the stars to emerge in the 1960s was Capucine. With elegant good looks, the actress had first become an international model and while modeling in the United States landed her first major film roles. Acting and English lessons added to her casting appeal. She appeared in Hollywood films opposite many big stars but she had little to do in any of them except to provide a diversion and a love interest. Her best work came in comedies such as *The Pink Panther* and *What's New Pussycat?* Within five years Hollywood was finished with her and Capucine returned to Europe where she appeared mainly in support roles as her career slowed down.

One half of a pair of famous French sisters was Françoise Dorleac who had already appeared in eight films before she was 20 years old. With a versatile talent many thought her more gifted than her sister, Catherine Deneuve. Tragically Dorleac's career was cut short when she died in a car accident at the age of 25. She had by then appeared in 18 films.

Marie-France Pisier spent most of the 1960s working in small-budget films with an intellectual nature. Due to such non-commercial fare Pisier was not well known outside the country. A slowly growing reputation led her to bigger parts and her breakthrough films, *Celine and Julie Go Boating* and *Cousin, cousine.* Tempted by Hollywood, Marie-France made one film there. Although it was her 20th movie, it was the first one that required her to do a nude scene. The film was a poor vehicle and Pisier never went back to Hollywood. Through the 1980s she has been one of France's busiest actresses.

With a cool and icy beauty Catherine Deneuve combined a certain ladylike quality with sexuality. Early in her career she did nude scenes in many of her films but she never seemed to evoke the earthiness of Bardot. Her personal life has been turbulent, keeping her in the public eye. As an actress she has given some excellent performances and some terrible ones. Deneuve remained steadily busy until 1985 but has been in only one film since.

In the early 1970s a few actresses emerged who were mostly used as sex symbols. One was Maria Schneider who achieved international fame from the controversial *Last Tango in Paris*. To many it was lewd pornography, to others it was art. In any case it made Schneider a star. She was very busy for a few years but her personal life was erratic. On the set she was undisciplined. She has made only two films in the 1980s.

Dominique Sanda was a top fashion model in her teens and had posed nude for *Playboy* before her film career started. She enjoyed a prosperous decade in the 1970s and was able to break away from the sex goddess image with some fine work, usually in Italian films. Sanda came to appreciate the Italian cinema more than the French. Sanda's screen appearances have declined significantly in the '80s.

During the middle 1970s Isabelle Huppert came to prominence, working steadily in a variety of roles. *The Lacemaker* was the breakthrough film for her. Specializing in playing modern and complex female characters, Huppert has worked for many top directors including Jean-Luc Godard. She has fulfilled her fantasy of working in Hollywood on a couple of occasions—with disastrous results each time. Today she is one of the best known of the most recent wave of French actresses.

A contemporary of Huppert's is Isabelle Adjani who gave up a promising stage career in France to devote herself to films. Her work in *The Story of Adele H.* and *The Tenant* firmly established her as a French star. Adjani also gave Hollywood one shot and had a bad experience. Ten years later she tried again with even worse results. In between she did excellent work in a number of European outings, showing her versatility in parts that ranged from drama to comedy.

Marie-Christine Barrault had stage experience before turning to film but she was rare among these actresses in that she also had done a fair amount of television work first. She turned in solid performances before becoming a star in *Cousin, cousine*. Woody Allen took her to the United States for *Stardust Memories* and Barrault hoped that she would fare better than those who had tried America before her. Unexpectedly the film was trounced by critics and after one mainstream Hollywood tearjerker flop, Barrault's American odyssey ended.

Television and stage work were also responsible for Fanny Ardant's step into films. She earned worldwide attention and praise for her work in Truffaut's *The Woman Next Door* and since then has appeared in a series of films. She remains one of France's premier young actresses.

From Ardant's 11 films to Moreau's 84 these French actresses have combined to appear in 545 films.

Simone Signoret

During her youth Simone Signoret was considered sensual and attractive and was often cast as a prostitute or femme fatale. Later she became overweight, her face took on lines and the actress made no effort to hide the fact. Some male critics were upset and one wrote, "Her brooding face has become disagreeable . . . lost beauty is a more cinematic tragedy than some of the political causes she has followed." The loss of glamor was bad enough but the calculated rejection of it was even worse. Her acting ability shone through this so-called lack of glamor and Signoret delivered some of her best work in the last half of her career.

The actress was born Simone Henriette Charlotte Kaminker on March 25, 1921, in Wiesbaden, Germany, to French parents. She had two younger brothers and was the only daughter of André and Georgette (Signoret) Kaminker. At the time of his daughter's birth, André and his wife were in Germany as part of the French occupation of that country after the First World War.

Two years later the family returned to France and settled in a suburb of Paris. André was fluent in five languages and worked as a translator. Simone remembered wanting her family to be average, to be like other families but that they "tried to be middle-class and failed." Mrs. Kaminker used to dress as a maid when she picked up her daughter from school since most of the other children were picked up by servants. In reality the Kaminkers had no maid.

Mrs. Kaminker often took her daughter to the Comedie Française to see the classic plays and from then on Simone's only goal was to be an actress. Simone, like her mother, had a tendency to become involved in various causes, something which later led Simone to have trouble entering the United States. Mrs. Kaminker once returned a toothbrush she had bought after finding out it had been made in "Fascist Japan." Georgette also hid Jewish refugees from Germany in her apartment.

Simone just completed her education days after the German occupation of France in the Second World War. Her father left France to join de Gaulle in London and subsequently did a lot of broadcasting, writing and interpreting for the Free French. Money was scarce and Simone took part-time work tutoring in Latin and English. She then learned to type and went to work as a typist for a newspaper, the *Nouveau Temps*.

Through working on the paper she met a number of artistic people. Some of these new friends worked as extras in films. "I discovered people who were success haters," she said, "and with them I found a little bit of myself." This shy 20-year-old got work in films and found "something broke inside my shyness. My new friends taught me to regard acting as an honest job. They told me it was all right to want to act, all right to leave the typing job. Before that, I had never said anything to anybody about acting. It was stirring in me, but it was a secret."

Her screen debut came in *Le Prince Charmant* where she was paid $4 a day for one week's work. Simone did quit her job on the newspaper, which by then had become pro–German, remarking, "It was disgusting. I might have become a collaborationist myself, because at that time I had no conscience about anything." It was during this period, after her Jewish father left for England, that Simone took her mother's maiden name for safety and professional reasons.

The young woman continued as a film extra appearing in six features over two years time although never having very much dialogue. She even appeared briefly in the chorus of a stage play but was fired after a few months because she giggled too much while on the stage. On the side she took acting lessons. Those early jobs were beneficial for Signoret who felt she gained much needed experience and discipline from them. "For a young actor to be an extra is very frustrating but very good for him," she noted. "You learn to be on time for appointments. You are treated anonymously, and it is good for your health to be lost in the crowd. Also, you see a lot of actors acting."

The actress's first significant role came in the 1945 release *Les Demons de l'Aube* with Simone drawing good reviews for her work as a prostitute. That film was directed by Yves Allegret with whom the actress was then living. Before that the actress had had two brief liaisons. The first was with an actor named Daniel Gelin but Signoret declared, "Since Daniel and I were the same age, I was too old for him." A second brief affair was with 40-year-old director, Marcel Duhamel. The actress decided he was too old for her. Simone started living with Allegret around 1942. The couple married in 1947. By then she had had a son who died in infancy and a daughter born in 1946. The union ended in divorce in 1950.

Macadam featured the actress as a prostitute again and her good work in that film brought her to the attention of an international audience for the first time. The *New York Times* called her "saucy and alluring." Britain had noticed her as well and Simone made her first English language film *Against the Wind,* a dismal thriller. Simone worked steadily in France giving a series of good performances; as a prostitute in *Dedée d'anvers,* an actress in *L'Impasse de deux anges,* a slut in *Manèges* and a prostitute in *La Ronde.* The latter received a good deal of publicity in the United States after it was banned in New York state in 1951 as immoral.

In the summer of 1949 Signoret was on vacation on the French Riviera while singer Yves Montand was on tour there. "As soon as I met him, I fell in love with him," said Simone. "I left my husband and my home, which was bad. I left my child, which was worse. People didn't like it, but I had to do it." As soon as she got her divorce the couple married, in 1950, and despite some stormy times stayed married for 35 years until her death.

Simone Signoret with unidentified actor in *Casque d'or.*

After the marriage, Simone declared, "Yves wouldn't be happy if I worked all the time. So I decided that I would do only what I liked very much, and I have since made very few films." This yielding to her husband was of relatively short duration. After 1950 she appeared in only seven more films that decade. In the 1960s and 1970s, however, she was featured in 16 and 14 films respectively. She was as busy as any actress of that time even though Simone always insisted she worked less so as not to be away from Montand too often.

Starring as a turn-of-the-century underworld courtesan in *Casque d'or,* the actress got rave reviews and was voted Best Actress in a foreign film by the British Academy. More fine work followed in *Les Diaboliques* and *Les Sorcières de Salem,* the French film version of Arthur Miller's play *The Crucible.* Montand and Signoret starred in both the stage and film versions. Simone was again named Best Foreign Actress by the British Academy.

The film that moved the actress to the rank of international superstar was the 1958 British release *Room at the Top* with the actress cast as an unhappily married older woman taking one last shot at love in an affair with an egotistical and ambitious young Englishman, played by Laurence Harvey. The part was originally that of a Yorkshire housewife but was given to Simone when the producers could find no British actress they felt had sufficient sensuality for the role.

Her brilliant portrayal in that film brought the awards flowing in; Best

Foreign Actress from the British Academy; Best Actress at the Cannes Film Festival; and an Oscar as Best Actress from the American Academy. The Oscar was a landmark in that it was the first major acting Oscar to go to an artist who had never made a Hollywood film and only the second to go to a performer for a non–American motion picture.

Already in Hollywood shortly before the awards—accompanying Montand who was filming there—the actress felt the publicity ads touting her for the Oscar were silly. "It is not my money, I assure you. But it is so foolish I think." She did say, "I am in show business and I am an exhibitionist. And I know it is a great honor to win an Oscar."

The couple was denied admission to the United States in both 1949 and in 1957 under a law barring subversives and communists. They were finally allowed to enter in 1959 under the special provisions of a waiver for six months, not a regular visa. The couple was active in liberal causes and often signed petitions and manifestos such as the Stockholm Peace Appeal which called for the prohibition of nuclear weapons. The State Department never released details of the case but claimed it was about something "much more serious" than the Stockholm Appeal. Montand and Signoret had also visited Russia in 1956 and had been guests at a dinner with Khrushchev and other Soviet officials. Simone said, "We've been—ninety-nine percent of my country—involved in taking stands which the American government didn't like at all. It was enough to sign peace appeals to be barred. People of my generation have always been more or less involved with the Communists. I've never been a member—neither has my husband." Such run-ins with United States Immigration would gall the actress for years into the future.

Around that time Montand had a brief affair with actress Marilyn Monroe while they were shooting a film. "Don't ask me about Marilyn Monroe," said Signoret. "I've had a lifetime of Marilyn Monroe. That happened while we were apart. Now I never take a job during a period when Yves is working." She argued that it did not really affect her career, saying, "not that I'm sacrificing anything. It's just that between lousy scripts and being with him, I'd rather be with him. Of course I'm jealous too. There's good reason to be. A singer attracts more women than anybody else. His voice acts on their nervous systems."

The actress was flooded with offers from Hollywood. Some of them were silly and most wanted her to repeat her *Room at the Top* role. She turned them all down, saying, "I don't go to bed with boys young enough to be my sons and I won't play them. So I didn't work much after that. But I enjoyed doing it that one time. It was a damn good story . . . I got offered mountains of scripts in Hollywood, but they were all things Bette Davis didn't want to do 20 years ago."

The only mistake she made on that film was in taking a flat fee instead of a percentage of the film. Simone felt *Room at the Top* would not make any

Simone Signoret appears in the title role of *Madame Rosa*.

money and later, when she was proved wrong, laughed, "If I had accepted a percentage of the film, I'd have enough money to make my grandchildren rich."

That role marked a change in Signoret's film image as she changed from a femme fatale to more mature parts. She was 37 then and commented, "That is a difficult age for an actress to make such a choice. It means that when she is still pretty good-looking, she must decide that interesting parts are going to be on the other side of the line and that it is useless to hang onto those branches of youth." Over the next few years she appeared in several European films including being cast as the shrewish wife of Laurence Olivier in *Terms of Trial*. These films were little seen in North America and Simone drew mixed reviews.

She finally went to Hollywood for Stanley Kramer's *Ship of Fools*. Simone played a drug-addicted countess having an affair with the ship's doctor, played by Oskar Werner. The actress gave a riveting performance and earned a Best Actress Oscar nomination from the American Academy. Signoret's only comment about the picture was about Kramer whom she said was "no Jean-Luc Godard, but he knows it."

Playing a 55-year-old Jewish woman who showed the ravages of years in concentration camps, Simone appeared fat, tired-looking and wearing almost no makeup in *The Deadly Affair*. When she saw the rushes of the first day's shooting she gasped and remained upset and morose for the eight-week shoot. "It was difficult, something that women of my age pretend to take well but don't," she said. "I had to look older. You don't take this lightly. You don't say, 'how charming, how wonderful.' It isn't." Nevertheless she got used to it in real life. As she gained weight and as her face became more lined and took on more character she made no attempt to alter or hide the situation.

At the end of the 1960s Simone became embroiled with United States Immigration again when she tried to enter to do some television work. Simone refused to answer what she called "insulting" questions such as: "Are you a homosexual?" "Do you take drugs?" and "Are you planning to kill the President?" The result was that Signoret was given only a visitor's visa and not a work permit so she could not do the television work. "All it means to me is that now I won't have to go on TV and talk to Mr. Merv What's-His-Name," she said, "Now that I know I don't do TV I don't have to look good so I think I'll booze it up."

Through the 1970s Simone remained busy making films in Europe usually getting good critical notices in such outings as *L'aveu* where she played the agonized wife of Yves Montand and *Comptes à rebours* in which she played a gangster's girlfriend. Signoret had not been in a big commercial success since *Room at the Top* and offers from Hollywood finally disappeared.

Signoret came back to international prominence on the strength of the 1977 release *Madame Rosa*. She played a hideous and bloated old prostitute who survived the concentration camps and, too old to work the streets, set up a foster home for children of younger prostitutes in a Paris slum. It was a part with no glamor and Montand urged her to refuse it. But Simone said, "A role like that comes every 20 years. It is a cake. She is everything — liar, sincere, gourmand, poor, stupid, intelligent, warm, nasty. If I had said 'no,' and another woman had played it, I would have been sick."

The actress was aged ten years, her wrinkles were deepened, cheeks bloated with cotton and legs padded and wrapped in bandages. "To accept being 10 years older than you are, wear the worst costumes, the least flattering make-up, be subjected to camera angles that make you look bigger if you're big, swollen up if you're puffy, it was a big dive for me," said Signoret.

Her performance in that film was brilliant and she won unanimous critical raves and a French Cesar Award for her acting — equivalent to the Oscar. Of the award she said, "I'm glad to have it — I don't have false modesty — but a young girl should have been crowned. At the beginning of a career, an honor like that is useful." It was a meaty part and the actress reasoned that you just could not lose by playing such a character. A lot of media attention came her way and she noted, "When I was young and beautiful I never appeared on the cover of a magazine. And now at 57 I am on the cover."

Asked about how she acted and prepared for her roles, Simone said, "Basically you know nothing about this craft. And there is nothing to learn. As one ages, one needs less and less of its science. There are two schools of thought: There are those actors who explain to you that they know exactly how they're going to do the part . . . And then there is the other method, which is to have no method at all. This is mine." What she did do was to let the character take possession of her to become, as she put it, a "tenant of her skin." This possession sometimes lasted weeks after the film finished.

After *Madame Rosa* Simone appeared in just four more films before her death. In *Judith Therpauve* she was cast as a newspaper editor who tried to stop a press baron from taking over her paper. *I Sent a Letter to My Love* featured the actress as an old spinster who had spent her whole life looking after her brother who was confined to a wheelchair.

She refused to go to the United States to promote *I Sent a Letter to My Love* as she fumed again about the questions she would have to answer if she went. "The most stupid of which is if you intend to kill the President of the United States—which is particularly dumb, because after all this time they could see they do that very well themselves; it's senseless to look elsewhere. And then there are political questions." All along Simone insisted that she and Montand had never been members of the communist party saying, "We were engaged, but we did not marry."

Until the end she remained politically aware and active although not as vigorously as in her youth. In 1978 she sent a letter to the wives of 22 soccer players going to a World Cup match in Buenos Aires to memorize the names of 22 political prisoners believed held in Argentina and to ask questions. The actress was known to get out of a taxi in the middle of a trip if she thought the driver's conversation was stupid.

Montand was always under the watchful eye of his wife, and Simone remarked, "I detest women who come too close to him. Our friends are very carefully selected."

A new career as a writer opened up and Simone published two books of memoirs and one novel between 1976 and 1982. All were well received critically, became best sellers and were translated into English. The actress claimed she got more money from her first book of memoirs *Nostalgia Isn't What It Used to Be* than for any of her film roles.

Simone Signoret died on September 30, 1985, at the age of 64, from cancer. All of the French television stations devoted most of that night's broadcasting to specials about her. French President Mitterand led the nation in paying homage to her and said in a telegram to Montand, "During more than 40 years she has spoken to the hearts of the French people."

During the ill health of her final few years she kept on working "which is the big thing," she said. "All I ever really had in mind . . . if you'll excuse me for giving myself a little bouquet, I think I used age pretty well. I didn't cling to an appearance that would have been artificial. I got old the way women who aren't actresses grow old, the way the woman in the butcher shop does or a university professor or a prostitute. I got old. But I continued to work, as opposed to certain women who tried to hold onto their grand image, their dream image, and who didn't want to get out of that and couldn't work anymore."

Simone Signoret Filmography

Le Prince Charmant (1942)
Bolero (1942)
Les Visiteurs du Soir [The Devil's Envoy] (1942)
La Boîte aux rêves (1943)
Adieu Léonard (1943)
L'Ange de la nuit (1943)
Beatrice devant le désir (1943)
Les Demons de L'Aube (1945)
Le Couple ideal (1945)
Macadam [Back Streets of Paris] (1946)
Fantômas (1947)
Dedée d'anvers (1948)
Against the Wind (1948)
L'Impasse de deux anges (1948)
Manèges [The Cheat] (1949)
Four Days' Leave [Swiss Four] (1949)
Le Traque [Gunman in the Streets] (1950)
Ombre et lumière (1950)
La Ronde [Circle of Love] (1950)
Casque d'or [The Golden Helmet] (1952)
Thérèse Raquin [The Adultress] (1953)
Les Diaboliques [Diabolique; The Fiends] (1955)
La Mort en ce jardin [Death in the Garden; Evil Eden, Gina] (1956)
Die Wind rosé (1956)
Les Sorcières de Salem [Witches of Salem] (1957)
Room at the Top (1958)
Les Mauvais Coups [Naked Autumn] (1960)
Adua e le compagne [Love a la Carte] (1960)
Les Amours célébrés (1961)

Terms of Trial (1962)
Le Jour et l'heure (1963)
Dragées au poivre [Sweet and Sour] (1963)
Il giorno piu corto commedia umaristico [The Shortest Day] (1963)
Le joli Mai [narrator only] (1963)
Ship of Fools (1965)
Compartiment tueurs [The Sleeping Car Murders] (1965)
Paris, brûle-t-il? [Is Paris Burning?] (1966)
The Deadly Affair (1967)
Games (1967)
The Sea Gull (1968)
L'Armée des ombres [The Shadow Army] (1969)
Mister Freedom (1969)
L'aveu [The Confession] (1970)
Comptes à rebours [Countdown] (1970)
Le Rose et le Noir (1970)
L'Américain (1970)
Le Chat (1971)
La Veuve Couderc [The Widow Couderc] (1971)
Rude Journée pour la reine (1973)
Les Granges brulées (1973)
La Châir de l'orchidée (1974)
The Case Against Ferro (1976)
Police Python 357 (1976)
La Vie devant soi [Madame Rosa] (1977)
Judith Therpauve (1978)
Cher inconnu [I Sent a Letter to My Love] (1981)
L'Adolescente [The Adolescent] (1982)
L'Étoile du nord (1983)

Sources

Andriotakis, Pamela. "Simone Signoret," *People,* 9:55+, June 12, 1978.
Borger, Lenny. "Simone Signoret, French Screen and Stage Luminary, Dead at 64," *Variety,*
    320:6, 26, October 2, 1985.
Champlin, Charles. "Simone Signoret Sets the Record Straight," *Los Angeles Times,*
    June 4, 1978, Calendar sec., p. 49.
Current Biography 1960. New York: H.W. Wilson, 1961, p. 381–382.
The International Dictionary of Films and Filmmaking: Volume III: Actors and Actresses.
    Chicago: St. James Press, 1986, p. 575–576.
Lewis, Flora. "Simone Signoret — From Sultry Sirens to a Faded Floozy," *New York Times,*
    March 19, 1978, p. C19.
"Miss Signoret in U.S. on Waiver," *New York Times,* April 6, 1960, p. 46.
Pace, Eric. "Simone Signoret Dies in France at 64," *New York Times,* October 1, 1985, p. B6.
Quinlan, David. *The Illustrated Directory of Film Stars.* London: B.T. Batsford, 1981,
    p. 426.
Reed, Rex. "Signoret: 'I've Lived, My Friend,'" *New York Times,* January 12, 1969, sec. 2,
    p. 1, 13.
Sancton, Thomas A. "Adieu, Ma Belle," *Time,* 126:107, October 14, 1985.
Schumach, Murray. "Simone Signoret Discusses Films," *New York Times,* March 25, 1960,
    p. 21.
Shipman, David. *The Great Movie Stars: The International Years.* London: Angus &
    Robertson, 1972, p. 479–483.
"Simone Signoret," *New Yorker,* 37:89+, November 4, 1961.
"Subtle Poison," *Time,* 75:44, April 4, 1960.
Thomson, David. *A Biographical Dictionary of Film.* New York: William Morrow, 1975,
    p. 522.
Vinocur, John. "Simone Signoret," *New York Times,* May 3, 1981, sec. 2, p. 1, 15.
Weinraub, Bernard. "You Can See that I'm Not 20 Years Old," *Saturday Evening Post,* 240:
    39–41, February 25, 1967.

Jeanne Moreau

Jeanne Moreau first gained international fame by simulating an orgasm in a 1958 film aptly named *The Lovers.* So convincing was her acting that the film's director, Louis Malle, who was also Moreau's real-life lover, ended their relationship. Moreau has only enigmatically commented, "I knew that if I acted in the love scenes the way Louis wanted, he might like me as an actress but hate me as a woman. It was a gamble and I lost."

Jeanne Moreau was born in Paris on January 23, 1928, to Anatole Moreau the owner of a restaurant in Montmartre, La Cloche d'Or, which catered to artists, writers and entertainers. He met his wife Kathleen Buckley, an English dancer, when she dined at his establishment and complained about the food. It was an inauspicious start to a marriage which was doomed to fail.

In 1939 after losing his restaurant, Anatole was drafted into the army. Kathleen's British origins branded her an enemy alien during the Nazi

Jeanne Moreau in *Back to the Wall.*

occupation, and she, Jeanne and her younger daughter Michele lived on a small stipend in a shabby hotel in Paris. On the ground floor was a brothel and Jeanne remembered the lineups of German soldiers waiting to enter.

Jeanne was a good student and loved reading, tackling Zola at the age of 13. She lost all interest in her studies, however, after she saw her first play, a production of Anouilh's *Antigone.* The theater overwhelmed and fascinated her. Two days later she saw *Phèdre* at the Comedie Française. Although her father equated acting with prostitution, Jeanne was determined to go on stage. Her father slapped her when she told him her decision. Even though their relationship was close in later years, Jeanne's father was never reconciled to her career as an actress, and considered her life a failure. "For him," she commented, "it didn't fulfill the classic destiny of a woman." The awards she received for her work did not impress him. Her father thought it was a crazy world that would bestow honors on an actress.

Fortunately a helpful neighbor recommended an acting coach who prepared Jeanne for an audition at the Conservatoire National d'Art Dramatique. She was accepted at once, and studied there for a year before debuting at the age of 19 in Turgenev's *A Month in the Country* at the Comedie Française.

The next year she became the youngest member of the Comedie and remained with this group for four years until 1952. Cast in 22 roles during this period, she was well grounded in classical technique.

Moreau's parents had divorced while she was at the Conservatoire and Jeanne's mother and sister returned to England. In 1949 Jeanne married a young actor named Jean-Louis Richard, from the Theatre National Populaire. Their son Jerome was born two days after the wedding. The marriage lasted only a year but the couple did not divorce until 1965 and have retained both a friendship and a professional collaboration.

Moreau considered her tenure at the Comedie as "a prison term" from which she desired liberation. She was upset that the stars rarely gave newcomers a chance. "The established actors would take roles they didn't want," she said, "just to keep others from having them."

Jeanne spent the next year with the Theatre National Populaire and then moved on to a boulevard production of *The Dazzling Hour*. When the star fell ill, Moreau took over the lead role and her excellent acting caught the attention of the critics. She stayed with this play for two years and then worked in about a dozen other shows ranging from Cocteau's *La Machine Infernale* to Shaw's *Pygmalion*.

Working in the theatre during the evenings, Moreau spent her days trying to establish herself in films. Her first picture in 1948 was *Last Love* and she earned only $300 for her role which was third-billed. Jeanne's attempts to become a movie star were frustrated. Although she made 19 films between 1949 and 1957 none brought her much critical or box office acclaim. Cast in B movies that were limited to murder mysteries and melodramas, Moreau's roles ran the gamut from waitress, whore, daughter of a whore, to nurse and murderess.

Many producers did not think Jeanne was pretty enough for movies. Her features were unusual, she had dark circles under her eyes and her mouth turned down at the corners. She was often heavily made-up in her early films in an attempt to make her conform to the prevailing standards of attractiveness. Moreau called this period of her career a "cinematic adolescence" and resented being compared to Bette Davis, although she later came to admire this actress.

Yet Moreau was very successful on the stage. In 1956 she was a sensation in Tennessee Williams' *Cat on a Hot Tin Roof*. Director Louis Malle saw one of her performances and, also aware of her film work, realized that no one had used her potential on the screen. Malle, himself, was just starting out as a director, and he hired her for his first feature *Frantic* in 1958. Jeanne played the role of a woman who plotted with her lover to murder her husband. Jeanne's agent thought she was foolish to accept a part in a film directed by "one of these guys nobody's even heard of who doesn't even film for money." Moreau fired her agent.

Malle decided that Moreau had a natural sensuality, magnetism, and expressive face that should not be masked by cosmetics. By using harsh, rather than flattering lighting, and by letting the camera linger on her face, Malle revealed the dramatic depth of Jeanne's theatrical range of emotions. He ushered in a new way of photographing women and Moreau became a symbol of sophisticated seductiveness. The actress and director became involved in a love affair.

Moreau remembered feeling liberated about her appearance when Malle insisted, "Don't worry about how you look, just be yourself." "And suddenly I felt free," said Moreau, "as though I had come out of a prison." Although Moreau never grew to like her face she did become accustomed to it. "I have nothing in me to make me look exceptional," she said. "Yet I wanted to become exceptional. I wanted to become part of the world of magic. I wanted the public to find my ordinary self extraordinary."

She continued to appear in other films in 1958 and 1959 but it was in *The Lovers* (1958) that both she and Malle attained international recognition. Jeanne played a bored housewife who takes a lover and then deserts her husband and child. Moreau claimed the idea for the project was her own. The film was considered risqué at that time, especially the scene where Moreau was shown in close-up having an orgasm. At first the Ministry of Cultural Affairs in Paris refused to release it. When it was finally shown, it was a great success and won a prize at the Venice Film Festival. Moreau was labeled the "Brave New Woman," the "Woman Who Had Lived," and the "Jeanne d'Arc of the Boudoir."

Ironically, Malle was threatened by Moreau's portrayal of sexuality in his film, and their affair ended. Moreau felt the problem was that Malle "could no longer stand to see me as others then saw me — and as only he had seen me until then." They remained on friendly terms and continued to work together. She appeared in two more of Malle's projects, *The Fire Within* and *Viva Maria*.

Moreau's role in *The Lovers* designated her as an actress of passion and worldly experience, and many of her future roles cast her in the same type of character. One French critic observed, "Jeanne Moreau suggests a praying mantis who devours her mate after indescribable pleasure." In some ways her private and professional life became intertwined and Moreau often had affairs with costars or directors. She prepared herself for films "like a woman getting ready for marriage" and remarked, "My life is strewn with emotional obstacles that trip me over and end up in becoming films. When they're finished, I feel like a convalescent, physically and spiritually impaired."

She worked with several French New Wave filmmakers like François Truffaut and Jean-Luc Godard, and almost every other director of note including Roger Vadim, Joseph Losey, Orson Welles, Peter Brook, Michelangelo Antonioni, Luis Buñuel, John Frankenheimer, Marcel Ophuls, Tony Richardson, Philippe De Broca, Jean Renoir, Elia Kazan, Paul Mazursky, and Rainer Werner Fassbinder.

It was Truffaut, however, who rescued Moreau from her depression after the split with Malle. She had moved from Paris to a house in Versailles and was brooding about being 30 and wondering whether it was worthwhile continuing in films. It was during this time that she met Truffaut and he introduced her to a group of intellectuals and filmmakers that revived her enthusiasm for acting. She also had an unbilled bit part in his 1959 film *The Four Hundred Blows.*

In the next decade she appeared in one memorable film after another beginning with Brook's *Moderator Cantabile* in 1960 in which she again played a bored housewife with a wandering eye for one of her husband's workmen played by Jean-Paul Belmondo.

During the shooting, her son Jerome was hurt in an auto accident in a car driven by Belmondo. The boy was in a coma for 14 days but made a full recovery and returned to boarding school in Grenoble. Jerome would grow up to become a book binder in Canada.

Moreau next worked with Antonioni in *La Notte* playing the wife of Marcello Mastroianni in a film about the disintegration of a marriage. Moreau found Antonioni to be distant and exacting, forcing the actors to film at night. "He's not a director you feel you can reach out and touch," she said. "It was a lonely movie and it left me a miserable memory." She never worked with him again.

One of her most famous roles followed in Truffaut's *Jules et Jim* where she was cast as Catherine, a woman loved by two men in a doomed three-way relationship. Moreau thought the film was important because it was one of the first to show that a woman might love more than one man at once, even though her character had to be punished for it by drowning herself. The film has since become a classic, but despite its success, Moreau only appeared in one other Truffaut film *The Bride Wore Black* (1968). She always remained close to Truffaut, however, and considered him a special friend.

Other challenging roles for Moreau included Jackie Demaistre in *Bay of Angels* in which she played a compulsive gambler, and Celestine in Buñuel's *Diary of a Chambermaid.* Not all of her films were well received and one critic complained, "Too bad that a first-rate actress so often has to squeeze her victories out of second-rate scripts." Losey's *Eva* was poorly edited and not widely distributed, and Jeanne's portrayal of Mata Hari did not match the Garbo version, an actress to whom she was often compared. English-language films such as *The Train* with Burt Lancaster, *The Victors* with Eli Wallach, and *The Yellow Rolls-Royce* with Rex Harrison did not serve her well.

Moreau preferred filming in France and explained, "I am used to making my movies in the austerity of French settings and studios. . . . In Hollywood they make you wait five hours to say three words. I prefer the informality of filmmaking in France. It's related, there's a feeling of being . . . among friends. . . . You can live without Hollywood. Look at Belmondo. He's never been there. He doesn't speak a word of English. But that has not stopped him from becoming an international success."

In 1965 Moreau costarred with Brigitte Bardot in *Viva Maria!* directed by Malle and shot on location in Mexico. It was her 44th film. The media went wild over the fact that two femme fatales were working in the same movie. "The whole world thinks this film is a kind of contest," said Jeanne, "a contest between Bardot and Moreau. All those people are wrong. Between Brigitte and me there is a sort of complicity. There's no rivalry between us. Between us there are only differences."

Bardot was described as having the "pouty, sulky magnetism of a beautiful animal" while Moreau had "the more studied sexuality of the mind." "Films have never shown the kind of relationship that can exist between two women," Moreau continued in connection with working with Bardot. "Men like to think that women must be constantly jealous of each other, never trusting, never in rapport. That is not true, of course."

Moreau was very open about her sensuality and once remarked, "There are men one goes through like a country," which prompted an observer to note "and she is a well-traveled woman." Moreau was not defensive about being called promiscuous nor was she concerned about nudity in film. "People want to see what's behind the clothes, but they forget that behind *that* there's still something else," she said referring to a person's inner spirit and mystery. Later she joked about her reputation for loose morals: "Now that I'm getting older, people have more respect. And maybe that's a conventional unconscious attitude towards women: 'She's older now, so she fucks less.' As you are no longer such a hot piece of cake, they can allow themselves to be more respectful."

Moreau's fantasy was to own a big house "where I could live with a man I loved, and where there'd be enough space for every man I'd ever loved in the past to have a room to himself, and we'd all live there together."

"Many people fall in love with her," said Marcello Mastroianni. "I did. And she loves you in return. But just till the end of the film." Moreau's friend, writer Marguerite Duras, described Jeanne as "the reconciliation of the romantic and the modern. In love she subordinated herself entirely to men," Duras said, "yet she holds her life and career in her own hands."

Moreau believed that many of the males in her country were afraid of what she represented. "The basis of a happy marriage for a Frenchman has always been a stupid wife. I . . . am not stupid," she emphasized. "I have the strength to abandon a situation. Men want to believe abandoned women have tears in their eyes. It frightens them to discover a woman can pack up and go as easily as a man can."

Yet for all her bold talk, Jeanne lived a quiet life staying at her estate near St. Tropez for long periods and visited her friends Truffaut, Duras and Florence Malraux, daughter of writer André Malraux. In 1965 Moreau had become involved with fashion designer Pierre Cardin, an affair that lasted for several years in the 1960s.

Despite all her lovers Jeanne was described by Mastroianni as having "an emptiness in her" which only her career could fill. "If I weren't an actress," she once remarked, "I would have been a hysteric." One writer noted that Jeanne's heart was "like an enormous room that is always cold. A man comes in, lights a fire, the flames swallow everything and then die down. When there are only ashes left, Jeanne shivers. She knows you cannot bring the cinders back to life; you have to light the fire. This makes her sad. So she is always looking for the one man who will not let the flames die down." She has yet to find him.

Moreau was an instinctive performer who had nothing but disdain for actors who spent hours discussing the motivation for a simple act like picking up an ashtray. "One should never search for meaning in a script," she said. "When the work is over, the meaning comes out by itself." Her technique was described as "mainly visual: what she says always tells less than what she does . . . a subtle vocabulary of gesture and expression."

Acting was such an integral part of her existence that she claimed, "Acting is not a profession at all: it's a way of living — one completes the other . . . The love, suffering and happiness I experience in life appear in my movies." Moreau also saw acting as making herself vulnerable — a state which frightened her. She described the actor's personality as "fuzzy" and felt when assuming a character "you lose youself in order to assume the inner rhythm, one might say the inner dance of another person." Sometimes such intensity had dangerous effects. During the shooting of *Moderato Cantabile* (1960) the producer recalled, "She started drinking wine in the morning, duplicating the troubling habit of the suicidal character she played."

Surprisingly Moreau selected her films on the basis of the director rather than character, explaining, "If I get concerned with what kind of part I would like to play, I would then start to wonder what kind of roles would be good for me, good for my career, pleasing to the public." With a good director she felt any character could be convincingly developed.

In 1962 Moreau had a bad scare when she was operated on for uterine cancer. This confrontation with the possibility of imminent death only made her work harder after she recovered. Her output remained prolific and she appeared in nine films between 1966 and 1969. They ranged from *Mademoiselle* based on a Jean Genet novel about a bitter pyromaniac to *Le Corps de Diane* about a lesbian who kills her husband. These films met with varying response, but Moreau always seemed to rise about her vehicles. She had the experience of working with interesting directors like Orson Welles, Tony Richardson, Philip De Broca, and Jean Renoir. Tony Richardson said, "Jeanne is more informed, committed and passionate than any actress I know." And he knew her well. Their love affair led to the breakup of his marriage to Vanessa Redgrave.

Moreau was still intrigued by the idea of being in love and claimed it influenced her pleasure in acting. "It keeps me in a sensitive state," she said, "and makes me conscious of my power. Most people don't have the energy for

Jeanne Moreau and Roger Coggio in *The Immortal Story*.

passion, and so they give up and go to the movies." She insisted that fame meant nothing. "You can't make love to it, although I like men to dream about me."

Moreau made 20 films during the 1970s. Most were not released in the United States. She did make several in Hollywood, however, including a western *Monte Walsh* with Lee Marvin, *Alex in Wonderland* directed by Mazurasky, and *The Last Tycoon* directed by Kazan and costarring Tony Curtis.

In fact Moreau was honored by Americans at the San Francisco film festival in 1974 which paid tribute to her art. Four of her movies — *The Lovers, Jules et Jim, Bay of Angels,* and *Diary of a Chambermaid* — were screened and clips were shown of her 25-year career. Moreau attended the festival and was available for a discussion period after the screenings. That year she also returned to the stage in Paris, performing in a Peter Handke play.

Although Moreau had been very independent both personally and professionally, she said, "To me, to be free means free to choose whose slave I want to be. I always want to enslave myself." By 1970 Moreau was still reluctant to endorse women's liberation mainly because of her aversion to politics of any kind, but she did support the theory of equal pay for equal jobs. "We have to stick together," she said referring to men and women. "It's impossible to consider men as enemies. Personal relationships are going to be hell if we do."

Yet Moreau soon gained a reputation for being, if not an outright feminist, then at least a sympathizer. This came about when she wrote the script for, acted in, and for the first time directed a film — *Lumière* in 1976. The story was about four actresses — Moreau played one of them. It dealt with their interactions with men and society but above all it explored the idea of intimacy in women's friendships. "It is about the life women lead when we are alone together," said Moreau. "I didn't do this as an activist or a feminist, though I am for equality. But I thought it was necessary to show that intimacy that is only possible among women alone." Moreau considered the language of the film to have a feminine quality. "There are not the competitive words that men have," she explained. "We rarely talk of sex the way men do, in terms of I've had this one, I've had that one."

In her work she tried to convey the emotional inner life of women. "We support each other," she said of females. "There is a very strong premonition of each other's pain, if it exists. We have this sense of loneliness. Men are lonely and they struggle to overcome it. We don't try to overcome it," she felt about women. "We know we are lonely in the major events of our bodies, of our lives."

Moreau described *Lumière* as a very personal film but said it was not strictly autobiographical. She chose the title meaning light as a symbol of the stage spotlights. She remembered being in the darkened theater audience watching the actors lit up on the stage. It made a profound impression on her. "I got so excited," she recalled. "I thought that I was not destined to be in the dark; my vocation was to be in the light, to live in that extraordinary dimension and escape that darkness, that most people have to live in."

Moreau chose Keith Carradine for one of the major male roles because he had an innocent American quality that reminded her of Gary Cooper. Directing a film made Moreau realize the anxieties involved in the job. She had several sleepless nights before shooting began and remembered that Truffaut would also pace his room during the night before filming began, while Losey was so nervous he had trouble breathing, and Buñuel ritualistically touched every object on the set. Once shooting began she had no trouble establishing a rapport with the actors and crew.

Moreau became disgusted with questions from the American press asking her why she turned to directing. "If I was a young male director you wouldn't ask me that," she said. "I've been asked why so many times I want to say just 'Because.' Why does everyone ask me this? Why shouldn't I be the one who decides the action?"

Moreau thought there was less prejudice against women directors in France than in the United States noting that one American producer complained, "We have enough problems already, we don't need that one."

Some observers accused *Lumière* of being critical of men. Moreau took exception to this and insisted, "A film that featured mostly men would never be said to be hard on women. For once women are in first place."

Moreau had no intention of giving up acting for directing. In fact she directed only two other features. *L'Adolescente* in 1979 was a study of a young girl's coming of age, and *Lillian Gish,* a biographical movie of that famous star. *Lumière* and these two films all met with critical success.

Moreau acted in 11 films in the 1980s. Most notable were *The Trout,* her third film with Losey, and *Querrelle,* Fassbinder's last film before he died. Moreau adored working with the German director finding him stimulating, scary, caring, and intense.

She also maintained her link with the theater by taking a few stage roles and in addition she had recorded several albums of songs which proved to be popular in France.

Moreau seemed undaunted by aging and was uninterested in having plastic surgery. She thought that perhaps Europeans were more tolerant of the older woman than Americans, and liked to tell the following anecdote. "There was a period in the 17th and 18th centuries where the women were very powerful in France, in the courts. Powerful not only through sex but through intelligence. Some of these women were talked and written about as though they were beautiful, and then you discover that Madame De la Clos was 72. Because the agility of the mind has always been considered in the amorous French imagination, as a pleasure."

In 1977 at age 49 Moreau married 37-year-old William Friedkin, director of such films as *The French Connection* and *The Exorcist.* It was his first marriage and her second. They had a brief civil ceremony in Paris. The marriage lasted two years. Moreau thought the marriage ended because their work kept them apart. "He was in Boston preparing a film, . . . and I was away in France preparing *L'Adolescente.* I felt he resented that, she said. "It was as if I had deserted him. But after all I am a filmmaker too."

Moreau had no plans to retire from acting. In 1986 at the age of 58 she completed her 84th film. As writer François Sagan said of her: "Startling, scandalous, seductive, are words for Moreau; never touching, tender, pitiable. Not at all. You never catch her preparing a bechamel sauce or mothering babies. You always see her with a cigarette holder . . . sunglasses . . . She is a true star . . . She has never become frozen, fixed, defined. She is intelligent, as great actresses are, despite all the nonsense that's been said on the subject. Though she is a femme fatale, with all the violence, cruelty, and power the term implies, she is also a child . . . Alfred de Musset, the 19th-century French poet said that a door must be open or closed; Jeanne Moreau would not agree. She would say that a door must swing. All her life she has been that door, swinging in the winds of love, the squalls of passion, the hot breath of ambition, or the drafts of loneliness, always moving."

Jeanne Moreau Filmography

Dernier Amour (1948)
Meurtes [Three Sinners] (1950)
Pigalle-Saint-Germain-des Prés. (1950)
L'Homme de ma Vie (1951)
Il est minuit (1952)
Docteur Schweitzer (1952)
Touchez pas au Grisbi [Grisbi; Honor Among Thieves] (1953)
Dortoir des grandes [Inside a Girls' Dormitory] (1953)
Julietta (1953)
Secrets d'alcove [The Bed] (1953)
Les Intrigantes (1954)
La Reine Margot (1954)
Les Hommes en blanc [The Doctors] (1955)
Gas-Oil (1955)
M'Sieur la caille [The Parasites] (1955)
Le Salaire du Péché [Wages of Sin] (1956)
Les Louves [The She-Wolves] (1956)
Jusqu'au dernier (1957)
L'Étrange Monsieur Stève (1957)
Trois Jours à vivre (1957)
Echec au porteur (1958)
Ascenseur pour l'échafaud [Frantic; Lift to the Scaffold] (1958)
Le Dos au mur [Back to the Wall, Evidence in Concrete] (1958)
Les Amants [The Lovers] (1958)
Les Quatre Cents Coups [The 400 Blows] (1959)
Les Liaisons dangereuses (1959)
Five Branded Women (1959)
Le Dialogue des Carmélites [The Carmelites] (1959)
Moderato cantabile (1960)
Une Femme est une femme [A Woman Is a Woman] (1961)
La Notte [The Night] (1961)
Jules et Jim (1961)
Eva (1962)
La Baie des anges [Bay of Angels] (1962)
Le Feu follet [A Time to Live and a Time to Die; The Fire Within] (1963)
The Trial (1963)
The Victors (1963)
Peau de banane [Banana Peel] (1963)

Le Journal d'une femme de chambre [Diary of a Chambermaid] (1964)
The Train (1964)
The Yellow Rolls-Royce (1964)
Mata Hari—agent H-21 [Mata Hari] (1964)
La Peau douce [Silken Skin. Voice only] (1964)
Viva Maria (1965)
Chimes at Midnight [Falstaff] (1966)
Mademoiselle (1966)
Sailor from Gilbraltar (1966)
Le Plus Vieux métier du monde [The Oldest Profession] (1967)
La Mariée était en noir [The Bride Wore Black] (1968)
Great Catherine (1968)
The Immortal Story (1968)
Le Petit Théâtre de Jean Renoir [The Little Theatre of Jean Renoir] (1969)
Le Corps de Diane (1969)
Monte Walsh (1970)
Alex in Wonderland (1970)
Comptes à rebours (1970)
Cannibales en Sicile (1971)
Dead Reckoning (1971)
L'Humeur vagabonde (1971)
Mille Baisers de Florence (1971)
Chère Louise (1972)
Nathalie Granger (1972)
Joanna Francesa (1973)
Je t'aime (1973)
Les Valseuses [Going Places; Making It] (1973)
La Race des 'seigneurs' (1974)
Hu Man (1974)
Le Jardin qui bascule (1974)
Souvenirs d'en France [French Provincial] (1975)
Mr. Klein (1976)
Lumière (also director) (1976)
The Last Tycoon (1976)
L'Adolescente (also director) (1978)
Your Ticket Is No Longer Valid (1980)
Les Uns et les autres (1980)
Plein sud [Heat of Desire] (1980)
La Débandade (1981)
Lucien chez les barbares (1981)
Mille Milliards de dollars (1981)

The Trout (1982)
Querrelle (1982)
The Wizard of Babylon (1983)

Lillian Gish (also codirector) (1984)
Sauve-toi Lola (1986)

Sources

"Actresses," *Time,* 85:78–83, March 5, 1965.
Archer, Eugene. "Actor's Actress," *New York Times,* section 2, March 5, 1961, p. X7.
Buckley, Michael. "Jeanne Moreau," *Films in Review,* 34:599–603, December 1983.
Collins, Larry and LaPierre, Dominque. "The Name Is Moreau," *New York Times Magazine,* March 21, 1965, p. 46+.
Current Biography 1965. New York: H.W. Wilson, 1966, p. 283–285.
Curtiss, Thomas Quinn. "Moreau Lights *Summer Fires,*" *New York Times,* section 2, August 8, 1965, p. 7.
Dibbell, Carola. "The Asymmetrical Woman: Jeanne Moreau at 48," *The Village Voice,* 21:14+, November 15, 1976.
Duras, Marguerite. "Jeanne Moreau," *Vogue,* 146:101+, November 15, 1965.
Eder, Richard. "Premiere Film for Premier Actress," *New York Times,* June 30, 1976, p. 26.
"France's Bette Davis," *Newsweek,* 55:100, February 15, 1960.
"Full Moreau Dance-Card," *Variety,* 302:26, August 25, 1982.
Gilliatt, Penelope. "Profiles," *New Yorker,* 54:44+, March 13, 1978.
Ginsburg, Mark. "Jeanne Moreau," *Interview,* 12:60–62, December 1982.
Harwood, James. "11 Hours of Jeanne Moreau Tribute," *Variety,* 276:7+, October 30, 1974.
The International Dictionary of Films and Filmmakers: Volume III: Actors and Actresses. Chicago: St. James Press, 1986, p. 453–455.
"Jeanne Moreau," *American Film,* 9:15+, July–August 1984.
Joffee, Robert. "Honored but Elusive Moreau," *Washington Post,* October 28, 1974, p. B3.
Klemesrud, Judy. "No Longer in Love with Cardin, but Faithful to His Clothes," *New York Times,* October 6, 1970, p. 60.
Krebs, Albin. "Notes on People," *New York Times,* February 9, 1977, p. C2.
"Milestones," *Time,* 109:76, February 21, 1977.
"Moreau," *Variety,* 281:1+, November 19, 1975.
"Moreau—She Lives to Love," *Life,* 62:39+, January 20, 1967.
"Off Screen and On," *Saturday Evening Post,* 238:86–88, April 10, 1965.
Quinlan, David. *The Illustrated Directory of Film Stars.* London: B.T. Batsford, 1981, p. 340.
Sagan, Françoise. "Moreau," *Vogue,* 175:398+, November 1985.
Shipman, David. *The Great Movies Stars: The International Years.* London: Angus & Robertson, 1972, p. 373–377.
Thomas, Kevin. "Jeanne Moreau: 'I Lead an Incredible Life,'" *Los Angeles Times,* section 4, November 28, 1974, p. 1+.
————. "Lights on 2nd Career for Jeanne Moreau," *Los Angeles Times,* section 4, December 2, 1976, p. 1+.
Thurman, Judith. "Jeanne Moreau," *Ms,* 5:50+ January 1977.
Turan, Kenneth. "Jeanne Moreau," *Washington Post,* June 25, 1976, p. B1+.
"Vogue a la Moreau," *Time,* 96:23, December 28, 1970.
Wlaschin, Ken. *The Illustrated Encyclopedia of the World's Great Movie Stars and Their Films.* London: Salamander, 1979, p. 205–206.

Anouk Aimee

The career of French actress Anouk Aimee has had a number of ups and downs over the years. Several times she has been on the verge of superstardom only to be derailed by a series of bad films, or one of her own self-imposed periods of retirement. Anouk first retired while still a teenager and later took seven years off when she married actor Albert Finney. Directors continued to seek her out though, and she has given some memorable performances with 57 films to her credit.

The actress was born Françoise Sorya in Paris, France, on April 27, 1932, the daughter of two actors. Her schooling took place in that city and then she studied dance at the Marseilles Opera and drama in Paris under René Simon. One day the 15-year-old was walking down the street with her mother when they were stopped by a director named Henri Calef, whom the mother knew. Calef was looking for a young girl for a film he was shooting and Françoise found herself making her film debut that year, 1947, in the melodrama about jealousy and love called *La maison sous la mer.*

The character she played in that film was named Anouk and the actress recalled, "People on the set kept calling me Anouk." From then on she billed herself as Anouk. Her next film followed quickly and the writer on that one, Jacques Prevert, came up with Aimee (beloved) as a surname for the actress. For her first nine films she billed herself just as Anouk, but since then has always used Anouk Aimee.

Prevert was so impressed by Aimee's acting that he wrote a script especially for her, *The Lovers of Verona,* a variation of *Romeo and Juliet* with the teenager cast as the stand-in of a film, Juliet, in love with a studio carpenter. It was her first major role and brought her to the attention of Rank, the big British film company, who was looking for a French girl to pair with Trevor Howard in a thriller *The Golden Salamander.* At just 17 years old Rank signed her to a three-year contract. The media touted her as potentially one of the biggest British stars of the 1950s. Film success came to her easily as did film work. "I never worried about it," she said, "I just took it for granted."

Yet she did not become a popular star in England. The projects scheduled for her were cancelled or filmed with others as Aimee took two years off. First she married Edouard Zimmermann in 1949, a brief union that ended in divorce. Then she married director Nico Papatakis in 1951 as well as giving birth to a daughter that year. That marriage ended in divorce in 1954. After her daughter was born she admitted to having lost interest in acting. About her lack of ambition in general, she commented, "I was never an actress with a flame."

When she returned to films she worked mainly in France during the early 1950s doing well as the girl with a weak heart who seduced a soldier and then died in *The Crimson Curtain.* Several forgettable films followed in Germany

Anouk Aimee in *A Man and a Woman*.

and then a few more in France. She was well received critically as a girl remembering her lovers while being interrogated by the police in *Les Mauvaises Rencontres* but it was a box office flop. By 1957 her stardom had faded to such an extent that she took a very small, and unbilled, role in *Pot-Bouille*.

Anouk appeared in several more pictures in the 1950s but she was not impressive. Her best work from that period was in *La Tête contre les murs*. She also had a support role in *The Journey,* only her second film made in English. Regardless of her vehicles or her work, directors continued to seek her out, seeing in her a quality of erotic tenderness and an extremely photogenic face.

Aimee attracted international attention again in 1960 when she appeared in Fellini's *La dolce vita* where she received excellent notices portraying a loose lady. She teamed with him again a few years later as Marcello Mastroianni's wife in *8 1/2*. Working with the Italian director, she said, "That was when for the first time I began to understand something about acting and even to enjoy it; Federico taught me to relax, taught me to think about what I was doing, taught me to have some pride in my work and not just carry on like a puppet. I'm an instinctive actress, not a technical one, and Fellini taught me how to live with that and how to accept that I might need six months or even a year between films just to recharge."

Another notable film from 1960 was *Lola* by Jacques Demy in which she played a dancehall girl and got some outstanding notices. One critic called her work in that film an "exquisite performance, a breathless, electric, vulnerable supremely sensuous being." Anouk worked mostly in Italy during the first half of the 1960s making many films, most of them of poor quality. "I had a difficult time just after *Dolce vita* because I thought all Italian directors were going to be as good as Fellini," said the actress, "and they certainly weren't." One of her worst outings then was as a lesbian queen in *Sodom and Gomorrah* while her best work came in *Il terrorista* and *Il successo*.

Director Claude Lelouch's first feature *A Man and a Woman* (1966) proved to be the biggest film in Anouk's career. A songwriter named Pierre Barouh had an idea for a film which he told to his friend Lelouch. The director then went to see actor Jean-Louis Trintignant. His wife was present and suggested her friend, Aimee, for the female lead. Anouk's agent did not like the idea and told her to reject the role but the actress's intuition prevailed. *A Man and a Woman* was a banal love story about a man and a woman, both widowed, who met and found new love. The public enjoyed it and it became a huge hit worldwide.

That film was shot in just three weeks by a crew of 12 who did all their own lighting and makeup. *A Man and a Woman* won an Oscar as Best Foreign Film while Aimee was nominated for an Oscar as Best Actress. The British Academy named her Best Foreign Actress for her work in that film. The actress was in big demand again particularly in the United States. "But you don't build a career around one film," Aimee said, "and you certainly don't move to another country because of a few awards."

With commitments to honor she did a few more European features and then a couple of American films. Most of these did nothing to advance her career. Anouk appeared in Sidney Lumet's *The Appointment,* shot in Rome, for a reported fee of $150,000 but the film was so poor it was not released in most countries. Equally abysmal was *Justine* which had been on the planning boards for ten years and involved a change of directors in midstream.

"When I did finally go to Hollywood to do that disastrous screen version of *Justine* we worked for six months with Joseph Strick and then abruptly the studio removed him and brought in George Cukor," said Anouk. The actress felt you could not finish with one director what you had started with another. "You just can't change directors on a film, it's as simple as that, only once you get inside a big studio they abandon all the basic rules of artistry and you end up with a mess like *Justine*." That film was a box office disaster and Aimee has made no American or English-language films since.

On the set of *A Man and a Woman* Anouk had met Barouh, who had a part in the film, and married him in 1966 only to be divorced within a couple of years. She began to see Albert Finney and they married in 1970 and divorced in 1978. Aimee retired from films and was not seen on the screen between 1969 and 1976. "I really didn't ever plan to act again after we married," said Aimee.

Anouk Aimee *(in sunglasses)* **on location in Rome for filming of** *The Appointment.*

"I'd been at it a long time, there was no script around that I particularly wanted to make, and I genuinely thought that maybe I should take up painting or writing instead. I even bought an easel on which the canvas turned slowly from white to yellow as it lay untouched in a corner of the house. While the marriage was good, I saw no point in being an actress; when it began to fail, I went back to work."

After that retirement Aimee appeared, as usual, in some mediocre films and some excellent ones. Her best work came in *Salto nel vuoto* for which she was named Best Actress at the Cannes Film Festival. She was also named Best Actress for her performance in Bertolucci's kidnap drama *The Tragedy of a Ridiculous Man.* For *Mon Premier Amour* she acted also as coproducer to raise the money. "In the end, if you believe in a project enough, then you probably have to do it all yourself," she said. "It's no good waiting for other people to do all the setting up for you especially now that film money is so tight all over the world."

Aimee admitted she never really understood ambition or a single-minded dedication to acting. Even though she enjoyed the work she has never felt the need to act all the time. "My own luxury has always been choice. I'd rather wait and not have the money for a new car than do the film and hate it afterwards. All that really matters is getting the right director. Bad scripts or poor costars can be dealt with, but if you've got the wrong director you may as well go home ... But I'm lucky in that I've always been able to work with the best—Carne, Prevert, Fellini, Lelouch, Bertolucci."

Recently she starred in Lelouch's *A Man and a Woman: 20 Years Later* which, as its title suggests, was a remake of his earlier hit with the same people brought up-to-date. Aimee was praised for her acting again. Anouk still looked youthful at 54 but the film itself was an incomprehensible jumble and panned by most critics.

For the actress who once said, "I did nothing to have a career; it's not a word that suits me," she has succeeded almost in spite of herself and is now committed to continue. "Other actresses come and go," she said, "I just seem to stay around. Not always in the right movies, maybe, but considering the mistakes I've made privately and professionally it's a miracle I'm still here at all. And now I think I will work; no more retirements unless, of course, something very special happens."

Anouk Aimee Filmography

La Maison sous la mer (1947)
La Fleur de l'âge (1947)
Les Amants de Vérone [The Lovers of Verona] (1948)
The Golden Salamander (1949)
Conquêtes du froid (1951)
Noche de tormenta (1951)
La Bergère et le ramoneur (voice only) (1952)
The Man Who Watched Trains Go By [The Paris Express] (1952)
Nuit d'Orage (1952)
Le Rideau cramoisi [The Crimson Curtain] (1953)
Forever My Heart [Happy Birthday] (1954)
Contraband Spain (1955)
Ich suche Dich (1955)
Les Mauvaise Rencontres (1955)
Nina (1956)
Stresemann (1956)
Tous peuvent me tuer [Anyone Can Kill Me] (1957)
Pot-Bouille [The House of Lovers] (1957)

Montparnasse 19 (1957)
La Tête contre les murs [The Keepers] (1958)
Carve Her Name with Pride (1958)
The Journey [Some of Us May Die] (1959)
Les Dragueurs [The Chasers; The Young Have No Morals] (1959)
La dolce vita (1960)
Lola (1960)
Le Temps d'un reflet (1960)
Le Farceur [The Joker] (1961)
L'imprevisto (1961)
Quai Notre-Dame (1961)
Il giudizio universale [The Last Judgment] (1961)
Sodoma e Gomorra [Sodom and Gomorrah; The Last Days of Sodom and Gomorrah] (1962)
Les Grands Chemins [Of Flesh and Blood] (1962)
Otto e mezzo [8 1/2] (1963)
Il giorno più corto [The Shortest Day] (1963)
Il terrorista (1963)

Il successo (1963)
Liolà (1963)
Le voci bianche [White Voices] (1964)
La fuga (1964)
Il Morbidone (1965)
La stagioni del nostro amore [A Very Handy Man] (1965)
Lo scandalo (1966)
Un Homme et une Femme [A Man and a Woman] (1966)
Un Soir, un train (1968)
Model Shop (1969)
Justine (1969)
The Appointment (1969)
Si c'était à refaire [If I Had to Do It

All Over Again; A Second Chance] (1976)
The Mandarins (1976)
Mon premier Amour (1978)
Salto nel vuoto [A Leap in the Dark; Leap into the Void] (1980)
Les petits Matins (1980)
Tragedia di un uomo ridiculo [The Tragedy of a Ridiculous Man] (1981)
Qu'est-ce qui fait courir David? (1982)
Il generale dell'armata morta (1983)
Viva la vie (1984)
A Man and a Woman: 20 Years Later (1986)

Sources

Ager, Cecilia. "50 Million Frenchmen Call Her 'Ah Ah!'" *New York Times,* April 9, 1967, sec. 2, p. 13.

Bender, Marilyn. "French Actress Takes on Role of a Shopper Here," *New York Times,* April 10, 1965, p. 21.

Buck, Joan Juliet. "Anouk Aimee," *Vogue,* 176:408+, November 1986.

Durham, Michael. "Aimee—It Means 'To Be Loved,'" *Life,* 62:85–6, May 19, 1967.

The International Dictionary of Films and Filmmakers: Volume III: Actors and Actresses. Chicago: St. James Press, 1986, p. 9–10.

Morley, Sheridan. "Enjoying the Luxury of Choice." *Times (London),* December 14, 1981, p. 7.

"On the Road Again with Anouk Aimee," *Life,* 9:74–5, August 1986.

Quinlan, David. *The Illustrated Directory of Film Stars.* London: B.T. Batsford, 1981, p. 4.

Shipman, David. *The Great Movie Stars: The International Years.* London: Angus & Robertson, 1972, p. 2–4.

Thomson, David. *A Biographical Dictionary of Film.* New York: William Morrow, 1975, p. 1–2.

Wlaschin, Ken. *The Illustrated Encyclopedia of the World's Great Movie Stars and Their Films.* London: Salamander, 1979, p. 164.

Leslie Caron

Discovered dancing in French ballet, Leslie Caron was quickly spirited to Hollywood while still a teenager. She began a long series of American films in which she was mostly known for her dancing prowess and featured usually as a gamine or waif-like orphan. More and more the emptiness of those films annoyed Leslie. Caron began to complain. Soon she had a reputation as a difficult actress and she and her studio parted company. Leslie gave up film dancing permanently and returned to Europe where she got a chance to display her acting talents and did some of her best work.

She was born Leslie Claire Margaret Caron on July 1, 1931, in Boulogne-Billancourt near Paris, France. Her father Claude Caron was a French chemist who lived a respectable middle-class existence "with pretensions" as Leslie recalled. Mrs. Caron was the former Margaret Petit who was born in Topeka, Kansas, and trained in ballet in Seattle. Later, in the 1920s, Margaret achieved a degree of success as a dancer in musical comedy productions in New York City. After marrying, the couple made their home in France. Margaret gave up dancing and raised her daughter and younger son in the Paris suburb of Neuilly.

No longer a dancer herself, Mrs. Caron channeled the desire through her daughter and Leslie began ballet lessons at a young age. According to Leslie, Mrs. Caron regretted giving up her career and advised her daughter, "It's better to count on yourself than on your husband for the good things in life." The child received her education at the Convent of the Assumption in Paris. During the Nazi occupation of that city Leslie and her brother were sent to live with grandparents in Cannes.

After the liberation of Paris Caron returned and took up ballet in earnest, studying at the Conservatoire de Paris. In 1946 she began her professional career with the Ballet des Champs-Elysees where she danced bit parts. Within a couple of years she had moved up to lead ballerina with the company and became an immediate hit with the public in 1948 as the principal dancer in *La Rencontre*. One of those who saw that ballet was the American actor Gene Kelly. Kelly was impressed by the teenager's ability and went backstage to congratulate her. Leslie recalled, "He came to my dressing room, but I wasn't there. I'd finished my job, and there was too much gushing and goo and I didn't like it, so I scrubbed my face and went home. But let's face it, I was very good."

For the next couple of years Caron continued with her ballet career in Paris and on tour until 1950 when Gene Kelly returned to Paris to find a leading lady for his upcoming film *An American in Paris*. Gene remembered the teenaged ballerina, found her, gave her a scene to study and arranged a screen test where he played opposite her. The film was flown to Hollywood and viewed by the film's producer and director. Approval of Kelly's selection was given and three days later Leslie, accompanied by her mother, was on a plane flying to Hollywood.

Caron was happy to be away from ballet and said, "You have no life at all. A few francs a week, not enough to live on. Work all day and night. You are so tired and sweaty when you finish you throw on any kind of clothes, you don't care, and hurry home to sleep." Working on *An American in Paris* was not a pleasant time for the actress who said, "The experience was one long pain and I still don't know how I got through it. I was completely lost. I knew nothing about movies and I knew no English. Everything you heard me say in that film was said phonetically."

That film was a lush, musical extravaganza which was well received by the public and the critics, with Leslie drawing particular attention. Reviewers enthused about her and emphasized her "puckish" and "elfin" qualities. Metro-Goldwyn-Mayer (MGM) signed her to a longterm contract and she was next seen in *The Man with a Cloak,* a forgettable drama which made no impact. It was notable in that Leslie was cast as an orphan for the first time. The actress would often find herself playing a young gamine even as she aged. Leslie grew increasingly hostile to that type of role and soon was tagged as being a "difficult" actress.

When she first arrived in Hollywood Leslie had a somewhat straggly hairstyle. This was soon remedied by studio hairdressers. So naïve was Leslie that one day during the middle of the picture she was shooting she arrived on the set with a homemade haircut that did not remotely match any previous shots. Director Vincente Minnelli fumed, "She used a bowl." Initially she lived in a small apartment over a garage cooking for herself and her brother, who had replaced Mrs. Caron as chaperone. The brother had gotten a job as a messenger boy at MGM.

In 1951 Leslie married George Hormel II, heir to the meat-packing fortune. The couple divorced in 1954 with George testifying that Leslie preferred "the intense artistic life to life with me." Caron commented some years later, "I married wrongly because of Hollywood." The film *Lili* (1953) was one of the high points of her early Hollywood career with Leslie cast as a teenage orphan who got a job working for a puppeteer in a circus. Shooting during that film came to a standstill when the actress refused to allow her ragamuffin character of the early part of the film to become glamorous at the end. Every morning after makeup Leslie disappeared "to take the stuff off my face and spit on my hair to straighten it out."

Shortly before *Lili* was released Leslie returned to the ballet stage in New York. MGM gave permission "only because it thought *Lili* was going to be a terrible failure and there was some doubt even of its release." To the surprise of the studio *Lili* enjoyed great success as did Caron. For her work in that film the British Film Academy named her Best Foreign Actress and the American Academy nominated her for an Oscar as Best Actress.

The Glass Slipper featured Caron in a straight version of Cinderella and then she starred, as an orphan, opposite Fred Astaire in *Daddy Long Legs* in which the pair danced. Said Astaire, "She is a fine artist, conscientious, apt, serious. She hesitates to attempt anything either in dance or acting unless she is absolutely sure of herself. Leslie will hold up production for many minutes, or hours, on some occasions, until she feels complete control of what she's about to do. I consider that a most commendable trait." Her reviews for that film were excellent. *Gaby,* another musical, was poorly received.

Leslie Caron serves a meal in *Fanny*.

By then Leslie was more frustrated with Hollywood and went to Europe where she appeared in a stage play in Paris and next played in *Gigi* on the London stage. MGM tried to get her to come back to star with Kelly in *Les Girls* but the actress refused. Her contract still had several years to run but she claimed she did not care if she ever returned to Hollywood. She changed her mind, however, when MGM filmed *Gigi*. Leslie came back to star as the young orphan wooed by Louis Jordan. The film won the Best Picture Oscar. It also marked the end of her screen dancing. "Now I'll see whether I can get by on my acting," she said.

When she worked on *Gigi* in London she met theater director Peter Hall. They married in 1956, had two children and divorced in 1965. "There's the chance of a woman's losing her personality when she marries," said Leslie, "but it is a part of her dignity to maintain it ... I cannot bear to be represented as a good housewife by my publicists. I cook and make clothes only out of a lack of creative things to do."

After the divorce from Hall the actress commented, "I had an inkling before I married Peter that he was too ambitious to include me in his artistic life, that he wanted to relegate me to making the cucumber sandwiches. After all, I wasn't Oxbridge. I was a not-quite respectable film star. But I was so eager for bad plumbing and so starved after Hollywood for an interesting theatrical

Leslie Caron struggles with David Opatoshu in *Guns of Darkness*.

life that I thought I'd take a chance." Caron noted the couple lived elegantly on "my money" and that "one day when it became clear to me that I wasn't going to be taken seriously, I flew out of the nest."

At the end of the 1950s Caron appeared in a couple of Hollywood clunkers and a couple of European films which were somewhat more kindly received. That concluded her MGM contract. Caron had no regrets. She did not leave Hollywood permanently, however. In 1960 she appeared in *Fanny,* an odd film from the Broadway musical, without the songs. Critics panned it but it did fairly well at the box office.

A couple more forgettable vehicles followed until she landed the lead role in the British production *The L-Shaped Room.* Leslie played a lonely and pregnant woman living in a bed-sitter in a shabby London boardinghouse. The British Film Academy named her Best Actress on the basis of that film and the American Academy again nominated her for an Oscar as Best Actress.

The director of *The L-Shaped Room* was Bryan Forbes and Leslie said to him, "Teach me not to smile. Wipe the smile off my face, because this is drama; you've got to teach me how to act without smiling . . . Even now I feel furious with myself because, whenever there's a still camera pointed towards me, my MGM training makes me smile. I don't like it. You can see it on all the people who came from that era because there was no question of them not smiling for the camera."

Breaking away from the stereotyped roles she had played in Hollywood elated the actress who said, "I had a girlish face and I guess I was pretty good at playing juveniles so it made good business sense for that to be my pigeon-hole. They just changed the partners and the costumes and that was it." In the future the actress hoped "my characterizations will be greatly different from the adolescent parts I've been in. Grace Kelly proved that an actress need not be emotionally mixed up nor have an offensive bosom for the public to like her."

Caron bristled when she thought about the "strange little girl" roles she had so often essayed for Hollywood and the battles she had fought with the studio bosses over them. "I got the feeling I was some sort of freak, because I wasn't pretty in the conventional sense," said Leslie. "The publicity written about me was filled with adjectives like 'gamine' and 'elfin'—another way of saying I was very plain. I got so used to being thought plain and somewhat dull that I came to believe it ... I got to what I have now through knowing the right time to tell terrible people to go to hell."

The whole Hollywood scene had been offensive to Caron. She was contemptuous of what passed for taste in the film capital and fought against what she termed "swimming-pool values." She said, "I had to get away from the silly publicity nonsense of Hollywood, appearing at the Mocambo with whomever they chose for you, visiting hospitals just to publicize a film, being photographed with bunnies and being always cute. That's not me. And the agonies of sitting in a chair and having someone curl my hair the wrong way became unbearably painful. They never had the decency to let me know what film I was doing next. I had to read about it. Everyone was sheep—but I am not sheep." During her Hollywood contract days she was often suspended and once even set up a dancing school "to have enough money to refuse scripts I didn't like." Leslie declared, "My stay in Hollywood was a long and slow form of nervous breakdown really. By the time I left, I was a total wreck."

Despite her aversion to Hollywood she was lured back in the mid–1960s for three films, all comedies and all poorly received by critics. Leslie was a school teacher who succumbed to the charms of Cary Grant in *Father Goose;* a psychoanalyst who succumbed to the charms of Rock Hudson in *A Very Special Favor;* and a widow who succumbed to the charms of Warren Beatty in *Promise Her Anything.*

In real life she did succumb to Warren Beatty and when she left Hall it was to an affair with Beatty. Hall named Beatty as corespondent in his divorce action and rumors circulated that Caron and Beatty might wed. Leslie had no such intentions and laughed, "Warren Beatty only wants to marry his next Academy Award. The man really is a megalomaniac."

At the end of the 1960s she made a couple better movies in Europe. The big-budget French film *Is Paris Burning?* did not do well critically or at the box office but Caron got good personal notices and was one of the few bright spots in the film. She starred in the Italian comedy *Il padre di famiglia* and did excellent work although the film received almost no distribution in North America. That role remained Caron's favorite and she felt she did her best acting in it.

American film producer Michael Laughlin and Caron married in 1969. Laughlin produced a few of her films but, like *Chandler* which was a detective story with Warren Oates and *Madron,* a western with Richard Boone, they were dismal and represented some of the worst work of her career. The couple split in the mid–1970s and divorced in 1977. Leslie commented, "He trifled with my work and forbade me to experiment."

In 1973 Leslie sold her house in Hollywood and moved back to her native France. She again recalled her early days under contract in the 1950s with loathing. "Hollywood frightened me. It was a frightening atmosphere. I don't know quite how to describe it, except that everything you did was reported. If you left the set to go to the toilet, they would write it down," she said. "When you did interviews there was always somebody from the studio who sat in. We were taught to be very mild in interviews and we had to be very careful. Under the studio rule you just had to obey. They would come at me with tweezers and say, 'Studio orders—we've got to pluck your eyebrows.'"

When she moved back to Paris she claimed she was almost unable to converse because "In L.A. I'd never thought or talked about anything important. My mind had become dull. So I felt utterly stupid when I got back to Paris. It took me a year to adjust." One motivation for Caron's return to France was her age. Leslie had passed 40 and felt Hollywood provided very few opportunities for an actress of that age.

"In America you have to play freak parts — to swing a hatchet — if you're in that age category. In France, you can still play love stories," she said. "I think Hollywood is really immature in its attitude toward extreme youth ... except for men. Men can work until they are 50, 60 or 70. Women's careers are ridiculously short, except for the stage. Hollywood is all geared for men because they are organized in a business-like fashion and can find themselves parts. They are all producers."

Back in Europe Leslie found there was no great demand for her at first and went through a few years with no screen appearances. "I thought my career was over," said Caron. "I'm not a juvenile any more and, after a while, producers just don't want to hear about you, however much the public may love you." She was optimistic they would notice her because, she joked, "After forty, there aren't that many who can still stand up. A lot of us fall by the wayside, get married, start drinking or taking drugs. Life gets too harsh."

Caron had left the United States because she never had a chance, in her view, to prove herself as a dramatic actress, always being thought of as a young song-and-dance girl. About her appearances in France, she said, "I get immense respect, as if I were some rare Egyptian cat. But not always the roles I want. . . . To the French I'll always be Gigi."

In 1980 she said she had no plans for remarriage adding, "I might live with someone, I suppose. But that's hard too. You see, I'm just not willing to adapt any more; to turn into an obedient, complacent woman. I'm much too independent now. It's hard living alone. But it's equally hard living with a man, I find. It has to be someone intelligent for a start, and that always seems to lead to conflict. So there's no answer." Later that year she met an Australian lawyer named Roger Vincent and the pair began living together.

The actress most admired by Leslie was Simone Signoret because "look at the parts she gets to play because of the way she looks. Me, I'd never even be considered for them." Finally the parts started to arrive for Leslie. The actress gave a brilliant performance as the housekeeper in *Serail* and then had a small role in Truffaut's *The Man Who Loved Women.* Caron did not enjoy working with Truffaut, complaining he gave her an eight-page scene and shot it as if it were two pages. "Truffaut put me in a straitjacket. He's rigid, severe. He made me nervous," she noted.

Leslie took chances on unusual roles and appeared in Ken Russell's *Valentino.* She played flamboyant Russian-born actress Alla Nazimova and got good notices for an odd part in this bizarre film. In 1980 she appeared in *Kontrakt,* a Polish film made for a total cost of $50,000 with the money supplied by the Polish government. "I've got a small percentage of *Kontrakt,*" said Leslie, "but I don't expect to make anything. Every scene was shot in one take because we couldn't afford film. We didn't have a crew—one cameraman held a single camera on his shoulders. To make good movies, you don't need money or equipment. You need brains and talent."

Since that film the actress has only appeared in two others but has kept busy in other ways. She has toured in a number of plays. It was on one such tour of Australia that she met Roger Vincent. Leslie even resumed dancing on the stage after an absence of decades. A collection of her short stories published in 1982 was met by generally favorable reviews.

"I think it's the end of progress if you stand still and think of what you've done in the past," she said. "I'd rather do a small film which has quality than a commercial film. I'm at war against corporate filmmaking. I think corporate dread-and-disaster films and their sequels are sick and unimaginative and undermine our profession . . . I keep on."

Leslie Caron Filmography

An American in Paris (1951)
The Man with a Cloak (1951)

Gloria Alley (1952)
The Story of Three Loves (1953)

Lili (1953)
The Glass Slipper (1954)
Daddy Long Legs (1955)
Gaby (1956)
Gigi (1958)
The Doctor's Dilemma (1959)
The Man Who Understood Women (1959)
Austerlitz [The Battle of Austerlitz] (1959)
The Subterraneans (1960)
Fanny (1960)
Les quatre verites (1962)
Guns of Darkness (1962)
The L-Shaped Room (1963)
Father Goose (1964)
A Very Special Favor (1965)
Promise Her Anything (1965)
Paris brûle-t-il? [Is Paris Burning?] (1965)
Il padre di famiglia [Head of the Family] (1967)
Madron (1970)
Chandler (1971)
Nicole (1972)
Purple Night (1972)
James Dean — the First American Teenager (1975)
Serail (1976)
L'homme qui aimait les femmes [The Man Who Loved Women] (1977)
Valentino (1977)
Goldengirl (1979)
Tous vedettes (1979)
Kontrakt [The Contract] (1980)
Chanel solitaire (1981)
La diagonale du fou [Dangerous Moves] (1984)

Sources

Bell, Arthur. "Bell Tells," *Village Voice,* 26:40, October 14–20, 1981.
"The Chic Caron," *Look,* 24:91+, June 7, 1960.
Current Biography 1954. New York: H.W. Wilson, 1955, p. 157–158.
d'Arcy, Susan. "A Parisienne in America," *Films Illustrated,* 6:90–91, November 1976.
Hutchings, David. "Leslie Caron Gets Back on Her Toes," *People,* 21:143+, May 14, 1984.
The International Dictionary of Films and Filmmakers: Volume III: Actors and Actresses. Chicago: St. James Press, 1986, p. 123–124.
Jennings, C. Robert. "A Waif Becomes a Woman," *Saturday Evening Post,* 236:22–23, September 14, 1963.
Katz, Ephraim. *The Film Encyclopedia.* New York: Thomas Y. Crowell, 1979, p. 210.
Kent, Leticia. "There's a Lot of Leslie Caron in Our Future," *New York Times,* August 28, 1977, sec. 2, p. 13+.
Lazarus, Charles J. "The Latest Thing from Gay Paree," *New York Times,* October 7, 1951, sec. 2, p. 5.
"McCall's Visits," *McCall's,* 85:10+, May 1958.
McClure, Hal. "Leslie Caron Goes Home," *Los Angeles Times,* May 18, 1973, sec. 4, p. 4.
Mann, Roderick. "Ex-waif is 49 and All Woman," *Los Angeles Times,* June 8, 1980, Calendar sec., p. 36–37.
_____. "Paris Piques Her Mind — and Morale," *Los Angeles Times,* January 26, 1985, sec. 5, p. 1.
"Miss Caron," *Newsweek,* 55:60, January 4, 1960.
Quinlan, David. *The Illustrated Directory of Film Stars.* London: B.T. Batsford, 1981, p. 77.
Shipman, David. *The Great Movie Stars: The International Years.* London: Angus & Robertson, 1972, p. 76–79.
Shipp, Cameron. "Mademoiselle in Blue Jeans," *Reader's Digest,* 62:137–139, February 1953.
Thompson, Howard. "Caron in Cameo," *New York Times,* May 26, 1963, sec. 2, p. 5.
Thomson, David. *A Biographical Dictionary of Film.* New York: William Morrow, 1975, p. 80.

Whitcomb, Jon. "Leslie Caron as Gigi," *Cosmopolitan,* 144:77+, May 1958.
Wlaschin, Ken. *The Illustrated Encyclopedia of the World's Great Movie Stars and Their Films.* London: Salamander, 1979, p. 178–179.

Brigitte Bardot

Brigitte Bardot was often defined by the term "sex kitten." With the exception of Marilyn Monroe no one before or after Brigitte Bardot has had such an impact on filmgoers. With a sulky look and a luscious face and figure, she exuded a sex appeal that was rarely matched. She became the biggest foreign film star of her time. Her personality took on the traits of her screen persona as she tried to become her image. It all ended suddenly when Brigitte quit the film business to live as a semi-recluse and devote herself to her causes. More than a decade and a half later the Bardot mystique remained larger than life.

Brigitte Bardot was born in Paris, France, on September 28, 1934, the oldest of two daughters in a well-to-do family. Mr. Bardot was an industrial engineer who owned a liquid-air factory. Mrs. Bardot managed a chic dress shop in the fashhionable district of Passy where the family lived. Growing up Brigitte lacked for nothing and led the easy and thoughtless life of a sheltered and spoiled French girl. She attended an exclusive, private girls' school and began ballet lessons at age seven. Regarded as an outstanding pupil in dance she won an excellency award from the Paris Conservatory when she was 13, but soon abandoned ballet. School vacations were spent at the family villa on the French Riviera.

Mrs. Bardot was ambitious for her daughter and pushed the teenager into modeling clothes for some of her designer friends. While her childhood was not an unhappy one, Bardot was not satisfied and later recalled, "When I was fifteen I was seeking something. Not just excitement—I don't know what it was. Perhaps a fulfillment of myself." In May 1950 she appeared as a model on the cover of *Elle,* France's foremost fashion magazine—an event that would change the course of her life.

That cover came to the attention of film director Marc Allegret who was interested in her fresh beauty. Allegret told his assistant Roger Vadim to get in touch with her with a view to casting her in a forthcoming Allegret picture. While that film was never made and although Bardot's screen tests were not promising, Vadim took her on as his protégée and urged her to quit school. Brigitte was not interested in school and needed very little urging to quit.

In the space of a few weeks Vadim became her boyfriend and got her bit parts in a couple of inferior films, the first being the 1952 release *Le trou normand*. The couple married in late 1952, having had to wait until Brigitte became of age. Mr. Bardot reportedly hated Vadim.

The actress did poorly in the first two films as well as in her next two films, both again being very small bit roles. Vadim had already started a publicity campaign for the actress by orchestrating a lot of newspaper coverage of his own wedding. He had connections with France's national weekly *Paris-Match* and arranged a two-page picture spread in that publication. After those first few dismal outings, Vadim came to the conclusion that if Brigitte could not get roles through her acting then she could by using her body. If he could not get her to the top as an actress he would move her there as a personality. "She didn't really have the vocation of an actress," noted Roger.

For the next few years, Bardot had small parts in a dozen films — mostly a series of stripteases, seductions, milk baths and almost nude bathing scenes. Wandering around the screen wrapped only in a brief towel became a Bardot trademark. She had become a starlet with a reputation for stripping but not much else. Impatient with not making much progress Brigitte was ready to quit but Vadim was determined his wife would be a big star and Bardot remembered, "He kept telling me that one day I would be Brigitte Bardot, the impossible dream of married men."

In some of those films such as *The Light Across the Street* and *Please, Mr. Balzac,* the actress had moved up to lead roles but no real acting was required and none was given. In her roles she always appeared wild, childishly provocative and as naked as the censors would allow in those films. Vadim selected all the parts for his wife and functioned as a screenwriter on some of her projects.

To get around his wife's lack of acting ability, Vadim built his legend by publicizing that she "was not an actress but a natural phenomenon. Brigitte does not act — she exists." Brigitte was to be the figurehead of his own philosophy of "sincere immorality" and media material stated that audiences didn't see an actress on the screen playing a role when they watched Bardot but saw "the real Bardot, all animality, sensuality and femininity unfolded." Vadim tried to twist logic to convince the audience that acting was old-fashioned, that previous screen stars were "silly little artists of make-believe" while Brigitte was authentic.

The big break came in early 1956 when producer Raoul Levy gave Vadim the opportunity to write, cast and direct a film of his own, with his wife as the star. That film was *And God Created Woman* in which Brigitte played an empty-headed, sex-crazed, lazy and unscrupulous woman. The film was poor and mostly concerned with sex but it went on to great commercial success, though a critical failure.

In press releases Vadim called his wife: "The young girl of today, typical of her generation." Bardot said, "I must resemble the whole of my generation, and that's why they have adopted me so nicely." Given her character in the film, many young people in France resented the implication and a controversy arose, which only helped the film. Roger leaked his rows with the censor to the press, further generating interest in the picture.

During the course of shooting that film Bardot, always headstrong and ill-tempered, started to live in the manner of her image. She pouted and sulked, surrounded herself with stuffed animals, had tantrums, flirted and overplayed the sex scenes. Engaging in Vadim's "sincere immorality," Bardot had an affair with the film's leading man and at the conclusion of the film Brigitte walked out on Vadim. Roger had his legend but lost his wife. The couple divorced in 1957. Over the years Bardot remained friendly with Vadim and later said, "I owe everything to Vadim. He alone knew how to guide me, sustain me, console me and teach me to be courageous and stubborn."

And God Created Woman was a huge success in the United States and England and made the actress an international superstar. The cult of the "sex kitten," of "B.B.," was born. In the United States a glut of Bardot films was rushed into the market to meet the demand. Some of them dated back to 1952. The actress was offered large sums of money to go to Hollywood to do films and was offered a reported $50,000 for three appearances on television's "Ed Sullivan Show." All those offers were turned down. According to her agent Brigitte just wanted "to stay in France, have fun, and work as little as possible."

Not everybody loved Brigitte. She was said to be a bigger star in England and the United States than in her native France. About her countrymen, the actress said, "I know they don't like me. They say I have no heart, that I am egotistical and unstable. They say I destroy love relationships and that I am a danger to the youth." Religious groups in various parts of the world denounced her wiggling while the French Jehovah's Witnesses announced she was eternally damned. The Vatican exhibit at the Brussel's World Fair in 1959 contained a large picture of Bardot, symbolizing evil. They had to remove the photo when it proved to be the most popular part of the exhibit.

According to one report B.B. "takes her clothes off almost any time, anywhere, in front of almost anybody—for publicity stills, for the movie cameras, because the director tells her to, or just because she happens to feel like it." A different report came from the actress who said, "And do you think it is fun to film scenes in the raw?" On those occasions she said she insisted on having a closed set except for the cameraman.

After the success of *And God Created Woman,* Brigitte appeared in several more similar films such as *The Bride Is Too Beautiful* and *Parisienne* which featured the actress disrobed as much as possible. Lovers came and went in great number and her behavior on the set grew more volatile as she swung between spitefulness and docility, between charm and petulance. Temper tantrums became more frequent as she alienated many of her coworkers. "That little woman," said actor Jean Gabin, "has done what 30 years of getting along with people couldn't do to me: Finally disgust me with the movies."

Brigitte Bardot in *Mam'zelle Pigalle.*

People who disliked her were definitely in a minority and "Bardolatry" was considered the wave of the future. Perhaps the single biggest box office draw in the world at the end of the 1950s, her appeal was said to be based on her child woman image. Even the intellectuals were impressed and Simone de Beauvoir published a book about the actress in 1961, seeing in her "an infantile, almost animal sexuality that freed her from all the inhibitions of adulthood." Actress Jeanne Moreau termed her a "real modern revolutionary character for women."

Her lack of acting ability did nothing to lessen her appeal. "Some people say I am not a very good actress, said Bardot. "Maybe so. But I have not had very much chance to act. Mostly I have had to undress. That is not acting, and I know it. I would like to be a good actress." At the height of her stardom she still had second thoughts about her life and said, "I feel that I have missed out in life. I should never have made mvoies, but now I'm in the rat race. At eighteen, I should have married someone stable, a real companion." Brigitte married actor Jacques Charrier in 1959. She bore a son Nicolas in 1960 and the couple divorced in 1963.

The year 1959 saw the release of *Babette Goes to War,* the first change-of-pace film for the actress who played a girl in the French Resistance who undertook a mission in enemy territory. The actress was fully clad in a uniform and helmet. This film was a deliberate move by Brigitte who said, "I am now spending my life trying to erase the Bardot legend ... I am going to be a girl without anything unhealthy or equivocal about her, and I am going to be good if it kills me. I want to be cute and tender and warm, in the hope that people will forget the idea that I am a brainless, bosomy girl. I can be more than that." She knew a change of image would be difficult since "all the stories that are offered me repeat one another. They still represent the Bardot myth, not the real me. I haven't minded people seeing me undressed when the plot calls for it. But now I want people to see the rest of me."

The change of image never really became established and although there was less nudity in her 1960s' films than in those of the 1950s, nudity remained her greatest claim to fame. Her sexuality, not her acting skills, brought in the public. She appeared in the courtroom drama *The Truth;* Jean-Luc Godard's *Contempt;* a comedy, *Adorable Idiot* with Anthony Perkins; and *Viva Maria,* another comedy in which Bardot and Moreau played soubrettes caught in a Mexican Revolution. *Dear Brigitte* was a comedy costarring James Stewart. In it Stewart's young son wrote a fan letter to B.B. who played herself. Bardot played a French countess in a British Western *Shalako,* which was filmed in Spain. It costarred Sean Connery. *The Legend of Frenchie King* had Bardot costarred with Claudia Cardinale in an alphabet battle of B.B. versus C.C.

Occassionally she got a good review but usually she did not. The vehicles themselves were of poor quality but Bardot remained a big box office draw, even though her popularity was down slightly from her peak in the 1950s. Sophia Loren had supplanted her as France's favorite actress. Charles de Gaulle had once received Bardot and said, "This young woman seems to be made of sterling simplicity."

The actress's personal life continued in turmoil and provided plenty of material for the media. In 1958 she made her first suicide attempt when she swallowed sleeping pills in her dressing room on a film set. Gilbert Becaud, a French singer, whom Bardot announced she would wed, was proclaimed as the cause. Becaud announced the next day to the press that Brigitte was annoying him. The humiliated actress overdosed the following morning.

Shortly after Bardot married Charrier he was drafted into the French Army. Jacques became the butt of so many jokes about his wife that he suffered a nervous breakdown. He had two more breakdowns and slashed his wrists after one of them. By the time he recovered, Bardot was dating director Henri-Georges Clouzot. Clouzot's wife slashed her wrists after learning about this state of affairs and then Charrier slashed his again. Some months later, on her 26th birthday, Bardot swallowed a bunch of pills and slashed her wrists. "I had messed up everything. I was a young, foolish girl, and I had damaged so many people," said the actress. "I damaged them through carelessness, and stupidity and foolishness, and I had nothing left to live for."

By the mid–1960s Bardot was becoming increasingly unhappy with being a public figure complaining that "for people like me, there is no place left to hide . . . No matter what I do, they continue to hound me . . . I tried to retire two years ago, so that I could be free and at peace. So I would not have photographers chasing me day and night, so that I could be on my own at last. But it has not happened that way. In some ways when I work I have finally more peace than when I do not. At least in a film studio I have guards, and the other people are professionals like myself. I don't have guards on public streets."

Even acting did not interest her. "All of this—most of this—bores me. I try to do my best, to be always prepared, but I am not an actress. Lady Macbeth does not interest me. I am just Brigitte Bardot. In the movies or out, I do not think I will ever be anything else . . . I am thirty, but there are things about me that are still fifteen. And that Brigitte Bardot, the one I see in the magazines and the newspapers, the one who is up on the movie screen, *that* Brigitte Bardot will never be sixty."

Bardot was then involved in animal rights, a subject which would concern her more and more in the future. The French passed a law in 1964 which ordered all animal slaughtering to be done with a stun gun rather than a club or a hammer. It was dubbed the B.B. Law since she campaigned for it so strenuously. Yet the following year she was quoted as saying, "I adore furs." Her collection of fur coats included zebra, sable, ocelot and otter.

Brigitte married Gunther Sachs in 1966; a union which dissolved in 1969. She has not remarried since.

She analyzed her own enormous appeal by saying, "I have become, without premeditation on my part, the symbol of female freedom. Of woman's sexual freedom . . . I am the only Bardot, and my species is unique. Many other girls will have fantastic careers after me. Some will have a lot more talent. But none of them will ever be Bardot."

By the early 1970s Brigitte still said, "I don't think I'm what is properly called an actress. That's perhaps my greatest strength. I express myself through instinct." She was getting old for a sex symbol and felt, "I shall know I am old the day I can no longer have the man I'd like." Once again she threatened to leave acting, "one day I'll leave it for good. Before it abandons me."

That day came when she was working on the 1973 release *Colinot*. One day she looked at herself in the mirror, saw herself in a silly turban, and was struck by the absurdity of her life as an actress. "I thought, as I looked at myself, 'Poor girl, what are you doing here?' I decided at that precise moment that between me and the cinema, it was a final divorce." She has not made a movie since.

Brigitte retired to her beloved French Riviera and spent most of her time avoiding the media and campaigning for animal protection—being particularly vocal in protesting the Canadian seal hunt. Lovers came and went. On her 45th birthday she gave a rare interview and said, of her age, "It's better to be old than dead." Curiously prudish about the state of cinema at the time, the actress commented, "It's true I helped liberalize morals. I was one of the

Brigitte Bardot and Charles Boyer in *Parisienne*.

first to appear nude in a scene. But it was in the script, and it was natural. Today it has gone too far. I'm not a prude, but all this showing of human flesh
on the beaches isn't beautiful."

Her son had been brought up by Charrier and his family, with Brigitte
saying, "I couldn't bring up Nicolas. I couldn't possibly have looked after a
baby. I needed a mother . . . I was completely uprooted, unbalanced, lost in
that crazy world." On her 49th birthday the actress took another overdose of
pills.

She was happier in her world of animals. She became increasingly involved with them and her behavior became more bizarre. In 1982 she led a raid on a dog pound that she considered inhumane. When one of her own dogs drowned in a neighbor's swimming pool, Bardot hired a detective to find the "murderer." Another time a friend brought six lobsters to Bardot's place for dinner. An enraged Bardot, not a vegetarian, threw them into the sea.

Her troubled years as an actress left their mark and Brigitte said bitterly, "I was no good as an actress. I never had the vocation. For 20 years I was cornered like an animal. I had crazy people stealing into my bathroom to take my toothbrush. I was treated as a husband-stealer. One woman wanted to disfigure me with a fork. Even the clergy made me the incarnation of evil."

She was preoccupied with death and admitted thinking of it daily. "It must be our punishment. And we deserve it. It's the decomposition that gets me. You spend your whole life looking after your body. And then you rot away."

In 1987 Bardot auctioned off about $750,000 worth of her jewelry and other possessions to raise money for an animal rights foundation that bore her name. She was then 52. The crowds were so large the sale had to be held in a huge conference center and a street closed off to traffic.

The Bardot mystique remained. "I gave my beauty and my youth to men," said Brigitte, "and now I am giving my wisdom and experience, the best of me, to animals."

Brigitte Bardot Filmography

Le trou normand [Crazy for Love] (1952)

Manina, la fille sans voile [The Girl in the Bikini; The Lighthouse Keeper's Daughter] (1952)

Les Dents longues (1952)

Le Portrait de son père (1953)

Tradita [Night of Love] (1954)

Si Versailles m'était conté [Royal Affairs at Versailles; Versailles] (1954)

Futures vedettes [Sweet Sixteen] (1954)

Le Fils de Caroline chérie (1954)

Un acte d'amour [Act of Love] (1954)

Helen of Troy (1955)

Doctor at Sea (1955)

La lumière d'en face [The Light Across the Street] (1955)

Les Grandes Manoeuvres [Summer Manoeuvres] (1955)

Cette Sacrée Gamine [Mam'zelle Pigalle] (1955)

Mio figlio Nerone [Nero's Weekend] (1956)

En effeuillant la Marguerite [Please, Mr. Balzac; Mam'selle Striptease] (1956)

Et Dieu créa la femme [And God Created Woman] (1956)

La Mariée est trop belle [The Bride Is Too Beautiful] (1956)

Une Parisienne [Parisienne] (1957)

Les Bijoutiers du clair de lune [The Night Heaven Fell; Heaven Fell That Night] (1958)

En cas de malheur [Love Is My Profession] (1958)

La Femme et le pantin [A Woman Like Satan] (1958)

Babette s'en va-t-en guerre [Babette Goes to War] (1959)

Voulez-vous danser avec moi? [Come Dance with Me] (1959)
Le testament d'Orphee (1959)
La Vérité [The Truth] (1960)
L'affaire d'une nuit [It Happened at Night] (1960)
La bride sur le cou [Please, Not Now!] (1961)
Vie privee [A Very Private Affair] (1961)
Les amours celebres (1961)
Le repos du guerrier [Love on a Pillow; Warrior's Rest] (1962)
Tentazioni proibite (1963)
Le mepris [Contempt] (1963)
Paparazzi (1964)
Marie soleil (1964)
Une ravissante idiote [Adorable Idiot; A Ravishing Idiot] (1964)
Viva Maria (1965)
Dear Brigitte (1965)

Masculin-feminin [Masculine-Feminine] (1966)
A coeur joie [Two Weeks in September] (1967)
Shalako (1968)
Histoires extraordinaires [Spirits of the Dead; Tales of Mystery] (1968)
Les femmes (1969)
L'ours et la poupee (1970)
Les novices (1970)
Les petroleuses [The Legend of Frenchie King] (1971)
Boulevard du rhum [Rum Runner] (1971)
Don Juan 1973 ou si Don Juan etait une femme [Don Juan, or if Don Juan Were a Woman] (1973)
L'histoire tres bonne et tres joyeuse de Colinot Trousse-Chemise [The Happy and Joyous Story of Colinot, the Man Who Pulls Up Skirts] (1973)

Sources

"Bardot Auction Boosts Animal Rights," *Globe & Mail*, June 19, 1987, p. A20.
Bender, Marylin. "Miss Bardot: Just an Old-Fashioned Girl Girl," *New York Times*, December 18, 1965, p. 32.
"Brigitte's Mentor," *New Yorker*, 35:34+, May 2, 1959.
Carlson, Peter. "Swept Away by Her Sadness," *People*, 20:34+, October 24, 1983.
"Confessions of a Femme Fatale," *Time*, 121:59, January 10, 1983.
Current Biography 1960. New York: H.W. Wilson, 1961, p. 17–19.
"The Discontented Countess," *Life*, 64.85–86, May 3, 1968.
"Flight from the Sexy?" *Newsweek*, 53:100, February 16, 1959.
Hamill, Pete. "No Place Left to Hide," *Saturday Evening Post*, 238:41–2+, May 8, 1965.
Howard, Toni. "Bad Little Bad Girl," *Saturday Evening Post*, 230:32–33+, June 14, 1958.
The International Dictionary of Films and Filmmakers: Volume III: Actors and Actresses. Chicago: St. James Press, 1986, p. 48–49.
"Notes on People," *New York Times*, September 29, 1979, p. 34.
Quinlan, David. *The Illustrated Directory of Film Stars*. London: B.T. Batsford, 1981, p. 27.
Schneider, P.E. "France's Fabulous Young Five," *New York Times Magazine*, March 30, 1959, p. 12+.
Shipman, David. *The Great Movie Stars: The International Years*. London: Angus & Robertson, 1972, p. 32–38.
"The Star," *Newsweek*, 51:68, January 6, 1958.
Vilallonga, Jose Luis. "The Sensational Brigitte Bardot at 38," *Vogue*, 160:169+, November 1, 1972.
Whitcomb, Jon. "Brigitte Bardot," *Cosmopolitan*, 145:72–77, November, 1958.

Capucine

With a classically structured face, tall slim frame and elegantly cool manner, Capucine became an international model of reknown before switching to film acting. After several years' work in the United States where she studied drama and perfected her English she made her Hollywood screen debut and enjoyed fame there for several years before her popularity just as quickly waned. Capucine returned to Europe and remained alive in films there, usually as support, with the occasional foray back into American productions.

She was born Germaine Lefebvre on January 6, 1933, in Toulon, France, into a wealthy family. Her father was an industrialist. "I had wanted to be a motion picture actress even since I was a child in Toulon," she recalled, "and used to see every film in which my favorite actresses, Greta Garbo, Katharine Hepburn, and Ingrid Bergman appeared."

Early on she changed her name to Capucine, the French word for her favorite flower, nasturtium, explaining, "I hated my real name. In France it's as common as Gladys." As a child she was rebellious and said, "I was very deliberate in changing everything that pertained to my childhood. I came from a very strict bourgeois family, and I knew I wasn't going to do anything they wanted me to do. I never obeyed the rules of childhood. I was always the girl who came home with egg on the face."

Educated at schools mostly in Saumar, France, Capucine got a bachelor of arts degree and her parents suggested she be a schoolteacher. When their daughter balked at that they next suggested she "work in a bank adding figures all day long." Capucine wanted something more glamorous and struck out for Paris. In the French capital she went to a newspaper office and asked if she would be good in photographs. They thought she might and Capucine began her career as a model. Not making much money at first, she took extra jobs. One of these was as an emcee at a Left Bank beatnik bistro where she introduced the acts and read poetry. In 1952 she held the same position on a cruise ship to the Canary Islands. One of the acts she introduced was Brigitte Bardot.

Soon she made enough money modeling to give up the extra jobs as she became one of the best-known French models. Couturiers such as Givenchy and Dior picked her to display their creations all over the world and she quickly became an internationally recognized model globetrotting to places like Rome, Vienna, Athens, Istanbul, Johannesburg, Buenos Aires and Madagascar.

Acting remained in her mind and while in Paris she took dramatic lessons and went to the theater as often as she could. She had long hoped that "fashion modeling might lead me to Hollywood." Capucine had actually made her film debut in a 1949 French release and appeared in two more French films in the 1950s but she only had bit parts. Having hoped for years to get a free trip to the

United States in some way—an unrealized dream—she decided the only way to get there was to pay her own way. In 1956 she arrived in New York, speaking no English and having just two telephone numbers of people who might help her. She began work as a model. Soon she met agent Charles Feldman who told her she would be good in films. The actress did a screen test for director Gregory Ratoff. The test was silent due to her lack of English but Ratoff was impressed enough to send her to Hollywood to work with speech and drama coaches.

Capucine spent the next three years learning the language and said, "I knew that if I was to succeed as a screen actress in Hollywood I not only would have to speak my lines correctly, but would also have to know the various shades of meaning of the words I uttered. In my opinion there is nothing more hollow-sounding than a foreign actress mouthing her words phonetically with only a vague sense of what she is saying."

During her training period the actress was offered several small parts but her agents turned them all down waiting until they judged she was ready for a choice role. That role came in *Song Without End* (1960), the dramatic story of Franz Liszt with Capucine cast as Princess Carolyne, the great love of Liszt. It was a wonderful role for an actress with virtually no experience and she got to wear 40 gowns with 2,000 yards of material after landing the part over one hundred other hopefuls. She got a lot of media hype and was called a new Garbo or Bergman. Her American film debut was less than auspicious, however, and she admitted, "I got ripped to pieces by the critics."

Nevertheless she was happy with her invasion of the United States and said, "I came to America like Christopher Columbus. I didn't know what I would find here. But, as with Columbus, it was my most successful trip." She became the female lead in several more Hollywood films including *North to Alaska* (1960) with John Wayne wherein an Alaskan gold prospector took a girl (Capucine) north from Seattle from his lovesick partner. Capucine did an attractive and spirited job in what was basically a male action film.

Walk on the Wild Side featured her as a hooker in a mature treatment of lesbianism and prostitution while in *Honey Pot* Capucine was Princess Dominique, "a glacially beautiful jetsetter" and one of three former mistresses and victims of a joke played by a very rich man. *The Lion* featured her as the love interest and point of tension between male leads William Holden and Trevor Howard. One reviewer commented she "looks as cooly beautiful in the jungle as in a boudoir." She and Holden began an affair on the set which lasted two years.

On screen she had a cool and poised persona and "glacial" was a term often used to describe her. As *Newsweek* put it, she was "as cold and remote as an icicle." Her best films from that period were comedies wherein she parodied her own persona. One of those films was *The Pink Panther* where she was the perfect comic partner for Peter Sellers, playing his treacherous wife.

Capucine with William Holden in *The Lion*.

Her other major film success was the comedy *What's New Pussycat?* with Capucine drawing excellent notices as a nymphomaniac who was treated by a philandering psychiatrist (Peter Sellers).

By 1965 her glory days as a leading lady in Hollywood were gone as demand for the actress diminished. Capucine left America and settled again in Europe where she indulged in her favorite occupations, said to be acting and eating. During her travels she had acquired exotic tastes and had consumed dishes such as chicken-entrail soup in Cambodia, sheep eyes in North Africa and honey bats in Mauritius. The actress got steady film work in Europe, although not as a lead. She was usually second-billed female and fourth- or fifth-billed overall.

Fraulein Doktor was a World War I spy melodrama with Capucine seventh-billed. She had a fifth-billed support role in *L'incorrigible*, a comedy about a con man. *Soleil Rouge* was a bizarre European-made western in which a samurai (Charles Bronson) and Toshiro Mifune fought the bad guys. The pair had an interlude with two prostitutes, as one reviewer noted, "with one played jocosely by the usually subdued Capucine."

More small roles followed including a part in *Arabian Adventure*, an action-packed costume fantasy; and one in *Jaguar Lives*, a rather dismal kung fu epic. *Aphrodite* was just silly soft-core porn and one critic considered her fortunate saying, "Capucine retires early from the picture, dignity intact."

One of her best appearances was in *Nest of Vipers* with Capucine cast as the mother of a girl who was the victim of another woman's revenge efforts. The actress got excellent notices. *Balles perdues* was a rather anemic detective spoof with the actress injecting brightness into the pedestrian material.

In the early 1980s she was in two Pink Panther films. The first was *Trail of the Pink Panther* which exploited the recent death of Peter Sellers, compiling mostly outtakes and reprised clips from older films of the series. *Curse of the Pink Panther* was a poor imitation with a new actor trying unsuccessfully to portray a Sellers-type bumbling Clouseau. Capucine had little to do in either film as her screen career seemed to slowly wind down. There simply were not many roles of any type, particularly for a woman past the age of fifty.

Capucine Filmography

Rendez-vous de juillet (1949)
Bertrand Coeur de Lion (1950)
Frou-Frou (1955)
Song Without End (1960)
North to Alaska (1960)
Le Triomphe de Michel Strogoff (1961)
Walk on the Wild Side (1961)
The Lion (1961)
I Don Giovanni della Costa Azzurra (1962)
The Pink Panther (1963)
The Seventh Dawn (1963)
What's New Pussycat? (1964)
The Honey Pot (1965)
Le Fate [The Queens] (1966)
Fraulein Doktor (1968)
Las crueles (1968)
Fellini — Satyricon (1969)

Soleil Rouge [Red Sun] (1971)
Jackpot (1975)
L'incorrigible (1975)
Per amore (1976)
Storia di truffe e di imbroglioni [Bluff] (1976)
Ecco noi per esempia (1977)
Ritratto di borghesia in nero [Nest of Vipers] (1977)
Giallo napoleano (1978)
De l'enfer a la victoire (1978)
Arabian Adventure (1978)
Jaguar Lives (1978)
Aphrodite (1982)
Trail of the Pink Panther (1982)
Balles perdues [Stray Bullets] (1983)
Curse of the Pink Panther (1983)

Sources

Hamilton, Jack. "Beauty Under Wraps," *Look,* 24:86+, March 15, 1960.
Harrity, Richard. "The Unknown Star from France," *Cosmopolitan,* 148:10–11, April 1960.
"The Hottest Icicle," *Time,* 86:89, December 10, 1965.
"Les Immortels du cinéma: Capucine," *Ciné Revue,* 63:38–41, August 25, 1983.
Katz, Ephraim. *The Film Encyclopedia.* New York: Thomas Y. Crowell, 1979, p. 204–205.
Lloyd, Ann, ed. *The Illustrated Who's Who of the Cinema.* London: Orbis, 1983, p. 71.

Françoise Dorleac

France produced two famous acting sisters in the 1960s and initially it seemed that Françoise Dorleac, the older of the two, would become the most successful. Françoise arranged for sister Catherine Deneuve, who used their mother's maiden name, to get her first film role. Observers found the older sister spicier and more emotional than the cooler and more sugary younger sibling. By the mid–1960s the pair were about equally famed; then Françoise tragically died in a car crash when she was just 25.

Dorleac was born in Paris, France, on March 21, 1942, the daughter of Maurice Dorleac who was a minor character actor on the French stage. Growing up she attended a convent school until she was 15 and took ballet lessons as a little girl. She threw herself into ballet with such energy that she kept dancing even after her toes were so raw they bled. Mrs. Dorleac recalled a definite difference between the two girls and remembered Françoise hurling herself at everything "with passion" while describing Catherine as a "tender, fragile little girl who loved candy."

The family consisted of four daughters and Françoise recalled Catherine as being very fragile and always ill with the result that Mrs. Dorleac spent more time with her than with the other three girls. "I understood the reasons," said Françoise, "but I was jealous just the same of the time she gave her." There would always be a rivalry between them.

At the age of ten the young girl made her stage debut and sporadically continued in the theater. She later began modeling for Christian Dior. When she was 15 she was dancing at a club with some friends when a photographer approached her and asked her to model for some fashion pictures. Dorleac agreed and a producer saw one of those photos and gave her a small role in a short film *Mensonges* (1957) which was shot during the summer holidays.

After convent school Dorleac went to a public school for a couple of years, but said, "I had terrible grades. I couldn't write compositions — it was very difficult." She transferred to the Conservatoire d'Art Dramatique in 1959 and studied there until 1961, concentrating on her real love — acting.

During her time at the school she appeared on the stage several times most notably in a run of several months duration as the title character in *Gigi*. Françoise found it difficult to get to class on time in the mornings and was always laughing. "They did not like this. It disturbed the class, but I couldn't help it, so I left school and went to work full time." By then she was already well established as a film actress. Always ambitious, the actress said, "From the time I am a little girl, I have wanted to act always, and be the finest actress I can."

Her first appearance in a full-length film came with a minor part in the 1959 release *Les Loups dans la Bergerie* which was about a group of gangsters who hid in a home for delinquents, exposing themselves as cowards thus destroying their image as heroes in the eyes of the kids. The next year she had a part in *The Door Slams* and the producers were looking for someone to play her younger sister. "I have a younger sister at home," said Dorleac, "why look for somebody else?" They did not and Catherine made her film debut.

The year 1961 was busy for Françoise who had appearances in five films. Most of the parts she had were minor and drew no critical notice. However, she was third-billed in *La Gamberge* and for most of the remaining films during her career she would be the top-billed female. *La Gamberge* was a satirical comedy with jokes about youth, television and journalism. Françoise played a young country girl who hitched a ride to Paris hoping to find a career and a Prince Charming.

Her first leading role came in *Arsène Lupin contre Arsène Lupin,* the story of the activities of the two sons of a famous turn-of-the-century burglar, Arsène Lupin, in the 1920s. Dorleac was adequate in the poor role of a love interest. More than any other film, *La Peau douce,* directed by François Truffaut, shot her to international fame. It was the story of a man's first extramarital affair in twelve years of marriage. Dorleac received excellent reviews as the air hostess with whom the man began an ill-fated affair.

La Chasse à l'homme (1964) was a weak comedy about bachelors reluctant to marry. Dorleac was one of the women trying to get a man to the altar. Fourth-billed overall and lead female, the actress was still billed ahead of Catherine who was in the same film and sixth-billed. Françoise said of her sister, "She dresses very different from me, in ribbons and lots of pink." Catherine used the zodiac to explain the differences and said, "I'm Libra (the passive, love-prone), and she is Aries (the ram), always running like that."

To create the kind of image Françoise wanted both off the screen and on, the actress spent hours on her clothes and hair and was said to design herself like a stage set. "It's extraordinarily important," she said, "I want to dress so that everybody tries to dress like me, and nobody can. I love it when you are completely dressed and you look naked. I wear chain belts to look fragile, like a slave. Every time I go out, even if it's six o'clock in the morning, when nobody can see, it's still important." It was important to her that she "keep a certain class, but look erotic."

Françoise turned in some of her best work in the last two years of her life. *Where the Spies Are* starred David Niven as a mild-mannered English doctor pressed into espionage. Dorleac was second-billed, playing a double agent, and was described by one reviewer as being "lushly effective." The film *Genghis Khan* was strictly a man's film but as the lead female Françoise overcame a weak part and appeared to good advantage as Khan's wife. The part had her age from a teenager into a woman in her thirties and it was one of her favorite roles.

The most crucial element of filmmaking to the actress was the director and

Françoise Dorleac in *Where the Spies Are.*

she said, "The most important thing for me in making a film is the director upon whom I must rely. If I have confidence in him, then I can work. Otherwise I am nothing." She was directed by Roman Polanski in *Cul-de-sac* and commented, "Polanski is completely preoccupied with film; he doesn't think about the actors as human beings at all. But I do not mind it; he is a brilliant director." In that offbeat comedy drama she played a bored and flirtatious wife and while she did not like the egotistical character she played, "Françoise gave an excellent performance and enhanced her acting reputation.

Despite acting success she remained insecure. "I find that with each picture, I become more insecure, less confident about my ability to do good work," Françoise said. She had not moved away from home until 1965, long after being established as a highly successful actress. The move came at the insistence of her mother. Mrs. Dorleac felt Françoise should learn to take care of her own home and prepare for life. Mrs. Dorleac found an apartment for her daughter, which was across the street from the family residence.

The actress's views on marriage were very traditional and she said, "It is a pity that a career takes away from a woman's femininity. To be a woman, one must be married and have children and raise a family. Until this comes I do not feel that I am a woman." But Dorleac never married saying, "I want to be loved without compromises."

She and Deneuve were reunited on the screen in the 1967 release *Les Demoiselles de Rochefort*. It was a musical about small-town life by Jacques Demy, the same writer director whose successful musical *The Umbrellas of Cherbourg* made Deneuve a big star. As twins, *Variety* said Dorleac and Deneuve played "with the right mixture of feminine guile, passiveness and stubborn aggressiveness when it comes to the men they want." In that film Deneuve was first-billed with Dorleac second and the rivalry was still in evidence. Dorleac said she had wanted her sister's part in *Les Demoiselles de Rochefort*. Of the films Deneuve had done, Françoise insisted that except for *Cherbourg* and Polanski's *Repulsion* they "were not worth making. I would have turned them down," she said, despite the fact the sisters had twice before appeared in the same film.

While the actress had never made a Hollywood film the idea had crossed her mind. "I would like to make a big film in Hollywood," she said, "but I am afraid of going there. I only want to do it when I am ready, when it won't be wrong for my career." Fame had come easily to Françoise, who once said, "My career has come without any trouble at all. I make money, but I spend it all. I don't know on what, on clothes, all sorts of things."

Her last film was *Billion Dollar Brain,* an unimpressive spy drama released after her death. Dorleac played a double agent and added a touch of glamour to an otherwise lackluster film. Near the end of June 1967, Dorleac was vacationing with Deneuve at a villa in the south of France at Saint Tropez. On the 26th of that month she was driving alone towards the Nice airport when she lost control of the vehicle, perhaps because of the wet road, and crashed into a concrete road sign. The car burst into flames and the actress burned to death. Françoise was just three months past her 25th birthday and had appeared in 18 films.

Françoise Dorleac Filmography

Mensonges (short) (1957)
Les Loups dans la Bergerie [The
   Damned and the Daring] (1959)

Les Portes claquent [The Door Slams]
   (1960)
La Gamberge (1961)

Le Jeu de la vérité (1961)
Tout l'or du monde [All the Gold in the World] (1961)
Ce Soir ou jamais (1961)
La Fille aux yeux d'or [The Girl with the Golden Eyes] (1961)
Arsène Lupin contre Arsène Lupin (1962)
L'Homme de Rio [That Man from Rio] (1964)
La Peau douce [The Soft Skin; Silken Skin] (1964)
La Ronde [Circle of Love] (1964)
La Chasse à l'homme [Male Hunt] (1964)
Where the Spies Are (1965)
Genghis Khan (1965)
Cul-de-Sac (1966)
Les Demoiselles de Rochefort [The Young Girls of Rochefort] (1967)
Billion Dollar Brain (1967)

Sources

"Françoise Dorleac—Gamine fatale," *Vogue,* 144:44, October 1, 1964.
"Françoise Dorleac, 25, Is Dead," *New York Times,* June 27, 1967, p. 39.
Harris, T. George. "Sister Stars of France," *Look,* 29:90–93, June 1, 1965.
Katz, Ephraim. *The Film Encyclopedia.* New York: Thomas Y. Crowell, 1979, p. 353.
Lloyd, Ann, ed. *The Illustrated Who's Who of the Cinema.* London: Orbis, 1983, p. 127.
Miller, Edwin. "An Actress Alone," *Seventeeen,* 25:164+, November 1966.
Quinlan, David. *Quinlan's Illustrated Directory of Film Stars.* London: B.T. Batsford, 1986, p. 121.
"Transition," *Newsweek,* 70:98, July 10, 1967.

Marie-France Pisier

Americans claimed Marie-France Pisier had a fleeting resemblance to Claudette Colbert while in Europe she was called the "thinking man's Brigitte Bardot." She worked for years in film without drawing much recognition at home or abroad. At 30, suddenly famous and in demand, the actress journeyed to Hollywood for a much publicized debut film there. The picture bombed and Pisier scurried back to France to continue her career, having satisfied her curiosity about the American film capital and her desire to make a commercial film. Hollywood would not figure in her future again.

Marie-France Pisier was born in May 1944 in Dalat, Indochina (now Vietnam), the daughter of Paula and George Pisier. George was a colonial governor of Halong Bay. When she was six the family was transferred to Noumea, New Caledonia, where the youngster spent the rest of her childhood, raised with an older sister and younger brother. Life in the French South Pacific was both comfortable and enjoyable for Marie-France who recalled, "It was the most beautiful childhood you can imagine. I was like a little boy, running barefoot on limitless beaches, riding horses in the surf with a gang of friends."

Six years later in 1956 the Pisiers divorced and Mrs. Pisier took her three children back to Paris on a cargo boat. They arrived with just two hundred dollars. Having spent so much time in the tropics the family was not used to Paris weather and found it unbearably cold. Three months after arriving in the French capital the family packed up for the South of France and settled in Nice. The children all became excellent students with Marie-France attending the Lycée des Jeunes Filles for five years while Mrs. Pisier worked.

The teenager found the example of her mother to be more than enough motivation to do well at school. Mrs. Pisier had been a medical student but gave up her studies when she married. After her divorce Mrs. Pisier could only obtain menial work—one job was putting stamps on envelopes on the night shift. Excelling at school was a way to secure her future since, Marie-France thought, "It was too risky not to be independent."

At school Pisier took part in stage productions and at 16 became involved with an amateur film and theater group. Her film debut came with a small part in the 1961 release *Qui ose nous accuser?* but a bigger break came her way the next year when she was discovered by François Truffaut. While Marie-France was performing in a play in Nice a newspaper critic was impressed enough to send his review and Pisier's picture to the director. Truffaut was looking for a girl to play in *L'Amour a vingt ans (Love at Twenty),* a short film that was the sequel to *The 400 Blows.* The director brought Pisier to Paris for a test and gave her the part.

For the next several years Marie-France combined university and films, making a couple motion pictures a year while pursuing her studies. She took degrees in both law and political science although she never practiced law. Despite her film work she had no trouble passing her exams and said, "Films were becoming more and more important to me and I didn't care if I passed the exams or not. So I did."

University officials were not always happy about her other career and when she once asked to do some course work by correspondence during a film shoot, the rector said, "Films were a quite inadequate excuse for anything." Pisier commented, "I think we are not so far from Molière's time, when all actresses had bad reputations and performers could not be buried in cemeteries with decent people." She continued with her education because it was important to her mother and to ease her own fears of having nothing to fall back on.

Before 1974 she had appeared in 16 films often in supporting roles in films of low budget with an "artsy" content and films with limited commercial appeal. She worked with Truffaut again in *Baisers volés (Stolen Kisses)* but most of her work received no distribution in the United States. "Truffaut was like a father in introducing me to the cinema and influencing me to become a cinephile," said the actress. Marie-France did not consider the way she was discovered to be unusual and remarked, "I never even realized that acting was work, a profession. That was the moment anyway, when the greatest compliment

Victor Lanoux *(left)*, Marie-France Pisier and Guy Marchand in *Cousin, Cousine*.

you could give an actor was to say he was 'natural.' The new wave was finding actors in the streets every day."

Souvenirs d'en France (1974) proved to be a breakthrough film for the actress as she got tremendous reviews and for the first time played a part that was not 'natural' for her. She moved on to another critical success with a role in *Celine and Julie Go Boating* and then an even bigger success the next year in *Cousin, Cousine*, in which she played the zany, neurotic and betrayed woman to perfection, earning a Cesar (French Oscar) for her work. These films turned her into a major star at home and brought her international recognition as well. Her image as an actress who appeared only in inaccessible intellectual films was still firmly entrenched and when she arrived on the set of a 1976 film with Jean-Paul Belmondo, the actor joked, "Here comes the star of the cinémathèque to honor us on a commercial set."

Pisier has also established a reputation as a radical feminist and took part in the 1968 student revolts in France. The actress explained, "It is most difficult to be young in Paris. French society is structured against the young. There are no jobs for university graduates." In 1976, along with other prominent French women such as Simone de Beauvoir, Marie-France signed a petition in support of legalized abortion. She admitted to having had an illegal abortion and ran the risk of being jailed. "And as for equality of the sexes, there is very little," said the actress, "French women are underprivileged." She did not feel it was any different in film and volunteered, "Any time a woman had a lead in a film they call it feminist."

Marie-France began living with lawyer Georges Kiejman in the early 1970s and the couple married a couple of years later. Kiejman was a practicing lawyer and often represented motion picture and record companies.

Pisier's new fame in Europe led to a screen test in Hollywood and the lead role in her first American film *The Other Side of Midnight* at a reported salary of $120,000. She played a French girl who was impregnated and abandoned during World War II by an American airman. The character aborts herself with a coat hanger, uses her body to become a top film star and many years later takes revenge. "It is what you Americans call a soap opera," said Marie-France, "I do not know how it will be received but I hope well, because I would like to make other films here."

Even though she had already made over 20 films, the Hollywood film was the first to require her to do nude scenes. The men were not required to appear nude. Nervous about it at first, she went ahead with the scene and then rationalized, "If a nude scene makes sense, if it adds to the mood and the motives of the characters, if it is necessary for the story, I have no objections. . . . If men in the audience want to look at me with sensuality in their eyes, so be it."

The Other Side of Midnight was a big budget feature with Marie-France getting a lot of publicity after landing her much sought-after role. In a massive understatement, producer Frank Yablans said of the film, "It is not the intellectual movie of the decade." The film was an abomination and panned by critics. The publicists even admitted it was dreadful.

Pisier had come to Hollywood against the advice of friends such as Jeanne Moreau, partly because she said, "I have always been in intellectual pictures that have had very good critiques but did not do very well at the box office. I wanted to do a commercial picture." She explained, "My idea was very cynical, that it would be good for me to make a commercial movie, and it would be helpful for directors in France who wanted to use me if I had a big success. I hate so much to be labeled the intellectual actress of the New Wave."

Pisier had also come to California to satisfy her curiosity about Hollywood and American filmmaking. "Hollywood," she said, "is like a clinic. Everyone comes here to get well, to find a career, a husband, stardom, to find something. I am one of the patients." She found the Hollywood set like an "enormous factory" where people worked ten times harder. In Hollywood an actor was "supposed to know what you're going to do. In France with the New Wave directors, you arrive to find out what you're going to do."

Marie-France Pisier and Raf Vallone in *The Other Side of Midnight*.

Marie-France maintained a tactful silence about *The Other Side of Midnight* saying only, "I don't know if I can tell the truth, it might be a little like spitting in the soup. . . . Anyhow, I thought I could be a good actress in a bad film. In France, I could play against the dialogue. If it's bad, I can slalom it; I can play it ironically. I didn't realize that I couldn't handle it in English. In English, I don't feel the words completely. I miss nuance."

The Other Side of Midnight was the only motion picture Pisier made in Hollywood. She quickly returned to France and expressed happiness to be going to work on "a small intellectual film. In France you feel much more like in a family."

Back in Europe Marie-France appeared in 18 films over a span of eight years (1977–1985). She reunited with Truffaut for *Love on the Run*, starred with Isabelle Adjani and Isabelle Huppert in *The Brontë Sisters* and portrayed fashion designer Gabrielle Chanel in *Chanel solitaire*.

Throughout her career Pisier has always been willing to take supporting roles in films even after becoming a major film star. "You don't have the picture on your shoulders, and you can take chances and enjoy the risks. I would always go back to supporting stars if it's a good part." Students spending a year abroad was the subject of *French Postcards*, with Pisier in a support role as part of the husband and wife team who ran the school. Pisier, said *Variety*, "developed an attractive and fasacinating character." In *Le Banquiere* she played the wife of a man who was lover to a journalist and banker (Romy Schneider) who dominated French financial circles in the 1920s. Marie-France put jealousy aside to side with her rival.

She did well in *The Magic Mountain* where she played a passionate Russian woman. Pisier was one of the characters in a Swiss sanitorium in an adaptation of the Thomas Mann novel about the pre–World War I decay of European society. In *L'As des as* she was cast as a reporter but had little to do in what was basically a vehicle for Jean-Paul Belmondo. *Hot Touch* was a dismal and poorly-made film about a jewel thief caper. The actress was little more than love interest to the male lead.

Marie-France was the female lead in *Le Prix du danger,* a sci-fi thriller about televised manhunts, and was one of many conquests of a womanizer in *L'Ami de Vincent*. She had the lead in *Les Nanas* which had an all-female cast in an update of Clare Booth's *The Women*. The action centered around Pisier whose ideas of liberated relationships toppled when her lover started to see other women. She gave an excellent performance while one of her worst came in *Parking*, a pop remake of the Orpheus legend. Pisier played Persephone, the fashion conscious niece of the Devil—a dismal film in all ways.

About her philosophy of acting, Marie-France Pisier commented, "I believe in taking chances. I'm suspicious about everything except that. My way is to feel fear. To be an actress can be quite scary."

Marie-France Pisier Filmography

Qui ose nous accuser? (1961)
L'Amour a vingt ans [Love at Twenty] (1962)
Les Saints ntouches [Wild Living] (1962)
Les Amoureux de France (1962)
La Mort d'un tueur (1963)
Young Girls of Good Families (1963)
Les yeux Cernes (1964)
Le Vampire de Dusseldorf (1964)
Trans-Europ-Express (1966)
No sta bene rubare il tesoro (1966)
Baisers voles [Stolen Kisses] (1967)
L'Ecume des jours (1967)
Nous n'irons plus au bois (1968)
Paulina s'en va (1969)
Le Journal d'un suicide (1971)
Feminin, feminin (1971)
Souvenirs d'en France [French Provincial] (1974)
Celine et Julie vont en bateau [Celine and Julie Go Boating] (1974)
Cousin, Cousine (1975)
Serail (1975)
Barocco (1976)
Le Corps de mon ennemi (1976)
The Other Side of Midnight (1977)
Les apprentis Sorciers (1977)
L'Amour en fruite [Love on the Run] (1978)
The Brontë Sisters (1978)
French Postcards (1979)
Miss Right (1980)
Le Banquiere [The Woman Banker] (1980)
44, ou les recits de la nuit (1980)
The Hot Touch (1981)
Chanel solitaire (1981)
Der Zauberberg [The Magic Mountain] (1982)
Meurtres sous protection (1982)
Boulevard des assassins (1982)

L'As des as [Ace of Aces] (1982)
Le Prix du danger [The Prize of Peril]
  (1983)
Der stille Ozean [The Silent Ocean]
  (1983)

L'Ami de Vincent [A Friend of Vincent] (1983)
Les Nanas [The Chicks] (1985)
Parking (1985)

Sources

Buck, Joan Juliet. "Marie-France Pisier," *Vogue*, 162:238+, May 1977.
Champlin, Charles. "Carrying a Brief for Film," *Los Angeles Times*, January 28, 1977, sec. 4, p. 1.
Chase, Chris. "At the Movies," *New York Times*, October 16, 1981, p. C8.
Katz, Ephraim. *The Film Encyclopedia*. New York: Thomas Y. Crowell, 1979, p. 915.
Lloyd, Ann, ed. *The Illustrated Who's Who of the Cinema*. London: Orbis, 1983, p. 348.
"New Faces of '77," *Newsweek*, 89:62, February 14, 1977.
"Newsmakers," *Newsweek*, 89:47, May 16, 1977.
Quinlan, David. *Quinlan's Illustrated Directory of Film Stars*. London: B.T. Batsford, 1986, p. 346–7.
Russell, Bruce. "A Hollywood Connection," *Washington Post*, February 10, 1977, p. D14.
Shearer, Lloyd. "Introducing Marie-France Pisier," *Washington Post*, March 6, 1977, Parade sec., p. 9+.
Stone, Elizabeth. "Marie-France Pisier: What's a Woman Like Her Doing in a Film Like That?" *Village Voice*, 22:39+, June 20, 1977.
Thomas, Kevin. "Marie-France Pisier: The Impossible Girl," *Los Angeles Times*, November 17, 1979, sec. 2, p. 6–7+.
Turan, Kenneth. "What's a Good Actress Like You Doing in a Movie Like This?" *Washington Post*, June 21, 1977, p. B1.

Catherine Deneuve

Catherine Deneuve has fascinated audiences with her cool beauty and detached, almost haughty aura. Whether playing the role of a whore or an upper class socialite, Deneuve appears aloof and withdrawn. Some detractors have interpreted this as simply a lack of talent, and believe she is unable to convey emotion, while critics who admire Deneuve perceive her as enigmatic and intriguing.

She was born Catherine Dorleac on October 22, 1943, in Paris, France. Both of her parents were actors and one of Catherine's three sisters, Françoise, also became an actress. Catherine adopted her mother's maiden name for professional purposes. Deneuve was a frail child and led a sheltered bourgeois life. One source even maintained that she was bottle-fed until the age of nine. Her father described her as very introspective as a child. "She was something of a hypocrite, too. It was always difficult to know what she really thought," he said. "She did not do well at school. Most subjects bored her. It is difficult for

Catherine Deneuve in a publicity photo.

me to talk about Catherine," her father continued, "because, though we are very close, I don't feel I know her all that well."

She rarely saw her father perform because of the social stigma associated with a stage career. Catherine's elementary education was in a Catholic girls' school, and then an exclusive high school. During her teens she had a few bit parts in films, and her older sister, Françoise, who was an ambitious actress, encouraged Deneuve to try out for parts. They appeared in several films together which were mainly low budget.

When she was 17, Catherine met director Roger Vadim who became her lover and the father of her son Christian who was born in 1962. The affair lasted a couple of years but neither wanted to marry. It took a great deal of courage for Deneuve to have a child at that time without being married. Catherine appeared in Vadim's film *Vice and Virtue* in which she played an innocent girl who was victimized by the Nazis. She was also cast as a rich girl, in a film produced by Vadim called *Et Satan conduit le bal,* and was in another film about vacationing couples. None of these films made an impact on Deneuve's career. Catherine was not overly concerned. Vadim remarked that in those years, Deneuve "never had that drive to be in films. But living with me, she wanted to get involved in that part of my life." Vadim also commented on Deneuve's shyness. "It's an extraordinary thing," he recalled, "but for the first year we lived together she hardly spoke at all. She was incredibly reserved."

Catherine became friends with Jacques Demy and his wife Agnes Varda, who were both directors. Demy cast her in his film *The Umbrellas of Cherbourg*. Styled like a Hollywood musical, the movie became a popular international success. Catherine played the daughter of an umbrella merchant, who is coerced into an unhappy marriage after her true love joins the army. Deneuve's lines were dubbed by a singing stand-in, yet Deneuve won rave reviews from critics and received the Best Actress award at Cannes in 1964. She only earned $5,000 for her work in the film.

Encouraged by the praise and attention she received, Deneuve became more enthusiastic about acting. "Before *Umbrellas of Cherbourg,* I did not take acting seriously," she told one interviewer. She credited Demy with giving her confidence. "Jacques made me feel that I am beautiful," she explained. "He sees, too, that I am sensitive. He made me learn to act, to love acting for the first time, to believe what I act."

Other directors became interested in working with Deneuve and she appeared in several films in the early 1960s. Her most memorable one from that period was Polanski's *Repulsion* in which she played a schizophrenic whose sexual obsessions lead to murder. "She looks like a professional virgin, but sexy," Polanski said of Deneuve. "Not sexy like Marilyn Monroe, nor with Bardot's bitchy Lolita quality," he continued. "She's like a man's niece that he takes on his knee. All those dirty magazines in France play her up; they think she's ripe for exploitation as a sex goddess because she had a kid out of wedlock. She hates that. She fights it."

Polanski had to convince Deneuve to do nude scenes. "It's an incredible deal to undress her because she's so shy," he said. "Deneuve did pose nude for a magazine layout, again at the behest of Polanski, who no doubt realized the publicity potential for his movie. *Playboy* published some stills from *Repulsion* showing Deneuve writhing on the floor naked, with the caption "Queen of the Parisian Cinema Sex Pots." Catherine was embarrassed by the exposure and later said, "It was a terrible, terrible mistake. I will never do anything like that again."

British fashion photographer David Bailey had taken the shots for the nude magazine spread. He and Catherine married on August 18, 1965. The ceremony was in London. The bride wore black and Mick Jagger was best man. The marriage lasted until 1970.

Polanski described his working relationship with Deneuve as "the best I've ever had." He found her to be very insecure about her talent, however, and noted, "She doesn't believe in herself; she thinks she will never be a great actress. She says she does it because it is the only thing she knows. I tried to convince her otherwise, because I think she has a talent, but she thought I was simply flattering her."

Most critics were impressed after seeing *Repulsion*. Catherine's performance was described as "simply splendid." She was said to have played the part with "haunting detachment," and was "secretive in nursing her obsession and starkly sad in her insanity." Deneuve was more modest about her accomplishment. "The hardest thing in film acting is not to play a crazy woman," she felt. "It is to walk across a room with no pockets in your dress, and still make the audience believe."

Polanski thought that Deneuve became too involved in her character and said, "Catherine was strongly influenced by the film. She got very nervous. Sometimes she would get the same look in life that she had on camera and I would think, 'In another two or three weeks she'll have gone round the bend.'" Perhaps Polanski was embroidering a bit for media effect, or else Deneuve was protective of her feelings because she told an interviewer that in one scene where she had to stab a man, "I am able to discard the emotion completely the moment we finish. You must never become so involved that you bring the role away from work with you. I stab the man again and again, he suffers horribly, there is blood everywhere. Then we finish, and right away we all laugh, and wipe off the blood, and go and eat lunch together!"

Deneuve continued to work with European directors during the next couple of years in films of varying quality. In 1967 her international reputation soared again when she appeared in Buñuel's *Belle de Jour*. Deneuve played Severine, the wife of a physician, who fulfills her masochistic fantasies by working part-time in a brothel. Buñuel structured the film so that the audience was never certain if Severine's experiences were real or merely products of her imagination.

Deneuve was required to be nude in many of the scenes, a state she found "excruciating." She fortified herself with liquor in order to lose her inhibitions. In one shot she is stripped half naked, strung up from a tree and whipped.

Deneuve explained her approach to the character of Severine: "Buñuel called me an Anglo-Saxon, someone with a static visage, a constant deadpan. We kept it that way . . . It corresponds to my own nature . . . My theory of acting . . . is to communicate through nuances—by keeping things very natural, simple, hidden, dissimulated." Deneuve considered *Belle de Jour* to be her best film.

Michel Deville who directed Deneuve as an 18th-century coquette in a comedy called *Benjamin,* described Catherine's technique by saying, "It's not really a question of expression. Even the great Garbo didn't change her expression that much. She just created a mood around her, and Deneuve is growing more and more capable of the same . . . There is something very cold and untouchable about her. She hides herself," Deville stated. "She's an enigma and mystery."

Deville enjoyed working with Deneuve. "She is wonderful to direct," he said. "She is a violin you can set vibrating." Other directors were equally

Catherine Deneuve comforts Terence Hill in *March or Die.*

enthusiastic. "Her great virtue," said Demy, "is that she is absolutely at the service of the director."

Deneuve appeared with her sister, Françoise Dorleac, in *The Young Girls of Rochefort,* directed by Demy. It was another light musical but this time critics were disappointed with the production. The film became significant, however, as the last movie in which the sisters performed together. In 1967 Dorleac died in a car accident. Deneuve was devastated by the tragedy and her marriage to Bailey began to crumble. Bailey once told the sisters that between them they made the perfect female. After Françoise's death he wondered if he was married to "half a woman." Yet it was Catherine who wanted the separation and Bailey claimed to be "still mad about her."

Deneuve kept busy working. Omar Sharif was her costar in the historical drama *Mayerling.* Catherine played a baroness, and critic Judith Crist noted,

"Miss Deneuve successfully lays to rest any delusions...about her being able to act beyond simulating a lovely blank-eyed marble statue." One of the reasons Deneuve accepted the role was her love for extravagant costumes. "I have a passion for furs," she explained.

In Jean Aurel's *Manon 70* Catherine had a 15-minute bathtub scene. Said Aurel of Deneuve, "She was superb, and only complained when the water got cold."

Deneuve went to the United States to film *The April Fools*. She was lured by the $250,000 salary. Catherine played the wife of a prosperous New Yorker. She leaves him and runs off to Paris with a more attentive lover, played by Jack Lemmon. Said Jack of his costar, "She's very young, but she's a woman. That's for damn sure." The movie made little impression on the critics but the American press was fascinated by Deneuve and she was written up in the *New York Times, Time, Look, Newsweek* and *Life*. While in New York Deneuve studied English and took dance classes with Martha Graham.

Deneuve had no plans to establish a career in the United States, however. "I can't retain my Frenchness over here," she explained. "My French temperament, the fact that I want to live in France, my accent, these are all going to work against me," she said of her opportunity to stay in America.

Deneuve became more secure about her acting talent with each film that she made. She cultivated a discreet, remote persona. "I try to do things as simply and naturally as possible," she explained of her acting methods. "I hate the word effort. I like things that are not obvious." Demy described her technique as subtle and noted, "Her real value on camera is in close-ups."

Deneuve also had a duality that worked perfectly for roles requiring a mixture of innocence and perversity. Vadim described her as "very clean even when she was acting on an erotic level." Polanski cast her in *Repulsion* because he wanted "an angelic girl who could kill a man with a razor."

Catherine was very aware that her main appeal was her looks, however. "A woman's beauty on the screen has to be a dream for other people," she felt. This dependence on her appearance made her insecure about aging. When she was only 24 she worried, "How long can it last? It can't go on." She used a great deal of makeup even in her youth, and dyed her hair blonde to transform herself from a pretty to a strikingly beautiful woman. Deneuve also loved luxury, sumptuous houses, jewelry, extensive wardrobes and furs. Her stardom separated her from her own generation. In 1968 when Paris youths were storming the barricades, Deneuve was being chauffeured around Manhattan in an air-conditioned limousine.

Catherine's instincts were extremely bourgeois but her life, in many ways, ran counter to the status quo. She not only had an illegitimate child, but her career, not marriage, was the focus of her life. "A woman has three security valves," she commented, "a man, a child, a job; in my code it stands in that order, yet in my real life, the order is reversed."

For someone like Deneuve who found it difficult to reveal herself to anyone, the mask of an actress was wonderfully safe. Deneuve described herself as totally pessimistic. "It's tough on earth, that's all I believe in. Life is a jungle. You eat or get eaten," she said. Yet Deneuve was, despite her icy exterior, a woman of deep feelings. "Passion is the only way out," she believed. "For me, the greatest luxury on earth would be to be able to abandon myself to passion."

Deneuve continued to work steadily in films, mainly in Europe. She was directed by Truffaut in *The Mississippi Mermaid,* a love story costarring Jean-Paul Belmondo. One critic compared her to the frosty heroines of Hitchcock films, and noted a resemblance to Grace Kelly.

Buñuel cast her as a young orphan corrupted by her guardian (Fernando Rey) in his film *Tristana.* Deneuve got good reviews and her performance was described as "magnificent," "perfect," "precise" and "magnificently controlled."

In the early 1970s she costarred with Marcello Mastroianni in a couple of films. Their collaboration flowered into a romance and Catherine gave birth to his daughter in 1972. The affair with Marcello continued for about three years.

Deneuve's films were of varying quality in the 1970s. She appeared in gangster films, comedies, and melodramas with directors such as Ferreri, Szabo, Lelouch and Demy. In 1975 she was cast as a high-class callgirl in another American film *Hustle,* directed by Robert Aldrich and costarring Burt Reynolds. The American public, however, was more familiar with Deneuve as the woman who appeared in television ads for Mercury cars and Chanel perfumes.

As Deneuve approached 40, her roles increasingly exaggerated her dual persona. As one observer noted, earlier in her career Deneuve epitomized "woman as destroying angel — a whore with a heart, not of gold, but of glass." In one of her more recent films *The Hunger,* directed by Tony Scott, Deneuve as a vampire "outwardly unmarked by age, has decayed to the core with centuries of lust and self-regard. Yet her innocence remains, almost to the end, unsullied, her tenderness for her dying partner David Bowie sincere and touching, her seduction of Susan Sarandon no mere acquisition of fresh meat but an act of carnal and spiritual love."

Deneuve was once anxious that "one day I'll be a forty-year-old cynical woman going from affair to affair." Yet at that age she was lovelier than ever and lived contentedly in Paris with her two children. "Forty is not so old anymore," she realized. Nor was she concerned about working with younger male costars such as Gerard Depardieu in *Fort Saganne,* the tale of a legendary swashbuckler of the Sahara in the early 1900s.

In the 1980s Deneuve tried to select roles that challenged her. She appeared in *Love Songs* because her character must juggle a husband, family, career and lover without breaking apart. In the murder drama *Scene of the Crime,* directed by Andre Techine, Deneuve played a middle-aged single mother, a part that paralleled her real life. Yet Deneuve did not identify with her screen persona. "The image is just a distillation of what you seem to be," she said. One critic felt that *Scene of the Crime* proved that Catherine was "a more and more resourceful actress as she grows older."

In 1985 Deneuve's face was chosen by a popular poll to be the model for the sculpture of the mythological woman who symbolizes the French Republic. She succeeded Brigitte Bardot who had previously had the honor for 15 years. Deneuve was surprised that she was chosen for this exalted symbol since her affairs and illegitimate children had often been the subjects of malicious gossip. Deneuve felt that the choice reflected "something interesting in the turn of the mentality, of what the ideal working woman would be today. She's someone who has children on her own ... who's trying to manage both things." Deneuve had never felt a part of the women's liberation movement, but she was aware of conditions for women and signed a highly publicized petition demanding abortion rights for women in France.

Catherine Deneuve has made over 60 films during her career. Her work is vital to her. "When I'm making a movie, I am all right," she explained. "I know I am a good actress and I feel the flow of life moving through me and into the camera."

Catherine Deneuve Filmography

Les Collégiennes (1956)
Les Petits Chats (1959)
Les Portes claquent (1960)
L'Homme à femmes (1960)
Les Parisiennes [ep. Sophie] (1961)
Et Satan conduit le bal (1962)
Le Vice et la vertu (1962)
Vacances portugaises (1962)
Les Plus Belles Escorqueries du monde (1963)
Les Parapluies de Cherbourg [The Umbrellas of Cherbourg] (1964)
La Chasse a l'homme (1964)
Un Monsieur de compagnie (1964)
La costanza della ragione [Avec amour et avec rage] (1964)
Repulsion (1964)
Le Chant du monde (1965)
La Vie de château (1965)
Das Liebeskrussell (1965)
Les Créatures (1966)
Belle de Jour (1967)

Les Demoiselles de Rochefort [The Young Girls of Rochefort] (1967)
Benjamin ou Les memoires d'un puceau (1968)
Manon 70 (1968)
La Chamade (1968)
Mayerling (1968)
The April Fools (1969)
La Sirene du Mississippi [The Mississippi Mermaid] (1969)
Tout peut arriver [Don't Be Blue] (1969)
Tristana (1970)
Peau d'âne (1970)
Henri Langlois (1970)
Ça n'arrive qu'aux autres (1971)
Liza [La Cagna] (1971)
Un Flic [Dirty Money] (1972)
L'Evénement le plus important depuis que l'homme a marche sur la lune [The Slightly Pregnant Man] (1973)
Touche pas la femme blanche (1973)

*Fatti di gente perbene [La Grande
Bourgeoisie; The Murri Affair]*
(1974)
La Femme aux bottes rouges
(1974)
Zig-Zag (1974)
L'Agression (1975)
Hustle (1975)
Le Sauvage [Lovers Like Us]
(1975)
Si c'etait a refaire [Second Chance]
(1976)
Anima persa (1976)
March or Die (1977)
Coup de foudre (1977)
Casotto (1977)
L'Argent des autres [de Chalonge]
(1978)
*Si je suis comme ca c'est la faute de
papa [When I Was a Kid, I Didn't
Dare]* (1978)

Ecoute voir (1978)
Ils sont grands ces petits (1979)
A Nous deux [Adventure for Two]
(1979)
Courage, fuyons (1980)
Le Dernier Metro [The Last Metro]
(1980)
Je vous aime (1980)
Le Choix des Armes [Choice of Arms]
(1981)
A Second Chance (1981)
Le Choc [The Shock] (1982)
*Hotel des Amériques [Hotel of the
Americas]* (1982)
L'Africain [The African] (1983)
Fort Saganne (1983)
The Hunger (1984)
Paroles et Musiques [Words and Music]
(1984)
Love Songs (1985)
Scene of the Crime (1987)

Sources

"Angel Catherine Deneuve Devil," *Look,* 32:62–66, April 30, 1968.

Brantley, Ben. "Serene Queen," *Harper's Bazaar,* 120:204+, February 1987.

Burke, Tom. "Belle de Jour Comes Across," *New York Times,* August 18, 1968, section 2, p. D13.

"Catherine Deneuve," *Life,* 66:32–34, January 24, 1969.

"Catherine Deneuve's New Film," *Harper's Bazaar,* 117:298+, March 1984.

"Catherine of France," *Esquire,* 65:143–145, April 1966.

Current Biography 1977. New York: H.W. Wilson, 1978, p. 98–101.

"Deneuve: Making It in America," *Newsweek,* 72:42+, August 26, 1968.

"Deneuve's Mission," *The Vancouver Sun,* May 12, 1987, p. E7.

Haber, Joyce. "Deneuve—A Very Private Household Face," *Los Angeles Times,* April 13, 1975, calendar section, p. 23.

Hamphill, Chris. "Catherine Deneuve," *Interview,* 6:22–26, October 1976.

Hotchner, A.E. "Why Catherine Deneuve Gets Depressed," *McCall's,* 105:177+, October 1977.

The International Dictionary of Films and Filmmakers: Volume III: Actors and Actresses. Chicago: St. James Press, 1985, p. 190–191.

"New Movies," *Time,* 91:106+, April 26, 1968.

"Over 40," *Harper's Bazaar.* 118:176, August 1985.

"People," *Time,* 109:70, April 4, 1977.

Quinlan, David. *The Illustrated Directory of Film Stars.* London: B.T. Batsford, 1981, p. 127.

Shipman, David. *The Great Movie Stars: The International Years.* London: Angus & Robertson, 1972, p. 125–128.

Taylor, Angela. "French Star Is Feminine," *New York Times,* December 15, 1964, p. 53.

Maria Schneider

At the age of 20 Maria Schneider gained international fame in one of the most controversial films ever made, *Last Tango in Paris*. Her sweet cherubic face and lovely body were shown off to best advantage. It was a hard act to follow and Schneider has never since made such a great impact in the movies.

Maria Schneider was born on March 27, 1952, in Paris. She was the illegitimate daughter of actor Daniel Gelin. Her mother, a Rumanian-born woman, ran a bookstore in Paris. Maria had an older and younger brother. Her mother was bohemian, divorcing and remarrying the same man twice, not Maria's father. Home life was not conventional. Maria remembered, "In grammar school the children were very cruel and would yell, 'Your mother is a bitch.' Of course they did that to anybody who was black, or Jewish or illegitimate."

Her relationship with her father was not close. Maria met him when she was 16 and was not impressed. "He's an old actor now, and quite frustrated that he didn't do more," she said. "When he met me, he was not nice. He's an egotist. . . . He exists, but he means *nothing* to me." Gelin did send her a telegram wishing her good luck when she started filming *Last Tango in Paris*.

Schneider left home at the age of 15. She was bisexual and had experimented with drugs. "My mother thought I was a lesbian junkie," she recalled. Her mother was pleased, however, when she got the part in *Last Tango in Paris*. Although she tried heroine and cocaine, Schneider realized the dangers of these drugs and gave them up in favor of marijuana. Maria was a child of the '60s, wearing hippie-style clothing and no makeup. When she moved out on her own she became part of the Montparnasse crowd of artists and, without formal training, she landed a role as a dancer in a French stage comedy called *Superstition*. She also obtained bit parts in a couple of films including *Madly* with Alain Delon and *The Old Maid* with Annie Girardot. Her first major role was in a Vadim film *Helle* in which she played a young existentialist.

Schneider was also an extra in a Bardot picture, and became part of her circle which included Warren Beatty for a while. Beatty told Schneider that he thought she would have a promising career in films and they have remained friends. Maria dropped out of the Bardot entourage, not wanting to be one of the people that "court and follow her."

In 1972 *Last Tango in Paris,* directed by Italian filmmaker Bernardo Bertoluccci, was released. Schneider had the female lead role of Jeanne costarring with Marlon Brando. The movie was a sensation and critics seemed to love it or hate it.

Bertolucci had originally offered the part to Dominque Sanda who turned it down because she was pregnant. He then auditioned 100 actresses for the role

Maria Schneider being pursued by Marlon Brando in *Last Tango in Paris*.

of Jeanne. Bertolucci finally picked Schneider because she seemed "a Lolita but more perverse" and because she was totally uninhibited when he asked her to disrobe. As the part called for a great deal of frontal nudity, this was an important criterion. When she had to take off all her clothes for a screen test, Bertolucci said, "She became much more natural." He was also impressed by her figure which was full-breasted but slim in the hips.

Last Tango in Paris was an intense film about an older man (Brando) and his encounter with a young girl (Schneider). They meet when both are looking for an apartment. As they explore it, they suddenly become attracted to each other and have spontaneous sex. Although complete strangers, they lease the apartment and meet there frequently. Brando's character is cynical, sad, frightened and violent. Jeanne is fascinated and repelled by her lover. Brando's wife has just killed herself and he is devastated by the failure of love. He vents his anger in crude sex with Jeanne, refusing to tell her anything about himself, including his name. He also does not want to know anything about her. Everything is reduced to an elemental physical level as though communicating through the body is the only honest interaction. Gradually Brando begins to talk about himself, and in an emotionally riveting monologue, he describes the harshness of his childhood. By the end of the film he is ready to add a spiritual dimension to his relationship with Jeanne and even offers to marry her. She has become totally disenchanted with his brutality, however, and just as he is about to reveal his name, she shoots and kills him.

Many people were outraged by the explicitness of the film and considered it pornographic. Yet more sensitive observers recognized it for the masterpiece that it was. Said director Robert Altman, "I walked out of the screening and said to myself, 'How dare I make another movie?' What it has done is give me a twenty-year jump in my career. The level of honesty it achieved was fantastic — not the sexuality but the emotional honesty. My personal and artistic life will never be the same."

Critic Pauline Kael hailed it as a "breakthrough" film and said it was a "landmark in movie history . . . This must be the most powerfully erotic movie ever made, and it may turn out to be the most liberating . . . Brando and Bertolucci have altered the face of an art form."

Schneider was called "a stunningly natural new performer" by *Time* magazine and Brando's acting was considered outstanding by many critics. Some feminists were offended by the fact that Maria was often fully nude while Brando never took his clothes off even during the love scenes. Schneider, who considered herself a feminist, objected to this condemnation. She defended Brando saying that because he was aging he had a complex about his body. In her broken English (which she said she learned in the movies and in bed with lovers), Maria explained, "He is getting old. Heavy. He's no more so beautiful. . . . He's not so free as I am. I'm more beautiful than he is."

Schneider was indeed lacking in any self-consciousness, and was "as unabashed about her ripe-bodied nudity as a 2-year-old." Another explanation for Brando's modesty came from Bertolucci. He claimed that Brando's film character was an extension of himself, and even though he did take some footage of Brando nude, he decided not to use it because he felt he would be exposing himself. He also justified Brando's wearing clothes by saying that he wanted to show a paternalistic relationship and Brando would seem more fatherly with his clothes on. This is strange logic in a film that showed sodomy and every conceivable position in sexual intercourse.

As for Schneider, the nudity and sexual simulation in the film did not bother her at all. "People are sick who say this film is pornographic," she emphasized. "It is a film about loneliness and anguish more than it is about sex." Nevertheless, she displayed more frontal nudity than any other actress in a major film had before, and was dubbed "the pin-up girl of the Decadent Decade" and the "Establishment's Linda Lovelace."

Because of the intimacy of their roles, Brando tried to put Schneider at ease in his abrupt way. They went for a walk at their first meeting, and Brando said, "Maria, you're going to have to put your finger up my rear so let's get to know each other." Then he led her into a bar and insisted they just look into each other's eyes for a while without talking. The next day he sent her flowers. People wondered if Maria and Marlon were having sexual relations offscreen and if the on-screen sex was more than just acting. Maria denied it. "We were never screwing on-stage," she said. "I never felt any sexual attraction for him, though my friends all told me I should. But he's almost 50, you know."

Since Schneider talked openly on just about any topic, she was probably telling the truth. "Maria is never false," said Bertolucci. "She doesn't know falsity." Bertolucci felt that Marlon taught Schneider a lot during filming: "Marlon gave her fantastic assurance," he said. "She lost her fears with him . . . it was Marlon who imposed the rhythm."

Maria also credited Brando with helping her but never felt subordinate to him. "Brando gave me his blah-blah once the first day and tried to be very paternalistic with me," she recalled. "But I kept him laughing and it really wasn't any father-daughter relationship. Brando is a man who is still a child — a bit ambivalent."

What she did pick up from him were his "vibrations." That heavy, very slow movement. His ability to size up a scene in an instant and then do it perfectly naturally. In the movie, his character takes that girl and teaches her a lot of things, makes her stretch, makes her explode. That's what he did to me as an actress."

She and Brando established a fine rapport. "We got near very quickly," said Maria. "We had something together. He learned from me, and I learned from him. I learned about camera angles from him, and how to hit your marks at the right time when the camera is going." Her explanation for their affinity was, "We're both bisexual and it's beautiful."

Brando was an actor who improvised brilliantly but had a hard time remembering lines. Cue cards were stuck up all over the set, and he even asked Bertolucci if he could write lines on Maria's rear end.

The character of Jeanne was extremely submissive. At first this made Maria "nervous and furious." "I am not at all submissive," she said, "and that bothered me. At first I thought, 'Bertolucci you hate women.' But I no longer think the film is a putdown of women. Because at the end, after Paul says they'll marry and have children, Jeanne makes the final decision and she rejects him." She did rebel while filming. In a scene where she is sodomized by Brando and her character is meant to be degraded, Schneider was supposed to yell out "family secret, family secret," instead she shouted "freedom, freedom."

There were aspects of Schneider that did correspond to her character of Jeanne, however. She felt very free sexually and also saw herself as cynical. She also felt that, like her character, she was not intellectual but physical. "I make love with a lot of people. Sometimes very violent," she admitted. "Without knowing them or anything . . . I don't feel like getting married . . . I need a lot of different sensations from different people. Not just one person . . . I never stay with anybody more than two or threee months," she added. "I've had quite a few lovers for my age. More men than women. Probably 50 men and 20 women. I'm incapable of fidelity."

Schneider said she was attracted to women because they were more open than men. "We speak the same language," she explained. "Men, they get afraid sometimes, I don't know, they get afraid of me; because I was so young, much younger than them, and I was not looking for what they were proposing—security, possessions . . . I still have men lovers but I don't want to live with them. They bore me so quick—just a wall."

Asked if her interest in females had to do with her father's rejection of her, Schneider replied, "Maybe before, but I have passed through that." Sometimes the sheer volume of her experience frightened her. "I keep thinking that I am going to die young, in an accident," she said. "It's just a feeling I've got because I've done so much in such a short, short time."

Despite the instant stardom that *Last Tango in Paris* brought her, Schneider was not caught up in the glitter of the movie world. "I love it when I'm with the camera," she explained, "but not all the other things. This business is all blackmail—that's why you have to have power. I'm anti-star. I'll never have a makeup man or hairdresser or driver."

Schneider was not seduced by the celebrity scene either. On a trip to New York she was introduced to Andy Warhol but felt that he treated her like a show business product. She cut short a dinner with him explaining that she thought it was better to leave than to become aggressive or hostile. She returned to her hotel to write postcards to friends back in Europe and hand-stamped "Bullshit" on each one of them.

Schneider shocked one American reporter by speaking candidly on intimate topics, by playing loud rock music during the interview, and by going to the bathroom in the middle of a conversation but leaving the door open so that it could continue.

She was not interested in being loved by her public. "I don't give a damn what people think. I've always been against everything in the world. I never had any myths. I'm not a symbol of anything. I'm Maria, I'm just Maria."

Some people considered Schneider arrogant. They say that "I push myself, that I impose myself when I go somewhere," she commented. "Well I'm quicker than other people. I see things more quickly. I get it faster."

Schneider was serious about acting, however. "I believe in what I'm doing," she said. "I don't want to do movies for money. I just want to make movies about things that I believe in, like young people, or about things that I oppose, like the bourgeoisie, the war, capitalists." Of course this was the idealism of youth and Schneider would later work just for money in some inane vehicles. She was paid only $4,000 for *Last Tango in Paris*. Maria did not consider herself a Marxist, but saw herself as full of contradictions politically. "I try to reach people through art, not politics," she said. "Movies are my destiny."

Maria was interested in doing modern projects rather than the classics. "I learned to be an actress in life, in the streets. I don't believe in acting lessons,"

Maria Schneider in a publicity shot.

she said. "For me they are really bad. I once spent four days at the Actors Studio in Paris, and it was not for me. It was not *real.* It was all technique. I feel that is damaging to acting, and in life."

Schneider predicted that she would never be able to match the experience of making *Last Tango in Paris* and so far this has proved to be true. "I don't think I'll ever get the chance to do another film like that!" she said, " . . . where the crew and actors are so together. The crew was not making an atmosphere of . . . you never got the feeling of voyeurism that I got with Vadim, when I made a film called *Helle* with him."

Several films that Schneider worked in were released in 1974–75. *Reigen (Dance of Love)* was by German director Otto Schenk and starred Senta Berger. It was a sexploitation film with couplings between prostitutes and a count, soldiers, a playwright as well as a maid and the son of rich people.

La Babysitter, directed by Carlo Ponti and costarring Sydne Rome and Robert Vaughn was about a rich kid who is kidnapped. Schneider played a young sculptress who ends up babysitting for him and managed to return him to his parents. She was described as more "intense, thin and introspective" than in *Last Tango in Paris.*

During the filming of *La Babysitter* Schneider created a scandal when she had herself committed to a mental hospital in Rome. The problem started when Maria quarreled with her lover Joan Townsend, daughter of Robert Townsend, the president of Avis Rent-a-Car, and author of *Up the Organization.* Joan was found wandering around the Rome airport in an hysterical state. The police took her to a psychiatric hospital. When Schneider was notified, she checked herself into the same hospital to be with her lover.

La Babysitter producer Zev Braun gave a statement to the media: "Yes it's fascinating," he said of the episode, "except when we're in the middle of making a picture. Joan, whom I know and call Joey, has a totally different kind of lifestyle than most of us. When Maria sees her emotionally upset, she has to get into the same thing. They're unconventional people."

Ponti remarked that it was the first time he had to visit an actress in an asylum. "This affair is very sad," he commented, "humanly sad." Schneider had not lost her flair for dramatics during this crisis. The press photographed the two women posing behind the barred windows of the hospital, and both *Time* and *Newsweek* ran the pictures.

Braun said he would not fire Schneider from the movie. "She's a terrific little actress," he noted. "She needs discipline in films . . . Despite what's been going on . . . Maria's a very innocent character. She needs a father." Braun, however, was not prepared to take on this duty. "Oh no, not me," he asserted. "Carlo's the father." Maria was quickly released, while Joan was transferred to a private clinic.

A more successful experience was the filming of *The Passenger,* directed by Antonioni and starring Jack Nicholson. Schneider was excited about working with this director. He was also very positive toward her. "He is quiet and very peaceful and open in many ways," Maria said. Nevertheless, she worried he would be hard on her "because of the way he treat the actors; but he was real with me, with me . . . he was different . . . and we mix very well." Schneider received about $30,000 for *The Passenger.*

The film was about a reporter (Nicholson) who is disenchanted with his work and hurting from a failed marriage. On an assignment in Africa he takes on the identity of a man who had died in the hotel in which he was staying. Nicholson's character was a study in alienation, a man attempting to escape from himself. It was a fine movie but Schneider's role was merely a dramatic device to advance the story. Nevertheless, she did the most with the little she had to work with and was charming and magnetic when on the screen.

Schneider fared less well in Buñuel's *Le Femme et le Pantin* in 1977, and was fired before filming was completed. The reasons were never made public although one observer claimed, "Buñuel tried 35 takes of the same shot with her before finally throwing in the towel." This was not the first time Schneider had been dropped from a film. Bertolucci fired her during the shooting of *1900* for unspecified reasons.

Two other films in 1977 did see Schneider in the credits—*Donna in Guerra* and *Caligula*. The latter film gained notoriety for its vulgarity and accusations of pornography were leveled against it. Starring Malcolm McDowell and based on a story by Gore Vidal, the movie showed a decadent Rome under the syphilitic Tiberius and epileptic Caligula. Maria had one of the minor roles in the film.

Schneider has since appeared in half a dozen other roles but the vehicles were lackluster. *Mama Dracula,* for example, starring Louise Fletcher, was yet another tedious vampire spoof described as an "anemic farce" by one critic. Maria played a police detective and was said to look "profoundly bored" in her role. Her latest film to date *Balles Perdues* (1983) was a light detective spoof whose male lead was pursued by a bevy of femme fatales.

Maria Schneider was an actress whose personal life was often more fascinating than her films. Her exotic eroticism, outspokenness, and wild behavior attracted much attention. Bertolucci successfully captured her unique quality in *Last Tango in Paris.* No director, including Bertolucci himself, has been able to duplicate this accomplishment.

Maria Schneider Filmography

Les Jambes en l'air (1970)
Madly (1970)
La Vieille Fille [The Old Maid] (1970)
Helle (1971)
What a Flash (1971)
Ultimo Tango a Paris [Last Tango in Paris] (1972)
Cari Genitori (1973)
Reigen [Le Baiser; Dance of Love] (1974)
Professione: Reporter [The Passenger] (1974)
La Babysitter [Babysitter] (1975)
Merry-go-round (1977)

Violanta (1977)
Lo sono Mia (1977)
Donna in Guerra (1977)
Voyage au jardin des morts (1977)
Caligula (1977)
Een vrouw als Eva [Une Femme comme Eva; A Woman Like Eve] (1978)
La Derobade [The Getaway; Memoirs of a French Whore; The Life; Confessions of a Streetwalker] (1979)
Haine (1979)
Mama Dracula (1980)
Balles Perdues [Stray Bullets] (1983)

Sources

"Buñuel Sacks Schneider," *Variety,* 286:35, February 23, 1977.
Haber, Joyce. "Maria Has Herself Committed," *Los Angeles Times,* section 4, February 20, 1975, p. 11.
_____. "Maria's First Tangle in California," *Los Angeles Times,* section 4, May 26, 1975, p. 10.
Katz, Ephraim. *The Film Encyclopedia.* New York: Thomas Y. Crowell, 1979, p. 1024.

Klemesrud, Judy. "Maria Says Her Tango Is not Blue," *New York Times,* section 2, February 4, 1973, p. 13.

Lloyd, Ann, ed. *The Illustrated Who's Who of the Cinema.* London: Orbis, 1983, p. 394.

Michener, Charles. "*Tango:* The Hottest Movie," *Newsweek,* 81:54–58, February 12, 1973.

"Milestones," *Time,* 105:48, March 3, 1975.

Probst, Leonard. "Maria Schneider of *Last Tango,*" *The Village Voice,* 18:79, February 8, 1973.

"Self-Portrait of an Angel and Monster," *Time,* 101:51–55, January 22, 1973.

"Transition," *Newsweek,* 85:45, March 3, 1975.

Wade, Valerie. "Brando's *Tango* Partner: What Next for Her?" *Vogue,* 161:174+, April 1973.

Dominique Sanda

Mysterious, beautiful Dominique Sanda was hailed as the new Greta Garbo of the 1970s. She worked with Europe's best directors including Bernardo Bertolucci, Vittorio De Sica and Luchino Visconti, in films that met with critical acclaim. Success came quickly and effortlessly to Sanda but her career began to wane in the 1980s. Although she continues to work, her roles have been fewer and less exciting.

Sanda was born Dominque Varaigne in March 1948 in Paris, France. Her father was an electronics engineer and she described her parents as "very Catholic, very French and very rigid." Sanda's brother was 17 years her senior and she felt lonely as a child. "I lived on dreams," she said. Dominique was educated in a convent. She then wanted to study painting at the Beaux-Arts but her parents were against it. Sanda became rebellious. Explaining her parents' opposition, she remarked, "For them the Beaux-Arts meant dirty, bearded young men who would bring me home late at night after having drugged me and raped me behind an easel. And then, a daughter who paints is a daughter lost to society. Their society. The one they still call 'good.' So naturally, I took it into my head to do everything to blow it up, this society. Now I know that society will not blow up," she added. "It will collapse all by itself, like a rotten fruit with a 'plop.'"

Sanda did study for a brief time at the Beaux-Arts after all, but she gave it up because "it was an exhausting and solitary experience." At 15 Sanda got married but it only lasted a year. "It was nothing," she said of the marriage. "My parents told me to choose between not seeing him and marrying him. So OK, I got married. . . . He was a guy I had nothing in common with," she continued, "and he didn't do anything."

To earn some money, Dominique began modeling and by 17 was a top fashion model. She posed nude for *Playboy* and experimented with drugs. Her parents, she said, "reacted like good French Roman Catholic parents. Scandal

Dominique Sanda in *Damnation Alley*.

in the family. It was terrible. Fears, reproaches. Terror, in fact." Later she admitted, "The nudity was an act of personal vengeance against my very strict upbringing. Today it seems stupid." As to her drug use, she said, "It was past history. It's not interesting to talk about that, at least not for me. There are some things that are too personal to talk about in public." Dominique changed her surname because she did not want to embarrass her parents. She chose Sanda because it sounded Italian and was based on the name of someone she admired, the writer George Sand.

Director Robert Bresson was casting his film *Une Femme douce*. He saw a picture of Sanda in *Vogue* and decided to hire her. She had had no acting lessons or experience. The film dealt with Catholicism versus feminism and the theme suggested that liberated women were lost souls who were doomed.

Bresson was known for being very hard on actors and usually reduced actresses to tears. Sanda was not intimidated by him. "I argued with him," she recalled. "Maybe now I wouldn't dare to, but I had nothing to lose . . . I was only a beginner," she added. "So, with me, he was almost kind." By confronting Bresson, she gained his respect. "I told him you're not going to make me down. If you answer him and present him with another point of view," she said, "he stops and becomes interested. He wants to be God, he wants to flatten people in order to give them life. . . . In the Bresson film I had to be an object — just a bare outline, without color and shadow."

Yet Sanda was able to transcend this. As one observer noted, Sanda's participation in Bresson's film "sets up a pronounced resistance to the director's habitual and perverse repression of actors: if the 'liberated woman' is damned, she is also the most alive and vivid presence in the film."

Sanda believed that she was indebted to Bresson for introducing her to film acting. "What I owe most to Bresson is the discovery of the cinema," she explained. "For that I will always be grateful to him. Between the cinema and me it was, instantly, love. A crazy love. A passion." She also learned from Bresson how "to do away with all phony laughs, phony gestures, phony references. To go back to absolutely zero. It feels crazy at times — but it's the best starting point an actress can ever have. From there on, you can build whatever you please."

Dominique's sensuality, remoteness and tough vulnerable ambience came across clearly in her first movie. Maximilian Schell, who was directing and starring in *First Love,* chose her to play an innocent heroine whose sexual magnetism attracts both a father and a son. Schell found Sanda to be a natural actress. She improvised many of her scenes and learned to overcome her shyness. Word spread throughout the European film community that she was talented and would work for a low salary.

Bernardo Bertolucci was planning a film called *The Conformist.* He offered Sanda the role of a bisexual antifascist, a part that she came to consider the best work of her career. Bertolucci felt that Dominique had "charm and allure that are outside of our time today." The film linked homosexual repression to fascism and Sanda's gentle, free-spirited character was a contrast to the violent, authoritarianism of fascism. In one memorable scene she dances a tango with actress Stephania Sandrelli. The flowing sensuality of the women as they moved to the highly structured music symbolized freedom struggling with suppression.

Sandrelli had difficulty dealing with the fact that she was supposed to be less attractive and interesting than Sanda in the film. During the shooting of one segment, Sandrelli began crying. When Sanda asked her what the problem was, Stephania replied, "Oh God, I have to be the one who is less beautiful, the bourgeoise, the older." Sanda was upset that Sandrelli felt competitive. "It hurt me," she said. "I wanted her to know how much I needed her to help me."

Sanda's feelings about Bertolucci were more positive. "With Bertolucci," she said, "nothing is fixed, he changes all the time. It's not uncomfortable. It's magic. Even the camera seems to breathe. There's no need of explanation. Everything is done by suggestion. Since I was very timid, and I am still, when he wanted something and I was too reserved, he would act angry and then I would do it, to please him."

In 1971 Sanda, then 23, was deeply involved with French film star 44-year-old Christian Marquand. Some of Marquand's more notable films were *And God Created Woman* and *Lord Jim.* He was a close friend of Marlon Brando. His mother and sister designed clothes for Chanel, and another sister was married to actor Jean-Louis Trintignant who had starred in *The Conformist.* Dominique and Christian were introduced by a friend, and it was love at first sight. He had his big toenail mounted in a gold earring which Sanda wore in her ear. "It goes well with her pale complexion and personality," he said.

Marquand described Sanda as a witch. "All women have a certain amount of witch in them," he decided, "but with her, the strain is finely developed. Today being a witch is so accepted. It's almost bourgeois. With Dominique, it's like a film by Antonioni: You see the surface, but there are many layers beneath. She can see each of those layers. With a nature of this kind," he continued, "boredom is not possible." Marquand also concluded that Sanda was "slightly schizophrenic, and that gives her a great gift of poetry and a natural perception of things."

The couple had no plans to marry. Neither believed in it at that time. "Our affair," said Christian, "is between serious and the joy of the moment. We have no plan—we do as we feel from day to day." Sanda gave birth to a son in 1972. They bought a farmhouse 25 miles from Paris.

Sanda considered herself a serious actress and continued to perform in interesting roles. In *The Garden of the Finzi-Continis,* directed by Vittorio De Sica, she played a doomed Jewish daughter of an aristocractic family in fascist Italy. She received excellent reviews for her acting. De Sica described her as a baby. "Una bambina . . . with all the qualities and all the defects of the very young." He also found her mysterious and said, "With Dominique one must scrutinize, one must search out what she sincerely thinks and feels. It is all closed inside . . . she is undefined and ambiguous."

Sanda attributed her fame to her femininity. "In spite of everything, people still seek a certain image of the woman," she said. "And I believe that I am rather feminine." She also felt that her moodiness was an asset. "I am very emotional and sensitive," she noted. Dominique liked to apply this to filming because of "the schizophrenia of what one does; you change all the time, there are lots of facets . . . constantly changing one's skin. Being and no longer being. Losing myself and finding myself."

Many critics were in awe of Sanda's beauty. She had a natural loveliness

and wore no makeup or extravagant clothing offscreen. She dismissed this adoration by noting that she was, after all, a girl in her 20s, and many females looked good at this age. When one interviewer asked her about her appearance, Sanda replied, "Your question bores me."

Sanda did make some films "without any real pleasure. Just for the money," as she put it. "One must work in order not to be forgotten," she realized. But she hoped to be able to be more selective in the future, "to say no to all the trashy geniuses who make you film any old thing as long as it's commercial." On the other hand, she said, "If Fellini should ask me to make a film with him for nothing, I would do it on my knees."

Sanda made *Without Apparent Motive,* a minor French spy thriller, just for the money. Sanda was not enthusiastic about French directors. "Even Truffaut has been bourgeois and very light," she noted. "In Italy there are giants and gods," she said. One of her personal gods was Bertolucci. But when he offered her a role in *Last Tango in Paris,* which he had created especially for her, she turned it down. Her excuse was that she was pregnant, but she was also nervous about the sexual explicitness of the film, and felt it was not something she would ever want her children to see.

She worked steadily for the next few years making films. These included *Conversation Piece,* directed by Visconti. It was the story of an older bourgeois whose museum-like mansion is invaded by the younger generation. The film was a rave in Europe but poorly received in the United States. *Impossible Object,* directed by John Frankenheimer and costarring Alan Bates, was about a novelist that Sanda's character has an affair with. Frankenheimer called her "the most exciting young actress I've seen in years." The movie was not widely distributed, however. A film she made with John Huston and costarring Paul Newman also sank without a trace. Titled *Mackintosh Man,* it was so bad that it was barely released.

By 1975 Sanda's relationship with Marquand was over, and she was living with French painter Frederique Pardo. She married him about a year later but it did not work out. She recalled their time together as "very destructive, very negative. Life was so heavy and terrible with him," she said, "but it took me a long time to understand that I had to leave."

Her career, meanwhile, was at its peak. She was commanding $100,000 per picture in 1975, and had completed Bertolucci's *1900.* She played Ada, the wife of an Italian landowner (Robert de Niro), in this epic about the confrontation between the bourgeoisie and the peasants in Italy. The film took six months to shoot, but Sanda said, "With Bertolucci you don't notice the time . . . The thing I love about Bernardo is that with him, I'm never dull." Sanda had to develop much of the role on her own. "The character in the script was hardly structured," she said. "Bertolucci has an esthetic, photogenic idea of

Opposite: **Dominique Sanda relaxes in** *Caboblanco.*

me. He writes for me in images, which I then have to interpret, but usually, it turns out to be just what he had in mind," she decided. "That's why he prefers to always use the same actors. He reaches that deep understanding with them."

Expectations were high from the film community, but *1900* did not receive the critical praise Bertolucci usually earned. There were excellent sequences in the movie but as a whole it came across as simplistic and melodramatic.

For Bolognini's *The Inheritance,* Sanda won the Best Actress award at the 1976 Cannes Festival. The movie got almost no attention in the United States, however. *The Inheritance* was followed by a light sci-fi flick *Damnation Alley* with George Peppard and Jan-Michael Vincent. She chose to do this type of movie, saying, "It's a recreation, an escape. I wanted to not be too involved." More interesting was the film *Beyond Good and Evil* about Friedrich Nietzsche. Dominique was excellent as the bohemian Jewish woman whose love the German philosopher had to share with another man.

Sanda had a disappointing experience in 1979. She was flown to Los Angeles to read for a part in *The Formula,* starring George C. Scott. They went over the script together and then Sanda was told to wait in another room. Scott decided that he did not like the sound of her accent, and a humiliated Sanda was sent back to France.

A more successful venture was *Voyage en douce* in which she costarred with Geraldine Chaplin. It was about two female friends who take a summer vacation together. Sanda enjoyed working with Chaplin and admired her for being "frank, open and strong." Both the movie and the actresses rated mixed reviews.

Her next vehicle *Caboblanco,* a take-off on the Bogart classic *Casablanca,* was a complete disaster and the production was labeled "shoddy." Sanda's improbable costar was Charles Bronson.

Dominique's roles began dwindling in the 1980s. She noted the diminishing lack of opportunities and had her own theories for this decline. "For a long time it was easy for me," she said. "Everything was really lucky ... I received beautiful scripts ... Then it started to be a little more complicated. The stories were not as good. I had to make more decisions. My price went up ... Also, because I had made so many movies in costume, I wasn't offered anything modern."

Sanda was also inexperienced at pushing herself. She had never tried to become a star, and was accustomed to directors seeking her out rather than having to compete for roles.

Yet Sanda has a memorable screen presence even though she has been absent from film recently. As Louis Malle noted, "She goes straight to your subconscious, somebody to fill your dreams with. There is always the feeling that she is in the shadow, not the full light."

Dominique Sanda Filmography

Une Femme douce [A Gentle Creature] (1970)
Erste leben [First Love] (1970)
Il conformista [The Conformist] (1970)
Sans mobile apparent [Without Apparent Motive] (1971)
Il giardino dei Finzi Contini [The Garden of the Finzi-Continis] (1971)
La notte dei fiori [Night of the Flowers] (1972)
The Mackintosh Man (1973)
L'Impossible Objet [Impossible Object; Story of a Love Story] (1973)
Gruppo di famiglia in un interno

[Conversation Piece] (1974)
Steppenwolf (1974)
1900 (1975)
L'eredità ferramonti [The Inheritance] (1976)
Oltre il bene e il male [Beyond Good and Evil] (1977)
Damnation Alley (1977)
Utopia (1978)
Voyage en douce (1981)
Caboblanco (1981)
Une Chambre en ville [A Room in Town] (1982)
De weg naar Bresson (1984)

Sources

"Bella Bambina," *Time,* 100:91, July 10, 1972.
Blume, Mary. "Dominique Sanda—Garbo with a Gallic Accent?" *Los Angeles Times,* July 23, 1972, p. 1+.
Brady, James. "Class," *Esquire,* 84:122, August 1975.
Chase, Chris. "At the Movies," *New York Times,* April 17, 1981, p. C6.
Chelminski, Rudolph. "The Dominique Mystique," *Life,* 73:67–69, September 29, 1972.
De Vilallonga, Jose Luis. "Dominique Sanda," *Vogue,* 159:148+, April 1, 1972.
Dreyfus, Catherine. "Dominique Sanda," *Mademoiselle,* 82:172+, October 1976.
The International Dictionary of Films and Filmmakers: Volume III: Actors and Actresses. Chicago: St. James Press, 1986, p. 555.
"Is She a Witch?" *Look,* 35:71+, October 5, 1971.
Katz, Ephraim. *The Film Encyclopedia.* New York: Thomas Y. Crowell, 1979, p. 1013.
"Mystery Girl," *Newsweek,* 79:93, March 13, 1972.
"People," *Time,* 105:56, January 6, 1975.
"People," *Time,* 107:39, February 23, 1976.
"Personalities," *Washington Post,* December 14, 1979, B2.
Shearer, Lloyd. "Dominque Sanda," *Washington Post,* September 17, 1972, p. 10+.
Trebay, Guy. "Voice Centerfold," *Village Voice,* 26:59, April 8–14, 1981.
Wade, Valerie. "Dominique Sanda," *Los Angeles Times,* August 22, 1976, p. 33.
Warhol, Andy. "Dominique Sanda," *Interview,* 11:34–37, August 1981.

Isabelle Huppert

Isabelle Huppert is an actress of grace and subtlety who brings a natural quality to each of her roles. She began her career in her teens and her lovely red hair, freckled face, luminous green eyes and slender figure gave her the image of the French girl next door.

Her roles were usually profound and Huppert's characters rarely smiled. Many of her films used her innocent appearance as a contrast to the often complex characters that she portrayed. Isabelle was able to convey a sullen emotional detachment that, depending on the film, could be interpreted as shyness or alienation.

Huppert was born on March 16, 1955, in Paris, France, the youngest of four girls. Her sister Elizabeth is a well-known novelist and actress in France. Isabelle's father Raymond manufactured safes. Her mother Annick taught English and Isabelle is fluent in this language. Huppert's parents both came from Hungary.

After high school Isabelle enrolled at a university in Paris, the Faculte de Clichy, where she majored in Russian studies. In her spare time she accepted bit parts in several television dramas. This aroused her interest in acting and she transferred to the Conservatoire National d'Art Dramatique in Paris.

In 1971 Huppert landed her first film role in *Faustine et le bel été* and during the next five years she appeared in 15 other movies. Some of the parts were small but she did work with some important directors and in several landmark films. Huppert's career gained momentum early and kept rolling. "I never had to audition or screen-test much," she said. "Once you're working and they know you and your work, other things follow."

In *Cesar and Rosalie* she played Romy Schneider's kid sister. A 1974 film *Going Places* directed by Bertrand Blier became one of the most talked-about movies that year. It was about two loutish nihilists (Gerard Depardieu and Patrick Dewaere). Huppert played a nice young girl who leaves home and takes to the road with the two brutes. She gets slapped around in the movie and some critics complained that the film was immoral and sadistic; others compared it favorably to Godard's classic *Breathless*.

In Preminger's *Rosebud*, a film that was panned by reviewers, Huppert played a teenage girl searching for her friends. "He yelled so much," she recalled of the director. In 1977 Huppert appeared in *The Lacemaker*, directed by Claude Goretta. Huppert played Beatrice, a young hairdresser's assistant who falls in love with an upper-class university student whose superior status is apparent. He leaves Beatrice and she suffers a breakdown and is institutionalized. Huppert's understated approach quietly conveyed the passivity and despair of Beatrice, and many critics were moved by Beatrice's pitiful fate.

Some feminists saw *The Lacemaker* as a typically masculine view of woman as helpless victim. Huppert defended the movie saying, "A masculine vision exists — why not show it?" Huppert also felt that since life often involved failure, one had to sometimes portray characters that were defeated.

The role of Beatrice gave Huppert more attention as an actress than any previous work, and she was described by one reviewer as "extraordinarily expressive." She was voted the "Most Promising Newcomer" of the year by the British Academy of Motion Pictures.

Isabelle Huppert in *The Lacemaker*.

Huppert explained her technique when trying to develop a character. She looked for a "visual key" that would give her a reference point. For example, in *The Lacemaker* it was the small flat shoes of Beatrice that gave her the clue. "I try to give a different physical appearance to each character from the ones I did before," she said. "You look for an image to place the character before the film even starts, to express the psychology of the part. Fifty percent of your work is done when you can begin with this—the way she wears her hair, the way she moves and walks . . . I start by thinking about what might have happened to the character before the story began, and this preparation helps you to work on what's underneath—the unseen part, which has to be very much built in to your mind," she added.

After *The Lacemaker* Huppert appeared in a stage play and a couple of other films in 1977. Her next role in *Violette Noziere,* directed by Claude Chabrol, met with critical acclaim. *Violette* was based on the true story of an 18-year-old French girl who was an innocent student by day and a prostitute by night. She poisoned her parents but her mother survived and forgave her daughter. At the trial Violette revealed that she had deliberately planned the crime as a response to her father's incestuous attacks upon her.

Chabrol was interested in revealing the paradoxes in Violette: "a girl who commits the worst crime—and one the whole world dreams of—and as a result finds herself free of her anguish and deprivation; a girl who cannot bear the family world and destroys it while later on she finds herself by creating another which is almost identical to the one she rejected [she got married and had five children]; a girl who feels a prisoner at home finds a measure of freedom in prison. In short, she is both tragic and ridiculous ... it is very difficult to know if her act implies liberation from something. Maybe it's simply the freedom to live," he concluded.

Huppert, as Violette, was described as "strikingly vivid" and "extraordinary." Her characterization of Violette was almost the extreme opposite of Beatrice in *The Lacemaker,* and critics were impressed by Huppert's versatility. One reviewer called her performances "so markedly personal that they seem not to be performances at all." Isabelle won the Best Actress award at Cannes.

Huppert said she was attracted to both parts. "They could be the story of every woman," she said. "*The Lacemaker* is about the victimization of a woman whose internalized revolt ends up in madness, while Violette's is an externalized revolt that culminates in murder," Huppert explained. Speaking of Violette, Huppert added, "I'm fascinated by this kind of person. She's at once a murderess and a saint. There is a search for purity in her, and this is the image that led three heads of state to reduce her sentence and finally pardon her. I myself never thought of shooting my parents," said Isabelle, "but playing Violette was a way of expressing my own revolt.... What I like about both girls," she continued, "is that we start from a very ordinary level and gradually pass into the mythical.... Violette's story is a bit symbolic, a story about the unconscious, and it's less interesting to take it literally," said Huppert.

Huppert also described how her acting methods enabled her to undertake such diverse parts. She explained that she played Beatrice "in an understated way." She said, "It was very subtle. Violette too, internalizes her intentions but then acts violently. First, I construct in my mind everything that's under the surface: motivations, the subconscious ... but on the screen it suffices to show just a little bit. In film, an actor should do less rather than more, because the camera exaggerates everything, it's a sort of x-ray ... It's enough to *be* rather than *do.*"

This internalization of character affected Huppert's psychic life. "Every time I play a role, it follows me for two or three months afterward. During the shooting, I'm completely desensitized. I feel nothing. Then it's very painful because I identify with the character for such a long time," Huppert said. "Only later can I say it's over. Exorcised."

Chabrol called Huppert's concentration on the set "phenomenal" and said, "She literally took possession of the film after having absorbed the character. I confess I have never seen anything like it."

One of her next films *The Brontë Sisters,* directed by André Techine and costarring Isabelle Adjani and Marie-France Pisier, proved to be disappointing. Huppert, who played Anne, felt the film may have failed because "Techine is

Isabelle Huppert in *The Trout*.

very cerebral. It's a fault of many French directors maybe to be more theoretical than pragmatic."

There were very few directors that were more cerebral than Jean-Luc Godard. Huppert worked with him in her next film *Every Man for Himself* (1980) in which she played a prostitute. Said Huppert about working with Godard, "I was very surprised, there is not a word of improvisation with Godard. He is a maniac on the purity of the text. With him you rehearse very precisely."

Every Man for Himself received excellent reviews and critic Vincent Canby of the *New York Times* praised it as a "stunning original work." Huppert had no reservations about performing nude if it was "necessary for the script. If you start getting self-conscious about that," she said, "you'll go crazy."

Three other films in which Huppert appeared were also released in 1980. In *The Heiresses* she played Irene, a Jewish shopgirl who agrees to be a surrogate mother for a rich woman. The woman's husband falls in love with her, and his wife takes revenge by denouncing Irene to the Nazis.

The Heiresses was directed by Marta Meszaros, a Hungarian woman. Asked if she favored being directed by a male or female, Huppert felt that it made little difference, saying, "When a male director makes films, he uses the imaginative feminine part of himself, dealing with the world of images and sensations, rather than his masculine side." She did find that a woman director was less controlling, and explained, "We don't expect a woman to be that powerful." Yet she did not resent the authority of male directors. "As long as they are talented and good," she said, "I totally enjoy their authority over me—moral and artistic authority."

In *Loulou,* directed by Maurice Pialat and costarring Gerard Depardieu, she played Nelly, a bored middle-class housewife who becomes involved in an affair. The charged chemistry between Huppert and Depardieu made a simple movie electric. Pialat encouraged his actors to improvise and Huppert said that the director hated rehearsing "because he thinks that you can't find anything fresh and new." Depardieu objected to this way of working but Huppert was comfortable with improvisation and hoped to work with the director again.

Michael Cimino, an American director who had won an Oscar for *The Deerhunter,* had seen Huppert perform as Violette. He offered her a part in *Heaven's Gate* which was a western set in 19th-century Wyoming. She played a brothel madam who was loved by two men (Kris Kristofferson and Christopher Walken).

Saying that it is "the fantasy of every French performer to work in America," Huppert also clarified that this was not the only reason she accepted the role in *Heaven's Gate.* "The reality is that it's very difficult to act in another language . . . I could never pretend to be just another American woman in a Hollywood movie . . . I wouldn't do just anything in order to work. . . . Anything I've done, I've wanted to do," she said. "Here was the part and it was wonderful."

Unfortunately, the film was considered a disaster by critics. It was withdrawn for further editing but the recut version was not enough of an improvement to save the movie and it bombed at the box office.

Heaven's Gate was Huppert's 26th movie and she was only 25 years old. Interviewers asked if she was planning to take a break from acting, and Huppert joked that she was thinking of retiring. In actuality, her pace did not abate whatsoever, even though there was a certain stress involved in her work. "One is always forced into a pattern of seduction, either as the seducer or as the seduced. However, being the seducer is a lot of work too and not all that easy," she said. The main reasons for becoming an actress she felt, were to be loved and admired, yet she also saw the movie set as a kind of cocoon where she could withdraw from the world.

Huppert preferred not to watch her own films, believing that the effort she put into her work never matched the results on the screen. Still she was happy and confident about her talent, and continued to work prodigiously. She made *Clean Slate* with Tavernier, was directed by Godard in *Passion* and by Losey in *The Trout.* In 1983 she was especially praised for her role in *Entre nous* in which she played a housewife who falls in love with another woman. They leave their husbands and set up a dress shop together. That year Huppert also had a baby she named Lolita. When questioned about the choice of name, Huppert replied, "I know ... the connotation in people's minds, somebody who is a little perverse, ingenue ... sexy ... Maybe it says more about my sexiness than hers."

The child was born out of wedlock but Huppert was not concerned about the social stigma. "I'm an actress," she remarked. "Once you start doing a profession like this, it just puts you out of the conventions, you know."

In 1985 Huppert's sister Charlotte directed Isabelle in a film. The movie, called *Sincerely Charlotte,* was the story of a triangle between a pop singer, her ex-boyfriend and his new lover. It got decent, if not overly enthusiastic, reviews. Some of Huppert's most recent films such as *Cactus* which was filmed in Australia, and *The Bedroom Window* which was a Hollywood movie, were disappointing. In *Cactus* Huppert's emotional detachment worked against her for once, and her almost zombie-like acting could not save an already poor script.

Overall, however, Isabelle Huppert has been in an impressive array of films. She has tried to select roles that show the ambiguity and mystery of women as well as their practical side. "I can't play too straight characters," she explained.

Huppert described her talent in musical terms saying, "It's like you're an instrument: in life you play three notes. You have a thousand notes in yourself; suddenly a part makes you play on some obscure notes you would not have thought of. It's a beautiful musical metaphor, being an actress."

Isabelle Huppert Filmography

Faustine et le bel été (1971)
Le Bar de la Fouche (1972)
Cesar et Rosalie (1972)
Glissements progressifs du plaisir (1974)
Les valseuses [Going Places] (1974)
L'Ampelopede (1974)
Serieux comme le plaisir (1974)
Dupont Lajoie (1974)
Rosebud (1974)
Le Grand Delire (1974)
Aloise (1974)
Doctor Françoise Gailland (1975)
Le Juge et l'Assassin [The Judge and the Assassin] (1975)
Je suis Pierre Riviere (1975)
Le petit Marcel (1975)
Flashback (1975)
La Dentelliere [The Lacemaker]

(1977)
Des Enfants gates (1977)
Les Indiens sont encore loin [The Indians Are Still Far Away] (1977)
Violette Noziere (1977)
Retour a la bien-aimée (1978)
Les Soeurs Brontë (1978)
Sauve qui peut [La Vie; Every Man for Himself] (1980)
Orokseg [Les Héritières; The Heiresses] (1980)
Loulou (1980)
Heaven's Gate (1980)
Coup de torchon [Clean Slate] (1981)
La vera storia della signora della camelie (1981)
Les Ailes de la colombe [The Wings of the Dove] (1981)
Eaux profonds (1981)

My Best Friend's Girl (1982)
Passion (1982)
The Trout (1982)
Entre nous (1983)
Storia di Piera (1983)

Signe Charlotte [Sincerely Charlotte]
  (1985)
Sac de Noeuds [All Mixed Up] (1985)
Cactus (1986)
The Bedroom Window (1987)

Sources

"Behind the Wall," *Time,* 112:74+, October 23, 1978.
Bolotin, Susan. "Isabelle Huppert," *Vogue,* 174:262+, June 1984.
Buckley, Tom. "At the Movies," *New York Times,* July 25, 1980, p. C8.
Champlin, Charles. "A Rising Star in Roles of Fallen Women," *Los Angeles Times,* calendar
    section, July 27, 1980, p. 1+.
Corliss, Mary. "Journals," *Film Comment,* 16:4+, September/October 1980.
Current Biography 1980. New York: H.W. Wilson, 1981, p. 218–220.
Harvey, Stephen. "Isabelle Huppert—The Virtues and Pitfalls of Independence," *New York
    Times,* section 2, November 16, 1980, p. 15.
The International Dictionary of Films and Filmmakers: Volume III: Actors and Actresses.
    Chicago: St. James Press, 1986, p. 322–323.
"Isabelle Huppert's Life Outside of Conventions," *New York Times,* January 27, 1984,
    p. C8.
O'Toole, Lawrence. "Huppert Girl," *Film Comment,* 16:45–47, September/October 1980.
Simon, John. "The French Way," *New York,* 13:28+, October 6, 1980.
Yakir, Dan. "Innocents with Dirty Hands," *Village Voice,* 23:67–68, October 23, 1978.

Isabelle Adjani

International film success came Isabelle Adjani's way when she was just 20 years old. Even at that early age she had already won acclaim in France for her stage acting and was considered the best young actress to grace that country in years. Over the past decade she has turned in many fine performances and picked up numerous awards for her film work. Her experiences with Hollywood films have been much less satisfactory. Lured there first in 1978, she was cast in a bomb *The Driver* and then stayed away for almost ten years before finding herself cast in an even bigger flop, *Ishtar.* For the latter she could take some consolation in a large salary.

Isabelle was born in Paris, France, on June 27, 1955, to a German mother and an Algerian father, a former car salesman. She grew up and attended school in the working class suburb of Neuilly where she nourished a passion for theater and film. At 12 she earned a prize for a recitation she gave at school and began appearing in amateur stage productions. Attending films was a major recreation for her and she often spent weekends at the Cinemathèque in Paris where Adjani would watch up to 12 films in a day.

A terrified Isabelle Adjani in *Nosferatu the Vampire.*

Her entry into films came quite casually as Adjani remembered, "When I was fourteen I did a film during the holidays with other children. It was nothing to do with anything professional. One day I was coming out of school and someone asked me if I wanted to be in a movie. It was very simple." That debut film was *Le Petit Bougnat* in which she had a small part. Two years later someone remembered her in that film and gave her another bit part in *Faustine et le bel été,* also shot during the holidays.

Between those films Isabelle began her professional stage career in 1970 in a Lorca play at Reims, France, and then started doing television work in 1972 with an adaptation of a Molière work. France's renowned Comédie Française acting troupe was mounting the same play on the stage and cast Isabelle for the role she had essayed on television. Despite her lack of training or background she became a full member of that troupe in 1973 and played leads immediately.

Isabelle performed in works by the likes of Molière and Giraudoux in repertory and remarked that "playing repertory was fantastic. I felt structured by the work. It was like a driving force behind you." Critics raved about her stage work and called her a "phenomenon of her generation." During her stay with the Comédie Française Adjani took time off to appear in a film *La Gifle,* a comedy about an 18-year-old girl's problems with her estranged parents. Reviewers agreed that Isabelle played her part with "quivering charm" and stole the picture. It was a major hit in France but a flop in the United States.

The Comédie Française was impressed with the young actress to the extent that they offered her a 20-year contract. It seemed to be the chance of a lifetime—but there were strings attached. The contract forbade Adjani from working for anyone else on the Paris stage and allowed her to appear in films only if they approved them. The actress was already set for the lead in Truffaut's *The Story of Adele H.* but the Comédie rejected it. Isabelle responded by rejecting the contract and quitting the Comédie.

It was an almost unheard of action and aroused a good deal of national media attention. "I felt so guilty. I hid," said Adjani. "I vanished until the scandal disintegrated.... At the Comédie Française you just do what you are told to do. That is why I left. I will only do what I want to do." Her reaction to a long-term Comédie contract was similar to one she had when asked if she had plans to marry. "No my god! I like Simone de Beauvoir too much. I can't think about it. How can you sign a contract and say you will be in love with anyone or anything for twenty years? That's a kind of death. You talk about freedom of choice—a choice of which prison you want to get in."

Director François Truffaut was enthused by the acting work of Adjani and, when he offered her the lead in *Adele,* said, "I wanted to do a film with Isabelle very quickly because I thought that I could steal from her those precious things—the way her face and body express everything." When offered the part the actress's first response was that it would be risky and that she could not handle it. "I told him I wouldn't be able to perform it. I was too young. I couldn't trust myself." François convinced her however, and the actress immersed herself in the part, becoming obsessed by it. That film was the story of the tormented daughter of Victor Hugo who was consumed by her passion for a British lieutenant and drove herself to madness as she pursued him around the world. Her character was the only one of importance in the film and her performance was brilliant. The New York Film Critics voted her Best Actress and the Academy of Motion Picture Arts and Sciences nominated her as Best Actress. She became a high demand item in the international film world.

Roman Polanski cast her opposite himself in his film *The Tenant.* It was a shrewdly-done film about a paranoid breakdown of a bureaucratic clerk. Isabelle did fine work again as the girlfriend of a deceased woman who owned an apartment. Polanski rented the apartment from Isabelle's friend. Adjani admired the work of director André Techine and, after finishing *Adele H.,* approached him and said she wanted to work with him. The result was *Barocco,* a private-eye genre movie. Gerard Depardieu played a man who was killed by his double. The killer then took his place with his girlfriend, played by Isabelle. The film and the acting were poorly received. *Violette et François* was another weak vehicle for the actress who played one half of a couple in a picture about their trials and tribulations.

Isabelle Adjani in *Subway.*

Commenting on how she approached her craft, Isabelle said, "When I read a scenario, my first experience is a visual one. I see scenes and situations unfold first on the level of images, and then on the level of emotions. I next try to draw up a draft. The more structures you have to build on, the better you can construct a character that really works. The process must above all not be instinctive. Words and phrases always contain every nuance imaginable. The actor should not add to them."

After *Adele H.* the actress received many Hollywood offers but turned them all down, not finding them to be of a high enough quality. She finally succumbed to a role in *The Driver* because she had liked a picture previously done by the director, Walter Hill. It proved a bad choice. The film starred Ryan O'Neal as a highly skilled getaway driver pursued by Bruce Dern who played a very clever detective. Adjani played a gambler hired by O'Neal as an alibi. *The Driver* featured lots of screeching tires but had no plot. It was savaged by critics as a "bleak wreck of a film."

Over the years the actress steadfastly refused to discuss her private life with the press. She mentioned only that she had one brother and that her parents were happy with her career. It was an attitude that once earned her the Prix Citron (lemon) in France for her refusal to cooperate with the media. The actress agreed with the notion that there were few good roles for women in movies and added, "It's rare, incidentally, to find a director who really likes and knows how to look at a woman through a camera. . . . Directors and screenwriters tried to assume responsibility for me as a woman."

Better film vehicles came her way and she got good notices in Herzog's Dracula tale *Nosferatu* as an object of Count Dracula's desires. *The Brontë Sisters* was a biography of the tormented and repressed writing sisters and their doomed brother. Adjani was lead-billed as Emily. It was an excellent film with strong acting but was not a commercial success. Playing a young woman who had left her husband just after the wedding, Isabelle had a support role in *Clara et les chic types* and again managed to steal the show.

Quartet (1981) was an adaptation of the Jean Rhys novel of the same name with the actress playing a resilient woman of the 1920s. *Possession,* released the same year, was a psychological horror tale about a man who returned home after a long secret mission only to find his wife acting strangely. Isabelle played the deranged woman. She got excellent reviews for these films and was named Best Actress at the Cannes Festival for her work in both. As well, she won a French Cesar (equivalent to the Oscar) for *Possession.*

Comparing herself and other young French actors with an older generation, Adjani said, "The cinema of the young Delon and Belmondo aimed to produce stars. Everything hung on the star system. Producers thought of nothing else. But we're different. In a way we're like missionaries.... Superstars don't exist anymore. Ours is a different world. Full communication takes place between 'fictive people' on the one hand and 'everyday people' on the other—thanks to the development of the mass media."

For a change of pace the actress appeared in a light romantic comedy *L'Année prochaine si tout va bien* and did well with fluffy material. Another comedy was *Tout feu tout flamme* about father and daughter relationships with Yves Montand as the father. She went back to more somber material when she starred in *L'été meurtrier,* a psychological drama about a neurotic woman's obsession with a family shame. She drew rave reviews and one critic wrote that her performance "of a disturbed woman moving implacably towards madness is so electrifying it manages to forestall any questions one might have about the unlikely plot turns." Adjani won another Cesar award for her acting in that film.

Montelle randonnée was a taut thriller with Adjani in top form again as a pathological murderess who roamed about the country seducing and killing men. She was lead-billed in *Subway,* playing a bored wealthy woman who became involved with a man who hid out in the Paris Metro system to avoid pursuers. Filmed almost entirely in the subway, the picture soon took on cult status.

Isabelle had stayed away from American films since her debacle in *The Driver.* Ten years later she tried again. *Ishtar* was estimated to have cost $40 million to produce and worth not one penny of it. Much of the money was gobbled up by huge, $5 million plus each, salaries to the male leads Warren Beatty and Dustin Hoffman. Those two played aging song and dance men caught up in the Middle East. Adjani was a Middle Easterner and had little to do, appearing mostly in a veil. *Ishtar* labored long and mightily but lost a fortune. The only consolation for Isabelle was that she was paid around $1 million.

"I didn't want to be an actress. I swear it. I never, never did," said Isabelle. "I just met people, and in a strange way, it happened. There were opportunities, people made me work. Now I like it. It is a way of expressing myself, of having the opportunity of expressing myself. I love to act. I love to rehearse. I love to make a text alive. But I don't want to be completely filled with the poison of my work. I want to do other things."

Isabelle Adjani Filmography

Le Petit Bougnat (1970)
Faustine et le bel été [Faustine and the Beautiful Summer] (1972)
La Gifle [The Slap] (1974)
L'Histoire de Adèle H. [The Story of Adele H.] (1975)
Le Locataire [The Tenant] (1976)
Barocco (1976)
Violette et François (1977)
The Driver (1978)
Nosferatu — Phantom der Nacht [Nosferatu the Vampire] (1979)
Les Soeurs Brontë [The Brontë Sisters]

(1979)
Clara et les chics types (1980)
Quartet (1981)
Possession (1981)
L'Année prochaine si tout va bien [Next Year If All Goes Well] (1981)
Antonieta (1982)
Tout feu tout flamme (1982)
L'Été Meurtrier [One Deadly Summer] (1983)
Mortelle randonnée (1983)
Subway (1985)
Ishtar (1987)

Sources

Cott, Jonathan. "Striking Poses," *Rolling Stone,* August 26, 1976, p. 32–35+.
"Everyone Wants this Success Girl," *Vogue,* 165:135, December 1975.
Flatley, Guy. "At the Movies," *New York Times,* August 12, 1977, p. C7.
Gussow, Mel. "She Quit the Comédie Française for Truffaut," *New York Times,* October 26, 1975, sec. 2, p. 15.
The International Dictionary of Films and Filmmakers: Volume III: Actors and Actresses. Chicago: St. James Press, 1986, p. 7–8.
Katz, Ephraim. *The Film Encyclopedia.* New York: Thomas Y. Crowell, 1979, p. 11.
Lester, Peter. "The Story of Isabelle A.," *Interview,* 6:11–12, March 1976.
McBride, Joseph. "Isabelle Adjani Is Wise, but Letdown on Academy Visit," *Variety,* 282:7, April 7, 1976.
Monaco, James. "Today's French Actresses Are Picking Power over Stardom," *Village Voice,* October 27, 1975, p. 152+.
Shales, Tom. "Isabelle Adjani," *Washington Post,* March 8, 1976, p. B1+.

Marie-Christine Barrault

As a beautiful French blonde known for her onstage coolness, Marie-Christine Barrault was a serious dramatic actress who had worked extensively on the stage and in television before making her theatrical film debut. As with so many other foreign actresses, one of her films was a bigger than expected hit and enjoyed a long run in the United States. Following the pattern, this led to a couple of American films but not the big Hollywood career so often envisioned in these circumstances. The actress soon returned to make films in Europe.

Marie-Christine Barrault was born on March 21, 1944, in Paris, France. Mr. Barrault died when his daughter was quite young but the children grew up in fairly comfortable circumstances. Her uncle was Jean-Louis Barrault, a well-known French actor and stage director. Sensitive to her connections, in later years when asked if Jean-Louis had given her career a boost, she insisted, "Oh no, I grew up in a convent school absolutely away from him. He never helped me in any way. I don't think he was happy that I became an actress. My mother is a widow, and he thought I should have had a more serious job to earn money very soon to support her."

After high school Barrault was unsure of her future and briefly studied literature in London. She was soon back in France to devote herself to acting. Mrs. Barrault was opposed to acting as a career but one of the teen's aunts intervened in her favor and convinced the mother to permit her daughter to take acting lessons. Marie-Christine studied with a famous French acting teacher René Simon in 1963 and the following year she enrolled at the Paris Conservatoire where she spent the next two years.

While she studied acting she made numerous appearances on both stage and television. It was also during this period that Barrault married Daniel Toscan du Plantier, the scion of an aristocratic family. The couple would later have two children. By the early 1970s Daniel became the director-general of the huge French film company Gaumont.

Eric Rohmer's 1969 film *My Night at Maud's* was the actress's debut film. That picture dealt with the morality of sex, with the actress cast as a very pure young Catholic girl who eventually weds the male lead. One reviewer said she lent an aura of "attractive mystery" to the film and her notices were uniformly good. From there she went on to appear in a comedy *Le distrait* about an absent-minded young man who spread chaos in an advertising agency before he got the girl and succeeded on the job. Marie-Christine had a supporting role.

Next she played the female lead in two dramas. *Les Intrus* was about a pair of criminals who held a doctor's wife and child hostage while the banker got money to pay a ransom. Marie-Christine played the wife and drew mixed reviews. *John Gluckstadt* was set in Germany in 1860. John Hansen was down on his luck after six years in jail for armed robbery. Upon returning to the small town of Gluckstadt and unemployment, he married an illiterate servant girl. He saw his wife and child suffer in poverty as he drifted from one part-time job to another. The hostile townspeople named him John Gluckstadt and as he grew

Marie-Christine Barrault in one of her many films.

more desperate he accidentally killed his wife and had his child taken away. As the wife, Barrault gave a forceful performance, her best to date, and her reputation as a fine dramatic actress grew.

Cousin, cousine (1975) was a surprise smash hit and gave Marie-Christine international exposure and fame. Until that one was released none of her films except the first had received any exposure in America and she was almost completely unknown. All that changed after the film did turn-away business for months on end in cities like New York and Los Angeles.

That film, which top-billed the actress, was a comedy about family manners built around such rituals as death and marriage. It was a love story about two cousins, both unhappily married, who were having an affair with each other. Marie-Christine got rave reviews, as did the film, from almost all quarters. The film took awards at several festivals although it was initially banned in Spain, and Russia refused to buy it condemning it as "antifamily."

Gaumont produced *Cousin, cousine* but Barrault hotly denied that her husband helped to promote her career, saying, "I had been an actress for eleven years and he had been in the movies for only two years when I got this part." She had a nude scene in the film and remarked that it did not bother her at all. "I'm not very beautiful, you know. I'm not Brigitte Bardot. But to be naked is just a way of life. When I go on holiday, I'm naked all the time. Besides, you give much more of yourself when you cry or do a very dramatic scene than you do when you're naked."

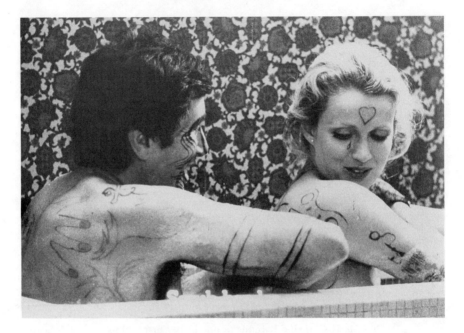

Marie-Christine Barrault and Victor Lanoux in *Cousin, cousine.*

The inevitable rush of Hollywood film offers followed on the heels of *Cousin, cousine* and Marie-Christine was tempted but unsure. "I just don't know, I don't want to be away from my home," she said, "I feel really French in my blood. I could do a film in a foreign country once, perhaps twice, but not more." Her husband hoped they would continue to be successful with French films, feeling, "That way we can still have big hits in America, but stay as we are — French." In the end Barrault refused the "crazy offers" from the United States, as she called them, at least for a few years.

She kept busy in Europe appearing in a variety of parts, some good, some less so. A support role in the big budget spectacular *The Medusa Touch* brought little attention, while her portrayal of the lead role in *L'État sauvage* garnered mixed reviews. That film took a dramatic look at a new African state in the 1960s. Marie-Christine played a French woman who left her dull civil servant husband to run off with an adventurer to Africa. Once there she left him to take up with the local Minister of Health.

Barrault played Guinevere of King Arthur's court in *Perceval le Gallois*, the story of a young man in medieval times who wanted to become a knight. In *Een Vrouw tussen hond en wolf* the actress played a woman whose sheltered life was shattered by violence, politics and love as she came of age during World War II. She got good notices in her top-billed role. *Ma chérie* was a well-made film about mother and daughter relationships. Marie-Christine portrayed a divorced, independent woman in her 30s with a 16-year-old daughter. She gave an excellent performance and *Variety* said she "sensitively portrays the difficulties of a woman and mother trying to keep her balance."

The enticements of America, if not Hollywood, proved too much to resist for the actress and she appeared in Woody Allen's *Stardust Memories* (1980). Barrault had been hoping to be used by someone like Robert Altman, whom she admired, but had never thought of herself as material for an Allen project. She got a call from him while on vacation on the French Riviera and found him gentle and very shy. Woody wanted to know her availability, how her English was, and to discuss the project with her in Paris. Barrault told him everything was fine and then spent the rest of the time before the meeting taking a crash course in English.

Woody had been impressed by her performance in *Cousin, cousine* and told her he was casting her as an American even though she was French because he couldn't find an American actress for the part. Marie-Christine was aware of the number of successful European actresses who had tried their luck in America to little effect. The actress felt she had a better chance to succeed because she was working with Woody Allen and the film was shot in New York, not Hollywood. "It's not just any old part and I won't be working in Hollywood. I hate the way of life there," she said, "I'm sure the spirit of New York is closer to Europe . . . it's nearer anyway. Los Angeles is another world."

Stardust Memories was soundly trounced by the critics and was an unexpected cynical film from the usually nebbish Allen. This bitter change of pace was as responsible for the poor reviews as anything else. Barrault, as one of the three women in the Allen character's life, gave a credible showing. The actress took her shot at a Hollywood film a couple of years later with *Table for Five,* an asinine tearjerker about an errant father (Jon Voight) who took his three kids on an ocean voyage to try and close the gap between them. Barrault was the woman whom he romanced on the ship. She did as well as could be expected with poor material. That marked the end of the actress's American experiment. All of her other films have been European projects.

Recently she has had support roles in *A Love in Germany* and *Swann in Love*. In *Les Mots pour le dire* she gave an excellent performance as one of two troubled women. Marie-Christine played a mother repatriated to France from Algeria after the independence. After her daughter's marriage, the mother sank into a bitter idleness and made her daughter's life a living hell. It was a subtle and gripping portrayal by the actress.

Her work in *Le Pouvoir du mal,* set in the 1920s, was less generously received. That film was about a poverty-stricken theological student who found himself in a metaphysical jam as lover to the wife of a rich weapons maker who had agreed to finance his university studies. Barrault was first-billed as the wife. The film had poor dialogue and most reviews were poor. *Variety* termed all the chief players "dreadful." Hopefully Barrault's next movie will do her credit.

Marie-Christine Barrault Filmography

Ma Nuit chez Maud [My Night at
    Maud's] (1969)
Le Distrait [The Daydreamer] (1970)
Les Intrus (1971)
L'Amour l'après-midi [Chloe in the
    Afternoon] (1972)
John Gluckstadt (1974)
Cousin, cousine (1975)
Du Côté des tennis (1976)
The Medusa Touch (1977)
L'État sauvage (1978)
Perceval le Gallois (1978)
Een Vrouw tussen hond en wolf
    (1978)

Ma Chérie (1979)
Même les mômes ont du vague a l'âme
    (1979)
L'Amour trop fort (1980)
Stardust Memories (1980)
Josephs Tochter (1981)
Table for Five (1982)
Eine Liebe in Deutschland [A Love in
    Germany] (1983)
Les Mots pour le dire (1983)
Un Amour de Swann [Swann in Love]
    (1983)
Le Soulier de satin (1984)
Le Pouvoir du mal (1985)

Sources

Champlin, Charles. "Barrault at the Pinnacle," Los Angeles Times, November 19, 1976, sec.
    4, p. 1.
Crawley, Tony. "Woody's French Cousin," Films Illustrated, 9:172–3, January 1980.
"Les Immortels du cinéma: Marie-Christine Barrault," Ciné Revue, 65:20–23, January 10,
    1985.
Katz, Ephraim. The Film Encyclopedia. New York: Thomas Y. Crowell, 1979, p. 81.
Klemesrud, Judy. "U.S. Love Affair with Cousine," New York Times, October 27, 1976,
    p. 56.

Fanny Ardant

For Fanny Ardant success in film in her native France came easily and very
quickly. With appearances in only a couple of films behind her, Fanny was cast
as the female lead in a film by François Truffaut which led to international acclaim for the actress. Since then she has been one of France's busiest actresses,
working exclusively in that country, and has appeared in ten films since 1980,
seven of them since 1983. She has also been fortunate in working with many
top directors.

Fanny Ardant was born in 1952 in Saumur, France, a small town about
200 miles southwest of Paris. She described her family as bourgeois but
without much money. Mr. Ardant was in the French army and the family spent
a number of years living in Monte Carlo where Fanny spent most of her
girlhood. After high school she attended Aix-en-Provence University and
graduated with a degree in political science.

Fanny Ardant takes aim in *Confidentially Yours.*

Mr. Ardant hoped his daughter might become a diplomat but instead Fanny drifted to London where she spent some time working as a model. Not satisfied with modeling, Ardant returned to Paris in 1974 and enrolled at a drama school. That same year she made her stage debut and acted in all the French classics such as those by Racine and Giraudoux as well as works by Shakespeare.

Fanny Ardant and Jean-Louis Trintignant in *Confidentally Yours.*

Five years went by with Fanny doing a lot of stage work and some French television before she made her film debut. Her father was not happy with his daughter's career choice. Fanny said, "He does not like much the theater and the cinema. He does not like the actor's life. But I do think that parents have the right to be afraid of what their children do. And I have always been very close to my father."

Also in 1974, Fanny married. It was a brief union that only lasted two years before divorce in 1976. Fanny refused to discuss the marriage. A daughter, named Lumière, was born in 1975. In the early 1980s the actress vowed she would never marry again, saying, "I am too afraid of marriage. Not afraid of the other half but of myself. I do not want to be . . . in jail." She also remarked that she cherished fantasies "of a family with a father, a mother, a lot of children, in a beautiful house in the country. Just because my life is not like that, I don't say such a dream is rubbish."

Television work brought her to the attention of the film world and Fanny made her cinema debut in *Les Chiens* (1979). That film was a parable of modern France protesting the increased use of trained guard dogs by private citizens. After the dogs "accidentally" attacked some immigrant African workers and youths, violence erupted. Ardant had only a small part and did not attract any notice. The following year she was in a Claude Lelouch film, *Les Uns et les autres* which covered the time period 1936 to 1981 and looked at the impact of history on the lives of several couples in different countries. Once again the actress's part was too small to attract critical attention.

Fanny continued to do stage work and felt she would never abandon it entirely due to her love for the classics, saying, "Because I love the word, I love the music of the word. In the theater, I want to sing, I want to fly. I don't want to say, 'Pass me the salt.' To act well in Racine, you can spend your whole life—there is always something you have to work on, you never get to the end of it." For Ardant, acting was a way of getting out of herself. "When I was a little girl, I stayed home all the time reading books. I was too tall and too skinny. Not very pretty," she said. "Sometime I think that the whole circle of France was closing in. But when I entered theater school I realized that onstage I could dare to do anything."

Director François Truffaut became aware of her work and cast her as the female lead in *The Woman Next Door* (1981). It was the story of a man and a woman who had a traumatic love affair, separated and met again years later when both were married to others. Ardant moved into the house next door to the man's (Gerard Depardieu) and soon the couple resumed their affair. The liaison ended when the woman shot the man and then killed herself. Fanny got excellent notices and received worldwide acclaim and recognition.

The actress accompanied Truffaut to New York to publicize the film after having some doubts about the trip "afraid to be the little dog following the master." Working with François was a happy experience for her. She felt, "Mr. Truffaut's camera views all women lovingly. In his movies, the woman is glorious." After just three films, two years, and only one major role Fanny Ardant was an international star.

Director Alain Resnais cast her in *La Vie est un Roman*, a poorly received drama that was considered pretentious and boring. Reunited with Truffaut in 1983, Ardant was lead-billed in *Vivement dimanche*, a mystery/comedy that paid homage to Alfred Hitchcock. The story was about a real estate dealer accused of having murdered his wife's lover. The mystery was unraveled by the man's secretary (Ardant) who was secretly in love with him. Reviews of her work were excellent and *Variety* said of Fanny, "This film is a real showcase, putting forward not only her considerable physical charms but also a remarkable talent for elegant comedy."

When asked if she was happy then the actress replied, "Ah, no. I do not care about happiness. Happiness is not the most important thing in life. The most important thing is to be full, to be filled up! To be alive, Not to be like a dead man who gets up in the morning, goes to work, then goes to sleep."

Playing the title character in *Bevenuta*, the story of a woman's passionate and impossible love for a married man, the actress was cast as a musical virtuoso involved with an Italian magistrate. Good notices were the order of the day again with adjectives such as "dazzling" used to describe her performance. The film *Swann in Love* was less satisfactory with the actress in a support role in that adaptation of Marcel Proust's novel of the same title. Reviews ranged from mixed to disappointed.

Alain Resnais used her again in *L'Amour a mort* set in a town in Southern France on the site of an archaelogical dig. A philosophical examination of love, religion and death, the film did not do very well at the box office. One of the actress's worst vehicles was *Les Enragés,* an obvious melodrama about a pair of young ruffians who terrorized a movie star (Fanny) at her country villa. The film and the acting were almost universally panned by the critics.

Fanny next was seen in *L'Été prochain,* a sentimental story about a large family which was torn apart. It told of their trials and tribulations, and eventual reunification in a happy ending. Fanny played the eldest daughter in a family of six children of Philippe Noiret and Claudia Cardinale, with a rocky marriage to Jean-Louis Trintignant. The film was slick and manipulative but was well received, as was Ardant's work.

Constantin Costa-Gavras, known for his almost documentary style dramas, directed *Conseil de famille,* an unusual vehicle for him since it was an ironic comedy about a family of burglars. Top-billed Fanny was more than adequate as the wife but the film itself was perhaps too offbeat to catch on. She recently received good notices playing a major role in Ettore Scola's epic saga, *The Family.*

Success had come so swiftly that Fanny had never gotten used to it and its advantages. She remarked, "It's like a dream! At every single moment I have felt that I don't have the right to these things. But whenever a very big car stops in front of the hotel, I say to myself, 'Ah, this is just like in the movies.'"

Fanny Ardant Filmography

Les Chiens (1979)
Les Uns et les autres (1980)
La Femme d'à côté [The Woman Next Door] (1981)
Le Vie est un Roman [Life Is a Bed of Roses] (1983)
Vivement dimanche [Confidentially Yours] (1983)
Benvenuta (1983)

Un amour de Swann [Swann in Love] (1983)
L'Amour a mort (1984)
Les Enragés (1985)
L'Été prochain (1985)
Conseil de famille (1986)
La Famiglia [The Family] (1987)
Melo (1988)

Sources

Amiel, Mireille. "Fanny Ardant," *Cinema 83,* n.297:29–34, September 1983.
Chase, Chris. "At the Movies," *New York Times,* October 30, 1981, p. c8.
"Fanny Ardant," *Esquire,* 97:64–66, February 1982.

Chapter 4
German Actresses

Germany has long been at the forefront of world cinema. Among the continental European countries, it is rivaled only by Italy and France in the number of top flight directors produced. Depsite this, Germany has produced only a handful of actresses who have achieved international fame. They have never had a director like Sweden's Bergman who introduced a number of actresses to a global audience. Of the six women in this section, three were actually born in Austria and a fourth in Poland. Only two were born in Germany.

From Austria, Maria Schell went to Switzerland as a young girl where she took her stage training before moving on to the German cinema. The 1950s were her glory years as she made films in at least seven different countries, aided by her fluency in several languages. Schell specialized in playing mournful and weepy characters, but always facing adversity with a sunny smile. Hollywood actually ignored Maria so she took the initiative and came unheralded to display her talents. A decline in work due to miscasting and her temperamental personality shortened her American film career. By the mid–1960s her days as a star were over. Maria got little work for a time but then bounced back and was busy again—this time as support instead of as the star.

Romy Schneider was only 15 when she made her first film and had done ten by the end of her teens—mainly support roles in German schmaltz films. Moving to Paris, Romy sharpened her acting skills with a wider variety of roles and started to draw excellent notices for her work. She was equally adept at drama or comedy. Schneider was an extremely busy and versatile actress whose career was cut short by sudden death at the age of 43.

As with most other countries Germany produced a couple of sex goddesses during the heyday of that type, the late '50s through the '60s. One was Senta Berger. She believed that an actress was never really a star until she had made it in Hollywood. For awhile Berger alternated back and forth between Europe and America but in Hollywood she was cast in uniformly poor vehicles which only stressed her as a sex object. By the 1970s Berger limited herself to European films in which she turned in some decent work when given the chance. Berger's career has slowed markedly in the 1980s.

The other sex goddess was Elke Sommer who appeared in 29 films from 1959 to 1963 and soon became a European star. Her roles were forgettable — prostitutes, models and simpletons — but her face and figure weren't. Hollywood molded her into even more of a sex symbol and she became a huge success there, something few foreign actresses have been able to achieve in the modern era. Older now, Elke has kept very busy in films due to her willingness to take on different roles, play comedy, and take support billing instead of the lead role.

Hanna Schygulla came to prominence after she appeared in several films directed by Rainer Werner Fassbinder. Feeling stifled in Rainer's orbit, Hanna left and has since worked with many of Europe's top directors, in several countries. Her roles have often been complex and she has delivered consistently excellent work becoming German's finest, and one of Europe's best, dramatic actresses. Schygulla succumbed to the lure of Hollywood where she was miscast in a mindlessly violent epic *Delta Force,* starring Chuck Norris.

The latest German actress to rise to stardom is Nastassja Kinski. She was only 14 when she made her film debut and her appeal has been partly sexual and partly childish. *Tess* was her breakthrough film and since then her critical and box office success has been mixed with some big wins and some big losses. While there has been critical division over her work, all seem to agree that Kinski is a fascinating actress.

These six women collectively have appeared in 299 films.

Maria Schell

Cast most often in the role of a long suffering woman, Maria Schell perfectly essayed the part of a weepy and emotional female who could cry a seemingly inexhaustible supply of tears on cue. Coupled with her "golden look" and a winsome smile which was often used excessively and inappropriately, Schell had a sensuality which was said to bring out the best in men, not the beast in them. Fluent in four languages, Maria became a true international star and her first score of films originated in seven different countries. Her peak years were in the middle 1950s when she earned major acting awards. Her career then went into a steady decline as Hollywood woefully miscast her and the public lost its taste for crying and suffering female roles with the coming of the women's liberation movement.

The actress was born Maria Margarethe Anna Schell on January 15, 1926, in Vienna, Austria. She was the oldest of four children, two boys and two girls,

Maria Schell in a publicity photo.

all of whom would enter the acting profession with brother Maximilian being the best known besides Maria. Father Herman was a Swiss playwright who lived and worked in Vienna while mother Marguerite was a Viennese actress who would later run the acting school at the Conservatory of Arts in Berne, Switzerland.

Maria was involved in the nursery dramas put on in the household and made her first public appearance in a grade school play when she was just six years old. Over the years she appeared in several more school theatricals as well as being an avid playgoer. Schell would later claim that by the time she was about five she had already decided her future — she would act.

To avoid Hitler, the Schell family moved to Zurich, Switzerland, in 1938 and all acquired Swiss citizenship. Maria spent a year in convent school and by age 15 was begging her father to let her study acting. Mr. Schell refused, however. Aware of his own limited success and the financial instability of the artistic world, he told his daughter to take a business course to have something to fall back on. The teenager went to work as an apprentice in a bookdealer's shop to wrap books and learn secretarial routine. She was paid $11.50 a month. She also took a typing course.

Fate intervened the next year when a friend of Maria's mother was looking for a girl for a small part in a picture he was making. When he saw Maria, he asked her to read for the part and after he heard her he offered the 16-year-old the lead part in the 1942 release *Steibruch* in which she played a 12-year-old and billed herself as Gritli Schell. Her career as an actress was launched.

After this film Mr. Schell relented. Secretarial work was forgotten and Maria enrolled at Zurich's School of Theatrical Arts. The next year the young actress appeared in her second film and made her stage debut. Schell credited her parents with bringing their children up to be independent and her mother for giving her "the foundation of my self-discipline. From her I learned that what you undertake you must complete to the best of your ability.... It was my mother who gave me the courage not to be afraid of a powerful dramatic style."

For the next half dozen years Schell worked exclusively on the stage in various Swiss cities performing in both classical and contemporary pieces. She worked her way up to a salary of $150 a month with the State Theatre of Berne near the end of the decade. One of her early stage directors recalled the teenaged Maria and commented, "It was all there at 17. The tremendous intensity and ambition, the radiance and the look of sentimental innocence, the specific Schell personality."

In 1948 with a few more brief film appearances to her credit Maria left Switzerland and headed back to Vienna where she planned to become a member of the famed Burgtheater Repertory House. She got sidetracked, however, and never made it. A film director named Karl Hartl met her in a cafe, was taken with her intensity, and on the spot offered her the lead in his film *Der Engel mit der Posaune (The Angel with the Trumpet)*. It was her first adult role.

She delivered a magnetic performance in that film which led to stage work in Vienna, a few more films and also drew the attention of British film executive Alexander Korda. Schell was flown to England where Korda offered her a seven-year contract. Schell refused, saying she did not want to leave Vienna. Even when offered four months off a year, the actress declined. Finally Korda suggested his offer was a good chance if only to learn to speak English. It was

Maria Schell and Hardy Kruger in *So Long as You're Near Me.*

enough for Maria, who recalled, "That convinced me, so I signed the contract. In London, I learned to speak English in three months."

She made several films in England over the next couple of years including an English language remake of *The Angel with the Trumpet* with her best performance coming in *The Heart of the Matter.* She was also active on the stage and in European films, appearing in 21 films from 1950 to 1957.

Her European pictures pushed her on to international stardom. Maria was voted Germany's most popular actress every year between 1951 and 1956 except 1953 and quickly became that country's highest paid film star. The Schell smile was as famous in Germany as the Marilyn Monroe walk was in the United States. Fluent in French, German, Italian and English, Schell had appeared in Swiss, Austrian, French, Italian, British and German films by 1957. The following year she added United States films to her list.

Her best performances came in *Die letzte Brücke (The Last Bridge)* for which she won the 1953 Best Actress Award at the Cannes Film Festival and *Gervaise* for which she gained the Best Actress Award in 1956 at the Venice Film Festival. Other memorable performances came in Visconti's *La notte bianche (White Nights)*, *Une Vie (End of Desire)* and *Die Ratten (The Rats)*.

While her films dealt with widely varying subjects, they all had the habit of putting Schell in the middle of a mournful plot in which she unfairly suffered and cried buckets of tears. In *Gervaise* she lost her husband, son and lover while she endured death by drowning in *Liebe*. As a doctor kidnapped by Yugoslav partisans, Schell died trying to save her children in *The Last Bridge* while in *Rose Bernd* the actress lost her baby after yielding to a lover. In *The Rats,* her character went insane after selling her baby to another woman.

This type of role suited Schell and her public. Of her intense acting style, Schell explained, "I drive to the center of the being I must become until I know it as I know my own. But more than that, I want the parts I play to represent not one woman but all women . . . *the* woman. I am trying to separate truth from reality."

Despite her awards and European stardom, Hollywood had not beckoned so Maria made the first move. She journeyed to Hollywood in the spring of 1957 armed only with an invitation to the Academy Award ceremonies. When she arrived no one met her and no flashbulbs popped, but within a few days she had snared one of the most sought-after parts in Hollywood.

MGM was doing a big budget adaptation of *The Brothers Karamazov* and for the main female part of Grushenka had hoped to land either Marilyn Monroe or Carroll Baker. Schell attended a cocktail party the day she arrived and the film's producer, Pandro Berman, was impressed with her but had not heard of her and did not know if she could act. After a hastily arranged private screening of *Gervaise,* he decided she could act and arranged a reading with director Richard Brooks. While she was nervous at first, she marshalled her forces and the next day harangued Brooks and star Yul Brynner "like a Prussian drill sergeant" about why she should get the part then intended for Baker instead of the much smaller one offered to her by Brooks. For personal and business reasons Monroe had been eliminated. Baker was eliminated shortly thereafter and Maria got the part of Grushenka—her first Hollywood role.

The spring of that same year (1957) Schell married a German film director named Horst Hackler who had been assistant director on *The Last Bridge*. The couple took up residence outside of Munich and they had a child in the early 1960s.

Hollywood may have ignored Schell previously but they made up for it by focusing on her with a vengeance as she made *The Brothers Karamazov*. *Time* magazine did a five-page spread on the actress just before the film was released and Brooks waxed eloquently about the sort of spiritual sensuality she brought to the screen as opposed to the more earthy quality of a Monroe or a Jayne Mansfield. It was Brooks who said Maria didn't give men sweaty palms, while another film executive said, "That smile. It doesn't arouse the cad in a man. It brings out the uncle."

The *Time* article went on to bring out Schell's dark side. She was accused of being ruthless and ambitious, and suffering from egoism and avarice. A French actor was quoted as saying he never hated anyone as much as Schell while a German director claimed he wanted to slap her face every time he thought about her. To the cast and crew of *Une Vie* she was openly known as "the monster" while a French director considered her to be the worst experience of his life.

The negatives were summed up by a director, who said, "Maria is an unmitigated egomaniac. For her, nobody else really exists. She lets nothing but nothing interfere with her career. She is a pure power type. What love means to most women, fame means to Maria." She was also charged with being a tightwad who overworked and underpaid her personal staff, saved on hairdressing by having it done free at the studio and negotiated all her own contracts to avoid legal fees. It was said Schell tried to direct her directors even when she was wrong and, in the words of *Time,* "though Maria can think like a man when she has to, she all too often talks like a stubbornly opinionated woman."

Schell quickly and hotly denied all the allegations and the press was kept busy. Probably there was little or no truth in the stories but setting veracity aside a great deal of publicity was generated just before *Karamazov* was released which wouldn't hurt the box office at all. No doubt it was needed as Schell was close to unknown in the United States.

On the set Schell caused no problems except for her weight. When she signed for the picture Brooks asked her to lose 20 pounds. Maria agreed but arrived on location at the same weight. Brooks told her again and when the actress asked why, Brooks gritted his teeth and said, "You are not sexually attractive." The actress gave back a quantity of verbal abuse but then lost 15 pounds in two weeks.

The Brothers Karamazov became a box office success but Schell was not well received by the critics for turning a complicated character into one with a perpetual giggle. A few more American films followed with equally dismal results. Notable was the western *Cimarron* where Maria flashed her famous smile endlessly, even during her childbirth scenes, much to the detriment of the film. Miscasting had soured her three years in Hollywood and she never lived up to the hype of being a new Ingrid Bergman.

She made several more European films by 1963 but then the offers dried up as the long-suffering female character went out of vogue. Save for one small role Maria would be off the screen for five years. Publicly she had announced the hiatus was to spend more time with her family but the reality was that there was little demand for Maria Schell. She was just 37 years old.

While she may have had acting limitations, when cast to her strengths she was one of the best. Director Ray Boulting said, "She is the greatest actress I have ever directed — a tremendous talent." She brought tremendous energy, intensity and concentration to her work. For *Die Ratten* in which she played a female refugee, she went to East Berlin to have her hair done Soviet style and bought the threadbare clothing she wore in the film off the back of a woman in a refugee camp.

Between takes on the set, she would ask for a glass of water not in her own voice but in that of her character while the interpretive notes she wrote on her script were often not in her own hand but in what she imagined to be the handwriting of her character. She often phoned her director in the middle of the night with questions. Once she asked the director to let her run a few more takes of a scene while he was off the set. The scene called for Maria to run down eight flights of stairs and when the filmmaker returned after several hours Schell had done 43 takes of the scene.

In 1968 she worked her way back into films and has appeared in a score of them since—mainly in supporting or cameo roles—in both American and European vehicles. The films have run the gamut from atrocious to excellent. She was cast against a butch Mercedes McCambridge as the two fought for control of a women's prison in *99 Women*. She has also appeared in *Night of the Blood Monster*, *The Odessa File*, *Voyage of the Damned* and had a cameo in *Superman*.

Maria did well in *Just a Gigolo* where she was cast as David Bowie's mother. She had one of her infrequent starring roles in *Nineteen Nineteen* (1985) in which she and Paul Scofield portrayed ex-patients of Sigmund Freud who relived the past in 1970's Austria. Schell gave a fine, understated performance in that film. No longer a superstar or leading lady, Maria will likely continue to appear in films as long as she can get parts. Her desire to act is as intense as her performances themselves. She once said about acting, "I love it, every moment of it. It's not only the money. There's more glory in it than money. To be wonderful in front of everybody, that's the real reward. To be known. To be somebody."

Maria Schell Filmography

Steibruch (1942)
Matura Reise (1943)
Nach dem Sturm (1948)
Wiener Kavalkade (1948)
Der Engel mit der Posaune [The Angel with the Trumpet] (1948)
Maresi (1948)
Der Angeklagte hat das Wort (1949)
Die letzte Nacht (1949)
Es Kömmt ein Tag (1950)
The Affairs of Dr. Holl (1950)
The Magic Box (1951)
The Angel with the Trumpet [English language version] (1951)
So Little Time (1952)
The Heart of the Matter (1952)

Der träumende Mund [Dreaming Lips] (1952)
Bir wir uns wiedersehen (1953)
Tagebuch einer Verliebten [Diary of a Lover] (1953)
Solange Du da bist [So Long as You're Near Me] (1953)
Die letzte Brücke [The Last Bridge] (1953)
Angelika (1954)
Napoléon (1954)
Die Ratten [The Rats] (1955)
Urgano sul Po (1955)
Herr über Leben und Tod (1955)
Gervaise (1955)
Liebe [Love] (1956)

Rose Bernd [The Sins of Rose Bernd] (1957)
Le notte bianche [White Nights] (1957)
Ungarn in Flammen [narrator only] (1957)
The Brothers Karamazov (1958)
Une Vie [End of Desire] (1958)
Der Schinderhannes [Duel in the Forest] (1958)
The Hanging Tree (1959)
Hellas [As the Sea Rages] (1959)
Cimarron (1960)
Das Riesenrad (1961)
The Mark (1961)
Ich bin auch nur eine Frau [Only a Woman] (1962)
L'Assassin connait la musique (1963)
Zwei Whisky und ein Sofa [Rendez-vous in Trieste] (1963)
Who Has Seen the Wind? (1965)
99 mujeres [99 Women; Island of Despair; Island of Lost Women] (1968)
Le Diable par le queue [The Devil by the Tail] (1969)
La Provocation (1969)
Heidi Comes Home [Heidi] (1969)
El proceso de las brujas [Throne of Fire; The Bloody Judge; Night of the Blood Monster] (1970)
Such a Pretty Cloud (1971)
Dans la poussière du soleil [Lust in in the Sun] (1971)
Chamsin (1972)
Die Pfarrhauskomödie (1972)
The Odessa File (1974)
Change (1974)
The Quack (1975)
So oder so ist das Leben (1975)
Voyage of the Damned (1976)
Folies Bourgeoises [The Twist] (1976)
Superman (1978)
Schöner Gigolo — armer Gigolo [Just a Gigolo] (1979)
Die erste Polka (1979)
La Passante de Sans-Souci (1981)
Nineteen Nineteen (1985)

Sources

Current Biography 1961. New York: H.W. Wilson, 1962, p. 411–413.
"The Golden Look," *Time,* 70:40–45, December 30, 1957.
"The Honeyed Newcomer," *Newsweek,* 50:100, July 15, 1957.
The International Dictionary of Films and Filmmakers: Volume III: Actors and Actresses. Chicago: St. James Press, 1986, p. 558–9.
Katz, Ephraim. *The Film Encyclopedia.* New York: Thomas Y. Crowell, 1979, p. 1021.
Lloyd, Ann, ed. *The Illustrated Who's Who of the Cinema.* London: Orbis, 1983, p. 392.
"Maria Schell," *New Yorker,* 37:100–102+, October 28, 1961.
Quinlan, David. *The Illustrated Directory of Film Stars.* London: B.T. Batsford, 1981, p. 417.
"Tears Pay Off for Maria," *Life,* 43:99–104, July 15, 1957.
Thomson, David. *A Biographical Dictionary of Film.* New York: William Morrow, 1975, p. 508.

Romy Schneider

Romy Schneider began her career as the sweet teen princess of German schmaltz movies. She then moved to Paris, lost weight, learned to dress in chic designer clothes, had an affair with handsome actor Alain Delon and was offered roles as the seductress in an array of international films. The latter and most creative period of her career saw her in challenging parts in mostly European films. Just when Schneider was consolidating her reputation as a first-class actress, she was stricken by a heart attack and died. By then she had made over 60 movies.

She was born Rose-Marie Albach-Retty on September 23, 1938, in Vienna, Austria. Her mother combined the words Rose-Marie into the pet name Romy. Schneider's father Wolf Albach-Retty was a leading actor in the Vienna Volkstheater. Her mother Magda, a plumber's daughter, was a star of the German stage and screen. Wolf's mother had been a famous Viennese actress. Romy's younger brother deviated from the family profession and became a physician.

Romy's parents were popular movie stars in Hitler's Germany. The couple survived the war, but their marriage did not, and they later divorced. Magda and Romy remained in Germany and Magda remarried in 1953. Romy adopted her mother's maiden name—Schneider.

Romy, a Catholic, attended convent schools until the age of 14. In 1953, the year she gave up her formal education, she began her movie career. A Berlin producer suggested that Romy be cast as Magda's screen daughter in a treacly film called *When the White Lilac Blooms Again.* The movie was a success and Romy's career was launched. Over the next several years Schneider worked in many German films. Most were light historical romances.

Dubbed versions of these productions were released in the United States. Americans were able to see *The Story of Vicki* in which Schneider played a young Queen Victoria, and *Forever My Love* in which she starred as Princess Elisabeth of Austria. This latter film was an edited pastiche of three German films known as the *Sissi* series. The dubbed vehicles were too fluffy to merit any critical enthusiasm in America but Schneider was a box-office favorite in Europe. Director Ernst Marischka, with whom she worked in the majority of her early movies, complimented her by saying, "Without ever having taken an hour of instruction, this girl is the greatest acting talent I've encountered in thirty years of making movies." One German observer remarked, "She has passed the stage of prodigy; she has the makings of another Marlene Dietrich." She did have a few serious roles during this period including a remake of the classic *Mädchen in Uniform,* yet she was offered few parts that demonstrated her range.

By 1958 Schneider was eager to break away from typecasting, claiming she was "fed up to here with princesses." Her cute and innocent image was beginning to wear thin and she was mocked as "Germany's most publicized virgin," or "Shirley Tempelhof." Even fees of $200,000 per picture did not compensate for the lack of stimulation.

Schneider was ambitious and so was her mother. Magda, who managed to find herself a small part somewhere in most of Romy's German movies, was anxious to launch her daughter in Hollywood. Romy even tried to get a

Romy Schneider in *Forever My Love*.

contract with the Disney studios. Magda boasted to American reporters that eventually American producers "will see in her a modesty and beauty that will make her their idol."

In the meantime, Romy was cast in yet another Viennese romance, *Christine* (1959). The movie was shot in Paris and Schneider's costar was Alain Delon. They began an affair which was to last for about eight years. Romy bade farewell to Germany and moved in with Delon. The German press castigated her for abandoning a lucrative career. "To German filmmakers I had become a sponge that must be squeezed to the last drop," Schneider recalled.

Romy distanced herself from her German background and took up life in Paris with enthusiasm. "The French have taught me to dress, to live, to sleep, to love — everything," she declared. She also improved her acting skills on the Paris stage. Directed by Visconti in John Ford's *'Tis Pity She's a Whore,* Romy discarded her coy mannerisms and learned to develop a fully-realized character. She later toured Europe in Chekhov's *The Sea Gull* in which she played the role of Nina. Romy received excellent reviews for her theater work, quite an achievement considering that French was not her native tongue. She became fluent in English and Italian as well, and said, "I always try to speak the language of the country in which I find myself."

Schneider was above all else, a natural actress. She had no patience for techniques like Method acting. "Acting is acting," she once remarked. "You know what to do. My mother always quoted a director who said, 'Damn it, don't think, act!'"

Romy's film career did not suffer outside Germany. She was as busy as ever, appearing in films such as Orson Welles's *The Trial*. A major breakthrough came in 1962 when Romy was seen in an episode of Visconti's *Boccaccio '70*. She played a young contessa who discovers that her husband is visiting prostitutes. She decides that she too may as well charge the count for services rendered. Schneider's acting was praised and she gained international recognition for this part.

Carl Foreman cast her as a violin student forced to become a prostitute during the war in *The Victors*. Foreman was impressed by Schneider's discipline and said, "She is almost frighteningly professional." He also noted that beneath her cool reserve was a warm personality. "Like a flower that reacts to sunshine, she reacts in the same way if she feels genuinely liked or loved," he said.

In Otto Preminger's *The Cardinal*, Romy played a girl who falls in love with a priest and is later a victim of the Gestapo. Although Romy was seductive in her films, sex appeal was not her dominant quality. "If the bosom matters, I'm out," she remarked. "My physique helps me, but not in the sense understood for Bardot," she added. "It serves me . . . it has never borne me. I know that I can't repose on it."

Schneider went to Hollywood to film the comedy *Good Neighbor Sam*, costarring Jack Lemmon. Critics admired her comic talents and called her "fascinating." Romy seemed blasé about the Hollywood publicity circuit. "Parties, parties—everybody is bored and noisy," she complained. "I have a bad reputation because I don't do little things which are supposed to make a star. . . . In Europe I go out only when I like to go out."

Romy made a few more American films including *What's New Pussycat?* but the majority of her films were European or British. She was seldom involved in German projects, however, even though she would have been welcome there. The Germans were proud of her success but Schneider felt that German producers "refused to understand me."

Schneider and Delon were living openly together in Paris. In the early 1960s this was considered quite scandalous so Romy told the media she was engaged to be married. The press "made me feel like a whore," she said. She had no intention of giving up her career to play housewife and remarked, "The cinema was in my skin. I couldn't give it up nor did Alain wish me to. I was not made for the kitchen." Romy saw herself as sentimental and romantic. "I like men who kiss the hand, and I hate the twist and love the waltz," she said. Yet she realized that she was not an easy person to live with. "I have too many moods. Sometimes I think I am too ambitious," she noted. "While my private life is the more important, I know I could never leave my profession." Delon was

Romy Schneider in *Triple Cross*.

known to stray, and as one observer commented, "At first he ran after her. Now she runs after him." The many separations required for location shooting did not help their relationship and by 1965 Delon ended the affair. Schneider married West German director Harry Meyen-Haubenstock in 1966 and they had a son David.

She remained active in movies and made this comment about actors and her ideas on selecting roles: "We cannot be bourgeois and timid; we must show all sides of life. I am ready to do and to play anything that is intelligent and real." Romy described herself as "proud, hot-tempered, impatient," and she was never intimidated by authoritarian directors. She had a shy side, however. "The more you are timid," she said, "the more you fall back into yourself, the deeper grow the roots of your sensations and sentiments." This, she believed, helped one to become a greater actor.

In the 1970s her output was prolific and she worked with Losey in *The Assassination of Trotsky* playing the murderer's mistress. She was cast as the Empress Elizabeth in *Ludwig,* directed by Visconti and costarring Helmut

Berger. Other important directors she worked with were Bertrand Tavernier and Costa-Gavras. Schneider once remarked, "I am an actress who relies a lot on the director. It was one reason why I didn't get on with Chabrol: he just left me alone in front of the camera, which I can't stand."

One of her best roles was as Leni in *Group Picture with Lady*, based on the Heinrich Böll novel. She played a tough German woman whose family and fortune are destroyed by World War II. Schneider had to age from a teen to a middle-aged landlady during the course of the film. Other strong roles were in *The Most Important Thing Is Love* and *A Simple Story* for which Romy received a Cesar, the French equivalent of an Oscar, in 1975 and 1978 respectively. *A Simple Story* was directed by Claude Sautet and it was Romy's fifth film with this director. One writer noted that "Visconti idealised her on the screen; Sautet showed us a woman of flesh-and-blood."

Romy had divorced her first husband Harry in 1975 and married her personal secretary Daniel Biasini that year. They had a daughter, Sarah. Daniel and Romy separated in 1977. It was also a difficult year because Harry committed suicide. Schneider had remained close friends with Harry and was saddened by his death. Her health suffered and she had a kidney removed. In 1981 she was devastated by a further tragedy. Her 14-year-old son David fell onto an iron railing and was killed. "She never recovered from the death of her son," said Yves Montand, with whom she had made several films. "It is difficult to say whether one can ever heal after an emotional shock like that."

Romy made the film *La Pasante du Sans-Souci* in which she played a mother whose son dies. She dedicated the film to her own son. It was the last film she ever made. Schneider was found dead in her Paris apartment on May 29, 1982. At first suicide was suspected since Romy had been depressed by her son's fatal acccident. It was determined, however, that she died of a heart attack. She was only 43 years old.

Perhaps director Claude Sautet best understood Romy Schneider's appeal when he described her as "a mixture of poisonous charm and virtuous purity. She is as elevated as a Mozart allegro but aware of the power of her body and her sensuality. Romy is vivacity itself, an animal vivacity with all its extremes of moods—from the most masculine aggressiveness to the subtlest gentleness. Romy is an actress who transcends the everyday, who has an ethereal quality which is the preserve of only great stars."

Romy Schneider Filmography

Wenn der weisse Flieder wieder blüht
[When the White Lilac Blooms
Again] (1953)
Mädchenjahre einer Königin [The Story
of Vicki] (1954)

Feuerwerk (1954)
Der letzte Mann (1955)
Die Deutschmeister [Mam'zelle Cricri]
(1955)
Sissi (1956)

Kitty und die grosse Welt (1956)
Sissi, die junge Kaiserin (1957)
Robinson, soll nicht sterben [The Girl and the Legend] (1957)
Monpti (1957)
Sissi-Schicksaljahre einer Kaiserin (1958)
Scampolo (1958)
Mädchen in Uniform (1958)
Die Schöne Lugnerin (1959)
Die Halbzarte (1959)
Christine (1959)
Ein Engel auf Erden [Angel on Earth] (1959)
Katia [Magnificent Sinner] (1960)
Plein soleil [Purple Noon; Lust for Evil] (1960)
Le Combat dans l'île (1961)
Die Sendung der Lysistrata (1961)
Forever My Love [An edited version of the three Sissi films] (1962)
Le Procès [The Trial] (1962)
Boccaccio '70 (1962)
The Victors (1963)
The Cardinal (1963)
Good Neighbor Sam (1964)
What's New Pussycat? (1965)
La Voleuse [Schornstein No. 4] (1966)
10:30 P.M. Summer (1966)
Triple Cross (1966)
Otley (1968)
La Piscine [The Swimming Pool] (1969)
My Lover, My Son (1970)
Qui? [The Sensuous Assassin] (1970)
Les Choses de la vie [The Things of Life] (1970)

La Califfa (1971)
Max et les ferrailleurs (1971)
Bloomfield [The Hero] (1971)
César et Rosalie (1972)
The Assassination of Trotsky (1972)
Ludwig [Ludwig: Twilight of the Gods] (1973)
Le Train (1973)
Le Trio infernal [The Infernal Trio] (1973)
Un Amour de pluie [Loving in the Rain] (1974)
Le Mouton enragé [Love at the Top; The French Way] (1974)
L'Important c'est d'aimer [The Most Important Thing Is Love] (1975)
Les Innocents aux mains sales [Dirty Hands] (1975)
Le Vieux Fusil [The Old Gun] (1975)
Une Femme à sa fenêtre [A Woman at Her Window] (1976)
Gruppenbild mit Dame [Group Picture with Lady] (1977)
Mado (1978)
Une Histoire simple [A Simple Story] (1978)
Last Embrace (1979)
Bloodline (1979)
Clair de femme (1979)
Lo sconosciuto (1979)
La Mort ed direct [Deathwatch] (1979)
Garde a Vue [Under Suspicion] (1980)
La Banquière (1980)
Fantasma d'amore [Ghost of Love] (1981)
La Passante du Sans-Souci [La Passante] (1981)

Sources

"Actresses," *Time*, 80:38, December 14, 1962.
"Britannia Uber Alles," *Newsweek*, 51:106, February 10, 1958.
Current Biography 1964. New York: H.W. Wilson, 1965, p. 369–370.
"The Infernal Trio," *Films Illustrated*, 4:410, July 1975.
The International Dictionary of Films and Filmmakers: Volume III: Actors and Actresses. Chicago: St. James Press, 1986, p. 560–561.
Jennings, C. Robert. "Romy Schneider," *Saturday Evening Post*, 236:36–38, November 23, 1963.
Katz, Ephraim. *The Film Encyclopedia*. New York: Thomas Y. Crowell, 1979, p. 1024–1025.

Lloyd, Ann, ed. *The Illustrated Who's Who of the Cinema.* London: Orbis, 1983, p. 394.

"Lovely Romy Goes Home," *Life,* 54:45+, June 14, 1963.

"People," *Time,* 106:63, January 17, 1977.

Quinlan, David. *The Illustrated Directory of Film Stars.* London: B.T. Batsford, 1981, p. 418.

"Romy Schneider," *Good Housekeeping,* 160:24, March 1965.

"Romy Schneider," *Films and Filming,* n.335:4–5, August 1982.

"Romy Schneider, Austrian-Born Screen Actress, Dead at 43," *Variety,* 307:4+, June 2, 1982.

"Romy Schneider, European Film Actress, 43, Dies," *Washington Post,* May 30, 1982, p. B4.

"Romy Schneider: She Gave Up Royalty," *Look,* 26:38+, September 11, 1962.

"Romy Schneider, the Actress, Dies in Paris Apartment at 43," *New York Times,* May 30, 1982, p. 28.

Shipman, David. *The Great Movie Stars: The International Years.* London: Angus & Robertson, 1972, p. 464–467.

Talese, Gay. "Arrivederci, Romy," *Esquire,* 60:112, November 1963.

Thomson, David. *A Biographical Dictionary of Film.* New York: William Morrow, 1975, p. 509–510.

"The Tragic Last Years of Romy Schneider," *Photoplay,* 33:68, August 1982.

Wlaschin, Ken. *The Illustrated Encyclopedia of the World's Great Movie Stars and Their Films.* London: Salamander, 1979, p. 191.

Senta Berger

Senta Berger was one of those foreign actresses who was convinced that one was never really a star unless, and until, one achieved stardom in the United States—no matter how famous one might be at home. Berger had her shot at Hollywood fame, made a number of pictures there and received a degree of media hype. The roles, however, were uniformly terrible. Senta returned to Europe to get the few decent roles which she has had. One reviewer said she was "full-faced, full-bosomed, full-hipped—a frankly full female" and most of her parts have cast her as decoration or sex object. She has been very busy as an actress and in less than 30 years has appeared in 84 films.

Senta was born in 1941 in Vienna, Austria, the daughter of a Czech father who composed café music, and a Hungarian mother—a combination that "produces the best mixture of Viennese," joked Senta. The actress grew up in wartime Vienna and saw her father go off to prison camp. It was a time of poverty for mother and daughter. Mrs. Berger often had to resort to stealing eggs to feed the family. Senta remembered the city burning and recalled, "It was like tiny fragments of stars. I still get sick when I hear an ambulance." She also remembered frequent trips to bomb shelters.

As a child she studied ballet and then turned to modeling. By the latter part of the 1950s she had appeared on the covers of many European fashion

Senta Berger in a publicity photo.

magazines. Bored with a career as a cover girl, she took up acting and studied with Max Reinhardt in Vienna. Soon she appeared in plays ranging from Shakespeare to Tennessee Williams and won critical praise for her work.

Senta made her debut in films in 1957 having bit parts in a few movies that year and the next. *The Journey* (1958) about the 1956 Hungarian revolution, in which she again had only a bit part, was her first English-language feature. Several more films followed until she got her first major billing in *The*

Good Soldier Schweik. Adapted from the famous novel of the same name, it was an excellent film and Berger was singled out as showing "promising talents."

A major break came when actor Richard Widmark signed her for a violent thriller he was producing, *The Secret Ways* (1961). That film was a cliché-ridden cloak and dagger melodrama which was so bad the audiences laughed at the serious parts. The only good thing *Variety* had to say about the picture was that it brought Berger to American theater screens. That publication described her as "a well-proportioned blonde bombshell with the culinary sounding name of Senta Berger, in a preposterously irrelevant role incorporated into the film apparently for purely decorative reasons."

The year *The Secret Ways* was released was Senta's busiest as she appeared in nine films. And as bad as *The Secret Ways* was, it did launch her on a Hollywood career although most of those American roles would be little better in quality than her first. *The Victors* was a three-hour blockbuster about World War II with a multitude of stars in a series of vignettes. Senta made an impression as a woman who sold sex for gifts and food. *Jack and Jenny* was a frivolous comedy with the actress involved in plenty of nudity and bed scenes.

Berger moved back and forth acting in both Europe and Hollywood. Her European roles were not always high quality either. *A Full Heart* was a comedy/drama about a poor German boy who won a lot of money and then indulged in the sweet life with, again, lots of time spent in bed. *Major Dundee* was a rugged action picture which starred Charlton Heston in a Cavalry versus the Indians yarn. Senta was only in the picture to provide a bit of romance to break up the violence, yet one critic felt that, among her American films, this was the only one which did her "appeal justice."

A variation on that type of role came in *Cast a Giant Shadow,* the fictional biography of West Pointer Col. Mickey Marcus who aided in the establishment of Israel. Berger did well as a busty fighter for Israel who provided a love interest for star Kirk Douglas. Her character was admittedly totally fictional. *The Quiller Memorandum* was a well-produced spy drama devoid of gimmicks and well received by the critics. Senta played a schoolteacher who "looks attractive" and provided another romantic interlude.

The first love in her life had been Vienna television director Peter Maar. Said Senta, "He was the first victim of my career. Peter had too little money, and he was too proud when I started to earn more than he did. There were crises over nothing." A natural brunette, the actress often found herself as a blonde in her films and commented, "It bothers me to put on a blonde wig for movies because nobody really takes blondes seriously, as women or actresses."

By the middle 1960s she was at the peak of her Hollywood popularity and said, "My future is bright if I get good parts in good pictures. If I have to struggle anymore—then, no, I'm not going to make it. I've had all the struggling

I want." The film capital publicists claimed that within Berger they found "a hint of Paulette Goddard, a flicker of Hedy Lamarr, quite a lot of Ava Gardner." And Hollywood was where she wanted to be. "It's okay to be famous at home," she said. "To have kids follow me and shout, 'Senta, Senta,' that's fine—but you're nothing unless you make it in Hollywood."

Good parts in good films did not materialize in California, however, and Senta made very few films there in the future, having to content herself with European projects. The actress claimed she never minded being a sex object, saying, "I like it when I walk and when men look at me and appreciate that I am a pretty woman. It's like being in a perfume bath."

Peau d'espion was a spy film about trying to stop the defection of a French scientist to Red China. Berger got good notices as the wife of a man who sold scientists to the East. *The Ambushers* was one in a series of Matt Helm spy films starring Dean Martin. In this poor film, the actress had nothing to do but look good.

By the end of the 1960s Senta was married to director Michael Verhoeven. The actress had a small role in *Paarunger,* the first picture directed by Michael. Senta and her husband had formed a company Sentana, which had raised two-thirds of the film's $188,000 budget. Eight years later Sentana produced *Mitgift* with Michael again directing. Senta starred in that detective story about a woman who collected men, tired of them and then had them killed.

Through the 1970s Senta continued as top-billed or lead female in most of her European outings. *De Sade* was a biography of the Marquis de Sade with plenty of sex and sadism. Berger played the sister of a homely and frigid woman whom de Sade married. She drew good reviews. One of her worst vehicles was a farce about prehistoric man and his first encounter with prehistoric woman called *When Women Had Tails.* Savaged by the critics, one of whom called it "embarrassingly low-class," it apparently did well enough at the European box office to spawn a sequel the next year, *When Women Lost Their Tails,* which was as bad as the original.

Berger lent good support in a violent underworld film about mayhem and vengeance titled *Le Saut de l'ange* and was also effective as a nurse in *White Mafia,* a satirical attack on the medical profession. One of her best performances came in *Die Moral der Ruth Halbfass,* which was based on a real life case in Dusseldorf about the glamorous wife of a wealthy industrialist who cheated on her husband and plotted his death with her lover. Said one reviewer, "Senta has expanded her acting potential to impressive dimensions."

Cross of Iron was an antiwar film from the German point of view. Berger did well in a brief and predictable role as a nurse who ministered to, and went to bed with, James Coburn. In *La giacca verde* the actress played a beautiful film star who distracted a famous symphony conductor who suffered a mental crisis while leading his orchestra. It was a well-played character study with

Senta Berger in *Cross of Iron*.

Berger getting good notices. Another excellent performance came in *Nest of Vipers* wherein Berger played a woman who seduced the young friend of her son. The boy fell in love and planned to marry a girl who was a student of Berger's. The actress's character then became jealous and took revenge.

In the 1980s Senta appeared on the screen only a couple of times as her career waned. *The Flying Devils* was about an aerial circus troupe trying to perform a difficult somersault for a large sum of money. The son in the troupe strayed from home, and sidetracked the dream with Senta who played a journalist twice the boy's age.

Senta compared herself to Sophia Loren. She remarked, "We have the same measurements, only I'm three inches shorter." Summing up her off-screen life, Senta commented, "This is the way I am at home — not very complicated, not too seductive, just myself. . . . I've never been able to be morbid or pale. I'm practical, earthy, quite normal and much too healthy."

Senta Berger Filmography

Die unentschuldigte Stunde (1957)
Die Lindenwirtin vom Donaustrand

(1957)
Der veruntreute Himmel (1958)

The Journey (1958)
Katia (1959)
Ich heirate Herrn Direktor (1959)
Der brave Soldat Schweik [The Good Soldier Schweik] (1960)
O sole Mio (1960)
The Secret Ways (1961)
Das Wunder des Malachias (1961)
Immer Aerger mit dem Bett (1961)
Eine hübscher als die andere (1961)
Junge Leute brauchen Liebe (1961)
Adieu, Lebewohl, good bye (1961)
Ramona (1961)
Es muss nicht immer Kaviar sein (1961)
Diesmal muss es Kaviar sein [The Reluctant Spy] (1961)
Das Geheimnis der schwarzen Koffer [Secret of the Black Trunk] (1962)
Sherlock Holmes and the Deadly Necklace (1962)
Das Testament des Dr. Mabuse [The Terror of Dr. Mabuse] (1962)
Frauenarzt Dr. Sibelius (1962)
The Victors (1963)
Jack and Jenny (1963)
The Waltz King (1963)
Kali-Yug, Goddess of Vengeance (1963)
Kali-Yug, Part II [The Mystery of the Indian Temple] (1963)
Volles herz und leere taschen [A Full Heart and Empty Pockets] (1964)
Major Dundee (1965)
The Glory Guns (1965)
The Spy with My Face (1966)
Du suif dans l'Orient (1966)
Our Man in Marrakesh (1966)
The Poppy Is Also a Flower (1966)
Cast a Giant Shadow (1966)
The Quiller Memorandum (1966)
Lange Finger (1966)
Peau d'espion [A Spy's Skin; To Commit a Murder] (1967)
Operazione San Gennaro [The Treasure of San Gennaro] (1967)
The Ambushers (1967)
The Miracle of Father Malachios (1967)
Paarunger (1967)
Diabolically Yours (1967)

If It's Tuesday, This Must Be Belgium (1968)
Istanbul Express (1968)
Les Etrangers (1969)
De Sade (1969)
Cuori solitari (1969)
Quando le donne avevano la coda [When Women Had Tails] (1970)
Der Graben (1970)
Casanova (1970)
Percy (1970)
L'amanti dell'orsa maggiore (1971)
Le Saut de l'ange (1971)
Roma Bene (1971)
Wer im Glashaus liebt...Sancorsiap (1971)
Mamma dolce, mamma cara (1971)
Un anguilla da trecento milioni (1971)
Cobra (1971)
When Women Lost Their Tails (1971)
Causa di divorzio (1971)
The Scarlet Letter (1972)
Amore e ginnastica (1972)
Die Moral der Ruth Halbfass (1972)
Reigen [Merry-Go-Round, Dance of Love] (1973)
Bisturi, la mafia Bianca [White Mafia] (1973)
Di mamma non ce n'è una sola (1973)
L'Uomo senza memoria (1973)
La bellissima Estate (1974)
The Swiss Conspiracy (1975)
Il ventre nero della signora (1975)
Mitgift [Killing Me Softly] (1975)
Lonely Hearts (1975)
La Guardia del corpo (1975)
La Padrona (1975)
Progliaccio d'amore (1975)
Signore e Signori buonanotte (1976)
Cross of Iron (1977)
Ritratto di Borghesia in Nero [Nest of Vipers] (1978)
Sentimenti [Sentiments and Passions] (1978)
La giacca verde (1978)
Das chinesische Wunder (1978)
I Miss You, Hugs and Kisses (1979)
The Flying Devils (1985)
Killing Cars (1985)

Sources

Katz, Ephraim. *The Film Encyclopedia.* New York: Thomas Y. Crowell, 1979, p. 109.
Lloyd, Ann, ed. *The Illustrated Who's Who of the Cinema.* London: Orbis, 1983, p. 39.
Quinlan, David. *Quinlan's Illustrated Directory of Film Stars.* London: B.T. Batsford, 1986, p. 39.
"Senta of Vienna," *Look,* 28:87–90, October 6, 1964.
"She's Paulette, Hedy and Ava, All in One," *Life,* 59:80, September 10, 1965.

Elke Sommer

Elke Sommer was one of many European actresses who became an international star in the 1960s primarily for her sex object image. With a provocative figure, a baby face and very blonde hair, Elke was in great demand. Many of her movies were bad and a lot of critics were of the opinion that she could not act at all. Like most women in her position, Sommer wanted to be taken seriously as an actress and not just be known for her body. It did not work out that way but her career endured and Elke wore very well in films, still appearing after almost three decades which is a remarkably long life for a sex goddess. Her creative satisfaction, however, had to come from other areas—notably painting.

The actress was born Elke Schletz on November 5, 1940, in Berlin. Her father was a Lutheran minister and the family lived in a town 15 miles outside of Nuremberg. By the time she was two Elke was said to have already been reciting verse. As a youngster she had a classical education and picked up the schoolgirl nickname of "Schluffi" which meant "Sniffing Around."

Mr. Schletz was 50 when his daughter was born and he died 14 years later. Elke recalled, "He always wanted a boy, and I was raised as a boy. I went to school with 500 boys and two other girls. I studied Latin and Greek. Until I was sixteen I dressed like a boy in hand-me-down slacks and sweaters. I never owned a dress except for confirmation." Living in an Allied-occupied Germany, the family lived in poverty and the actress said, "I milked ten cows a day for seven days a week for a dollar to get money."

After her father died Elke switched her education over to modern languages, hoping to become an interpreter. She was soon fluent in German, Spanish, Italian, French and English. The latter language was acquired when she took an au pair job in London at the age of 17. She was paid $8.50 a week and stayed nearly a year.

Next came a holiday to Viareggio, Italy, with her mother in 1959. The teenager went to a local dance and, like every other girl there, had a tag pinned on her as she entered. When the dance was over a man announced over the

Elke Sommer in *The Wicked Dreams of Paula Schultz.*

microphone that Elke's number had won — she had been chosen Miss Viareggio of 1959.

A movie producer came out of the audience to ask Elke to appear in his next film. Sommer brushed him off thinking he was not sincere but he and his wife showed up at the hotel the next day and offered Elke $1,500 to be in the film as well as paying all expenses for herself and her mother. Elke was convinced and made her film debut that year in *Das Totenschiff.*

Quickly she became a European star and by 1963 had appeared in over two dozen films made in several different countries including England. However, few had received any American distribution. Although she was directed by Vittorio De Sica for one film, most of her roles and vehicles were very forgettable. She played simple-minded country girls, prostitutes, models and trollops who committed suicide. In many of her films she was disrobed or scantily dressed. Elke was a sex object and followed in the tradition of Brigitte Bardot and Sophia Loren.

With her first paychecks she indulged in her passion for cars and very quickly had a collection of nine, ranging from the mundane, a Ford Fairlane, to the chic, a Jaguar. Elke regularly drove up and down the German freeways near her home at speeds in excess of 100 miles an hour.

As her popularity increased in Europe young girls began to imitate her hairstyle and clothes and Sommer's name and face became visible on such products as deodorants, lotions and hairsprays. Elke was so much in demand that she had been away from the cameras only 43 days out of three years at the beginning of the 1960s.

With all the attention it seemed inevitable that Hollywood would notice. Producer Sandro Berman was looking for a female to play the lead opposite Paul Newman in the 1963 release *The Prize* which became her first American film. Berman had seen one of Elke's German films and had been impressed, saying, "She was beautiful and wildly sexy. She was young and blonde and could play the Swede we needed. And she looked like she'd fit in Paul Newman's arms." In that film Elke led Nobel prize winner Newman through the streets of Stockholm and into romance. On the set she was said to have been so bubbly and refreshing that the crew nicknamed her "Alka Seltzer." Upon her Hollywood arrival, Sommer readily admitted that most of her film roles had asked nothing from her except "perfect teeth and a nice smile." Her hope was to be known as an actress instead of as a "star."

For the woman who once said, "I looked just like a boy until I was 17 years old — no lipstick, no makeup and no hairdo" and then went on to be one of the top European sex symbols, Elke found it was not enough for the Hollywood image makers. They decided to improve on the face and body which had been labeled perfect by some. The moulders at MGM told Elke to lose 10 pounds which she did. Next she was dispatched to a dentist who, after much searching, was able to find two next-to-invisible spaces which he then capped. It was also decided that Elke's blonde hair would be better rinsed out and lightened by several more shades. Her hair was then styled in a dozen or more ways until MGM decided the actress's original style was actually the best. Sommer was also ordered never to appear in public unless dressed to the nines. According to *Time* magazine she was a "packaged tomato."

Off screen she led a discreet and quiet life, declining invitations to Hollywood parties, commenting, "I've been to parties in Europe, I know what it's all about — to see and be seen. But it's not part of my job to turn up in a cocktail dress making awkward conversation. Why should I put on an act? Why should I give something of myself to the public if there's no need for it?" In 1964 she married writer Joe Hyams and the couple were still together two decades later.

Her one exception to the quiet life was in her driving habits. Elke obtained her license within a couple of days of arriving in the United States and raced her car up and down the freeways. Nabbed twice for speeding in a couple of weeks, Sommer remarked, "What business have policemen being out there at 5:30 in the morning? They should be home in bed."

In her spare time she read, composed and recorded her own songs, painted and indulged in a certain amount of controlled eccentricity. For breakfast it was said she consumed a concoction consisting of raisins, Rice Krispies, malt, maple syrup and chocolate sauce. "The press created me," said Elke, "I wouldn't dare to be normal."

After her first Hollywood effort Sommer divided her working time between the States and Europe with more and more of her films originating in the United States by the end of the 1960s. She became just as big a star in the United States as she was in Europe and was a much sought after talk show guest on American television.

Her critical reception remained poor and the idea that she might not be able to act at all preceded her on the set. When she filmed *A Shot in the Dark* (1964), it was reported that star Peter Sellers was so upset with her lack of acting ability that he wanted her removed from the picture. Director Blake Edwards brought the star around when he reminded him that Sellers had once boasted he "could act with a barn door." Elke responded, "I don't think I am a good actress yet, but I hope to become one. It's much more difficult for me as a blonde with a pretty smile than for a brunette who can go screaming about the room. Some people don't take me seriously. But they will."

Whatever acting limitations she may have had, Elke generated much enthusiasm from the press and with the public. Edwards attributed this to her screen projection of what he called an "image of astounding sexuality." A film magazine analyzed Elke's appeal and hailed her as "a mother goddess type whose physical presence in a picture awakens in the audience a realization of its unity with life."

In *A Shot in the Dark,* an Inspector Clouseau (Sellers) comedy, Elke did well and the *New York Times* described her as "a bright comic foil." Most of her vehicles, however, were of much poorer quality. *The Art of Love* was a dismal comedy about an artist who faked suicide so his conman roommate could cash in on the sudden demand for his pictures. Elke was little more than window dressing. As female lead in the crime thriller *The Money Trap* she acquitted herself well but the picture was not successful at the box office. Cast opposite Robert Vaughn in an inane spy picture *The Venetian Affair,* Sommer was again window dressing and ended up murdered in the film.

In *Deadlier Than the Male* she was one of the two female hit people for a syndicate who ran around London and the Riviera killing unsuspecting men by a variety of methods including spear guns, injections, time-bombs and exploding cigars. The women were caught in the end and the picture featured lots of bikini shots. Opposite Dean Martin in one of his Matt Helm spy flicks *The Wrecking Crew,* Elke and the rest of the cast was considered to be guilty of bad acting.

Percy was a British comedy about a male genitalia transplant which was panned both by audiences and critics. *Zeppelin* was an unbelieveable spy tale about the World War I dirigible. Elke played the wife and assistant of a German professor who had invented a new weapon.

Elke Sommer and Lee J. Cobb in *They Came to Rob Las Vegas*.

One of the best examples of the dismal type of roles Elke was saddled with came in *The Wicked Dreams of Paula Schlutz*, a film labeled "unrelievedly awful" by the *New York Times*. Elke played an East German Olympic star who escaped her country by pole vaulting over the Berlin Wall in her black lace underwear. Most of the rest of the story centered around showing novel ways for Sommer to become disrobed such as having her dress sucked off by a vacuum cleaner, her dress split by a climb and her sweatshirt removed by the weight of medals on her chest. While Elke had been the female lead in all these films but second or third-billed overall, she got top billing in *The Wicked Dreams of Paula Schultz* which was clearly the worst film of a very poor lot.

By the early 1970s Elke was getting fewer film offers from Hollywood. Demand had decreased due to her box office failures and the fact that she was getting old for a sex object. The actress did several films in Europe including *Percy's Progress*, the sequel to *Percy*, which did well abroad although a pronounced disaster at the American box office. Sommer indulged her flair for comedy by appearing in one film of another long-running British comedy series, *Carry On Behind*.

During the middle of that decade Sommer did stage work in the United States, appearing in *Cactus Flower* and *Born Yesterday* in between her film work. Her European roles were usually no better than her Hollywood ones. *Das*

Netz cast her in the role of a kittenish prostitute dressed all in leather and on the run from a killer. "I hope I'll still be sexy," said the then 35-year-old actress of her appearance in that film.

Elke had rarely spoken out about the sex object roles she was often relegated to until 1975 when she performed on the stage in Chicago. "Some idiot wrote a review of *Born Yesterday* in which he mentioned my 'obvious attributes,'" said Sommer. "That's what I resent so terribly. I don't mind this 'sex kitten' business in itself. I've heard it for twelve years. What I do mind is having to work twice as hard to get what's coming to me because of it — good parts, good reviews. . . . I mean, I didn't do anything to stop that 'sex kitten' image back when I began doing movies. But I sure didn't start it." The Chicago reporter who chose to report this also went on in his article, reprinted in the *Los Angeles Times,* to mock Sommer and to imply that she was indeed incapable of anything but a sex-object role.

Sommer remained fairly busy in films into the early 1980s although more often in support roles than in leads. In the comedy *The Prisoner of Zenda,* at least the fourth remake of that classic and another showcase for Peter Sellers in multiple roles, Elke had some good moments in a peripheral role. The actress was third-billed behind two males in *The Double McGuffin* but all three took a back seat to kids in a very inane mystery wherein a bunch of teens solve an assassination plot. Elke was cast as the Prime Minister of a small Middle East country who, inexplicably, spoke German. Even in that film geared to teens, the producers had Sommer give a quick flash of nudity in her minor role.

One of her better performances came in *Exit Sunset Boulevard,* shot in Los Angeles as a small budget feature by an experimental German filmmaker. It was about a German citizen who arrives in Los Angeles to claim an inheritance and his experiences with the American dream. Concerned more with content than form, it received no commercial distribution in the United States, relegated to the odd art house and Europe.

Invisible Strangler was a silly police manhunt thriller originally released in 1977 as *The Astral Factor* and then recut for a 1984 release. Once more Elke had a minor part, but in the words of one reviewer was "well-cast as a former beauty pageant winner." Since 1981 Elke has appeared in just four films. *Death Stone* (1986), her most recent, was her 71st film appearance.

The actress never received the kind of creative challenge she wanted on the screen and whatever talents she may have had were all too often shrouded and obscured by poorly written parts as bimbos, sex objects or prostitutes. More creative satisfaction came from her longtime hobby of painting and, in 1978, she had her first exhibition at a gallery in Southern California. Her subject matter was legends and proverbs from central Europe and her style was contemporary primitive.

Elke admitted that being a celebrity was a definite help in getting into a gallery, but when asked about the celebrity effect on sales, said, "I was afraid of that when I started exhibiting, so at my first exhibit I had twenty-two paintings, and I took my name off and put another name, E. Schwartz, on and didn't come to the gallery. Within four days everything was sold."

While she has never been taken very seriously by the film industry, Sommer has shown a definite facility for comedy and has delivered good performances on the few occasions a worthwhile part has come her way.

Elke Sommer Filmography

Das Totenschiff (1959)
Lampenfieber (1959)
L'amico del giaguaro (1959)
Am Tag als der Regen kam [The Day It Rained] (1959)
Uomini e nobiluomini (1959)
Freund von der Jaguar (1959)
Ragazzi del juke box (1959)
Ti diro . . . che tu mi piaci (1959)
La pica sul Pacifico (1959)
Femmine di lusso [Traveling in Luxury] (1960)
Himmel, Amor und Zwirn [Heaven and Cupid] (1960)
Urlatori alla sbarra (1960)
Don't Bother to Knock! [Why Bother to Knock?] (1961)
Douce violence [Violent Ecstasy] (1961)
Du quoi tu te meles, Daniela? [Daniela by Night] (1961)
Les mutins de Yorik (1961)
. . .und sowas nennt sich Leben (1960)
Zarte Haut in Schwarzer Seide (1961)
Geliebte Hochstaplerin (1961)
Les Bricoleurs [Who Stole the Body?] (1962)
Auf wiedersehen (1962)
Café Oriental (1962)
Nachts ging des Telephon [The Phone Rings Every Night] (1962)
Caprici Borghesi (1962)
Das Mädchen und der Staatsanwalt (1962)
Un Chien dans un jeu de guilles (1962)
Bahia de palma (1962)
The Victors (1963)
Denn die Musik und die Liebe im Tirol (1963)
Verführung am Meer Ostrva [Island

of Desire] (1963)
The Prize (1963)
Unter Geiern [Among Vultures; Frontier Hellcat] (1964)
Le Bambole [Four Kinds of Love] (1964)
A Shot in the Dark (1964)
Seven Tons of Gunfire (1964)
The Art of Love (1965)
The Money Trap (1965)
Hotel der toten Gäste (1965)
Wenn man baden geht auf Teneriffa (1965)
The Peking Medallion [The Corrupt Ones] (1966)
The Oscar (1966)
Boy, Did I Get a Wrong Number (1966)
Deadlier Than the Male (1966)
The Venetian Affair (1966)
The Wicked Dreams of Paula Schultz (1967)
The Invincible Sex (1968)
Las Vegas 500 millones [They Came to Rob Las Vegas] (1968)
The Wrecking Crew (1969)
Percy (1970)
Zeppelin (1971)
Baron Blood (1972)
Die Reise nach Wien (1973)
Einer von uas beiden (1973)
Ein Unbekannten rechnet ab (1974)
And Then There Were None (1974)
Percy's Progress (1974)
The Swiss Conspiracy (1975)
Carry on Behind (1975)
House of Exorcism [Lisa and the Devil] (1975)
Das Netz (1976)

On a Dead Man's Chest (1976)
The Astral Factor (1977)
The Thoroughbreds [later *Treasure Seekers*] (1977)
I Miss You, Hugs and Kisses (1978)
Fantastic Seven [Stunt Seven] (1978)
The Double McGuffin (1978)
The Prisoner of Zenda (1978)

Exit Sunset Boulevard (1980)
Der Mann in Pyjama (1981)
Jatsani kell [Fitz and Lily; Lily in Love] (1983)
Invisible Strangler [revised version of *The Astral Factor*] (1984)
Niemand weint fur immer (1985)
Death Stone (1986)

Sources

"Elke's Big Blitz on Hollywood," *Life,* 54:74–6, May 31, 1963.
Gordon, Stanley. "Elke Sommer," *Look,* 27:71–3, October 22, 1963.
Hyams, Joe. "A Season of Sommer," *Saturday Evening Post,* 237:70–72, April 18, 1964.
Katz, Ephraim. *The Film Encyclopedia.* New York: Thomas Y. Crowell, 1979, p. 1071.
"Packaged Tomato," *Time,* 82:58, July 12, 1963.
"People," *Time,* 106:50, November 3, 1975.
Powers, Ron. "The Mind, Matter of Elke Sommer," *Los Angeles Times,* August 15, 1975, sec. 4, p. 21.
Quinlan, David. *Quinlan's Illustrated Directory of Film Stars.* London: B.T. Batsford, 1986, p. 396.
"Tomorrow's Stars," *Good Housekeeping,* 160:24, March 1965.
Tuchman, Mitch. "Elke Sommer Paints," *Take One,* 6:22–3, November 1978.

Hanna Schygulla

Hanna Schygulla began her film career under the tutelage of German director Rainer Werner Fassbinder. She was the leading lady in nearly half of the films that he made, and established herself as one of the top European actresses. A few years before his death, Hanna felt overwhelmed by Fassbinder's intensity. She increasingly sought roles with other directors. In recent years Schygulla has been less selective about her work and has appeared in some commercial Hollywood and television roles that paid handsomely.

Hanna Schygulla was born on December 25, 1943, in Katowice, Poland, which was occupied by Germany during the war. Her father Joseph was a lumber merchant, but was away fighting with the German army when Hanna was born. He was captured in Italy by the Americans and sent to a prisoner of war camp in Pennsylvania until 1948. Hanna and her mother Antonie fled to Munich when the Red Army descended upon Katowice. Their first home was an abandoned railway car. Things improved somewhat when Joseph was reunited with his family. But "there were always fights about money," Hanna remembered. "I never wanted to be like people around me. I wanted more freedom."

Schygulla finished high school and then worked as an au pair girl in Paris. Her parents scraped together enough money to send Hanna to the University of Munich where she majored in Germanic and Romance philology with the intention of becoming a school teacher. She learned to speak fluent French and English.

A friend of Hanna's was studying acting at the Fridi-Leophard Studio in Munich, and one day Hanna went along to a class. She met Rainer Werner Fassbinder there and became intrigued by the stage. By 1967 she and Fassbinder were members of the Munich Action Theater. "I had been going with the intellect, studying to be a teacher, but I hadn't been satisfied. It was becoming less and less spontaneous for me and increasingly uncomfortable. I wanted something more sensual," Hanna explained of her decision to become an actress. "I rejected the idea of knowing how my life would be going on in a certain progression until I'm 65."

Fassbinder broke with the Action Theater and formed his own anti-theater. One of his actresses was stabbed and left paralyzed. Fassbinder called in Schygulla to replace her in *Antigone,* and as he remarked, "She became my star."

"With Fassbinder, we were taking ourselves seriously and yet not taking ourselves seriously," she recalled. "In the years '67 or '68 there was a rebellious spirit. We were innocent politically but we got into kind of hot stuff sometimes." The troupe performed in pubs and usually played to an audience of less than 20 people. "It was fun," Hanna said. "We did collages of classics — with much persiflage. . . . The students from the university would laugh and laugh. . . . Fassbinder would stage plays like they were movies, and his first movies like they were plays."

One of the Antitheater's productions, an adaptation of Goethe's *Iphigenie,* was filmed by director Jean-Marie Straub. The 23-minute film was released as *The Bridegroom, the Comedienne, and the Pimp.* Hanna played the comedienne. The movie received very limited distribution and little critical attention, but it inspired Fassbinder to write and direct a feature film *Love Is Colder Than Death,* starring Schygulla as a gangster's moll. The film was largely ignored by the 1969 Berlin Film Festival, but Fassbinder's next project *Katzelmacher* received critical acclaim and won the 1969 West German Film Critics prize. American reviewers were less enthusastic, and it would be several years before Fassbinder's work generated interest in the United States. Schygulla had the role of a small town girl who sympathized with a hated foreign worker, played by Fassbinder.

Hanna appeared almost exclusively in Fassbinder films over the next six years. She made only two movies with other directors. Neither made a great impact. She also performed in several television movies. Even most of these were directed by Fassbinder, although a couple of these television productions were by other directors such as Schlondorff and Lilienthal.

Hanna Schygulla in *The Marriage of Maria Braun*.

Her earliest films with Fassbinder were more experimental than highly developed pieces, but both director and actress were learning more and more with each project. Schygulla was never typecast by Fassbinder and she played a variety of roles ranging from a cool, composed actress in *Beware of the Holy Whore* to the sister of a fruit peddlar who drinks himself to death in *Merchant of Four Seasons*. Fassbinder would use ensemble players from the Antitheater, such as Ingrid Caven and Kurt Raab, in his films until about 1970.

In 1972 *The Bitter Tears of Petra von Kant* was released and played the New York Film Festival. It was a strange, depressing but excellent film, and Hanna was brilliant as a woman who abandons her lesbian lover and returns to her husband. Although reviews were mixed, American critics were taking more notice of Fassbinder.

His next film with Schygulla *Effi Briest* clinched his reputation as the greatest genius of the new German cinema. Schygulla was cast in the title role and played a young beauty who is married to a wealthy older man. Effi's affair with a handsome young officer results in a tragic end. The movie was a showcase for Schygulla and the *New York Times* called her "enchanting" and "stunning." "The film is essentially Hanna Schygulla's and she is splendid," enthused one critic.

Four more films with Schygulla were released after *Effi Briest,* although all had been shot earlier. None were Fassbinder projects and only Wim Wenders' *Wrong Move* and Jasny's *Clowns* gained much attention.

Even though *Effi Briest* seemed to be the start of an exciting international career for Hanna, she surprised the film industry by dropping out of acting entirely for a couple of years. She was partly afraid of success, and was worried about pushing herself too much. "I had the feeling I'd got stuck," she explained. "It was my first mid-life crisis . . . I isolated myself for a while to find out what would come up in me when I was not being told what to do by others. I felt I needed a change. I didn't like myself, so I took off."

She hitchhiked through the United States with a girlfriend for three months and traveled from New York south to New Orleans, through Texas, California and then New Mexico where she spent a day with elderly painter Georgia O'Keefe. "I really like old age when it still is young and has all the fire going," Hanna said of her visit to the artist.

During her period away from filmmaking, Schygulla took up yoga and Sufi and became a vegetarian. She spent time in a country house outside Munich with ten other artists, and also taught children at the Rudolf Steiner School where creativity is stressed. Summing up her experiences, Hanna said, "All I had was time, time, time."

She was lured back into films when Fassbinder offered her the title role in *The Marriage of Maria Braun*. She gave an excellent performance as Maria, an allegorical character whose shrewd and ruthless rise in life paralleled the "economic miracle" of West Germany. Hanna found it interesting to "portray something more cruel than I usually did," she said, "to get more into the cruel feelings I have. I've come across the monsters I am, so I want to get them out too. . . . What is out is almost gone."

The film took only four weeks to shoot and was, along with *Effi Briest,* one of the few Fassbinder films that had popular appeal with German audiences. Schygulla said the director was able to work quickly "partly because he knows his actors so well and they know him." She also liked the fact that Fassbinder allowed his cast a certain flexibility in interpreting their lines while he focused on "the movement and visual texture of a scene."

The movie was a great success in the United States and Schygulla received rave reviews. Andrew Sarris of the *Village Voice* wrote: "The beating heart of the film is Schygulla's," and *New York Times* critic Vincent Canby called her "splendid and mysterious." *Vogue* described her screen presence as having "the authority of the legendary, the patina of the classic. She gestures — with an eye, her chin, a foot — and the gesture is an assertion, has power. The persona is a stunning statement about woman, sex and power." Hanna won the 1979 Berlin Film Festival's Silver Bear Award for Best Actress and also received an Oscar nomination.

Remarking on her feelings about film acting, Schygulla said, "The camera represents so many eyes. There is pleasure in penetrating to so many other people. . . . You have to come up with the energy to cross through." She also liked the experience of taking on various personalities. "You want to get into the feeling of something more than just what your life is taking you through. It's adventuring within yourself into all the many possible people you are." Hanna explained that she always tried "to bring something enigmatic to a role, so people can fill in. You're revealing and concealing," she said.

Schygulla had a physical magnetism that did not depend on conventional standards of beauty. As one observer noted, her "pancake-faced, and some-what dumpy figure is so highly, though subtly, expressive that an elusive smile, a nuanced arching of the brows, or a slight hand gesture can transform her im-age into that of a vibrant beauty. To a large extent she has retained the distanced acting style she early developed, in avoiding the display of emotion but rather manifesting what has been deemed 'exaggerated understatement.'"

Her collaboration with Fassbinder lasted for three more films. She ap-peared in *The Third Generation,* a cynical look at terrorists, and *Berlin Alex-anderplatz,* a 15-hour television epic in which Hanna played a prostitute. The film was released in American cinemas in 1983 and was highly praised. "The viewer surrenders . . . to Schygulla, with her wicked, witty mouth," wrote Richard Corliss of *Time.*

Lili Marleen, her last film with Fassbinder, was inspired by cabaret singer Lale Andersen (called Willie in the movie) whose song "Lili Marleen" became popular during World War II with both the German and Allied troops. Schygulla starred as Willie and gave an affecting portrayal of a woman who is exploited by various factors during the war. The movie was a box office hit in West Germany but received mixed reviews in the States. Some critics found it melodramatic while those who liked it felt Schygulla gave a subtle per-formance.

By this time, Hanna had had enough of Fassbinder. "I had to save my sanity," she said bluntly. "I had to leave him, and Rainer couldn't understand it. He offered me a contract for life! It was laughable. . . . I would have drowned. Look, he was a superb director," she acknowledged. "I owe my career to him. But he was possessed—demonic. On the one hand, I found him poetic; on the other, I felt he was like a destructive force. He was all instinct. As a director, he saw the world in potent, dazzling images. he could reveal an entire relationship by the mere turn of an actor's head. He hated discussions— explanations. He wanted actors to surprise him," she continued. "And yet, he also needed to possess them, to manipulate them, to play masochistic games with them. All that didn't amuse me at all—and finally I had to leave."

Hanna made *Circle of Deceit,* directed by Volker Schlondorff. She did well in the role of Arianne, the German widow of a Lebanese businessman. Schygulla also was a favorite of the critics for her part in *La Nuite de Varennes,* a fantasy about Louis XVI's escape from Paris, directed by Ettore Scola. If Schygulla ever entertained thoughts of working with Fassbinder again, that

Hanna Schygulla with unidentified actor in *A Love in Germany*.

came to an end in 1982 when he was found dead from an overdose of alcohol and drugs at age 37.

At his memorial service, Schygulla cried out, "Who is going to take us to our limits now?" She once remarked, "I have always worked for other directors, but Fassbinder has been the dominant influence on my career." Describing the director's genius, Schygulla said, "He was the master of irritation . . . but then something would come along that was incredibly human, or simple. It was this mixture which produced a dynamic reaction in the spectator."

Fortunately Schygulla was not given much time to brood about Fassbinder's demise. Jean-Luc Godard offered her a role in *Passion,* his enigmatic project about making movies. Many critics and Godard fans were puzzled by the abstract pretensions of the film, and even Schygulla was confused about its meaning. "It's a difficult movie," she admitted. "I had to see it three times before I could piece it together. Working with Godard was like assisting a director in search of his own film," she noted.

An even more controversial film was *The Story of Piera,* directed by Marco Ferreri. Schygulla played a loose woman who introduces her daughter to sex with a man they pick up at a picnic. Hanna won the Best Actress Award at the 1983 Cannes Film Festival for her part. Many people in the audience were shocked by the subject matter and considered the film immoral. Hanna defended the movie and commented, "For me, playing the mother in *Piera* was incredibly fulfilling. I went into it knowing that the subject of incest was very touchy. But it was a role where, for once, the character was speeding ahead of me. You see," she explained, "I need to be in films that say something and to play characters who really live out their feelings. That's when I feel I'm being stretched out and challenged . . . I'm definitely not made for bourgeois parts," she decided. "I like roles that are illogical, chaotic, ambiguous."

Schygulla enjoyed working with Ferreri. "He dares to work in images that go straight to the root of people's emotions," she believed. "He is a man of vision, and he is fearless. Well, for me," she concluded, "fearlessness and vision are what filmmaking is all about."

In her next film *Sheer Madness,* directed by Margarethe von Trotta, Hanna played a college professor who tries to help a woman who is having a breakdown. The movie had a feminist perspective and was a fascinating portrait of psychological pain. Schygulla admired von Trotta's energy and courage as a filmmaker but wished her role in *Sheer Madness* had been blacker and more bizarre.

Andrzej Wajda, the highly acclaimed Polish director, gave Hanna the lead role in *A Love in Germany.* She played Paulina, a small town middle-aged German housewife, who falls in love with a young Polish prisoner of war during World War II. Although they both realize they are doomed by flaunting their affair, they defy the Nazi authorities and their personal tragedy becomes political.

Vincent Canby felt Hanna showed a new maturity, and said, "Miss Schygulla, I suspect, is one of the few actresses anywhere today who could succeed in making Paulina's love for Stani seem so erotic, and then to make that eroticism seem so important that it's worth the sacrifice of both herself and her lover . . . it is apparent that Miss Schygulla has at long last become one of the great European film actresses of our era."

Schygulla was now dividing her time between France and Germany. She had a home in Paris and one near Munich. Hanna never married but her recent beau was French screenwriter Jean-Claude Carriere, 54. Schygulla had often expressed an interest in working with American directors, particularly Stanley Kubrick, Woody Allen, Sidney Lumet, and Martin Scorsese.

Her faith in German films was declining. "I feel that at the moment German films are at a very low ebb, and the tide doesn't seem to be changing," she commented in 1983. "Since Fassbinder, no new voice has burst forth." Hanna felt that a new right-wing mood in the German film industry was discouraging any kind of courageous or challenging productions.

Schygulla's interest in Hollywood increased but she was cautious. According to one version she tried for the lead role in *Sophie's Choice* in 1982 but lost the part to the more commercial Meryl Streep. Another source claimed Hanna herself refused the part considering it too superficial. "I can only act when I feel there are hidden depths in a part and I am personally involved. . . . I don't want to be just a doll being rigged out in different costumes all the time."

In the end, the sparkle of Hollywood became too great to resist and Schygulla accepted a role in *Delta Force* starring macho-hero Chuck Norris. "It's the kind of film I'm amazed I did," said Schygulla of this mindlessly violent epic. She also appeared as Catherine in an NBC-TV miniseries, *Peter the Great*. She earned a six-figure salary for the project and had a free trip to Russia where the series was shot. Hanna's next role was in a comedy *Forever Lulu* that starred rock singer Deborah Harry and sex therapist Dr. Ruth Westheimer.

Schygulla once remarked that Fassbinder "brought out some special energy in me. He's still there, very much with me. There's never an end with Fassbinder." Perhaps the memory of his spirit will remain strong enough in Schygulla so that it will not be finished off by a lethal blow from Chuck Norris.

Hanna Schygulla Filmography

Der Brautigan, die Komodiantin, und der Zuhalter [The Bridegroom, the Comedienne, and the Pimp] (1968)
Liebe ist kalter als der Tod [Love Is Colder Than Death] (1969)
Katzelmacher (1969)
Gotter der Pest [Gods of the Plague] (1969)
Warum lauft Herr R amok? [Why Does Mr. R Run Amok?] (1969)
Jagdszenen aus Niederbayarn [Hunting Scenes in Lower Bavaria] (1969)

Whity (1970)
Warnung vor einer heiligen Nutte [Beware the Holy Whore] (1970)
Kuckucksei im Gangsternest (1970)
Der Handler der vier Jahreszeiten [Merchants of the Four Seasons] (1971)
Die bitteren Tranen der Petra von Kant [The Bitter Tears of Petra von Kant] (1972)
Wildweschsel [Jail Bait; Wild Game] (1972)
Fontane: Effi Briest [Effi Briest] (1974)

Falsche Bewegung [Wrong Move]
(1974)
Der Stumme (1975)
Ansichten eines Clowns [The Clowns]
(1975)
Die Heimkehr des alten Herrn (1977)
Die Ehe der Maria Braun [The Marriage of Maria Braun] (1978)
Die Dritte Generation [The Third Generation] (1979)
Lili Marleen (1980)
Die Falschung [Circle of Deceit]
(1981)

La Nuit de Varennes (1981)
Passion (1982)
La Storia di Piera [The Story of Piera]
(1982)
Maria Antonieta Rivas Mercado (1982)
Heller Wahn [Sheer Madness] (1982)
Berlin Alexanderplatz (1983)
Eine Liebe in Deutschland [A Love in Germany] (1983)
Il Futuro E' Donna [The Future Is Woman] (1984)
Delta Force (1986)
Forever Lulu (1986)

Sources

Buckley, Tom. "At the Movies," *New York Times,* October 26, 1979, p. C8.
Canby, Vincent. "Hanna Schygulla Achieves Greatness," *New York Times,* October 7, 1984, section 2, p. 17.
Current Biography 1983. New York: H.W. Wilson, 1984, p. 372–376.
Gruen, John. "Hanna Schygulla Charts a Fresh Course," *New York Times,* October 23, 1983, section 2, p. 19+.
"Hanna Schygulla," *Vogue,* 170:240+, February 1980.
The International Dictionary of Films and Filmmakers: Volume III: Actors and Actresses. Chicago: St. James Press, 1986, p. 561–562.
"Interview: Schygulla," *Vogue,* 173:58, December 1983.
Robbins, Jim. "Kollek, Schygulla Eye U.S. Growth," *Variety,* 323:20, July 2, 1986.
Stark, John. "Europe's Incandescent Hanna Schygulla Blazes in *Peter the Great*," *People,* 25:58–60, February 10, 1986.
Thomas, Kevin. "Schygulla: A Passion for Life," *Los Angeles Times,* November 28, 1979, section 4, p. 1+.

Nastassja Kinski

Nastassja Kinski made her film debut at the age of 14 and has been busy ever since. A bohemian childhood, a love affair with Roman Polanski, and a nude photograph of Kinski wrapped in a snake, all contributed to the legend that has surrounded her career.

She was born Nastassja (sometimes spelled Nastassia or Natassia) Nakszynski in West Berlin on January 24, 1961. Her father is the Polish-German actor Klaus Kinski and her mother is Ruth Brigitte, a writer. Home life was unconventional as the family moved from country to country following Klaus' film projects. Nastassja became multilingual and is still fluent in German, English, French and Italian.

Her parents had a passionate and emotionally demonstrative relationship.

Nastassja recalled her childhood as "wonderful," a mixture of "fights and tears, happiness and sweetness and breakdowns where we would destroy the house and then make up." Her parents' marriage lasted until Kinski was eight. Brigitte described living with Klaus as "like being onstage, every day and night, in Kafka. He was extremely jealous," she said. "It was as if he built a private religion around us: Madonna and Child." Nastassja also had similar memories of Klaus. "My mother wanted to work in movies, and people asked her to. But he just wanted her to be a mother, be a wife, be this Venus, a planet he could land on any time," said Kinski. She recalled her father's piercing blue eyes as being "like hell and the sky at the same time."

For two years after the split, Klaus wrote love letters to Nastassja and her mother. Then he met and married a Vietnamese woman and had a son with her. Nastassja also had an older half-sister also fathered by Klaus. For many years there was little contact between Nastassja and her father, and he had nothing to do with helping her become an actress. He was preoccupied with his new family and Kinski was hurt by her father's neglect. As a result she became extremely close to her mother. Brigitte took Nastassja to Caracas, Venezuela, where they lived with her lover, a painter. Nastassja considered her mother to be her best friend. "I love her because she always gave me freedom," Kinski said. Yet Brigitte was always there to protect Nastassja if she needed it. "For most parents, love means letting their child do what's good for them," Brigitte explained. "For me, love means letting her do whatever is within her. Maybe it's dangerous to let her act out her happiness, her fullness, her anger, but when I look at her face and know that she's happy because of the way she is, I cannot say no."

When Nastassja was 12 she began to seek independence "like an animal running wild, tasting all the honeys," as she described it herself. "My mother let me do it," she said, "and I think she was right; I think it's important for everyone to be able to go through that; now I don't have to."

Perhaps Brigitte thought that these experiences would help her daughter as an actress. "I always felt Nastassja would become an artist," said Brigitte. "Her father filmed her when she was two years old, and already she was a child-woman, with such sensitivity and such pain in her face—pain not as a woman would feel it, but as a flower, a rose would feel pain."

By this time Kinski and her mother had returned to Germany. Nastassja regularly went dancing at a rock and roll club in Munich and one night film director Wim Wenders came over to her and asked if she wanted to be in a movie. Kinski took time to think over the offer and decided to accept. "I did the part, mainly for the money," she said. "It wasn't much money, but it was a lot to me, and my mother and I needed it." The Wenders movie was the critically acclaimed *The Wrong Move*. Kinski played a deaf-mute juggler who falls in love with an itinerant older man. Her next projects, including *Passion Flower Hotel*, *For Your Love Only*, and *To the Devil a Daughter*, were minor.

Nastassja Kinski in *Tess*.

For Your Love Only was originally made for television in 1976 and later released theatrically in 1982. Kinski played a schoolgirl whose teacher is infatuated by her. *To the Devil* was a thriller in which a virginal Nastassja is saved from an evil occultist.

Stay as You Are brought more attention to Nastassja than her previous films. She played a student who seduces a married man (Marcello Mastroianni). Director Alberto Lattuada described her as a mixture of "poison and nectar." *Playboy* published nude stills from the movie which was accepted by Kinski. "I was brought up to believe that there is nothing shameful about the naked body," she commented. "Nudity does not bother me as such. It's beautiful and quite natural. But when pictures are taken out of films, and the context is lost, it's perhaps a different thing."

When Kinski was 15 she was introduced to a middle-aged Roman Polanski. It was Nastassja's mother who acquainted the two. Kinski immediately fell for him, and she and Polanski became romantically involved for about a year. "He introduced me to beautiful books, plays, movies," she said. "He educated me."

Polanski had just fled the United States after being charged with raping a 13-year-old girl. Kinski only saw a gentle side of Roman, however, and could not believe he would stoop to raping someone. "He was so nice to me," she insisted. She still considers him a close friend and cares deeply about his opinions. Polanski was planning a movie version of the Hardy novel *Tess of the d'Ubervilles.* He felt Nastassja would be right for the part of Tess and prepared her for the role by sending her to Los Angeles and London for acting lessons and to perfect her English. Polanski also gave her publicity by using her as a model in a 1976 issue of French *Vogue.*

Tess was a study of Victorian values, class structure, and women's rights, and Nastassja played the role of a girl who is raped by an aristocrat and punished for it, even though she was the victim. Kinski was interested in the fact that *Tess* focused on the theme of the sexual double standard, but she was hesitant to embrace feminism. "It's good it's coming up, women trying to get their rights instead of talking about it," Kinski commented. "Everybody should have the freedom to do what they want. But women are losing their femininity; they can't become men, and they shouldn't be against men."

Because of his own rape charge, Polanski was ostracized by some of the Hollywood elite, and there was doubt as to whether the film would be distributed commercially in the United States. When it did well in previews in New York and Los Angeles, Columbia decided to distribute *Tess* and the movie ultimately profited at the box office. Reviews were mixed but *Tess* won a Golden Globe Award for Best Foreign Film. Nastassja also won a Golden Globe for Best New Female Star. Said Kinski, "Acting is so easy; you learn it as you go along." She was completely dependent on the director and commented, "If you do things right, they tell you; if you do things wrong, they correct it. It has a kick to it. I love it."

American directors became aware of her talent and many of her subsequent films were made in the United States. Nastassja bought a co-op apartment in Manhattan. Francis Ford Coppola cast her in the box office flop *One from the Heart,* an overly romantic musical fantasy in which Kinski played a circus acrobat. Nastassja thought that Coppola was a genius as a director but was sometimes overwhelmed by his drive and energy. "He's almost like a monster—but not in a bad way—it almost frightens you," she remarked.

Even though *One from the Heart* was a disaster, audiences were fascinated by Nastassja's beauty. As *Time* magazine described it, "The camera loves

Nastassja Kinski. Every feature of her young body comes to life before its lens. The wide, gray-green eyes send out satellite signals of precocity or perversity. The dewy skin holds, on the left cheek, a tiny scar, like a bookmark in a turbulent autobiography. The lips, extravagantly full, can pout or preen or tauten resolutely or open in an elfin smile. The long Botticelli neck carries the eye to a strange and strong body, with delicate breasts, expressive musculature and the strong haunches of a peasant girl or a centaur. Kinski is a true camera animal because these disparate, classically mismatched parts combine sensationally well."

Critics were comparing her to a young Sophia Loren, Ingrid Bergman, Brigitte Bardot and even Audrey Hepburn. To this kind of praise, Kinski responded that it was far too soon in her career to mingle her name with such illustrious ones. "Oh no! Give me a break!" she protested.

Paul Schrader hired Nastassja for *Cat People,* a horror movie costarring Malcolm McDowell, about an incestuous brother and sister who transform into panthers. Schrader chose Kinski for five reasons he said: "One is we needed a girl who had an international quality. . . . Secondly, I needed a girl who was credible as a virgin. Thirdly, I needed a girl who could act. . . . I needed someone who had a sex goddess kind of beauty. And finally, I needed someone who would face up to the nudity." Schrader felt Kinski met all of these criteria. He also believed that if she lived in the States she could become a big star by learning "street idiom and gesture." In the meantime, during what Schrader felt was her transition period between a European and American identity, he cast her in a mythical role which did not require her to be from any one place. Perhaps Schrader was also partial to Kinski because of a romantic attachment. It was rumored that they were having an affair.

Most critics were disappointed with *Cat People,* although a few found the film to be brilliant and praised Kinski for her "edgy feral presence." Several, however, complained that Nastassja's voice was "flat," that it had "no music" or sounded "dubbed." Andrew Sarris of the *Village Voice* felt that Kinski had "an unvarying intensity."

After the lackluster box office receipts of *One from the Heart* and *Cat People* Kinski stated that she would also continue to make European films "because they are such a big part of me." She held true to her word, but did not have to worry about getting work in America either. Offers continued to roll in. A nude photo of Nastassja wrapped in a snake, which was published in several mass circulation magazines, also helped to keep her in the limelight. The photo which was taken by Richard Avedon became a best-selling poster and boosted Kinski's popularity. "I was so embarrassed," said Nastassja, "when I first told . . . some reporter about working with the snake. I went on and on about what a great feeling it was. I said, 'It was an amazing sensation, the way it moves through you body and through your legs,' and so on. Totally innocent. And then, of course, everyone took it the wrong way." Kinski did not feel that the poster was offensive, however. She described it as "beautiful, a work of art" and said, "I don't think that it is at all in bad taste." The poster actually was relatively modest. Kinski was posed in such a way that if she had been wearing a bikini, the same amount of flesh would have been visible.

Kinski's next film role in *Exposed* was another controversial venture, since the director James Toback was exploring the theme of sex and violence. Nastassja was attracted to the project because she respected Toback's persistence in finding a financial backer, and admired his obsession for and commitment to his work. Kinski played a young model who meets a violinist (Rudolf Nureyev) who is involved in combating international terrorism. The movie had many erotic scenes including a shot of Nureyev literally playing Nastassja with his violin bow. Some critics were offended by the sexuality. Jack Kroll of *Newsweek* called the film "a torrential wet dream," and advised Kinski about her dangerous need to be used by directors whose eccentricity overwhelms their artistry," although he also gave her "credit for daring to embody the disturbed visions of directors like Schrader and Toback."

Nastassja defended her choice of films, however. She even used $75,000 of her $500,000 salary for *Exposed* to reinsert four scenes that had been cut. Although she realized she was often an object of desire in her movie roles, and although she expressed an interest in doing roles with more dialogue and character development, she conceded that she was willing to be "a creature of the director's imagination. I want to get a glimpse of his eyes searching out things inside of me," she said. "I want to go to hell and to heaven for him. I want to make his dreams come true."

Kinski saw acting as a way of discovering her own self-identity as well, but she sometimes found the intensity of the work to be overwhelming. "A film is like a lover," she said. "You love so much you can't breathe." She also noted that the experience of filmmaking gave her the feeling of being "like chopped meat. You give your all, and suddenly, the sun goes in — cut! But you're not a machine. You can't just push a button. I go home crying every night."

Kinski disregarded the advice of critics like Corliss and Kroll and plunged into another fantastical film filled with incest, violence and sexual explicitness. *Moon in the Gutter* was directed by Jean-Jacques Beineix who had previously had a stunning success with his film *Diva*. This French production cast Gerard Depardieu as a dockworker haunted by the death of his sister, who was raped and left with her throat cut. Kinski played a rich girl who goes slumming in Gerard's neighborhood and becomes his lover. The movie had an abstract style that often failed to bring the disparate elements of the action together. When *Moon in the Gutter* was screened at Cannes, the audience booed it.

Nastassja, however, loved the film and always defended it. She also found it exciting to work with Beineix. "Sometimes when he said, 'Action,' I felt like exploding," Kinski said. "I wanted to cut myself in half and give something great, you know. It's wonderful when you are in such a visionary film, it pushes

Nastassja Kinski and James Toback in *Exposed*.

you toward another planet. I have never felt so cold and so hot as during this film."

Kinski also identified with the character she played. "The pain and the need and the struggle and the transcendent vision this Loretta has, I have," she said. As for working with Depardieu, Nastassja described him as "totally unpredictable. At one moment, he would turn on. At the next, he was — away. There was nothing in the middle. When he is on, he looks at you, and it goes through you. In the scene where I meet him for the first time, when I walked into the café and saw him, I have never had such a sensual experience in my real life as I had in that scene from cinema. There was no past, no future, only now. It was like . . . being bathed with Perrier. Everywhere." Continuing with her description of Depardieu, she said, "When he is there, he gives and is tender and it is wonderful. Then he goes away somewhere into his own head, and it's like just putting the knife in you. When he was there, it was like we were diving into each other's souls."

Beineix explained why he chose Kinski for the part: "The woman she plays resembles a star. With one look, she lights up Gerard's night. She is fragile and yet a hunter, dominating and perhaps dangerous. Nastassja was perfect for the role. I was completely seduced by her. I caressed her face on my editing table. But I found that she requires a lot of care, love and work. She makes great demands—and woe to the director who cannot satisfy them. You have to be strong with Nastassia. Otherwise she will devour you."

Despite the critical failure of *Moon in the Gutter,* Kinski's reputation as a fascinating actress did not suffer. She was cast as Schumann's wife Clara in *Spring Symphony,* a biographical film about their courtship. It was a fuller role for Nastassja in the sense that her character was more realistic than previous ones. Kinski was awarded the Bundespreis, the German equivalent of an Oscar, in 1983 for her acting as Clara.

Another challenging part for Kinski was in *Maria's Lovers,* costarring Robert Mitchum as Maria's father-in-law. The story was of a marriage that became tragic because Maria's husband was impotent even though they loved each other deeply. Kinski was superb as a woman filled with physical frustration who is at first hopeful and then despairing of her marriage.

A lighter project was *Unfaithfully Yours,* a slapstick comedy in which Nastassja played the Italian wife of a jealous orchestra conductor (Dudley Moore). It was her first commercially successful film since *Tess,* and Kinski got good reviews. Pauline Kael described her as "becoming more striking and assured—muskier, too." Director Howard Zieff had to convince the producers that Nastassja was capable of being comic. Even he had been surprised to see how "effervescent," "ebullient" and "full of vivacity" Kinski could be. "Her part is filled with energy," Zieff remarked. "She really has to go, and she's fabulous."

One of Nastassja's favorite experiences during filming was cursing in Italian. "I love slang," she said, "but I especially love to curse in Italian, you know? We used to live in Rome when I was little, and my father cursed all day, all the time. He cursed the traffic, cursed about money, cursed everybody. I found out cursing can feel so good."

A departure for Kinski was the role of Susie in *The Hotel New Hampshire,* based on John Irving's novel and costarring Jodie Foster. Kinski played the unglamorous part of an ugly lesbian who wears a bear suit until she finally realizes she is loved and accepted by her family. Jodie Foster had nothing but admiration for her costar and said of Nastassja: "Her intelligence shines through every spontaneous thought and yet she's completely unaware of her beauty, her perceptiveness, her inner strength. Her charm lies in her total lack of pretension—her naïveté coupled with fierce experience."

It seems that many who worked with her felt Kinski was special. Beineix called her "magical." John Savage, who played her husband in *Maria'a Lovers,* said, "People talk about her looks. But I think she's one of the best actresses I've worked with."

Her talent was definitely apparent in *Paris, Texas,* which was directed by Wim Wenders. Kinski was completely convincing as a girl from the American Southwest involved in a destructive relationship. The movie was a brilliant study of Texan lowlife and the depressing cultural milieu of that class. *Paris, Texas* won the grand prize at the 1984 Cannes Film Festival.

Nastassja's idol was actress Romy Schneider whom she considered "the ultimate woman. She's pain, strength, beauty, magic, loneliness, passion, everything." Kinski even regretted that she herself had not suffered more in order to convey the depths of emotion that Schneider did. Yet Nastassja did attempt to be emotionally open. "We're born, we're children, we're here in this incredible free world, we grow up, we're told to be afraid, we see that here we have been given this body and soul and sex and dreams but we have not been given the reason for our existence," Kinski elaborated. "We're unhappy, and it is very rare in life that we find a moment of ecstasy, a moment, like being born, or dying. . . . If we are not ready to die for a moment of emotion, what is the use of life?"

Nastassja had always wanted to marry and have a child. Even though her parents had divorced, Kinski still believed in family life. She had even reconciled with her father Klaus, and he was proud of his daughter's success. "Although we have had our differences in the past, everything is fine now," Klaus said. "I am delighted she has done so well. I never encouraged her to be an actress; nothing like that. She did it all on her own."

In 1984 Nastassja gave birth to a son. A few months later she married his father Ibrahim Moussa, 37, an Egyptian-born talent agent and film producer. She had known Moussa for several years and had at first lived platonically with him in his house in Los Angeles. Their friendship eventually developed into a romance. Moussa planned to take on a new career as an international representative for the Bulgari jewelry company.

Kinski decided to continue working as an actress but only occasionally. Since 1984 she has only made two films—*Harem* and *Revolution*. The latter starred Al Pacino in a historical epic that was a box-office and critical flop. Kinski played the predictable role of love interest for Pacino.

Nastassja Kinski Filmography

Falsche Bewegung [The Wrong Move; Wrong Movement] (1975)
To the Devil a Daughter (1976)
Leidenschaftliche Blumchen [Virgin Campus; Passion Flower Hotel] (1978)
Cosi come sei [Stay as You Are] (1978)
Tess (1979)
One from the Heart (1982)
Cat People (1982)
Reifezeugnis [For Your Love Only— originally made in 1976 for German television] (1982)
Fruhlingssinfonie [Spring Symphony] (1983)
Exposed (1983)
La Lune dans le caniveau [The Moon in the Gutter] (1983)
Maria's Lovers (1983)
Unfaithfully Yours (1983)
The Hotel New Hampshire (1984)
Paris, Texas (1984)
Revolution (1985)
Harem (1986)

Sources

Ansen, David. "Tasting All the Honeys," *Newsweek,* 97:60, February 23, 1981.

Bentley, Logan. "An Exultant Nastassja Kinski," *People,* 22:32, July 23, 1984.

Biskind, Peter. "Will Overexposure Spoil Nastassja Kinski?" *American Film,* 7:42–43, April 1982.

Corliss, Richard. "A Sensual Child Comes of Age," *Time,* 121:44+, May 2, 1983.

Current Biography 1983. New York: H.W. Wilson, 1984, p. 206–210.

Ebert, Roger. "Moonstruck Cannes: Kinski as Herself," *Washington Post,* May 23, 1983, p. B1.

Ferguson, Ken. "Nastassia Kinski," *Photoplay,* 33:40–41, December 1982.

Foster, Jodie. "Nastassia Kinski," *Interview,* 13:25+, February 1983.

————. "Nastassia Kinski," *Film Comment,* 18:50, September/October 1982.

Hibbin, Sally. "Nastassia Kinski," *Films and Filming,* 357:4–5, June 1984.

Hinson, Hal. "Who Can Resist Nastassia?" *Washington Post,* August 8, 1982, Parade section, p. 8+.

Jerome, Jim. "Nastassia Kinski's New Film," *People,* 17:101+, May 17, 1982.

Krucoff, Carol. "The Many Nastassia Kinskis," *Washington Post,* September 8, 1983 p. B1+.

Lawson, Carol. "A Sinister Plot Afoot?" *New York Times,* January 12, 1982, p. C11.

Lester, Peter. "After *Tess,*" *People,* 15:48+, April 13, 1981.

Lindsey, Robert. "Natassia Kinski," *New York Times,* January 18, 1981, section 2, p. D13+.

"Nastassia Kinski," *Harper's Bazaar,* 116:244+, March 1983.

"Nastassia Kinski," *Playboy,* 30:142+, May 1983.

"Nastassja Kinski," *Ciné Revue,* 65:58, February 21, 1985.

Quinlan, David. *Quinlan's Illustrated Directory of Film Stars.* London: B.T. Batsford, 1986, p. 243.

Simon, John. "Kinski," *Rolling Stone,* May 27, 1982, p. 32+.

Thomson, David. "Cats," *Film Comment,* 18:49–52, March/April 1982.

Chapter 5
Scandinavian Actresses

If it were not for Ingmar Bergman, Scandinavia would be poorly represented in terms of international actresses of repute. No one has done as much for actresses as the Swedish director. Four of the six women in this section came to fame via Bergman productions. He has been a prolific filmmaker and, coupled with his tendency to use the same people in repertory style and the fact that he is a good filmmaker, many of his actors have been propelled into the limelight. He is also a rarity among directors in that he provides plenty of interesting and complex roles for women.

Ingrid Thulin was the first of the director's stars to attain international recognition. Her peak years were in the 1960s when she was Bergman's brightest light. Her parts were intellectual and intense and quite often unsympathetic. Thulin appeared in many pictures outside Sweden, usually to good advantage.

Lesser known is Harriet Andersson who, in Bergman films, was most often used in the sexual roles—coarse and sensual lower-class females. Almost her entire body of work has been done in her native country and this is one of the reasons she has not achieved as high a degree of international success as the other Bergman women. Harriet has been much less active since 1976 when she reached 45 and faced the inevitable lack of roles for women of that age.

Bibi Andersson has teamed with Bergman for 11 films. She often took the role of a youthful and bubbly character. Tired of uncomplicated and innocent roles, Bibi worked for other directors for a chance at more sophisticated parts. Her performances have been consistently excellent and she kept busy into the middle 1980s.

The first non–Swede to be used by Bergman was the Norwegian Liv Ullmann who soon came to be the best known of all the Bergman actresses. Liv was trained in the theater in Norway before she had a personal and professional attachment with Ingmar. Liv specialized in gloomy and neurotic characters—women who were on the verge of a breakdown or already in the midst of one. By the 1970s Ullmann had supplanted Thulin as the director's brightest star and soon Hollywood offers came in. She accepted and was soon cast in a number of dreadful films. Liv limped home to deliver many more fine acting performances before devoting most of her time to social causes.

There were some Scandinavian actresses who achieved a measure of international fame without working for Ingmar—but not many. One was Anita Ekberg, a tall blonde who became a hot sexpot in the '50s and '60s. Her early career was all in Hollywood and it was there that her image was established. Her best work came in *La dolce Vita*. This memorable role gave her career a boost in Europe. It also showed she could act when given the chance. During the 1960s she worked both in Europe and the United States, but by 1970 demand for her services was low. Anita would make only seven more films, all low budget with no North American distribution. In the mid–1970s she was overweight and became a partner in a Rome car rental agency.

Britt Ekland, another Swede known more as a sex symbol than as an actress, did much of her early work in the English language. She got good notices in a couple of comedy vehicles opposite Peter Sellers. With a much publicized private life, Britt kept herself in the public eye while appearing mostly in films of low quality. The rather mindless pictures she has been cast in have frustrated her ambition to be a great actress. Still, she has kept busy.

These Scandinavian actresses have appeared in 295 motion pictures collectively.

Ingrid Thulin

From the almost repertory group of actresses used by Swedish director Ingmar Bergman, Ingrid Thulin was the most prominent and was called the third most famous Swedish film star, after Greta Garbo and Ingrid Bergman. At least that was true in the 1960s. By the end of the 1970s Liv Ullman had supplanted her. Thulin achieved her fame with intense and intellectual roles—parts that were often created especially for her by Bergman and which were usually unsympathetic. Thulin did well with some other Swedish and European directors but her plans of becoming a true international star were dashed by a particularly bad time in Hollywood.

Ingrid was born on January 27, 1929, in the town of Solleftea in the far north of Sweden near Lapland. Mr. Thulin worked as a fisherman and Ingrid's grandfather owned a store that sold furniture, perfume and toys. As a result she got all the shop's broken toys at Christmas.

As a youngster she loved going to the movies and her idol was child star Shirley Temple. Ironically that same Temple, then Shirley Temple Black, would refuse to serve as chairman of the 1966 San Francisco Film Festival in protest over the showing of *Night Games* by Swedish director Mai Zetterling. The film had a scene in which Thulin delivered a stillborn baby.

Recalling her childhood, Ingrid said, "I was an introverted child. My family lived in a small town in the north of Sweden, and I was very lonely. I had an artistic bent, toward painting and music, and then I drifted into acting when I was an adolescent." With no brothers or sisters, Thulin was naïve about films as a child. "I didn't know movies weren't real," she remembered.

As a teen she took ballet lessons for years but after being admitted to Stockholm's Royal Dramatic Theatre in 1948 devoted herself fully to acting. On the stage she gained experience with a variety of parts, ranging from the classical roles to comedy ingenues to music-hall singers. Later she performed at the Malmo Municipal Theater.

Work in Swedish films came her way and she made her debut in 1948. It was the first of almost a score of films she appeared in before Bergman found her. Much of the time she was unhappy with her roles and complained, "I always had to play femme fatale roles because I looked a little exotic for Sweden. I never looked like a Swedish woman. I had to play sophisticated ladies with low necklines."

None of these pictures received United States distribution with the exception of the American 1956 release *Foreign Intrigue* shot on location in Sweden and starring Robert Mitchum. It was a rather pedestrian 1950's cold war melodrama and Thulin recalled it as being originally made for American television but then given theatrical release instead.

Thulin's first marriage in 1951 to Claes Sylwander ended in divorce within a few years and in 1956 she wed businessman Harry Schein who had made a fortune by inventing a process to purify water. Schein later went on to found and head the Swedish Film Institute as well as to write film reviews for Swedish journals.

In 1957 Bergman was searching for an actress to play the demanding intellectual roles in his films. Being familiar with her work at the Malmo Theater, Ingmar chose Thulin who "brought a brooding, cinematically neurotic quality of her own to the director's increasingly metaphysical later works." It was a move which led to international recognition and praise for the actress who said, "My real career began when I went to work for Ingmar."

Wild Strawberries (1957) was her first film with Bergman and over the years she would appear in eight more of his films. In *Wild Strawberries* she was the brooding daughter-in-law who tangled intellectually with her father-in-law while her own marriage collapsed.

It set the tone for subsequent works with the director in which Ingrid's roles personified the victory of intellect over passion. Her roles combined suffering and sensuality as she underwent trauma after trauma. Unlike the roles for the other women in Bergman's group, Thulin's characters were usually unsympathetic. Despite this, she soon became the biggest star of the group

Ingrid Thulin in *The Cassandra Crossing*.

and prompted critics to say she "fills every corner of the screen with feminine sovereignty, beauty, sex and nerves — a star shining by its own power without reflection from irrelevant suns."

The next year (1958) she starred in *Brink of Life* as an anguished woman in a hospital recovering from a miscarriage, after conceiving against her husband's wishes. Ingrid gave one of her best performances in this role in which she was confined to bed for most of the film. She took the Best Actress Award at the Cannes Festival for her work — shared with costar Bibi Andersson.

Other Bergman films featured her as a woman masquerading as a young

Ingrid Thulin in *The Damned*.

boy in *The Magician*, a lesbian nymphomaniac in *The Silence* and a clergy-
man's mistress in *Winter Light*. The latter film was one of Ingmar's favorites
and of Thulin's performance the director said, she enacted "a monstrosity, a
primitive natural force." Working with Bergman was a pleasure for Thulin,
who said, "It's fun to work with him. We get very involved emotionally for
three months; then it's over and we say goodbye."

Between those films with Bergman she did a few others. One of these ventures was her first Hollywood film, the 1962 release *The Four Horsemen of the
Apocalypse*. MGM had enticed her to star with Glenn Ford. The actress had

been tempted by the prospect of working with director Vincente Minnelli. It was a multimillion dollar production and after having read the script, she was naïve enough to believe "if they were spending that much money, surely they would do something about that."

The actress found she could not conform to their standards of beauty and said, "After the first few rushes, it was obvious that it would turn out badly. Yet they went right on. Perhaps they couldn't convince themselves that all that money would end in disaster. I really did try to be as beautiful as they wanted." Fluent in several languages, Thulin tried to dub the dialogue but found the lines constantly changed to things she could not pronounce with the result that another voice was dubbed in for hers. Nothing could save the film which was both a critical and box-office bomb.

Ingrid would carry bitter memories of her Hollywood experience long afterwards. "It was the closest thing to being in a car factory making Cadillacs or Rolls Royces or Volkswagens," she remarked. With respect to Hollywood executives, she found them not to be "very dependable — little crazy people you couldn't trust." Whatever plans she had of international acting, she would never return to Hollywood although she would appear in a couple of United States-backed films that would serve her just as badly as had *The Four Horsemen*.

During the mid–1960s she appeared in a number of European films. She did not work with Bergman for five years during this period. Most notable was Resnais' *La Guerre est finie (The War Is Over)* set during the Spanish Civil War, with Ingrid giving an excellent performance as the long-suffering mistress of a Spaniard in one of her rare sympathetic parts. She was cast opposite Yves Montand. She also directed a 15-minute short in 1965 in which she also had a part.

Back with Ingmar, Ingrid had the small role of a dead mistress in *Hour of the Wolf* and then the wife/mistress in *The Rite*. That same year, 1969, Ingrid was outstanding in Visconti's *The Damned* as the Baroness Sophia in a film about decadence among the wealthy which allowed her a full range of emotion.

With Bergman Thulin always gave a good performance but with other directors the results were much more varied. Equally fine performances were given in the Resnais and Visconti films and Zetterling's *Night Games* but the rest were not as good, ranging all the way from terrible to totally wasted as in her few United States-produced ventures.

Cries and Whispers by Bergman featured Thulin, Ullmann and Harriet Andersson in a psychological study of three sisters. Ingrid was characteristically enigmatic, unhappy and suffering. In one of the more riveting scenes, the actress mutilated her genitals in order to avoid intercourse with her husband. It was another stunning performance by Ingrid.

That was her last appearance in a Bergman film for a dozen years until the pair collaborated again in the 1984 release *After the Rehearsal,* not one of the director's better efforts. Thulin's film work tapered off after *Cries and Whispers* but she still put in ten more appearances. Between roles she did stage work both in Europe and the United States, feeling, "Films are 'easier' but the stage is 'necessary.'"

The only film roles she accepted were those she found "artistically, and not necessarily commercially, rewarding." Ever since her directorial debut with the short film in 1965 the actress had wanted to try directing again. In 1978 she codirected, and appeared in *One and One.* That was followed four years later by *Broken Sky,* which Ingrid helmed alone.

Some of her films from the 1970s included *Moses — The Lawgiver* which featured Thulin as Miriam, sister to Moses, in a Biblical saga recut from television. *Monismanien 1995* was a futuristic nightmare of state dictatorship with the actress giving a good performance as a state investigator. *La Cage* was a two-character comedy-drama picture with Ingrid as a divorced wife who trapped her husband in a cellar to get even with him.

Her worst film from this period was *The Cassandra Crossing,* a hokey disaster epic about a trainload of disease-exposed passengers. The film was so bad it was unintentionally funny. The all-star cast, including Thulin, managed to give a collectively dismal performance. Her best film was *One and One.* The actress played a middle-aged artist who somewhat forced an older cousin to accompay her on a trip. The pair taunted one another in an affair that never took place in this Bergmanesque psychological drama. Thulin's acting was excellent.

Another picture of note was the campy *Madame Kitty* about a brothel operated by Nazis during World War II in which the girls spied on SS men and reported to the commander and to the madam (Thulin). Originally the film was banned in Italy where it was made. Director Tito Brass organized private screenings for the press, trying to elicit support. Producer Giulio Sbarigia then got the police to order Brass to cease holding such screenings. He prefered to wait for the appeals court ruling. The film finally was released with an X rating. It received only limited distribution.

Some of the magic and appeal which acting held for Thulin could be found in her remarks about one of her early Bergman features: "There's a moment in *The Silence* when I approached something — a moment, a feeling close to death. You work for 20 years and then you capture something. Now I've caught it, and I'll have to go on. You have to go on trying something else."

Ingrid Thulin Filmography

Kann dej som Hemma (1948)
Dit Vindarna Bar (1948)

Havets Son (1949)
Karleken segrar [Love Will Conquer] (1949)

Hjarter Knekt (1950)
Nar Karleken kom till Byn (1950)
Leva på "Hoppet" (1951)
Mote med Livet (1952)
Kalle Karlsson fran Jularbo (1952)
En Skargardsnatt (1953)
Goingehov dingen (1953)
Tva Skona Juveler (1954)
I Rok och Dans (1954)
Hoppsan! (1955)
Danssalongen (1955)
Foreign Intrigue (1956)
Aldrig i livet (1957)
Smultronsstaller [Wild Strawberries]
(1957)
Nara livet [Brink of Life; So Close to Life] (1958)
Ansiktet [The Magician; The Face]
(1958)
Donnaren (1960)
The Four Horsemen of the Apocalypse
(1962)
Agostino (1962)
Nattvarsgasterna [Winter Light]
(1963)
Tystnaden [The Silence] (1963)
Sekstet [Sextet] (1963)
Die Lady [Games of Desire; Frustration] (1964)
Der Film den Niemandsieht (1964)
Hangivelse [short—director and role]
(1965)
Return from the Ashes (1965)

Nattlek [Night Games] (1966)
La Guerre est finie [The War Is Over]
(1966)
Domani non siamo piu qui (1967)
Vargtimmen [Hour of the Wolf]
(1968)
Badarna [I, A Virgin] (1968)
Adelaide [The Depraved] (1968)
Riten [The Rite; The Ritual] (1969)
La cadutadegli dei [The Damned]
(1969)
Un diablo bajo la Almohada
(1969)
It Rained All Night the Day I Left
(1970)
Visknigar och rop [Cries and Whispers]
(1972)
N.P. (1972)
La Sainte Famille (1972)
En handfull kaerlek [A Handful of Love] (1973)
Moses—The Lawgiver (1975)
Monismanien 1995 (1975)
La Cage (1975)
Il viaggio nella vertigini (1975)
Salon Kitty [Madame Kitty] (1976)
The Cassandra Crossing (1977)
En och en [One and One—also codirector] (1978)
Brusten Himmel [Broken Sky—director]
(1982)
After the Rehearsal (1984)

Sources

Archer, Eugene. "Intonations from a 'Silent' Swede," *New York Times,* February 16, 1964, sec. 2, p. 7, 9.

Cowie, Peter. *Film in Sweden: Stars and Players.* London: The Tantivy Press, 1977, p. 61–68.

"Ingmar's Ingrid," *Time,* 83:76+, February 28, 1964.

The International Dictionary of Films and Filmmakers: Volume III: Actors and Actresses. Chicago: St. James Press, 1986, p. 610–11.

Jonas, Gerald. "Thulin Acts—but Isn't—a Tortured Bergman Female," *New York Times,* February 12, 1967, sec. 2, p. 13.

Katz, Ephraim. *The Film Encyclopedia.* New York: Thomas Y. Crowell, 1979, p. 1134.

Quinlan, David. *The Illustrated Directory of Film Stars.* London: B.T. Batsford, 1981, p. 456.

Thomson, David. *A Biographical Dictionary of Film.* New York: William Morrow, 1975, p. 560–61.

Harriet Andersson

Of the many actresses associated with the work of Ingmar Bergman, some considered Harriet Andersson to be the most versatile. Harriet was often used by the Swedish director to represent sensuality, both fully expressed or frustrated. Bergman frequently cast her as a sexual lower-class woman. A reviewer wrote that Harriet was "something of an outsider: a little coarse, sensual, dark and slatternly," giving much credibility to her performance. Working almost exclusively in Sweden has meant that Andersson's international fame has been more limited than if she had worked more extensivly abroad.

Harriet was born on January 14, 1932, in the southern part of Stockholm, Sweden. It was a poor part of town and the actress always felt that this made it easier to play lower-class roles in films. From the beginning, the young girl was determined to be an actress and left school at the age of 15 to study acting at a private drama school. To raise money for her tuition she held a number of parttime jobs including delivering newspapers at dawn and operating an elevator.

A Swedish film company, Sandrews, had enough faith in her to loan her 2,000 crowns to continue her training. They then hired her to work at a revue theater they owned. Oscar's was the name of the place, offering burlesque entertainment in a Swedish equivalent of Minsky's. Andersson worked as a dancer and was engaged to perform in a provocative and sexual manner. Soon she graduated to films and made her debut in the minor crime melodrama *While the City Sleeps,* released in 1950.

Andersson appeared in ten more films over the next two years, mostly in support roles, but made no great impression until she had a key role in *Defiance* (1952). Director Ingmar Bergman was impressed by Harriet's acting and spoke to *Defiance* director Gustav Molander. The latter was less than enthusiastic about the young woman, however, and told Bergman that she was not very promising.

Ingmar was not deterred by the remark, however, and cast her in the title role of *Monika,* a film he had written expressly for her. It was the story of a poor girl from Stockholm who tried to defy a crass society. The character was sluttish, self-centered and shallow, and redeemed for the audience only by the depiction of the grinding poverty of her childhood. Harriet drew high praise for her work and her display of "animal-like physicality." Bergman said, "There's never been a girl in Swedish films who radiated more uninhibited erotic charm than Harriet." The actress acknowledged the film as a good one but was less than happy with her own performance, saying, "I couldn't act at all."

Critics did not agree and neither did Bergman. Over the coming years the pair would collaborate on nine pictures. Next came *The Naked Night* in which the actress played a voluptuous bareback rider in a circus who becomes annoyed with the owner, also her lover. She embarks on a stage acting career only to be seduced, discarded and sent back to the circus by an actor who then heckles her from the crowd.

Smiles of a Summer Night cast her as a sexy and experienced maid. Both these roles featured unrepressed and unashamed sensuality. Bergman also cast her as a fashion model who seduces an elderly consul in *Journey into Autumn* and as a tomboy daughter who is afraid of sex, flat-chested and the victim of her parents' marital problems in *A Lesson of Love*.

Andersson made many more pictures during the 1950s. Most of them were not directed by Bergman although it was Ingmar's films for which she established an international reputation. Toward the end of that decade she married a farmer and for two years she lived in the country making no films, and having a baby. The life of a farmer's wife proved not to her liking and in 1961 she returned to motion pictures. The couple split up some years later and Harriet married the film director Jorn Donner.

Her first picture after the break was *Through a Glass Darkly,* the script which Bergman sent to the actress just after she had given birth. Harriet told him she could not do it but Ingmar persisted and Harriet returned to films. In *Through a Glass Darkly,* she was a woman trapped between a dull, unimaginative husband and a father who clinically studied her during a mental breakdown. It was a riveting performance and won for the actress the German Film Critics Grand Prize award.

Her first film for Donner was *A Sunday in September* where she played a put-upon wife whose marriage quickly degenerated. The following year they teamed again with *To Love,* the story of a widow having an affair. For her work in that film, Andersson was named Best Actress at the Venice Film Festival. "Harriet makes retakes unnecessary," said Donner. "I use two cameras because she hates to do scenes twice. She always is perfect the first time, so it keeps the budget down."

Besides films, the actress kept busy with stage work and had started with a company in Malmo in the mid–1950s. Other companies included the Intiman Theatre of Stockholm, the Halsingborg Town Theatre and regular appearances at Stockholm's Kunigliga Dramatiska Teaten. By the middle of the 1960s she was a major international film star with the *New York Times* describing her as looking "like a ripe plum" and calling her "one of the most exciting young actresses in the world."

She acted, she said, with "half of my head full of feeling and the other half full of technical concerns." Rejecting notions of stardom, Harriet commented, "I like to go to my work early in the morning like anyone else. Then, when it's finished, I can go home and lead my own life. If you are a star you never have this liberty." About her work and roles, she said, "I'm so bored with playing naïve virgins. Every time I read a script, I have to fight to add on a few

Harriet Andersson and Lars Ekborg in Ingmar Bergman's *A Summer with Monika.*

years and some experience, to make it more like me ... I just work, work, work. I have to keep working because the pay is so low, and I have a child to support." Andersson expressed an inclination to work in Hollywood for some of the California sunshine and salary if the right offer came along. But somehow it never did.

The closest she came was an English language film, *The Deadly Affair,* made in England, in which Andersson's talents were wasted in a passive role as James Mason's wife. *Rooftree* was the story of two couples who changed partners. The actress was cast as a Jewish girl who had spent time in a concentration camp and then found refuge in Sweden. Harriet gave a forceful and poignant

Harriet Andersson in *The Naked Night*.

performance. A change of pace came in *People Meet* where she got to display her comic skills in an erotic comedy with much bed-hopping. Harriet, as the heroine, wandered through brothels, boudoirs and dance halls giving a lusty portrayal. Many critics felt she was the best thing about the film.

She starred in Donner's *Anna,* a psychological drama about a woman reaching 40 and her problems with sex, husband and kids. The actress gave another excellent performance. Bergman used her again in *Cries and Whispers* in which Harriet gave one of her best performances as the dying sister. For most of the film she was on her deathbed, devoid of make-up, lines on her face accentuated by lighting and groaning and retching for help.

Andersson has been much less active since 1976 as she faced the decline in roles available to females over 40. In most of these films since that point she has been no longer first-billed, or even lead female. *Hempas bar* was a bitter-sweet nostalgic film about the 1950s which featured the alienation between a working class couple and their children. Harriet played the mother. She had supporting roles in *Linus eller* and *La sabina* and then worked with Bergman again in *Fanny and Alexander,* a sweeping family saga set in 1907. Her role as the middle-aged kitchen-maid in the household of the repressive stepfather was small but Harriet made her presence felt.

Raskenstam was a comedy based on the real life of a conman in 1942 who specialized in swindling money out of love-starved women, one of whom was played by Harriet. She was praised for "a vigorous, romping performance." Having made no United States films has limited the exposure Andersson has received internationally but she remains one of the few major actresses to emerge from Sweden since the end of the Second World War and is considered to be that country's most spontaneous and individual actress.

Harriet Andersson Filmography

Medan staden sover [While the City Sleeps] (1950)
Anderssonskans Kalle [Mr. Andersson's Charlie] (1950)
Motorkavalierer [Cavaliers on the Road] (1950)
Tva trappor over garden [Backyard] (1950)
Biffen och Bananen [Beef and the Banana] (1951)
Puck heter jag [My Name Is Puck] (1951)
Darskapens hus [House of Folly] (1951)
Franskild [Divorced] (1951)
Sabotage (1952)
Ubat 39 [U-boat 39] (1952)
Trots [Defiance] (1952)
Sommaren med Monika [Monika; Summer with Monika] (1953)
Gycklarnas afton [The Naked Night; Sawdust and Tinsel] (1953)
En lektion i karlek [A Lesson in Love] (1954)
Hoppsan! (1955)
Kvinnodrom [Dreams; Journey into Autumn] (1955)
Sommarnattens leende [Smiles of a Summer Night] (1955)
Sista paret ut [The Last Couple Out; Last Pair Out] (1956)

Nattbarn [Children of the Night] (1956)
Synnove Solbakken (1957)
Kvinna i leopard [Woman in Leopard-skin; Woman in a Leopardskin Coat] (1958)
Flottans overnan [Commander of the Navy] (1958)
Brott i Paradiset [Crime in Paradise] (1959)
Noc paslubna [Wedding Night] (1959)
Sasom i en spegel [Through a Glass Darkly] (1961)
Barbara (1961)
Siska (1961)
Lyckodrommen [Dream of Happiness] (1963)
En sondag i september [A Sunday in September] (1963)
For att inte tala om alla dessa kvinnor [All These Women; Now About These Women] (1964)
Att alska [To Love] (1964)
Alskande par [Loving Couples] (1964)
For vanskaps skull [Just Like Friends; For Friendship] (1965)
Lianbron [The Vine Bridge; The Vine Garden] (1965)

Har borjar oventyret [Adventure Starts Here] (1965)
Orsmen [The Serpent] (1966)
The Deadly Affair (1966)
Stimulantia (1967)
Mennesker modes och sod musik opstar i hjertet [People Meet] (1967)
Tvarbalk [Rooftree; Crossbeams] (1967)
Jag alskar, du alskar [I Love, You Love] (1968)
Flickorna [The Girls] (1968)
Der Kampf um Rom (1968)
Anna (1970)
Viskningar och rop [Cries and Whis-

pers] (1973)
Kallelsen (1974)
Tva Kvinnor [Two Women] (1975)
Monismanien 1995 (1975)
Hempas bar [Triumph Tiger '57; Cry of Triumph] (1977)
Linus eller Tegelhusets hemlighet [Linus] (1979)
La sabina (1979)
Fanny och Alexander [Fanny and Alexander] (1982)
Raskenstam [Raskenstam — The Casanova of Sweden] (1983)

Sources

Archer, Eugene. "Sweden's Electric New Star," *New York Times,* October 4, 1964, p. B9.
Cowie, Peter. *Film in Sweden: Stars and Players.* London: The Tantivy Press, 1977, p. 53–61.
The International Dictionary of Films and Filmmakers: Volume III: Actors and Actresses. Chicago: St. James Press, 1986, p. 17.
Katz, Ephraim. *The Film Encyclopedia.* New York: Thomas Y. Crowell, 1979, p. 30.
Lloyd, Ann, ed. *The Illustrated Who's Who of the Cinema.* London: Orbis, 1983, p. 10.
Thomson, David. *A Biographical Dictionary of Film.* New York: William Morrow, 1975, p. 8.

Bibi Andersson

Bibi Andersson was one of Ingmar Bergman's favorite actresses and she appeared in 11 of his movies. It was her association with Bergman that gave her international recognition, but Andersson has also worked with a variety of directors and has acted in over 60 films.

She was born Birgitta Andersson in Stockholm, Sweden, on November 11, 1935. Her father Josef was a businessman and her mother Karin, a social worker. Bibi had an older sister Gerd, who became a ballerina with the Swedish Royal Opera. The parents divorced when the girls were small, and Karin had a nervous breakdown when Bibi was about seven. Andersson recalled that the difficult circumstances caused her mother's problems, and she never perceived her to be sick. On the contrary, she felt her mother was fundamentally strong and was grateful that she encouraged Bibi's acting ambitions.

Andersson studied at the Terserus Drama School and from 1954 to 1956 at the Royal Dramatic Theater School in Stockholm, the same school that Greta Garbo had attended. While a teenager, Bibi worked as an extra in movies. Bergman saw her on one of the sets. He was directing television commercials at that time and hired her for a series of Bris soap ads. The slim, blonde, blue-eyed Andersson had a fresh, innocent, and simple quality that was perfect for a hygiene product.

Other directors also saw this quality in Bibi and in her first movie *Stupid Bom* (1953), she played a naïve and clean-scrubbed character. Most of her early films including the ones she made for Bergman typecast her in such roles. In 1955 he cast her in a small part in *Smiles of a Summer Night,* and it marked the beginning of a fruitful collaboration.

In Bergman's allegorical *The Seventh Seal* Andersson played Mia, an affectionate wife. As Peter Cowie wrote in *Film in Sweden,* "The long blonde hair, the milk-white skin, the ample mouth, the demure gaze: at one blow—in a single shot—the character of Bibi Andersson is caught by Bergman and registered by the spectator so that her Mia is forever a symbol of goodness and fidelity. She survives the plague and the ravages of Death while those more sophisticated and cynical must meet their doom."

In *Wild Strawberries* Bergman also used Sara's (Bibi's) sense of fun as a contrast to the bitter daughter-in-law, Marianne. Yet Bergman also revealed a darker side of Sara as glimpsed in a dream sequence that symbolized pitiless youth. Andersson played a pregnant teenager in her next Bergman film *Brink of Life.* At first her character is desperate for an abortion but soon her maternal feelings surface and she decides to have the child. Bibi shared the Best Actress Award at Cannes for this part. She would later win other European and British awards for her acting.

Three more Bergman films followed but none gave Andersson much scope beyond her bubbly, youthful image. She later recalled that she felt limited in these roles. Speaking of Bergman, she said, "It bothered me . . . he put me in uncomplicated roles, symbolizing simple, girlish things. I used to be called 'a professional innocent.'"

Other directors were offering Bibi more sophisticated parts in the early 1960s. In *The Mistress,* directed by Vilgot Sjoman, Andersson played a secretary who is infatuated by an older, married man. She betrays her fiancée to pursue him. No longer was Bibi the sweet ingenue. She portrayed a duplicitous woman full of tension and frustration.

Sjoman also gave her a challenging role in *My Sister, My Love.* Andersson played an 18th-century girl involved in an incestuous relationship with her brother by whom she becomes pregnant. Bibi received excellent reviews for her acting. Bergman finally recognized that Andersson, at 30, was ready for a mature part. He cast her as the nurse Alma in his psychological masterpiece *Persona.* Alma is to accompany Elisabet, a celebrated actress who has ceased talking, on a secluded rest vacation. Liv Ullmann played Elisabet. Bergman was struck by the physical resemblance of the actresses, and felt this would enhance the film which dealt with merging identities. Both Ullmann and Andersson

Bibi Andersson and Kathleen Quinlan in *I Never Promised You a Rose Garden.*

handled their difficult roles brilliantly. Ullmann had to elicit a response without uttering a word, while Andersson was solely responsible for the film's monologue. Alma undergoes a transition from a superficial chatterbox to a woman of disturbing emotional complexity. Elisabet in her calm silence begins to appear sane while Alma's incessant talking begins to sound completely mad. When Bibi read the *Persona* script, she was not flattered. "I didn't understand why I had to play this sort of insecure, weak personality when I was struggling so hard to be sure of myself and to cover up my insecurities," she said. Bibi then realized that Bergman was totally aware of her personality. "I was better off just trying to deliver that. It's a good way to know oneself. Sometimes I think artists instinctively are good psychiatrists," she added. "I also think all parts have to be based on oneself, otherwise they will never come across." Andersson used some of her personal experiences of sibling rivalry with her sister Gerd to understand Alma's symbiosis with Elisabet. The National Society of Film Critics in the United States voted Andersson Best Actress for her work in *Persona.*

Liv Ullmann became one of Andersson's best friends. They were often compared on a professional basis and had shared some similar personal experiences as well. Both had been involved with Bergman. Andersson had an affair with him, and Ullmann later lived with him and had his child. Bibi was often asked in interviews if she was jealous of Liv, and she sometimes felt pestered by these questions. "I'm so sick of people asking about Liv all the time," she said. "Liv is my best friend and I love her dearly. But I'm wonderful too."

Ullmann usurped Andersson of her position as leading actress in Bergman's films, but Andersson held no grudge. "The three of us are friends," she said. "It was painful only because I was afraid." Speaking of Bergman, she said, "There are so many actors who have worked with him, and if everyone should feel rejected because he works with someone else, you'd be in trouble. I myself wanted to take off and do other things as well."

She explained that she had to learn to rely on herself because she and Bergman were not "so much alike." He also had trouble dealing with her maturity and once told her, "I need a young you." Andersson respects Bergman's genius but feels she worked for him, not with him, and added, "For him, I'm still a little girl." Bibi was 41 when she made that statement.

She also found that although Bergman was a master at creating an environment of concentration on the set, he could also create "a mood that frightens people; you have to be very tense, and the discipline can be quite tough," she noted.

Andersson married Swedish director Kjell Grede in 1960 and had a daughter. The couple divorced in 1973. They remained friends and he directed her for the first time only after the divorce. The project was a Swedish television series. In 1978 Bibi married Per Ahlmark, a former chairman of the Swedish liberal party.

Bibi felt she had to make certain compromises in her personal life to maintain her career, especially when she was younger. "You were supposed to be happy in a family life," she said. "I was always asked the question, 'Would you choose a career before your private life?' It was very shameful to say, 'Yes.' No decent woman said, 'Yes.' So I always avoided the question by saying, 'Well, luckily enough, I haven't run into the problem' . . . I felt that it was not feminine to say, 'Yes, I really would sacrifice a lot in my private life,' but I knew I would be so miserable if I didn't work.' I think it's difficult to combine a career and a family life. . . . You have to find a man who is terribly generous and full of self-confidence not to be intimidated by a woman who is curious and likes contact with new people and makes you sit at home sometimes and wait," she concluded.

Andersson continued to essay a variety of roles and worked in several countries. She even accepted a role in an American western *Duel at Diablo*. It was a bad movie and most of Bibi's scenes were cut, but she did not regret doing it. Asked about why she agreed to appear in this movie, Andersson replied, "I had millions of maybe very childish reasons: coming to America, meeting people, seeing how films were made here, getting all that money. I knew that I would be out of place in a Western . . . but I just hoped that some miracle would happen."

Bibi Andersson in *The Kremlin Letter*.

Andersson also appeared in *A Question of Rape,* a Swedish/French production in which she played a woman held captive in her own apartment by an intruder. She then appeared in Mai Zetterling's *The Girls,* a movie with a feminist perspective. "Bibi finally superseded the docile status she held in her early films," noted *Film in Sweden* writer, Cowie. She went to Brazil to shoot *Black Palm Trees* and was then in an Italian/Swedish movie *Story of a Woman.* She made a couple of other films in the late 1960s and early '70s including Bergman's *The Passion of Anna, The Touch,* and *Scenes from a Marriage.*

In *Anna* she played a wealthy architect's wife trying to find purpose in her life. A similar role in *The Touch* saw her as the wife of a doctor (Max Von Sydow). Bored by the smug confines of bourgeois society, she has an affair with an American archaeologist (Elliott Gould). One observer wrote that her role in *The Touch* revealed Bibi as "the warmest, most free-spirited of Bergman's women.... Being more robust, her distress is more moving, and her doggedness more encouraging." As an embittered wife in *Scenes from a Marriage,* Andersson received her usual excellent critical notices. "Bibi Andersson," wrote one reviewer, "could not give less than the truth ... to anything she does."

Throughout the 1970s and '80s Andersson continued to be an international actress in a variety of roles. American director John Huston cast her as a prostitute in his flimsy spy thriller *The Kremlin Letter.* She then performed in a few French films. Her American career picked up again in 1976 when she and her daughter moved to New York City. Andersson had been questioned about her tax returns in Sweden, and Bergman had gone into temporary exile because of harassment by tax officials. The investigation was not the only reason she left Sweden. She felt she was becoming overly attached to her house. "It's on the water and quite grand," she remarked. "And I found I was taking work I didn't really want to do, just to keep up the payments ... I saw the movie *Burnt Offerings* about the people becoming slaves to a house. Pure archetypes ... I said 'I'm in prison.'" By moving to the States, Andersson hoped to broaden her horizons. "Part of an actress is aliveness, alertness, and it comes from not letting yourself stiffen," she said. "I wanted to see life, wanted to smell it, and I felt starving, mentally."

Andersson went to Hollywood and accepted a part as the compassionate psychiatrist in *I Never Promised You a Rose Garden*. She found the role "a difficult balance. . . . A psychiatrist has to cover her feelings; an actress has to uncover hers." In 1978 she appeared as Steve McQueen's wife in *An Enemy of the People*. The role of the gentle Dr. Stockmann in this Ibsen work was a departure for McQueen from his usual action-oriented films. Bibi agreed to take the part because, when she read the original Ibsen play, she found Mrs. Stockmann to be "a person of a certain earthy, coarse wryness." Later she said, "I think in the film I become simply a housewife."

Andersson found McQueen to be good-hearted and sensitive, and admired him for taking on the challenge of a role for which critics would later say he was miscast. The only problem Andersson encountered during filming was her accent. She tried to work on it, but found it difficult not to use her natural voice. "Somehow I don't feel I'm acting if I try to imitate a way of talking that's not my own," she explained. "I think the only way a foreign actor can work in America is if people will just accept the way that person speaks. But I also think American audiences want Americans," she added. "You're very lucky if you make it as a foreigner in films here. I notice American audiences don't like to read subtitles. Even a huge European success is a small success here compared to American films," Andersson noted.

Despite the language difficulties, Bibi made a few more American films inlcuding *Quintet* with Robert Altman. She commented on the inbred nature of Hollywood and said, "The danger here is doing film about film, so you end up eating your own tail. So much that goes on has nothing to do with the reality elsewhere." The celebrity cult in America was also something that Bibi was unaccustomed to. In a small country like Sweden she noted, "They treat no one like a superstar."

As well as a film career, Andersson had always remained involved with the stage. In Sweden she had performed in a range of plays by dramatists such as Chekhov, Ibsen, Shakespeare and Albee. She also appeared on the American stage and made her debut in 1973 in Washington, D.C., in Erich Maria

Remarque's *Full Circle*. She received critical praise for her acting although the productions in America usually had a short run.

Andersson felt that her acting ability had more to do with her emotional openness than with technique. "You have to keep alive your childhood, when you were soft and vulnerable," she explained. "It's a struggle to keep your vulnerability; we are all too good at putting up walls so we don't easily get hurt. Yet without that vulnerability, acting is very difficult."

She also remained receptive to an assortment of roles, and preferred not to be rigid about what was "ideologically correct. You can say, 'I will not compromise because this is not what I want to do,'" Andersson explained. "But then you will never have a chance to do what you want, because you will never be seen enough to get that opportunity. I have tried, to the best of my ability, to be as selective as I had the opportunity to be and yet not stop working because of moral reasons," she said. "I think I have a moral responsibility to myself as an actress, and that is that I have to work, because otherwise the instrument dries up."

She was not hesitant to play an evil woman. "Who said that just being a woman makes you a good person? Why should we liberate ourselves in that area? There are good persons, bad persons, characters of all sorts, and I hope they may also be played by women," Andersson said.

Bibi always memorized her lines before shooting began so she could concentrate on expression, but she did not like to overprepare because she wanted to remain free to improvise. She enjoyed acting and had no great ambitions to move into directing. "I find that my contribution seems to be in the nuances of things," she explained. "I like to be subjective and defend one piece of the whole and have somebody else defend the others and make the balance that way."

Andersson was not particularly worried about being an aging actress. Although she is pretty, she was never a femme fatale. "I don't mind being an adult woman," she said. "I find it interesting. Of course, It might be a problem if it didn't interest anyone else. I can't just do monologues, after all."

For a woman who has devoted her life to acting, career seemed an ugly word. "Career implies that you are on a staircase and you have to take one step up. I want to dismiss the whole idea of career," she stated. "I'm living my life, and I love to work." It was as simple as that for Bibi Andersson.

Bibi Andersson Filmography

Dum-Bom [Stupid Bom] (1953)
En natt pa Glimmingehus [A Night at Glimminge Castle] (1954)
Herr Arnes penningar [Sir Arne's Treasure] (1954)

Sommarnattens leende [Smiles of a Summer Night] (1955)
Flickan i regnet [Gril in the Rain] (1955)

Staden vid vattnen [Town by the Sea]
(1955)
Sista paret ut [Last Pair Out; The Last Couple Out] (1956)
Egen ingang [Private Entrance] (1956)
Det sjunde inseglet [The Seventh Seal]
(1957)
Smultronstallet [Wild Strawberries]
(1957)
Sommarnoje sokes [A Summer Place Is Wanted] (1957)
Nara livet [Brink of Life; So Close to Life] (1958)
Du ar mitt aventyr [You Are My Adventure] (1958)
Ansiktet [The Face; The Magician]
(1958)
Den kara leken [The Love Game]
(1959)
Brollopsdagen [Wedding Day] (1960)
Djavulens oga [The Devil's Eye] (1960)
Karneval [Carnival] (1961)
Lustgarden [The Pleasure Garden]
(1961)
Nasilje Na Trgu [Square of Violence]
(1961)
Alskarinnan [The Mistress] (1962)
Kort År Sommaren [Pan] (1962)
For att inte tala om alla dessa kvinnor [All These Women; Now About These Women] (1964)
On [The Island] (1964)
Juninatt [June Night] (1965)
Syskonbadd 1782 [My Sister, My Love]
(1965)
Duel at Diablo (1965)
Scusi, lei e favorevole o contrario
(1966)
Persona (1966)
Le Viol [A Question of Rape] (1967)
Flickorna [The Girls] (1968)
Svarta palmkronor [Black Palm Trees]
(1968)

Storia di una donna [Story of a Woman] (1969)
Una estate in quattro [L'Isola] (1969)
Taenk pa ett tal [Think of a Number]
(1969)
En Passion [The Passion of Anna; A Passion] (1969)
The Kremlin Letter (1970)
Beroringen [The Touch] (1971)
Ingmar Bergman [documentary] (1971)
Chelovek s drugoi storoni [The Man from the Other Side] (1972)
Scener ur ett aktenskap [Scenes from a Marriage] (1973)
Afskedens timme [The Hour of Parting] (1973)
La Rivale [The Rival] (1974)
Il pleut sur Santjago [It Is Raining on Santiago] (1975)
Blondy [Vortex] (1975)
I Never Promised You a Rose Garden
(1977)
A Look at Liv (1977)
An Enemy of the People (1978)
Justices (1978)
L'Amour en question (1978)
The Concorde—Airport '79 (1979)
Twee Vruowen [Two Women; Twice a Woman; Second Touch] (1979)
Barnforbjudet [The Elephant Walk; Not for Children; The Elephant]
(1979)
Quintet (1979)
Marmeladrupproret [Marmalade Revolution] (1980)
Prosperous Times (1980)
Jag rodnar [I Blush] (1981)
Berget pa manens baksida [A Hill on the Dark Side of the Moon] (1982)
Exposed (1983)
Svarte fugler [Black Crows] (1983)
Sista leken [The Last Summer] (1984)
Babette's Feast (1988)

Sources

Bachrach, Judy. "Bibi Andersson in America," *Washington Post,* April 29, 1977, p. E1+.
Champlin, Charles. "A Melancholy Bibi in L.A.," *Los Angeles Times,* October 8, 1976, section 4, p. 1.
Cowie, Peter. *Film in Sweden: Stars and Players.* London: Tantivy, 1977, p. 33–43.

Current Biography 1977. New York: H.W. Wilson, 1978, p. 12–15.
"Dialogue in Film," *American Film,* 2:33–48, March 1977.
Eder, Richard. "Bibi Andersson at 40," *New York Times,* February 23, 1977, p. C17.
Ferretti, Fred. "Bibi Andersson Says Swedish Police Harassed Her, Too, on Tax Matters," *New York Times,* April 3, 1976, p. 53.
The International Dictionary of Films and Filmmakers: Volume III: Actors and Actresses. Chicago: St. James Press, 1986, p. 16–17.
Katz, Ephraim. *The Film Encyclopedia.* New York: Thomas Y. Crowell, 1979, p. 30.
Lloyd, Ann, ed. *The Illustrated Who's Who of the Cinema.* London: Orbis, 1983, p. 10.
Quinlan, David. *The Illustrated Directory of Film Stars.* London: B.T. Batsford, 1981, p. 9.
Thomson, David. *A Biographical Dictionary of Film.* New York: William Morrow, 1975, p. 7.

Liv Ullmann

Liv Ullmann spent several years working in Norway on the stage and in films before a chance encounter led her to link up with Swedish director Ingmar Bergman, both professionally and privately. She soon became one of the director's regular actresses. Increasing international praise followed and by the mid–1970s Liv was the best known Scandinavian actress. The inevitable Hollywood offers came, followed by abysmal films. Liv returned to European films and also kept busy with stage work.

She was born Liv Johanne Ullmann on December 16, 1939, in Tokyo, Japan, the youngest of two daughters to Norwegian parents Viggo and Janna Ullmann. Viggo was an aircraft engineer working in Japan at the time. Not long after Liv's birth, the Nazis overran Norway and the Ullmanns fled Europe, taking refuge in Canada where they joined a colony of exiles on the outskirts of Toronto, dubbed "Little Norway."

Mr. Ullmann served with the displaced Norwegian airforce and in 1943 he suffered serious injuries when he accidentally walked into a moving airplane propeller. To obtain specialized medical treatment for him, the family moved to New York City but Viggo died shortly before the end of the war. Once peace was restored, the Ullmann family returned to Norway on the first available passenger boat and settled in the port city of Trondheim, 250 miles north of Oslo. Liv recalled nothing about her life in North America except what her mother told her. She did have a vague recollection of the Statue of Liberty, however.

Attending local public school, Liv found herself a loner and felt she was "awkward" with the boys, "not especially popular" with the girls and "very bored with her lessons." She was obsessed with her real or imagined flaws which included a flat chest and "ugly toes" and said, "I wasn't very beautiful as a teenager. My mother sent me to dancing school to make friends, so I could go to parties. But for me it was a failure.... There were always five girls too many—and I was always one of the five."

For solace, Liv turned to reading voraciously. Her mother ran a bookshop and after school the young girl went there and sat in a corner and read. Another source of comfort came from the stage. She formed a drama club at school for which she became a prolific writer of condensed classics as well as the principal actress. "I wrote all the best parts for myself," she laughed.

From early in her life Liv was convinced she wanted to be an actress and said that she knew she "wanted to go into the theater, that there I would be most alive. Life to me was onstage. I don't believe that you choose the theater because you're shy. Maybe shyness and insecurity come because you're a talented person. I chose the theater because that was my way of expressing myself."

When she was 17 she left school and journeyed to Oslo where she auditioned for the National Theatre School. She failed. Determined to become an actress, Liv convinced her mother to send her to England for eight months to take acting lessons. Returning to Norway with more acting skills than when she left, she auditioned in Oslo again. She failed again. "No talent," they said to her.

However, she did manage to get work with a repertory company in the small city of Stavanger where she promptly landed the lead role in *The Diary of Anne Frank* and earned rave reviews for her acting. After three successful years with that company Liv was welcomed with open arms by Oslo's National Theatre where she continued to play the serious and heavy roles from the classics such as Shakespeare, Ibsen and others, that she had played at Stavanger. "When I began I somehow thought I was a comedienne. But instead I was always the tragic heroine or the unhappy woman who loses her lover," said the actress.

In 1960 Liv married a psychiatrist Gappe Stang, even though she did not care for his profession, feeling analysis catered to self-indulgence and was "quite dangerous for people." Over the next five years the actress worked steadily on the stage and appeared in five films, mostly in small roles.

Her debut film was in 1957 and featured Liv bathing naked in a lake. It caused much consternation in the family as did the very idea of taking up acting as a profession. Her family thought the choice a disaster "especially my father's family," she said. "They wrote my mother: 'We're happy he's dead so he doesn't experience this!' But if you do well then it all changes. Suddenly I went around to family dinners again."

Liv might have continued to work anonymously in Norway except for a walk down a Stockholm street which she took with her friend Bibi Andersson in 1965. They bumped into Bibi's friend Ingmar Bergman who mentioned he had seen Liv act. Bergman then casually suggested they should do a film together. Liv agreed but thought Ingmar was just being polite and that nothing

Liv Ullmann in *Face to Face*.

would come of it. To her surprise, he called a few months later and cast Ullmann in *Persona*. It was the first of nine films they would make together. Liv was the first non–Swedish actor that Bergman used.

She was awestruck about working with the man she considered "the best director in the world" and said, "Every time Ingmar talked to me, I blushed and panicked. But because he is a great artist and greatly interested in people, I slowly started to speak." Ingmar recalled, "From the beginning when I worked with Liv I was always impressed by her passion of expressing herself—with her face, her body, her voice. Liv, like the best of all creative artists, has marvelous integrity and enormous faith in her own intuition."

In *Persona* Liv played an anguished actress who chose to become a mute and had a strange relationship with a neurotic nurse. The actress, with almost no dialogue, got excellent notices and started to build an international reputation. Another Bergman film was *Hour of the Wolf* in which Ullmann played a neurotic wife who followed the lead of her demented husband and drifted into insanity.

The Shame was Bergman's study of the effects of war and cast Liv as a violinist who tried to escape the devastation of battle. She was a destructive and tormented widow in *The Passion of Anna* and was cast as the indolent and self-centered sister of the dying spinster in *Cries and Whispers*. Her performances in these films were uniformly excellent and she received several Scandinavian acting awards as well as awards from the National Society of Critics in America.

After filming *Persona*, Liv and Ingmar began to live together and had a daughter about a year later in 1967. After some five years the couple split up, never having married, although they had divorced their spouses during the course of the affair. Many Norwegians were scandalized by Liv's lifestyle and she was subject to a barrage of hate mail. "Sweden is very free, so I was not afraid of the scandal there, but Norway is a prude country," she said. "I had been a married woman and I belonged to a family where even the theater was not altogether acceptable."

The couple remained friendly after they separated and made several more movies together. She always gave Ingmar a great deal of credit for her acting prowess and said, "Bergman taught me how little you can do rather than how much. I can now use much smaller means to express what I want to say . . . Ingmar gave me much more self-confidence than I had before. He listened to me. Living with him enriched me. I matured."

Between the Bergman films Liv continued to appear on the stage and did some movies for other directors. Most were poor, such as a thriller called *The Night Visitor* wherein Ullmann was the victim of a lunatic, and *Pope Joan*, a long-winded and pompous piece about a woman elected pope who was finally lynched after giving birth to a child. One of her best performances came with Swedish director Jan Troell in *The Emigrants* (1972) the story of Swedish immigrants to the United States in the 19th century. Liv's performance was lauded and the American Academy nominated her for an Oscar as Best Actress. She starred in the sequel *The New Land* the following year.

When asked about the reason for her success, the actress replied, "I don't become a character, I show a character ... I share a character. I share it not only with the audience but with myself. ... I hate the idea that you must become the character you're playing because if I did I would feel embarrassed and I easily feel embarrassed. I leave the character immediately after I do it."

Liv visited the United States in 1972 to promote *The Emigrants* and she said, "Oh, God, no! I'm not the type to become a Hollywood star. There are too many temptations that go with that way of life, and I don't want to lose my own life for a fake life. I only want to work with the good directors, wherever they are." The actress was popular, however, and Hollywood made her an offer she could not refuse. When she was first suggested to Ross Hunter, the producer of *Lost Horizon,* he said, "We don't want her, she's ugly and gloomy."

When she was taken to see Hunter, her smile was said to have won him over and Ullmann noted, "When I think of the fiasco that film was, I sometimes think it would have been better if I'd stayed gloomy." That film cost $6 million to produce and had Ullmann singing and dancing. It was a total bomb and even when it was later shown on television it could not draw an audience.

She quickly followed that with three more American turkeys: *Forty Carats, Zandy's Bride* and *The Abdication*. The one consolation was that she had been paid $10,000 to $20,000 per film in Sweden but made about $200,000 for each one done in the United States. Her attitude regarding Hollywood was understandably ambivalent. At one point, she said, "I like to be regarded as a star. I like to be at the center of things ... I like the glitter. It's seductive to get roses and cars and to have everything you say become suddenly important."

At other times, she said American actors were "grossly overpaid" and that the overpayment "can harm a performer." She said, "Hollywood is fun, but I'm a little bit afraid of it, and a bit ashamed sometimes at the way important work in the world is downgraded. ... You sit in your trailer and be 'special' and that is a lonely and ridiculous thing. In Sweden you're ashamed to drive around the streets in anything else than a Volkswagen, and that is healthier I think, a shame is having too much, than Hollywood, where the shame is in having too little privilege, too small a car."

About her Hollywood film, Ullmann said, "Of course, if I do another Hollywood picture I'll be more particular about the script, the director and the producer. But I had fun doing those films. ... Even knowing that I will never do something like *Lost Horizon* again is a good experience for me. I'm just sorry

Liv Ullmann in *Zandy's Bride*.

that it was the audience that had to suffer for my experience. . . . Professionally it made me rich and that's really all there is to say about *Lost Horizon*."

Ullmann escaped back to Europe and would make no more Hollywood films. Her greatest American triumph was when she appeared in New York in Ibsen's play *A Doll's House*. Back in Scandinavia, Liv teamed with Bergman in several more outstanding films. She starred in *Scenes from a Marraige* for which she was voted Best Actress by the New York Film Critics. Her work in *Face to Face* won her the same award and brought her an Oscar nomination as Best Actress. She has also starred in Bergman's *The Serpent's Egg* and *Autumn Sonata*.

On the issue of women, Liv said, "I think women become very confused because they're living out the unconscious lives of their men.... A woman is taught to want to please so many people. A man to please only himself.... More and more the whole world is coming to feel that a woman can do without marriage, but she's still a failure if she hasn't got a man to live with. I think a woman does want some kind of permanence in a relationship. She doesn't want somebody new every few years. I could live with somebody the rest of my life, without rings and papers, but with love. That would be ideal."

In 1977 she seemed determined to live in her native country, saying, "I have a strong bond with Norway where I mostly do theater. It's not good to stay away from home—you become rootless." A few years later she changed her mind and based herself in New York, explaining, "I'm tired of feeling that Norway is the only place where I belong."

By the end of the 1970s Ullmann had become an acclaimed author with her autobiography *Changing*. It was first published in Norway in 1976. When she made a promotional appearance for the book at a bookstore in Trondheim, she spent all morning in the shop with only one copy sold. Even that buyer did not want the author's autograph. The book became a worldwide best seller, however. A second volume, *Choices,* came out in 1985 and was equally successful.

She was less interested in acting and said, "Now I'd rather write than act. I get very easily bored with acting these days. Oh, I love the work, don't misunderstand, but somehow writing is more fulfilling for me. I seem to have spent so long playing miserable women who say lines I don't believe that it's wonderful to be able to write down my own thoughts for a change."

The fact that she was aging did not bother her and Liv commented, "Fortunately I'm not a person who looks a lot in the mirror. Still, I worry about my looks just like other women. However, I console myself with the thought my best things are all inside me. I've never believed that men liked me for my beauty or my body ... just as men seem to be attractive at any age, I like to think women can be too. I mean, I'd hope to be able to attract men even when I'm 70."

She did not completely quit acting, however. In the mid–1980s the actress appeared in a few undistinguished films including *The Wild Duck* and *The Bay Boy*. She had better luck with the 1987 release *Gaby—A True Story* where she was a commanding presence as the mother of a girl who had severe cerebral palsy but went on to become an accomplished writer. She was involved as a goodwill ambassador for UNICEF and spent a good deal of time working on famine relief and aid to refugees in countries such as Ethiopia and Somalia.

In her personal life she had been involved with a couple of men in the 1980s. One was a Yugoslav author and another was a New York scientist whom she found pompous and derisively nicknamed "the brain man." In late 1985 she married Donald Saunders, a Boston real estate broker.

On her career and her future, Liv said, "The older one gets in this profession the more people there are with whom one would never work again. But I'm an actress. God will punish me if I don't work.... There's less to believe in now. Fewer films that make you float out of the cinema.... Writing is the only thing I can stay with."

Liv Ullmann Filmography

Fjols til Fjells [Fools in the Mountain] (1957)
Ung flukt [Young Escape] (1959)
Kort År Sommaren [Summer Is Short] (1962)
Tonny (1962)
De kalte ham Skarven [They Call Him Skarven] (1965)
Persona (1966)
Vargtimmen [Hour of the Wolf] (1968)
An-Magritt (1968)
Skammen [The Shame] (1968)
En Passion [The Passion of Anna; A Passion] (1969)
De la part des Copains [Cold Sweat] (1969)
The Night Visitor (1971)
Pope Joan (1972)
Viskningar och rop [Cries and Whispers] (1972)
Utvandrarna [The Emigrants] (1972)

Nybyggarna [The New Land] (1973)
Lost Horizon (1973)
Forty Carats (1973)
Zandy's Bride (1974)
The Abdication (1974)
Scener ur ett aktenskap [Scenes from a Marriage] (1974)
Leonor (1976)
Face to Face (1976)
A Bridge Too Far (1977)
The Serpent's Egg (1977)
Herbstsonate [Autumn Sonata] (1978)
Couleur chair (1978)
A Look at Liv (1979)
Players (1979)
The Gates of the Forest (1980)
Richard's Things (1981)
The Wild Duck (1984)
La Diagonale du fou [Dangerous Moves] (1984)
The Bay Boy (1985)
Gaby — A True Story (1987)

Sources

Andrews, Emma. "Whirlpools of Passion," *Films Illustrated,* 10:8, October 1980.
Bennetts, Leslie. "Liv Ullmann Discusses Acting," *New York Times,* November 25, 1979, sec. 2, p. 29.
Cowie, Peter. *Film in Sweden: Stars and Players.* London: Tantivy, 1977, p. 44–53.
Current Biography 1973. New York: H.W. Wilson, 1974, p. 420–23.
Donnelly, Tom. "Liv on Love, Life, Reality and Ideals," *Washington Post,* June 23, 1973, p. C1+.
Eder, Richard. "Liv Ullmann: Actress, Mother and Now Author," *New York Times,* January 26, 1977, p. C15.
Flatley, Guy. "Liv and Ingmar Remain ... Such Good Friends," *New York Times,* April 9, 1972, sec. 2, p. 15+.
Green, Michelle. "Pages," *People,* 23:113+, April 8, 1985.
The International Dictionary of Films and Filmmakers: Volume III: Actors and Actresses. Chicago: St. James Press, 1986, p. 624–25.
"Just an Ordinary, Extraordinary Woman," *Time,* 100:77–82, December 4, 1972.

Katz, Ephraim. *The Film Encyclopedia.* New York: Thomas Y. Crowell, 1979, p. 1158–59.

"Liv Ullmann," *Time,* 93:71, January 10, 1969.

McConathy, Dale. "Liv Ullmann," *Vogue,* 161:158–9+, February 1973.

Mann, Roderick. "Liv's Easy to Love at First," *Los Angeles Times,* May 18, 1980, calendar sec., p. 31.

Michener, Charles. "How Liv Conquers All," *Newsweek,* 85:61–65, March 17, 1975.

Quinlan, David. *The Illustrated Directory of Film Stars.* London: B.T. Batsford, 1981, p. 464.

Raphaelson, Samson. "For the Love of Liv," *American Film,* 2:27–32, May 1977.

Shales, Tom. "Face to Face with Liv Ullmann," *Washington Post,* March 8, 1977, p. B1+.

"Spotlight," *Seventeen,* 36:82, March 1977.

Thomson, David. *A Biographical Dictionary of Film.* New York: William Morrow, 1975, p. 571.

Weitz, John. "Liv Ullmann," *Interview,* 13:96+, October 1983.

Anita Ekberg

Most of the internationally famous Scandinavian film actresses have come through the works of Ingmar Bergman. One who didn't was Anita Ekberg. Blonde, tall, buxom, and voluptuous, she soon graced the movie screens of the world, mostly as decoration and sex object. She proved capable of acting well when given the chance but rarely got the opportunity. Anita has graced more bad films than most, appearing in duds with titles such as *Little Girls and High Finance, Malenka, the Vampire's Niece, Fangs of the Living Dead* and *The Killer Nun.* Always in demand, she appeared in 45 films from 1953 to 1970 when her career began to wane.

The actress was born in Malmo, Sweden, on September 29, 1931, and had an untroubled childhood in provincial Sweden, growing up with six brothers and one sister. The only minor waves which arose occurred when she left school as a teenager to model hairstyles. Mr. and Mrs. Ekberg were upset with her career choice but soon relented. From hairstyles she moved on to model clothes for a wholesale dress house in Malmo. One day she was walking down the street in that city when a talent scout for the Miss Sweden contest approached her with an entry form. Anita thought he was just another masher and swiftly turned him down. Thinking it over later, she reconsidered, entered the contest, won, and became "Miss Sweden."

Ekberg picked up a bit part in a 1951 film — her debut — as a result of the beauty contest but the big opportunity was a trip to the United States as a guest of honor at the Miss America contest. Ekberg was not eligible to compete but she stole the show with her face and figure. She was said to have arrived with only five English words in her vocabulary — yah, no, hamboorger, El Morocco, and ice cream.

She made the rounds of model agencies getting professional tips. Eileen

Ford of the Ford Model Agency told her how to tilt her nose, suck in her cheeks and pull her neck out of her shoulders. These steps were supposed to give her a "more interesting face." The consensus was that Anita should lose weight and Ekberg returned to her native country to do just that and to learn more English. During that American visit *Life* magazine had reported her measurements as 36-24-38 while just a few years later the same publication listed them as 39½-23-36. Her earlier hip dimensions were said to have been too large for a United States model.

Ekberg did not stay home long and was soon back in the United States with her American film career launched in 1953. She also did a bit of modeling in the United States and Bob Hope took her on one of his yearly junkets to entertain the troops. Her first half dozen Hollywood films gave her only small roles with little to do. These included a bit in the comedy-drama *Take Me to Town*, a 10th-billed role as a guard in *Abbott and Costello Go to Mars* and a part as a handmaiden in *The Golden Blade*, an action-adventure costume epic set in Baghdad where Anita was required only to look good in scanty harem clothes.

Blood Alley featured her as a Chinese refugee with her charms hidden beneath bulky rags. She had no individual dialogue. In *Artists and Models*, Ekberg played foil to the comedy team of Martin and Lewis. *Man in the Vault* was a routine crime thriller and the Ekberg presence "means no more than lobby and ad art possibilities," said one critic. Even though her part was small, she was third-billed.

Publicity was beginning to turn the tide for the actress. Gossip and rumors appeared about her regularly in the press and she was briefly under contract to Howard Hughes. Nicknames such as "The Ice Maiden" and "The Iceberg" were attached to her—presumably due to her cool Swedish background. Intensive publicity campaigns were mounted and she became a bigger star and advanced to higher billing.

War and Peace, the epic adapted from Tolstoy's novel, was the film which brought her critical recognition. She lucked into the role of the opportunistic Helene when the actress originally selected took sick. Even though pitted against a stellar cast, Anita got excellent reviews.

For the next decade Ekberg would be a busy leading lady. Paired again with Martin and Lewis in *Hollywood or Bust* she, as a reviewer noted, "doesn't have much more to do than to display what nature has wrought in the fjords of Sweden, so it's still a big part." As one of a group of passengers forced to cope after their plane went down in the jungle, Ekberg was romanced by Robert Ryan and did well in the part.

Zarak was a formula sex and sand epic set in the desert with Anita getting to wear lots of scanty outfits but not do much acting. One of her better films was *Valerie*, a psychological drama set in the West with Anita in the title role. *Variety* said, "Miss Ekberg impresses as an actress as well as a scenic wonder."

Anita Ekberg in a publicity photo.

While the film was better than a lot of Hollywood offerings and Ekberg got uniformly good notices, *Valerie* did not do well at the box office. She was again simply decorative opposite Bob Hope and Fernandel in the comedy *Paris Holiday,* followed by a poor psychological thriller called *Screaming Mimi* in which the actress was again disrobed frequently.

War and Peace had been filmed in Italy and made Ekberg a big star in that country. She returned there for Fellini's *La dolce vita* in which she gave what was probably her finest film performance. She was cast as a world famous but empty-headed Hollywood film star in a story set in Rome about the decadent society of jetsetters. Ekberg's erotic dance was one of the film's highlights. She used her body for an erotic caricature in a riveting performance that earned high praise everywhere.

She was at the peak of her career as a sex goddess and known around the world. Red Skelton called her "a woman and a half" while George Gobel said, "They just don't make them that way no more." The actress rarely commented on the image, saying only, "I am not all body. I have a brain and I use it."

Anita Ekberg being lusted over by Jack Palance in *The Mongols*.

Anita married actor Anthony Steel in 1956 but they divorced in 1962. The next year she married actor Rik Van Nutter, a union that ended with a divorce in 1975.

La dolce vita had made her an even bigger star in Italy and she worked there exclusively for the next few years. Her best effort came in one of the episodes of *Boccaccio '70* in which a doctor fighting immorality was offended by a giant poster of Anita Ekberg on a wall opposite his apartment. The poster came to life and drove him crazy. It was another excellent performance.

During the 1960s she made films in a variety of countries although Italy remained her favorite. Hollywood used her in the usual way in *Four for Texas*, a western vehicle for Frank Sinatra and Dean Martin with Ekberg called upon to do nothing more than display cleavage. She did fairly well in *The Alphabet Murders*, a broad comic interpretation of an Agatha Christie whodunit.

That 1956 release marked the last time Ekberg would be the female lead in a major film. She kept busy and provided sex appeal in Jerry Lewis's comedy *Way . . . Way Out*, and did some mild sex scenes in *The Cobra*, an action picture about T-men fighting drug smuggling in the Middle East. The actress did well in one of the episodes of *Women Times Seven* as she vied with Shirley MacLaine for Michael Caine. She did another cameo for *If It's Tuesday, This*

Must Be Belgium. This spoof on American tourists found Anita called on once again to do little but look good.

After 1970, demand for Ekberg faded considerably and over the next 17 years she appeared in only seven films. In her prime she would have done that many in two years. The declining demand was partially due to her age and partially to a weight problem. *Newsweek* ran a photo of her in 1974 which showed her to be very heavy. "It is not fatness," said the actress. "It is development."

Of the films she has done after 1970, they have all been low budget releases and none have received distribution in North America.

In the 1970s she became a partner in a Rome car rental agency.

Anita Ekberg Filmography

Terras forster No. 5 (1951)
Abbott and Costello Go to Mars (1953)
Take Me to Town (1953)
The Golden Blade (1953)
The Mississippi Gambler (1953)
Blood Alley (1955)
Artists and Models (1955)
Man in the Vault (1955)
War and Peace (1956)
Hollywood or Bust (1956)
Back from Eternity (1956)
Zarak (1956)
Interpol [Pick-Up Alley] (1957)
Valerie (1957)
Paris Holiday (1958)
Screaming Mimi (1958)
The Man Inside (1958)
Nel segno di Roma [Sign of the Gladiator] (1958)
La dolce vita (1959)
Apocalisse sul fiume giallo [Last Train to Shanghai; The Dam on the Yellow River] (1959)
Le tre ecetera del colonnello (1959)
Les Cocottes [The Call Girl Business; Little Girls and High Finance] (1960)
A Porte chiuse [Behind Closed Doors; Behind Locked Doors] (1960)
Il Giudizio universale [The Last Judgment] (1961)
The Mongols (1961)
Boccaccio '70 (1962)

Call Me Bwana (1963)
Four for Texas (1963)
L'incastro (1964)
Bianco, rosso, giallo, rosa (1964)
Das Liebeskarussel [Who Wants to Sleep?] (1965)
The Alphabet Murders (1965)
Way ... Way Out (1966)
Scusi, lei e'favorevole o contrario? (1966)
Come impari ad amare le donne [How I Learned to Love Women] (1966)
The Cobra (1967)
Woman Times Seven (1967)
La Sfinge d'oro [The Glass Sphinx] (1967)
Das Geuisse etwas der Frauen (1967)
Malenka, the Vampire's Niece (1968)
If It's Tuesday, This Must Be Belgium (1969)
Blonde Koder fur den Morder (1969)
La Morte bussa due volte (1969)
Il Debito coniugale (1970)
Il Divorzio (1970)
I Clowns [The Clowns] (1970)
North-East of Seoul (1972)
Fangs of the Living Dead (1973)
Das Tal der Witwen [Valley of the Widows] (1974)
Death Knocks Twice (1975)
Suor omicidio [The Killer Nun] (1978)
Gold of the Amazon Women (1979)
Daisy Chain (1981)

Sources

"Beautiful Maid from Malmo," *Life,* 31:133–4+, October 8, 1951.
Katz, Ephraim. *The Film Encyclopedia.* New York: Thomas Y. Crowell, 1979, p. 384.
Lloyd, Ann, ed. *The Illustrated Who's Who of the Cinema.* London: Orbis, 1983, p. 136.
"Malmo Maid Makes Good," *Life,* 40:90+, January 16, 1956.
"Newsmakers," *Newsweek,* 84:56, July 29, 1974.
Quinlan, David. *Quinlan's Illustrated Directory of Film Stars.* London: B.T. Batsford, 1986, p. 134.
"Women Who Fascinate Men," *Look,* 20:57, March 6, 1956.

Britt Ekland

One of the questions asked most frequently about Britt Ekland was: "Can she act?" In many ways this was an unfair attack. In fact Britt turned in many fine acting performances, particularly in the last half of the 1960s when she reached her peak. A flamboyant offscreen life with a host of lovers gave her a great deal of media attention and her reputation became that of a celebrity. This tended to push the question of acting ability into the background. Britt became known more for her personal life than for her professional one.

She was born Britt-Marie Eklund in Stockholm, Sweden, on October 6, 1942, the only daughter in a family of four. Mrs. Eklund had once been a secretary and Mr. Eklund ran a fashionable clothing store. An expert curler, he later became captain of his country's national curling team, and eventually became president of the International Curling Association.

As a child, Britt remembered being "very heavy. God, I was brutal-looking. I always tried to be funny to make up for the fact that I was fat and ugly." After finishing private school, the teenager went on to drama school in Stockholm and then worked for a time with a traveling theater group. That experience led to her film debut in the 1962 Swedish release *Short Is the Summer.* In this story of tragic love and unrealized romance, the actress had only a small part and drew no critical notice. She billed herself under her real name but soon changed it by dropping the last part of her first name and anglicizing her surname from Eklund to Ekland. While made in 1962, *Short Is the Summer* did not receive American distribution until 1969.

One more film followed in Sweden and then Britt went to Italy for small roles in a few more pictures. One was *Il Diavolo,* a spoof on Italian characteristics. By then Ekland was a svelte blonde, a Nordic beauty. A talent scout for 20th Century–Fox spotted her in Italy and sent Britt to England for a film. It was a move which radically changed Ekland's career. English actor

Peter Sellers met the actress in England in 1964 and eleven days later they were married.

The new Mrs. Sellers got the female lead in two comedy films opposite Peter. *After the Fox* offered Sellers his usual range of zany impersonations. Ekland, disguised by an Italian brunette wig, was cast as his sister and got good reviews. Said one critic, "She shows up remarkably well in a small but pertinent role." In *The Bobo* the actress played a fortune hunter and got generally excellent notices. *Variety* wrote that "as a gold digger to stop all gold digging she is at once endowed with childlike naïveté and a witchiness that makes her the focal point of the entire male population.... She delivers surprisingly and should be in line for offers on her performance."

She remained in strong demand for years, usually being the top-billed female in her films. Yul Brynner starred in *The Double Man,* a thriller which used the double identity gimmick. Ekland played a woman involuntarily involved and a critic noted, "She tackles one or two tricky scenes with unexpected assurance." Her first Hollywood feature was *The Night They Raided Minsky's,* about early burlesque, with Britt performing well cast as the first girl to do a striptease.

Many of the films she appeared in were of low quality and required little of Britt. She was primarily used as a sex object. One such film was *Stiletto,* a forgettable melodrama based on a Harold Robbins' novel, which starred Alex Cord. With plenty of sex, violence and Mafia types, Britt did as well as could be expected portraying Cord's paramour. *Machine Gun McCain* was a predictable cops and robbers chase film. Ekland played a girl picked up by a crook who was planning to rob a bank. Her only function was as a love interest.

Once again she had nothing to do but function as a sex object in the crime thriller *Get Carter,* playing the fiancée of the male lead, Michael Caine. One of her scenes had her induce sexual fantasies on the phone and Caine remarked she would "physically turn on every man in the audience." Britt replied sarcastically, "I was acting, not living the role."

One of her poorest vehicles was *Percy.* It was the story of a man who lost his penis in an accident and then had a transplant. Wondering about the previous owner, the recipient set out to track down the first owner of the organ, nicknamed "Percy." Britt had a brief role as one of the women who had had dealings with Percy. *The Cannibals* was a modern adaptation of *Antigone* but it was too raw and rough for most and died a quick death at the box office even though Britt gave an excellent performance. "It's Britt Ekland as you've never seen her before," wrote one reviewer. "It's quite extraordinary that it is her — she's so very good."

Britt and Sellers had a daughter and then divorced in 1968 amidst much acrimony. The actress later said, "Men have basically never been monsters to me except Sellers." Peter replied, "She's a professional girlfriend and an amateur actress." By the early 1970s the actress was uncomfortable with her

Britt Ekland with John Cassavetes in *Machine Gun McCain*.

image as a sex kitten. She claimed that Sellers had given her that image and that she hated it. Britt was determined to become known as a great actress despite the fact that many critics gave her credit for little or no acting ability.

Good parts did not materialize for her during the first half of that decade, however. Britt played one of the inmates in *Asylum*, a thriller set in an insane asylum wherein a visiting psychiatrist had to guess which one of the inmates had once been the institution's director. *Baxter!* was a sloppy tearjerker about a young boy with a psychosomatic speech problem. Ekland was one of a pair of lovers who helped the boy before she died of pneumonia. That film was panned although Britt herself got some good notices. She was a James Bond girl in *The Man with the Golden Gun*. *Royal Flesh* was a silly period comedy. It was an embarrassment to all concerned.

Record producer Lou Adler and Britt became a twosome for awhile and produced a son in 1974. When they split up the actress took up with the rock singer Rod Stewart in her most publicized liaison. That union ended in 1977 and Stewart explained his method of terminating affairs: "Since I dislike confrontations ending relationships, I end live-in relationships by moving out of my home for a few days or weeks until a woman can find another place to live. This

has worked well in the past." It didn't work as well this time as Britt refused to leave until a judge ordered her to do so. Britt sued the singer for $10 million in palimony and later settled out of court for a sum she refused to mention except to say, "I can assure you the settlement's not half a million dollars."

During the last half of the 1970s her film vehicles remained undistinguished. She was one of the bare-breasted girls in *Casanova and Co.,* a comedy with the premise that Casanova was impotent and used a stand-in. In *High Velocity* Britt played the wife of a kidnapped corporation executive who fell for the charms of one of his would-be rescuers. *The Monster Club* featured Britt in a small role although she was a big enough name to continue to be the top-billed female.

The actress turned her hand to other ventures. She did a lot of television work, including game shows. She also made her stage debut in London in 1978 in a play called "Mate." This proved to be a disaster and it closed in three weeks. Ekland even released her first, and likely last, record. The disco single titled "Do It to Me," had a picture-disc with the nude image of Ekland pressed into both sides.

Writing was her next endeavor as she published her autobiography *True Britt* in 1981. It primarily detailed her active love life, outlining her marriage, ten short affairs (including Warren Beatty, George Hamilton and Ryan O'Neal), three long affairs (including Adler and Stewart) and two suitors, Lee Majors and Ron Ely.

On the question of her image, Britt was more resigned and commented, "Usually a sex symbol doesn't get the same kind of respect that a stage actress does. I can't change it now. So now I really don't mind the image. Now I'll use it to my advantage . . . I used to be confused with so many others. I was everybody. I was Elke Sommer and Sue Lyon and Julie Christie. Now I am definitely Britt Ekland and I love it. I think the people think of me as a celebrity. They know I'm an actress, but I don't have that much work out there."

Asked about the quality of her films, the actress said, "I didn't make that many bad ones—they were just not good. I made one great film—*The Night They Raided Minsky's.* It's a classic. . . . I have made 25 movies, but non, alas, has borne such scrutiny or provoked so much consternation and controversy as my private life."

She had not forsaken the quest for acting greatness and in the early 1980s insisted, "My whole ambitions for the future still revolve around my deeply cherished ambition to gain absolute recognition as one of the world's leading actresses." While she has appeared in more than half a dozen films in the 1980s, none have helped her to achieve her ambition.

Dead Wrong was a thriller about drug smugglers who used an unwitting fisherman to smuggle a cargo of drugs. Ekland was cast as an undercover agent

Opposite: Britt Ekland in a publicity photo.

who fell for the fisherman. Complete with lesbianism, catfights and mad scientists, *Hellhole* was a bad film about women in an asylum with Britt having a small part. *Fraternity Vacation* was a dismal sex comedy. Billed prominently with a "special appearance" card, Britt played a cocktail waitress and was visible on the screen for about 30 seconds.

In 1984 the 42-year-old Ekland married 24-year-old Jim McDonnell, drummer with the rock group Stray Cats. Summing up her career, Britt said, "I haven't had the career I wanted because I allowed it to happen. I chose to pursue my private life rather than my professional life. I want to reverse that ... I'm a good actress. I couldn't have had so many opportunities if there wasn't anything but looks. You can't live on that."

Britt Ekland Filmography

Kort År Sommaren [Short Is the Summer] (1962)
Det År hos Mie Han Här Varit (1963)
Il Comandante (1963)
Il Diavolo (1963)
Too Many Thieves (1965)
Caccia alla Volpe [After the Fox] (1966)
The Double Man (1967)
The Bobo (1967)
The Night They Raided Minsky's (1968)
Stiletto (1969)
Nell'anno del signore (1969)
Gli intoccabili [Machine Gun McCain] (1969)
Percy (1970)
I Cannibali [The Cannibals] (1970)
Get Carter (1970)
Tinto Mara (1970)
Endless Night (1971)
Night Hair Child (1971)
A Time for Loving (1971)

Asylum (1972)
Baxter! (1972)
The Wicker Man (1973)
The Man with the Golden Gun (1974)
The Ultimate Thrill [The Ultimate Chase] (1974)
Royal Flash (1975)
High Velocity (1976)
Casanova and Co. [The Rise and Rise of Casanova] (1977)
Slavers (1977)
King Solomon's Treasure (1978)
The Monster Club (1980)
The Hostage Tower (1980)
Dark Eyes [Satan's Mistress] (1981)
Erotic Images (1983)
Dead Wrong (1983)
Hellhole (1984)
Fraternity Vacation (1985)
Marbella (1985)
Love Scenes (1985)
Moon in Scorpio (1988)

Sources

Boyes, Malcolm. "Britt Ekland," *People*, 23:106+, May 20, 1985.
"But Can She Act?" *Look*, 35:41, March 9, 1971.
Katz, Ephraim. *The Film Encyclopedia*. New York: Thomas Y. Crowell, 1979, p. 385.
Kornheiser, Tony. "Slate of Affairs," *Washington Post*, May 2, 1981, p. F1+.
Lester, Peter. "On the Move," *People*, 13:65+, March 10, 1980.
Lloyd, Ann, ed. *The Illustrated Who's Who of the Cinema*. London: Orbis, 1983, p. 108.
"Newsmakers," *Newsweek*, 90:74, September 26, 1977.
Quinlan, David. *Quinlan's Illustrated Directory of Film Stars*. London: B.T. Batsford, 1986, p. 134–135.

Index

A